RAF Bomber Command
1936–1968

RAF Bomber Command 1936–1968

AN OPERATIONAL AND HISTORICAL RECORD

KEN DELVE

Pen & Sword
AVIATION

First published in Great Britain in 2005 by
PEN & SWORD AVIATION
an imprint of
Pen & Sword Books Ltd
47 Church Street
Barnsley
South Yorkshire
S70 2AS

ISBN 1 84415 183 2

Typeset by Concept, Huddersfield, West Yorkshire
Printed and bound in Great Britain by
CPI UK

Pen & Sword Books Ltd incorporates the Imprints of
Pen & Sword Aviation, Pen & Sword Maritime, Pen & Sword Military,
Wharncliffe Local History, Pen & Sword Select,
Pen & Sword Military Classics and Leo Cooper.

For a complete list of Pen & Sword titles please contact
PEN & SWORD BOOKS LIMITED
47 Church Street, Barnsley, South Yorkshire, S70 2AS, England.
E-mail: enquiries@pen-and-sword.co.uk
Website: www.pen-and-sword.co.uk

Contents

CHAPTER ONE

Introduction and Overview

During the Second World War Bomber Command flew around 390,000 sorties for the loss of 8,953 aircraft on operational missions; that number does not include another almost 1,400 that crashed in the UK whilst airborne on an operational mission. The cost in aircrew lives was over 47,000, to which must be added those killed in accidents or training – a further 8,000 plus; it is generally accepted that the total of lives lost is around 55,000. What did the six years of the bombing offensive achieve? Supporters and critics were active at the time and in the 60 years since the end of the war the argument has raged even more fiercely. As with all history the benefits of hindsight and access to previously classified documentary sources has to be balanced by the researcher's removal in time and context from the period under study. To understand truly decisions, policies, actions and attitudes is all but impossible. This book covers the entire period of Bomber Command from its origin in 1936 to its demise – into Strike Command – in 1968. Whilst all periods of the Command are covered it is inevitable that the major focus is on the period of the Second World War. The book has been divided into five main sections: an Introduction and Overview, which sets the framework for the development of Bomber Command and includes both policy and politics; an Operations chapter, which focuses on the combat operations of the Command; a brief look at each of the operational Groups; an overview of aircrew training; and, finally, an Aircraft chapter, looking in chronological sequence at all operational aircraft types – and one ballistic missile used by Bomber Command. The annexes provide a variety of historical data.

It seems appropriate to open this overview with a few words from the most famous of Bomber Command's leaders, Sir Arthur Harris: 'There are no words with which I can do justice to the aircrew under my command. There is no parallel in warfare to such courage and determination in the face of danger over so prolonged a period.' These words from Bomber Command's wartime leader, Air Marshal Arthur T. Harris are a fitting tribute to the sacrifice made by the Command in six years of war. Only one force on the Allied side was continuously involved with active operations against the German homeland – RAF Bomber Command. The day the war started a Blenheim of 139 Squadron flew a reconnaissance sortie to locate German shipping and for the next six years the Command took the war to the enemy, at first with limited effect but from 1942 with increasing resources and greater accuracy, and with an ever greater impact.

Origins and doctrine
Strategic bombing theory was developed in the latter years of the First World War and was a combination of the German raids on England and the Allied, especially Royal Flying Corps/Royal Air Force, bombing campaign, although this was only just starting to get into its stride when the Armistice was signed in November 1918. Despite the fact

Bomber Command suffered 55,000 aircrew casualties in the Second World War; a number of squadrons lost 1,000 aircrew during the war.

that strategic bombing had not really been evaluated in the First World War it became a central tenet of air power theory in the post-war period. In part this was because it was the one independent decisive (potentially) role that the air forces could perform. For the RAF this was enshrined as the Trenchard Doctrine: 'the nation that would stand being bombed longest would win in the end ... to win it will be necessary to pursue a relentless offensive by bombing the enemy's country, destroying his sources of supply of aircraft and engines, and breaking the morale of his people.' This doctrine of a war winning bomber force remained the focus of doctrine with the major air forces throughout the 1920s. In May 1928 Trenchard, whose views still carried great weight, circulated a forceful memo to counter: 'an unwillingness on the part of the other Services to accept the contention of the Air Staff that in future wars air attacks would most certainly be carried out against the vital centres of commerce and of the manufacture of munitions of war of every sort no matter where these centres were located.' He

Bomber Command Badge: In front of a thunderbolt gules winged grey, an Astral Crown Or (elements of this badge were subsequently used in the Strike Command badge). The thunderbolt represents Bomber Command's striking power and the Astral Crown is indicative of the success of its operations. Motto: 'Strike Hard Strike Sure'. The badge was approved in March 1947 by King George VI.

stated that the RAF doctrine was to 'break down the enemy means of resistance by attacks on objectives selected as most likely to achieve this end' it being better to attack munitions at source (the factory) than on the battlefield – this would become a well-rehearsed argument by Bomber Command throughout the Second World War. It would, he believed, have greater effect for less effort, and would include dissuading workers from working in the factories. 'The Hague Convention allows for military targets, including production centres. What is illegitimate, as being contrary to the dictates of humanity, is the indiscriminate bombing of a city for the sole purpose of terrorising the civilian population.' Bomber Command would later take great care to stress the military significance of its city targets, whilst the German propaganda machine would refer to the *Terrorflieger*. The other Chiefs of Staff in their respective memos were not convinced, and also expressed concern over being bombed in return; it must be remembered that this was a period when the independence of the RAF, in part budget-driven, was under threat and the arguments, as such tri-Service 'debates' usually are, was writ large with vested interest.

The debates were largely hypothetical at the time as the RAF's bomber strength in the early 1930s was pitiful with five night- and six day-bomber squadrons, all with slow biplanes with very limited bomb loads, hardly the material with which to deliver an aerial bombardment of any significance.

Although the stagnation of the 1920s, which in military terms had been a dismal decade for all of Britain's armed forces, had started to change in the early 1930s both doctrine and equipment were outdated and with little immediate prospect of improvement. In terms of aircraft there was a glimmer of hope with the issue of Specification B.9/32 for a 'twin-engined medium bomber of good performance and long range', although the requirement for a 720 mile range and 1,000 lb bomb load was not particularly inspiring! Two of Bomber Command's early stalwarts – the Wellington and the Hampden – were a result of this Specification. The following year saw Britain wake up to the realities of a changing Europe. A Foreign Office appraisal of 1933 stated that Germany '... controlled by a frenzied nationalism and resolved to assert her rights to full equality, will proceed to the building of formidable armaments on land and especially in

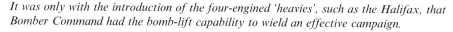

It was only with the introduction of the four-engined 'heavies', such as the Halifax, that Bomber Command had the bomb-lift capability to wield an effective campaign.

the air.' The Government suggested that the Services draw up expansion plans; the Defence Requirements Committee sat from November 1933 to February 1934 and in its report gave priority to the establishment by the RAF of a Home Defence force (including bombers) strong enough to counter any attack. Expansion Scheme A was announced in July 1934 to provide the basis for a deterrent force and a training establishment on which future expansion could be based; under this scheme the RAF would be ready for war in eight years (1942). The old One-Power standard, which had seen planning based on France as the 'enemy' had to shift to reflect the reality of the growth of German power and belligerence. It was all very well to talk of an offensive bomber force capable of attacking targets in the Ruhr and Rhineland districts of Germany, the two main industrial areas, but quite another to make it a reality (even on paper). The initial solution was one of numbers over capability; create the squadrons even though the equipment might not be right as better aircraft could follow in due course. This was a mixture of financial constraint and lack of suitable aircraft; the latter would continue to plague the Command into the middle years of the war. As an indication, it cost £245,000 to acquire twelve Hawker Hart light bombers and £83,000 to operate them; in comparison it cost £375,000 to acquire ten Vickers Virginia heavy bombers and £139,000 a year to operate them. The financial aspect became a secondary consideration with Expansion Scheme C (May 1935) stating that: 'Financial considerations were to be secondary to the attainment of the earliest possible security.' In July the Air Staff confirmed the strategic doctrine: 'Provided a sufficient weight of air attack could be brought to bear on the Rhineland-Ruhr-Saar area, Germany's armament industry would be paralysed, which would in turn preclude her from maintaining an army in the field.'

The bomber force was organised into regional commands, such as the Wessex Bombing Area, and all were part of the Home Defence organisation, fitting neatly with the bombing offensive being seen as 'attack as the best means of defence.'

By the time that Bomber Command formed on 14 July 1936, Expansion Scheme F (dated February 1936) was on the table. This called for a bomber force of 68 squadrons, with 990 aircraft, and was scheduled for completion by March 1939. Like the previous Schemes, and those that followed over the next two years, it was overly optimistic. Paper squadrons don't fight wars and when Expansion Scheme H called for 1,659 bombers in ninety squadrons it was obvious even to the optimists that it was unrealistic, even though it was not scheduled for completion until 1943. For the first Commander-in-Chief of Bomber Command, Sir John Steel, aircraft were only one of the problems to be faced; of equal importance was personnel – aircrew and ground crew – as well as equipment, including bombs, and airfields. Lack of suitable weapons was to prove a major embarrassment to Bomber Command in the early part of the war and the problem could be traced back to a 1932 Air Staff decision that there would be no requirement for a bomb heavier than 500 lb and that the 250 lb bomb would be the standard weapon. The need for airfields further north to cater for Germany as the main target led to Expansion Period airfields from Norfolk to Yorkshire, with the latter county, along with Lincolnshire, becoming the heartland of Bomber Command. This expansion did not really start until 1935, with old First World War sites being looked at as part of a major search for airfield sites. The basic requirement was for a large patch of level ground for a grass airfield, the current bombers requiring little in the way of prepared surfaces, along with support facilities such as hangars, technical, administration and domestic buildings.

The impressive C-Type hangar became typical of bomber airfields of this period, although the exact facilities varied between locations. The provision of aircrew, and training in general is covered in a separate chapter. By the mid 1930s aircraft manufacturers

The late 1930s saw a large number of new airfields under construction for Bomber Command, such as Finningley in South Yorkshire.

who had been finding it hard to survive official disinterest in the 1920s were being called on to produce large numbers of new aircraft and it is remarkable that they were able to respond as well as they did. A great deal of criticism has been levelled by some commentators on the poor quality of equipment with which the RAF entered the war, an argument that could equally be aimed at the likes of tanks and other military equipment, but it takes time to design, develop and produce advanced items such as aircraft. It was only in 1935 that a medium/heavy bomber philosophy was adopted, based on the bomb lift of the proposed new types, and there was much debate on the subject at Air Staff and Government level. However, on the outbreak of war the Command was still substantially composed of light bombers and it would be 1943 before it lost the last of these. Indeed it was only in 1936 that two of the Command's most advanced types – both light bombers, the Fairey Battle and the Bristol Blenheim, entered service. Perhaps the most significant decision was the issue of Specification B.12/36 for a four-engined bomber of 250 mph cruise, 1,500 mile range and 4,000 lb bomb load. It was also to have the latest navigation equipment, plus power-operated gun turrets, including a four-gun rear turret. This was starting to sound like a real strategic bomber – but the war would be well underway before the products of this Specification were ready for service. In the meantime, the expansion plans had to go ahead with whatever was to hand. Continued examination of overall air doctrine and assessment of the enemy air strength and employment, including tactical and strategic air operations in the 1936 Spanish Civil War, led to a revision in the expansion plan. In October 1938, Expansion Plan M was approved, which envisaged a strength of eighty-two bomber squadrons (1,360 aircraft) by April 1941, and with renewed focus on defensive requirements by increasing the number of fighter squadrons. Meanwhile, doctrine was being turned into reality and the Joint Planning Committee (JPC), with its eyes firmly fixed on offensive bombing, envisaged a three-phase campaign:

1. Countering the all-out German air offensive by attacking *Luftwaffe* installations.
2. Countering the German land offensive by attacking ground forces.
3. A war-winning air offensive against German industry and transport.

The JPC also stated that: 'the offensive employment of our own and Allied bombers is the only measure which could affect the issue during the first weeks of the war. The three classes of objective are:

1. Demoralise the German people, by methods similar to those we foresee the Germans themselves using against us, [so that] their Government might be forced to desist from this type of attack.
2. Discover and attack some target, the security of which was regarded by Germany as vital to her survival during the limited period within which she hoped to gain a decision over us, [so that] she would be forced to divert her air attacks to our own aerodromes and maintenance organisation.
3. Inflict direct casualties upon the German bombing aircraft, either in the air or on the ground, or upon their maintenance organisation; the intensity of German attacks would be directly and quickly affected.

The overall philosophy was translated into 'Planning for a War with Germany' and in late 1936 the Air Targets Intelligence sub-committee developed the Western Air (WA) plans and these became the focus for Bomber Command's strategic planning. On 13 December 1937 the Command was instructed to commence detailed planning for WA1 (German Air Force), WA4 (German Army concentration areas and lines of communication) and WA5 (manufacturing centres), with planning to be complete by 1 April 1938. It was a massive task and was carried out with incomplete information on the targets and an over-optimistic appreciation of bombing capability. A Bomber Command appraisal of the list suggested that only the third was realistic as the others comprised targets of an inappropriate nature for offensive strategic bombers, a stance that would be taken by bomber leaders, especially Arthur Harris, at various times throughout the war.

The WA Plans underwent a number of modifications over the next few months but by mid 1938 had settled down as:

WA1   German Air Force organisation and associated industries.
WA2   Reconnaissance of Home Waters and East Atlantic, in co-operation with the Royal Navy.
WA3   Convoy protection in Home Waters and East Atlantic.
WA4   German Army concentration areas and lines of communication.
WA5   Manufacturing Resources; WA5(a) Ruhr, WA5(b) Inland waterways, Ruhr, Baltic, North Sea ports, WA5(c) Outside of Ruhr.
WA6   Stores, especially oil.
WA7   Counter-offensive in co-operation with Royal Navy in defence of sea-borne trade.
WA8   Night attacks.
WA9   Kiel Canal and associated waterways.
WA10   Shipping and facilities, especially the Baltic.
WA11   Forests and crops.
WA12   German fleet in harbour or at sea.
WA13   Administrative centres, especially Berlin.

An indication of the optimism of the bomber theorists was a suggestion that an offensive against the Ruhr, especially the coking plants and power stations, would, 'Prevent Germany waging war on a large scale in less than three months.' This outcome could be achieved with 3,000 sorties, at a cost of 176 bombers, by knocking out twenty-six coking plants and nineteen power stations. With hindsight of the first years of the war this level of optimism seems incredulous!

Whilst plans were being prepared, the Command was undergoing a major reorganisation as aircraft types and roles were concentrated into individual Groups and units moved to more appropriate airfields within the new structure. The progress made in the two years since the Command was formed was incredible and those who criticise Bomber Command's performance in the first years of the war fail to recognise just how much had been achieved in such a short period. Despite the optimism expressed above, Ludlow-Hewitt (C-in-C since September 1937) clearly stated that his Command was: 'Entirely unprepared for war, unable to operate except in fair weather and extremely vulnerable in the air and on the ground.' These words proved to be far more prophetic. However, the military always has to play with the cards it has and Bomber Command was to enter the war with a far from ideal hand. The arrival of the Wellington, the first squadron equipping in late 1938, was one positive indication but by the outbreak of war there were only six operational squadrons with this type. It could have been worse; Bomber Command may have gone to war in September 1938 when the Munich Crisis took Europe to the brink of war. Most parties knew that the Allied 'sell-out' provided only a respite and that war with Germany was inevitable; for the RAF the extra year was crucial.

To war

At the outbreak of war in September 1939, Bomber Command had an average daily availability of 500 aircraft (total aircraft establishment was 920 aircraft) organised in fifty-five squadrons controlled by five operational Groups. No. 1 and No. 2 Groups were equipped with light bombers – Fairey Battles and Bristol Blenheims respectively – and the other three Groups (3, 4 and 5) with twin-engined 'strategic bombers' – Handley Page Hampdens, Armstrong-Whitworth Whitleys and Vickers-Armstrongs Wellingtons respectively.

On 2 September all aircraft of the Advanced Air Striking Force (AASF) were ordered to deploy to France, the Battles of No. 1 Group duly crossed the Channel, one ditching *en route* but with the crew being rescued. There were effectively four operational Groups left in the UK – Nos 2, 3, 4 and 5 – with No. 6 Group taking on the training role to administer the Group Pool squadrons. These latter units were squadrons within each Group which were given the task of training the crews arriving from Flying Training Schools to a standard whereby they were fit to join operational squadrons and of providing a pool of replacement crews. Any expansion of Bomber Command was faced with a number of hurdles, the most important of which were availability of aircraft, crews and airfields. Each of these aspects was to cause major problems in the early years of the war and in almost every instance the solution was, in some respects, a compromise. The overriding consideration throughout the expansion of the Command was that of maintaining the attack on Germany. Lead times required for new aircraft, airfield construction and the training of aircrew had an effect on the speed with which the expansion progressed.

Bomber Command was in action on day one of the war, a number of Blenheim reconnaissance sorties later followed by a Hampden/Wellington force in search of German shipping were conducted, whilst on the first night of the war Whitleys flew over

Blenheim of 44 Squadron at Waddington; the Squadron had re-equipped by 1939 and the Blenheim's bombing activities with Bomber Command were confined to No. 2 Group.

the Ruhr dropping propaganda leaflets. The Ruhr was a most appropriate destination in Germany for this first, albeit only with paper, visit by Bomber Command as it was the Ruhr that was to receive a great deal of the Command's effort once the bombing offensive was launched.

This pattern of activity of daylight searches for shipping and night leaflet dropping was to be the focus of Bomber Command's war for the next few weeks; only small numbers of aircraft were involved and little action took place, although there were early indications of bomber vulnerability such as the loss of five Hampdens on a shipping sortie on 29 September. There appears to have been little reaction to this high level of losses from an attack with no result in terms of damage to the enemy. October and November were quiet months although in addition to limited operational flying a number of exercises were flown, such as that on 22 November to, 'Investigate the factors of time and concentration of aircraft in attacks on targets situated in a relatively small area' and that on 28 November on ships in the Belfast area to, 'Give training and experience in the delivery of concentrated and rapid attack upon warships located in or near harbours.' The latter exercise involved sixty aircraft from Nos 3 and 5 Groups. Despite losses and lack of success to date, the general opinion was still that aircraft could find and hit their targets and that they would be able to defend themselves. Indeed, the report on an attack on 3 December appeared to confirm this view: 'Twenty-four Wellingtons carried out an attack upon enemy warships anchored in the vicinity of Heligoland. A total of sixty-three 500 lb semi armour piercing (SAP) bombs were dropped; a direct hit was obtained on a cruiser and probably on a second. At least three bombs were dropped so close to enemy warships as to make it likely that damage was caused and casualties were sustained. Heavy anti-aircraft fire was encountered and some twenty enemy aircraft, including Me 110s, were seen, some of which attacked. One Me 109 was shot down and one appeared to have been hit. Three of our aircraft were hit but all returned safely to their bases.' This report would seem to suggest that all was well and later that week the Air Ministry ordered attacks on naval forces in German estuaries 'as soon as possible.' On 14 December twelve Wellingtons from 99 Squadron were sent to patrol the Elbe Estuary and the Frisian Islands to attack shipping – and it was a disaster. Under fighter attack and in the face of heavy flak half of the attacking formation became casualties; not a promising start to the new campaign. Two days later the Commander-in-Chief presided over a conference of his Group commanders and senior staff to, 'Examine the existing operating procedures with a view to making such modifications as might be considered desirable in the light of the experience gained in war conditions.' The ink was hardly dry on the minutes of this meeting, which had reached no firm conclusions, when a second disastrous operation took place. On 18 December No. 3 Group sent twenty-four Wellingtons from three squadrons to patrol the Schillig Roads and Wilhelmshaven to report upon any enemy naval forces. 'In Wilhelmshaven a battleship, two cruisers and four destroyers were seen in the harbour and alongside. They were not therefore attacked. There was heavy anti-aircraft fire and some twenty-five Me 109s and Me 40s (sic) attacked – at least twelve of which were shot down. Twelve of our aircraft failed to return, of these two are known to have descended into the North Sea on the way home.' One initial reaction to this disaster was an Air Ministry order suspending attacks on naval forces until the armouring of the Wellington's fuel tanks had been completed.

So with new aircraft types promised and a major growth in numbers, Bomber Command entered the first winter of the war. With a political injunction against attacks on land targets, the rationale for the strategic bombers had disappeared. The doctrine of bombing the enemy heartland and destroying his industrial capability had been removed at a stroke by the politicians. This was not so much on humanitarian grounds, although the American President had requested both sides to refrain from unrestrained bombing, but more because of a belief that the German bomb lift, i.e. weight of bombs to a target, was greater than that of the RAF.

Whilst the Wellingtons endeavoured to find and attack German shipping, the Whitleys were operating over Germany at night – but only dropping leaflets. This propaganda leaflet-dropping campaign (*nickelling* as it was called by Bomber Command) continued throughout the war. The first real test for the daylight bombing campaign came in December 1939 when, on a number of occasions, formations of Wellingtons were intercepted by fighters and suffered heavy losses. Another pillar of doctrine, that bombers flying in close formation using mutually supportive fire from their gun turrets could defeat fighter attack, was shattered. The number of sorties had been small and

Wellington R3213 of 38 Squadron; the Squadron was part of the Marham bomber force in No. 3 Group.

Equipped with fleece-lined suits the crew climb aboard their Whitley for another cold trip over Germany.

taken overall the losses were still seen as acceptable – and by no means an indicator that an offensive over the Ruhr would not succeed. Nevertheless, from January the Wellingtons and Hampdens joined the night leaflet campaign as there were no suitable bombing targets and it was an excellent way of giving crews practice in night operations. Losses from these sorties were low, as the Germans had not yet developed a night defence system.

One of the major dangers faced by the bomber crews was severe weather, icing being a particular hazard. The Whitley was prone to wing icing and, despite the use of anti-icing aids such as *Kilfrost* paste, the only real solution was to avoid the icing layers in the cloud. Given the poor performance of the aircraft and the often inadequate Met forecast this was easier said than done – once icing had been detected the only option was a descent in search of warmer air.

April/May 1940 brought a number of developments. The German invasion of Denmark and Norway in April gave Bomber Command a new set of targets, and on 11 April a small force of Wellingtons attacked the airfield at Stavanger in Norway – the first intentional bombing attack on a land target in Europe. The same month saw Hampdens fly the first of a new type of mission: minelaying. *Gardening*, as these sorties were code-named, was to become a major part of the Command's work over the next five years. Finally, the German invasion of France in May led to a dramatic and short-lived tactical employment of the AASF Fairey Battles in attempting to stem the enemy armoured columns – with much heroism, and crippling losses among aircraft and aircrew.

The Blenheim squadrons were also heavily tasked in this period; indeed between 10 May (the date of the German invasion) and 25 June, the Blenheims operated on all but four days – flying 1,616 sorties for the loss of 104 aircraft.

By early June the battered remnants of the Bomber Command light bomber force had left France and returned to airfields in England; No. 1 Group had effectively ceased to exist.

The most significant event in May was the lifting of the ban on attacking targets in Germany; the first attack took place on the night of 15 May on oil and rail targets in the Ruhr area – the strategic offensive had started. As major industrial towns were concentrated in the relatively small geographic area of the Ruhr, this part of Germany was to be the focus of much of the bomber effort until the last months of the war. Italy's entry into the war in June provided additional targets for the bombers.

With the launch of bombing raids on Germany the focus of attack on industrial centres was intended to, 'Cause the continuous interruption and dislocation of industry, particularly where the German aircraft industry is concentrated.' On 4 June a new directive had been issued to Bomber Command but with the rider that: 'The initiative lies with the enemy; our strategic policy is liable to be deflected by the turn of events from the course we should like to follow. The Command was instructed to pursue its campaign against German industry but to be ready to assist in countering any invasion.

With the launch of the bombing offensive the Command endeavoured to attack industrial targets in the Ruhr, this being deemed the area most likely to produce results as it was a major industrial area, often referred to as the 'weapon smithy' of the Reich. It was a major mining centre for coal and produced large quantities of coke to feed its own industries and those of other areas. It was home to major industrial towns such as Bochum, Dortmund, Duisburg and Essen, the latter being home to the massive Krupps works. However, the very nature of this industrial centre meant that it had a permanent haze, which made it very difficult for bombers find targets visually. All of these places became regular targets for the Command, as did places such as Gelsenkirchen where the two hydrogenation plants of Gelsenberg-Benzin and Hydrierwerke-Scholvern between them produced 575,000 tons of aviation fuel a year. In addition to the actual industrial targets great importance was attached to the comprehensive rail and canal network that linked Germany's industrial centres. Indeed, the importance of the rail network became one of the Command's justifications for its area bombing of cities.

A new directive was issued on 13 July, which stated that the primary aim was to, 'Reduce the scale of air attack on this country with the aircraft and oil industries being the priority targets'. The Air Staff directive also recommended concentration of effort against a limited number of targets rather than the widespread attacks that had been made so far. It listed ten aircraft factories and five oil installations as the main targets, and it also estimated that bombers would have to hit an aircraft factory with 140 of the standard 500 lb bombs in order to have any effect. Secondary targets included communications centres. However, Portal as AOC-in-C considered the directive too restrictive and sought, and received, authority to be more flexible in his choice of targets. A new target category was added on 30 July with the Command ordered to attack power stations, the experts having decided that these were key targets that if destroyed would seriously disrupt German industry. Power stations featured in the summary of operations over the next few years, some as daylight attacks by the light and medium bombers, others as an aiming point within an area attack on a city. A summary in August showed that the Command had expended 41 per cent of its effort, in terms of bomb tonnage, against *Luftwaffe*-related targets and a further 21 per cent against oil targets.

The decision to include Operational Training Unit aircraft on *ops* was in part based on the desire to increase the number of aircraft operating each night but more particularly to provide trainee crews in the latter stages of their course with easy and relatively risk-free operational experience, the favoured mission being night leaflet-dropping over France. The first such *op* was flown by three OTU aircraft on the night of 18/19 July.

The increased threat from U-boats brought Bomber Command into this aspect of the maritime war, the first specific attack being made against the U-boat pens at Lorient on 2/3 September by thirty-nine Hampdens. A directive of 21 September instructed the Command to allocate three squadrons employed on minelaying to be transferred to attacks on U-boat targets. The same directive dictated a continued focus on the oil industry and also mentioned Berlin: 'Although there are no objectives in Berlin of importance to our major plans, it is the intention that attacks on the city and its environs should be continued from time to time when favourable weather conditions permit. The primary aim of these attacks will be to cause the greatest possible disturbance and dislocation both to the industrial activities and civilian population generally.' By the end of September the immediate threat of invasion had receded and the bomber effort was able to focus once more on the strategic offensive, with the light bombers of No. 2 Group contributing to the night attacks, although Blenheims also flew cloud-cover and anti-shipping operations.

The weather in October frustrated the attempt to return to the offensive over Germany, although it was fog at the home airfields that caused the greatest number of losses. On a bad night the Command could lose 10–20 per cent of the bombers to crashes in England; of seventy-three bombers that operated on the night of 16/17 October, fourteen crashed because of fog over their bases (and only three were lost over enemy territory). There had been a similar situation the previous month, as recounted by Ken Wallis (103 Squadron Wellington L7586): 'At this stage of the war we had orders only to drop bombs if we could identify a military target and so we brought ours back until we could drop them on a harbour target in Holland. This meant of course that we had used more fuel than planned. As we flew over the North Sea we received a message that all aircraft were being diverted to Scotland – not an option for us, we didn't have the fuel. Using the *Darkie* system we eventually persuaded someone that we had to try to land at an airfield on the east coast and so made for Binbrook, not that far from our own base. The fog was extensive and despite pass after pass over the airfield, during which we could dimly see the Chance Light, a landing was impossible and each time I just glimpsed a building or obstruction at the last moment and put the Wellington into a steep climb. The petrol gauges had been reading empty for some time and I requested permission to bale out the crew. I was told to fly a little further north – at which point both engines stopped. All the crew were able to get out but I was pretty low when I jumped. It was impossible to see where you were going to come down and I landed heavily and was knocked out, also damaging my back.' So much for the crash: the subsequent few hours are also worth recounting: 'When I came to I was near a hedge and had no idea where I was, the fog was still thick and moisture was dripping off the hedge. A few shots from the Mauser pistol that I always carried with me and a Policeman found me. He took me to a

Pair of 50 Squadron Hampdens. The Hampdens of No. 5 Group played a lead role in minelaying in 1940.

Tour lengths for aircrews varied throughout the war but by 1942 the normal tour was thirty operations for Main Force. At certain periods of the war the chance of survival for this 50 Squadron crew would have been poor.

nearby large house and the owner was persuaded, with some reluctance, to take pity on a poor pilot. The owner was making tea as he couldn't sleep and he grudgingly offered me a cup. When I asked to use his phone to call my base and check on my crew he was less than happy – until I offered to reverse the charges. At 6.00 am the next morning the maid arrived and I was looking forward to a good breakfast, especially after I gave her the chocolate and orange I had not eaten from my flying rations. No such luck. The Squadron Commander picked me up in his car at 8.00 am and we then picked up the rest of the crew from some cottages – they had done somewhat better than I had and had been plied with brandy for much of the night!' They went to the crash site but little survived of the aircraft except the tail, Ken acquired the fabric from the part of the fin with the mission marks painted on it and this now hangs in the hall of his house. After this incident he was given 10 days leave and then it was back to operational flying.

October was a quiet month for the Command because of bad weather but on the 24th it acquired a new commander when Portal moved up to become Chief of the Air Staff, his place being taken by Air Marshal Sir Richard Peirse. The strategy for the winter offensive was laid out in a directive of 30 October; it was not new in that oil was to be the priority target, followed by aircraft component and aluminium factories. However, the overall stated aim was for, 'Regular concentrated attacks on objectives in large towns and centres of industry, with the primary aim of causing very heavy material destruction, which will demonstrate to the enemy the power and severity of air bombardment and the hardship and dislocation which will result from it.' This core doctrine remained with Bomber Command to the end of the war, although it is interesting to note that oil and the aircraft industry became the focus of the USAAF's daylight bombing offensive from 1942 onwards, whilst Bomber Command concentrated on area bombing of cities of industrial and communications importance. The directive also called on the

Command to continue its contribution to the maritime war; indeed it could only reduce this involvement with prior agreement from the Admiralty. Agreement was reached to reduce the minelaying force to one dedicated squadron.

It must be remembered that at this stage of the war Bomber Command's nightly aircraft availability was limited, and a night when around 100 bombers operated was close to a maximum effort. The attack on Hamburg (16/17 November) was the largest to date but only comprised 130 aircraft; the raid was mounted in retaliation for the attack on Coventry the previous night. Only half the crews reported bombing the target and it is likely that if night photographs had been available from all of them that the true percentage would have been far lower. Evidence was beginning to mount that the bomber offensive was failing to have any major effect as bombers were unable to find or hit targets. Other developments in this first full year of war included consideration of tour length for aircrew – and the introduction to service of new bomber types. Discussions on tour lengths had been prompted by concern over the strain of continual operational flying; the 'squadron commander's discretion' policy was gradually replaced by a fixed tour of 200 operational hours, which equated to thirty to thirty-five *ops*, the policy being circulated to Group commanders on 29 November. Although this calculation changed at various times during the war the basic tour length was generally around thirty *ops*, more for Pathfinder crews and with some targets only counting as half an operation.

New aircraft – new problems
Three new bombers had entered service in 1940 and all had suffered problems even before they became operational. The Stirling entered service with 7 Squadron in August and amongst the problems noted by Command was that, 'It appears that a small degree of icing will invariably cause the aircraft to become unstable'. The Manchester joined 207 Squadron in November and the Command recorded: 'Losses due to failure of bearings and a tendency to catch fire in the air after an engine failure'. The Halifax started with 35 Squadron the same month and after an initial favourable impression, it, too, began to experience problems. All three types started their operational careers in the first months of 1941. The major increase in bomb lift that these new bombers promised was vital to the Command's plans. The planners also had other concerns. Bomber Command's airfields had also started to suffer through heavy use and lack of facilities, and with a forecast that by 1943 some 170 bomber airfields would be needed to accommodate up to 9,000 heavy bombers, drastic action was required.

During the first few months of 1941 there were a number of developments in terms of targets, weapons and aircraft. Oil having been determined as a weak link in the German military-industrial establishment, Bomber Command was directed, on 15 January, to concentrate on oil targets: 'The destruction of German synthetic oil plants will reduce the enemy to such a shortage of oil within the next six months that there will be widespread effects on German industry and communications, while it is even possible within this time an appreciable effect may be felt in the scale of effort of her armed forces.' The basis for this 'rosy picture' was an estimate by the economic warfare experts that 6.7 per cent of the total bomber effort, if applied to key oil installations, could reduce production by 15 per cent and produce the result outlined in the directive, which also listed seventeen key targets, nine of which were given priority for attack. The Command had attacked one of these, at Gelsenkirchen, on the night of 9/10 January but of the 135 bombers that flew on the attack less than half claimed to have attacked the target. Only one Whitley was lost. The German night defences were still poor but as the

The Stirling was the first of the 'heavies' to enter service, with 7 Squadron in summer 1940 and with its operational debut in early 1941.

1,000 lb bomb being prepared for loading into a Wellington of 115 Squadron; until the introduction of the High Capacity (HC) 4,000 lb blast bomb ('cookie') the 'thousand-pounder' was the most effective explosive weapon in the Command's arsenal.

offensive was stepped up in 1941 the defenders became far more efficient and loss rates became a major cause for concern in Bomber Command. Oil installations at Rotterdam were attacked on 10/11 February, the significant point being that this was the first Stirling operation.

The light bombers (Blenheims) had been contributing to the night war but in regard to their numbers the effort was small-scale. A new role was found for them in January 1941 with the *Circus* operations; these daylight *ops* were escorted by fighters and the bombers' main role was that of 'encouraging' the *Luftwaffe* to intercept so that the fighters could engage them.

Just as the Command was settling down to a planned offensive it was issued with a new priority directive. This directive of 9 March changed the emphasis to naval targets, especially those connected with U-boats, as the war in the Atlantic was going badly. However, the wording was kept vague to allow a wide range of target options, especially those in 'congested areas where the greatest morale effect is likely to result.'

As far as weapons were concerned, the 4,000 lb blast bomb, often referred to as a 'cookie', was introduced in late March – this bomb would play a major part in the campaign against industrial cities. More squadrons were being formed and the new heavy bombers were in service, which meant that a greater weight of bombs could be delivered each night, and the training system was turning out an adequate supply of aircrew. March had also brought a definitive policy on tour lengths; a standard tour was set at 200 operational hours, to be followed by a six-month rest and then a second tour of 200 hours.

Despite the introduction of heavy bomber types from late 1940 onwards, it was the medium bombers, primarily Wellingtons, which continued to shoulder the bulk of the Command's operations. In June 1941 the operational force comprised forty-nine squadrons:

Heavy	Halifax	2 squadrons
	Manchester	3 squadrons
	Stirling	2 squadrons
	Fortress	1 squadron
Medium	Wellington	21 squadrons
	Hampden	6 squadrons
	Whitley	6 squadrons
Light	Blenheim	8 squadrons

Canadians had been part of the Bomber Command since the start of the war but on 12/13 June Wellingtons of 405 (Vancouver) Squadron made the first operational sortie by an RCAF squadron, four aircraft taking part in an attack on rail yards at Schwerte. The Squadron had formed at Driffield in April and the RCAF contribution would continue to grow over the next few months, leading to an all-Canadian operational Group – No. 6 (RCAF) Group.

The Unit Establishment of bomber squadrons at this time was 16+2 per squadron, although the Hampden units had three flights to give 24+3 and the single Fortress squadron (90 Squadron) had nine aircraft. As always, bare statistics paint only part of the picture and the paper strength was far greater than the true operational strength. Problems with the new aircraft types meant they were slower to enter service than planned. In the first half of 1941 heavy bomber production was only 54 per cent of that predicted and the expansion plan had to be continually revised in the light of this and other factors. Loss rates had started to increase as the German defences built up and became more effective. Finally, whereas it had been predicted that a bomber would survive twenty-five operational sorties the average was running at around half that – with implications for aircrew and aircraft. Churchill was convinced of the value of the bomber weapon and the War Cabinet approved a higher priority of resources for bomber production, plus acquisition of American aircraft. Britain had limited resources,

The Manchester was not a success, mainly because of problems with its Vulture engines – but the basic airframe provided much for the Lancaster.

including manpower, and there was a continual juggling of these resources to meet each new crisis. To achieve the required bomber strength of 4,000 front-line aircraft by spring 1943 would mean the production/purchase of 22,000 bombers. All attempts were to be made to achieve this figure and combined with a conservation policy (i.e. an attempt to reduce losses) by Bomber Command, it was considered to be achievable. However, by January 1942 the Command was forty squadrons short of its target, although in terms of aircraft this was partly offset by increased aircraft strength per squadron.

A new directive of 9 July stated that: 'It is accepted as a principle of this plan that the successful attack of a specific target at night can only be undertaken in clear moonlight. It follows, therefore, that for approximately three-quarters of each month it is only possible to obtain satisfactory results by heavy concentrated and continuous attacks on large working-class and industrial areas in carefully selected towns .... The weakest points in his armour lie in the morale of the civilian population and in his inland trans-portation system ... direct main effort towards dislocating the German transportation system and to destroying the morale of the German population as a whole and of the industrial workers in particular.' In other words, the directive proposed pinpoint targets whenever conditions (moonlight) permitted but outside of that to concentrate on 'area' targets that contained elements of the primary target systems such as transportation. This was essentially to remain Bomber Command operational doctrine for the rest of the war.

The directive included a list of targets drawn up with the help of the Railway Research Service; nine major rail centres were listed for attack, two each in Cologne and Duisburg, plus Duisburg-Ruhrort, Hamm, Osnabruck, Schwerte and Soest. The scale of German rail movements was massive, a typical daily figure for Hamm being 10,000 movements, the vast majority of which was military. In addition, Cologne, Duisburg and Dusseldorf were listed for attack on moonless nights. Other priority targets included inland waterways, such as the Dortmund-Ems Canal and the Ems-Weser Canal, plus the synthetic rubber plants at Huls and Schopau. The list of secondary targets included Bremen, Frankfurt, Hamburg, Hannover, Mannheim and Stuttgart.

'Only one-in-three bombers within 5 miles of target'

At the same time that this directive was being implemented the Command's effectiveness was under the spotlight. The Cherwell Commission examined 100 raids on 28 targets between 2 June and 28 July, with 650 'target photos' used for the assessment. The Butt Report was issued on 8 August and concluded that only one in three bombers were within 5 miles of the target, with an even worse figure of one in ten for the Ruhr area. This was devastating news to those under the impression that bombers had been achieving reasonably precise attacks against industrial targets. Whilst some called for the virtual disbandment of Bomber Command and the allocation or resources elsewhere, others concentrated on addressing the problem of accuracy. Bomber Command's immediate retort was, 'Do photographs indicate such important factors as the loss of skilled workers killed or injured, or the loss of time during periods of air-raid alarms and post-raid disorganisation, the disruption of transport facilities serving factories and building yards, aggravated by the adverse impressions made on the workers' morale.' These were valid points but could not disguise the fact that the Command was achieving far less than it had been claiming in recent months.

Whilst this depressing news was being debated the first of a series of navigation and bombing aids – *Gee* – entered service in August 1941, although it was to be many months before its use was widespread but it did point the way forward. In the meantime there

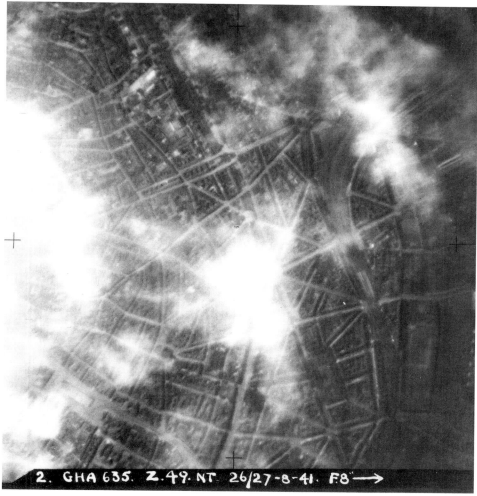

2. GHA 635. 2.49. NT 26/27-8-41. F8 →

Bombing photographs were used to assess the accuracy of the attack; Cologne from a 49 Squadron aircraft on the night of 26/27 August 1941 when, in clear conditions, ninety-nine bombers attacked the city. Intelligence Officers would compare the photos against maps and assess where the bombs fell.

was little alternative but to carry on as before – Bomber Command was, after all, the main method of striking back at Germany and this important morale point should not be forgotten. The same month brought a supplementary directive that added a number of minor towns to the target list, all connected with the German rail transportation system. The night of 29/30 August saw the operations debut of the RAAF, with 455 Squadron Wellingtons taking part in the attack on Frankfurt. The Squadron had formed in June and as with the Canadians a large number of Aussies had been serving with the Command since the start of the war; however, there was less pressure applied to create 'national' squadrons and combine them into a Group – so no Australian operational Group was formed.

A number of other reports and studies were undertaken in 1941, one of which looked at the reasons for aircraft losses. It had always been considered that a sustained loss rate of around 4 per cent was acceptable – or at least tolerable in terms of main-taining operational capability. However, studies showed that whilst German defences were improving and losses to enemy action on the increase, the incidence of losses not directly related to enemy action was also on the increase, and on a number of occasions was 2 per cent. The two main components of this were fuel shortage (26 per cent of incidents) and 'bad landings' (24 per cent). Although these were put down as 'non operational' it was often the case that enemy action played a part – damage to fuel systems leading to fuel shortage or damage to aircraft systems contributing to 'bad landings'.

Fuel was always a problem and many crews had nail-biting experiences of, 'Will we make it, won't we make it'. Bomb and fuel loads were specified by Group, although the Station – and to some extent the Squadron – could query the calculation and make adjustments. Crews had no choice in the matter, although bomb loads were sometimes 'adjusted' by dropping one or more 1,000-pounders in the North Sea on the way to the target in order to lighten the load. One of the main reasons for adding a Flight Engineer to the crew of the four-engined heavies was to manage aircraft systems, including fuel. Crews treated it as a matter of importance to get the best out of the engines, including fuel consumption and Captains who could nurse the aircraft in this way were always more popular. Some squadrons ran competitions to see which crews could achieve the most economical fuel consumption, and ground crew would always dip the tanks to see just how much was left (aircraft fuel gauges were notoriously unreliable). There were many unknowns once the bomber was airborne, the most worrisome of which was unreliable Met forecasts. The commonest reason for shortage of fuel was inaccurate wind forecasts – a strong headwind made all the difference to a thirsty bomber. So too did cruising altitude, icing and a number of other weather-related factors. Add to that evasion, with engines on higher power and burning more fuel and the potential for disaster was always present. Many crews began their return flights knowing that fuel was going to be tight – would they end up in the sea, would they make it to an airfield in

The geodetic structure of the Wellington fuselage proved rugged and even with the fabric burnt away and part of the structure damaged aircraft frequently made it home.

Stirling of 218 Squadron; the Shorts bomber became the primary equipment for No.3 Group.

Eastern England, or might they just get back to their own base? Having reached England safely it was time for another glance at the fuel gauges – enough to get home or should a landing be made at the nearest airfield? There were strong reasons to press on to home base; it was a familiar airfield to land on at night, it was better for the operational readiness of the squadron and the Mess and perhaps a local pub beckoned. Many crews pressed on, many made it, some took to the silk having had engines cough and die *en route*, others crash-landed (always dodgy at night) and some picked up a light or used the Darky (An emergency radio navigation aid) system to find another airfield.

It was certainly true that the Germans' somewhat *ad hoc* defensive system was growing; for example, in August the XIIIth Air Corps was formed with two searchlight Divisions, three signals Regiments, day fighter units and a night fighter Division. A Bomber Command report of August showed that of 3,449 sorties some 6.9 per cent reported interceptions and of these, 36 per cent turned into fighter attacks. Reports appeared to flow thick and fast within the Command and in September the Bomber Command Operational Research Section (ORS) was formed under Dr B. G. Dickins. This was to be an incredibly important and influential organisation and the ORS is quoted frequently in this book. They were given four main areas of study:

1. Bomber losses.
2. The success of bomber operations.
3. Vulnerability of bombers.
4. Radar and Radio problems.

The study of daylight operations was added later. The ORS combined the expertise and knowledge of scientists, technicians and operational personnel and its contribution cannot be too highly stressed. Its reports pulled no punches and whilst highly classified and with a limited circulation their recommendations were often acted upon.

Loss rates had risen in the latter part of the year and a new directive of 13 November introduced a policy to, 'Conserve our resources in order to build a strong force to be available by the spring of next year.' This was in part a reflection on the losses for the raid of 7/8 November and the AOC, Peirse, saw this as a slur on himself and his Command. He pointed out that most decisions were taken in close consultation with a wide range of experts and with consideration of the overall tactical environment – and that plans sometime went awry. This was not an isolated spat between Bomber Command and the Air Ministry staff (with Portal as CAS) and within weeks Peirse had gone, although this move was not officially connected with such disagreements.

This difficult year of 1941 year closed with the testing of another accuracy aid – *Oboe* – which showed great potential; Stirlings of 7 and 15 Squadrons used the new equipment during an attack on Brest but this was a one-off for fear of the equipment falling into enemy hands should one of the aircraft be shot down. Tests continued through December and *Oboe*-equipped Mosquitoes flown by Pathfinder crews were eventually to prove one of the most successful combinations of the war – but that success was still some way off, although a crystal-ball gazer may have started to see a bit of light at the end of the tunnel. At the end of the year the Command had 56 operational squadrons, of which 27 per cent were heavies. It had operated on 240 nights in 1941, dropping 31,000 tons of bombs, of which 12 per cent were incendiaries; it also flew 1,250 mining sorties on which 1,055 mines were laid. The next year was without doubt a turning point in the capability of Bomber Command.

Growing power

The conservation policy was maintained during the winter of 1941/42 in order to build up strength for a renewed offensive from the spring, when weather conditions would improve. Politics dominated the first few weeks of the New Year; a temporary C-in-C, AVM Baldwin held the reins from 8 January pending the arrival in February of the new bomber chief, AM Arthur T. Harris. Despite continued support from Prime Minister Churchill, the Command was under pressure; the influential Ministry of Economic Warfare (MEW) added its voice to the detractors with a report of 4 February stating that, 'The MEW depends directly on the Director of Bombing Operations to resist, in the higher levels any unsound tendencies to dilute, by-pass or emasculate policies which have been agreed between ourselves [the MEW Bombing Target Information Committee] and the Air Staff as being unsound in the respects which are within our respective provinces .... Bomber Command is still paying more attention to techniques and operational problems than to economic strategy, though there are signs that this phase is now passing.' Optimism of a change of attitude would prove premature for all the Commanders, Harris was the most dogmatic – indeed stubborn – in terms of the focus of bombing strategy as he saw it and he had an aversion to panacea targets.

The determined – indeed dogmatic – head of Bomber Command from early 1942 was Arthur 'Bomber' (or 'Butch') Harris.

It was in this overall situation that Arthur Harris took over the Command on 22 February. He arrived at Bomber Command HQ with the determination to prove that his was indeed the decisive weapon of the war. Although Harris's main focus was to be on achieving a front-line strength of 4,000 four-engine bombers, the first new type to enter service in 1942 was a Blenheim replacement, the Douglas Boston commencing its operational career in February.

Although a new operational Directive took effect the same month (before Harris took over), which approved area bombing of cities, it also cited that aids such as *Gee* would, 'Confer upon your forces the ability to concentrate their effort to an extent which has not hitherto been possible under the operational conditions with which you are faced ... and will enable results to be obtained of a much more effective nature.' The primary objective was still that of 'the morale of the enemy civilian population and in particular of the industrial workers.' The directive was accompanied by a list of suitable cities, with Essen top of the list, along with the bomb tonnage required to inflict critical damage; in the case of Essen this was given as 1,000 tons of bombs. The Air Staff also stated that the Command should focus on a particular target until the required bomb tonnage had been dropped and the desired level of destruction achieved. The final point was that each attack should be led by *Gee*-equipped aircraft to ensure accuracy, which in effect was the first real proposal for a 'target marking' force. The question of how best to employ the new aid had been under debate and trial within Bomber Command for some time and the next result was the *Shaker* technique. This tactical plan used three waves of aircraft, the first two of which comprised aircraft with *Gee*:

First wave: Illuminators dropping triple flares to illuminate the target from Zero hour.
Second wave: Target Markers dropping a maximum load of incendiaries from Zero+2.
Third wave: The Followers (Main Force) with a mainly HE load over the target from Zero+15.

When Arthur Harris took up his post Bomber Command had a total average availability (aircraft with crews) of only 378 aircraft, and only 69 were 'heavies'. He summarised his initial views: 'The bomber force of which I assumed command, although at that time very small, was a potentially decisive weapon. It was, indeed, the only means at the disposal of the Allies for striking at Germany itself and, as such, stood out as the central part in Allied offensive strategy.' This was despite, 'A lack of suitable aircraft in sufficient numbers, absence of efficient navigation aids, and deficiency of trained crews.'

All of these aspects were addressed in the coming months. Although bomber production had been given a high priority by Beaverbrook the 'heavies' were slow in coming off the production line, with only sixty-seven new four-engined aircraft being delivered in the first quarter of 1942, a major limitation on re-equipment and expansion plans. The situation with medium bombers had improved with the American Lend-Lease programme, types such as the Boston being acquired for No. 2 Group, but the one and only B-17 squadron in the RAF had given up its Fortresses – a combination of poor performance and lack of commitment from the Americans as to future supplies; the 'heavies' would have to come from British sources. It was therefore significant that on 3/4 March the Avro Lancaster made its operational debut.

The capability of the bombers to hit pinpoint targets was proven the same night, with an attack on the Renault factory at Billancourt. This was followed up a few nights later with an accurate attack on Essen, using *Gee* on a large scale for the first time. *Gee* did not, however, help with all Ruhr targets as the industrial haze continued to hamper accurate attacks. The month ended with a devastating attack on the Baltic port of Lubeck and when Harris looked back on his first weeks in command it was mixed picture. The new aids showed promise but his Command had lost ninety aircraft in the six weeks to the end of March, losses in aircraft and crews that were hard to replace. In terms of crews he had instigated a number of studies and one immediate result was the adoption of a single-pilot system, which immediately freed-up a large number of qualified pilots. Another member of the crew would take on the role of Pilot Assistant and be given a certain amount of pilot training for emergencies and to help the pilot. Harris also focused on what his crews were doing; he expected commanders to rest crews when operational requirements were light, but he also expected trained aircrew to fly two operational tours and two training tours – and he did not want aircrew posted to other Commands or ground tours. His expansion plans were hit by an Admiralty demand for eight and a half squadrons to be transferred to Coastal Command, mainly for employment in the Battle of the Atlantic. The argument closed at six squadrons, with Harris 'agreeing' to release three Whitley, two Wellington and one Hampden. The maritime war once more became the focus of attention with the spring campaign priorities being:

1. To destroy enemy ports, ships and the mainspring of his great offensive against our ocean convoys.
2. To inflict the maximum damage on German and German-controlled war industries . . . in the course of such operations it is now part of our policy to create havoc in those German towns and cities which house the workers on whose efforts the Nazi war machine is dependent.

The latter phrase would spell increasing misery for German civilians, especially when a 'de-housing' campaign was proposed. This strategy was debated at the highest levels and the War Cabinet established the Singleton Committee to review the arguments and determine 'what results are we likely to achieve from continuing our air attacks on Germany at the greatest possible strength during the next six, twelve and eighteen months respectively. Various developments took place before the Committee made its report.

A daring but costly daylight raid by Lancasters on the MAN factory in Augsburg caused another spat between the Ministry of Economic Warfare and Bomber Command when the MEW expressed the opinion that it had the, 'Gravest doubts whether this attack was planned, in the light of the intelligence available, to hit the enemy where it would hurt him most.' Harris was forceful in his reply that the, 'MEW allows no weight to the other, over-weening, factors which strategy, tactics and technicalities bring to bear on such an operation.'

The Whitley bowed out of Bomber Command's front-line on 27/28 April, two aircraft of 58 Squadron taking part in an attack on Dunkirk. This was not the last time that Whitleys appeared over enemy territory as they were back in action for the Thousand-Bomber raids and the OTUs continued to send aircraft on leaflet dropping

Lancasters entered service in 1942 an soon became the main focus of production, eventually equipping the majority of Bomber Command squadrons.

missions. A few days before, 23/24 April, the town of Rostock was subjected to the first of four consecutive nights of attack, a test of the policy of concentrating on a single target. It appeared to work in as much as damage, including the important Heinkel factory, was heavy whilst bomber losses (8 out of 520 over the 4 raids) were light.

On 5 May Harris received a modified directive that once more placed the aircraft industry as the first priority, with factories at Augsburg, Leipzig, Regensburg, Warnemunde and Wiener-Neustadt given particular mention. It also added industrial targets in France to the list, although these were already under attack, the main aim being to, 'Discourage the nationals of enemy-occupied countries from working in German controlled factories.' Three provisos were given for target selection: economic importance, ease of identification and maximum morale impact with the minimum of casualties. The attack on the Renault factory at Billancourt showed what could be done, and the Philips factory at Eindhoven was listed by name.

Harris was an experienced bomber leader and he was convinced that this was still a war-winning weapon, though he knew he would have to prove it to its many detractors. The three Thousand Bomber raids of May-June 1942 were designed to prove this point and large areas of Cologne, Essen and Bremen were destroyed. On the first of these attacks, 30/31 May, Cologne was targeted by 1,047 bombers, by far the largest force assembled by the Command and only achieved by using aircraft from the training Groups. This was an incredible achievement when it is remembered that when Harris took command a few months previously his available force was less than 400 bombers. By the end of the third raid, Harris felt that he had a convincing argument – and there was the added bonus that loss rates had been reasonably low as the defences had been swamped. Nevertheless he still had to defend the role of his Command and on 17 June sent a note to Churchill, who fortunately was almost unwaveringly supportive of the bomber offensive. In part this said: 'An extraordinary sense of lack of proportion affects outside appreciation of Bomber Command's operations. What shouts of victory would arise if a Commando wrecked the entire Renault factory in a night, with the loss of seven men!

Preparing a 4,000 lb 'Cookie'; this High Capacity (HC) blast bomb proved very effective.

What credible assumptions of an early end to the war would follow upon the destruction of one third of Cologne in an hour-and-a-half by some swift-moving mechanized force which, with 200 casualties, withdrew and was ready to repeat the operation twenty-four hours later? What acclaim would greet the virtual destruction of Rostock and the Heinkel main and subsidiary factories by a Naval bombardment! All this and far more has been achieved by Bomber Command – yet there are many who still avert their gaze, pass on the other side, and question whether the thirty squadrons of night bombers make any worthwhile contribution to the war.' They were forceful and appropriate comments, with barbs at the other Services that coveted the resources of Bomber Command. Harris would continue to fight such battles for the rest of the war and as the Command's destructive potential increased so too did its detractors, especially those seeking the moral high ground. As reported in the British Press in July Harris made his intentions clear: 'The German people have been told to expect devastating air raids every night and every day, rain, blow or snow. The man who gave them this message, in a broadcast in German, is Air Marshal Sir Arthur Harris, who took over as Chief of Bomber Command last February. He promised to scourge the Third Reich from end to end.' This may have been wishful thinking in 1942 but by late 1944 it had become a reality.

Just before this series of raids the Singleton Committee Report had been issued (20 May) and concluded that: 'The bomber strength of the RAF is increasing rapidly. I have no doubt that if the best use is made of it, the effect on German war production and effort will be very heavy over a period of twelve to eighteen months and such as to have a real effect on the war position'. He also concluded that with the exception of a number of attacks accuracy was still a problem and that a trained target-finding force would greatly increase the efficiency of the bombing.

It appeared that the, 'Corner had been turned' and it is certainly true that despite a number of crises that the Command was subsequently to face, the general trend was one of increased effectiveness. However, despite the rhetoric above, all was not well, especially with the new bombers. The Manchester had been faring particularly badly and had a loss rate almost double that of the Stirling; an ORS report ascribed this in part to the fuel system. 'The Manchester has two main petrol tanks and two small ones, whereas the Stirling has fourteen', with the implication being that damage to the fuel system was more crucial in the Avro bomber. They could also have cited the continued problems of overheating with the Vulture engines and the all-round poorer performance that made the Manchester more vulnerable. It became apparent over the next few months that the aircraft lowest and slowest in the bomber stream were those that suffered the highest loss rates. The Halifax was also criticised in an ORS report as its loss rate of 5.3 per cent in 1,467 sorties in the year to June 1942 was not sustainable. The report concluded that most losses were to night fighters and two main problems were cited: poor exhaust shrouds made the Halifax easier to find and once found the aircraft was not manoeuvrable enough. The latter suggestion was further investigated in conjunction with a review of the experience levels of pilots in No. 4 Group. This report concluded that: 'There is no reasonable doubt that pilots on their first two operations have a casualty rate well above the average and that those who had survived twenty sorties had a rate well below the average. This must be aircraft related as the Lancaster does not suffer the same problem. The record on lightly defended targets is good; the problem comes on highly defended targets. New pilots are a bit nervous of the aircraft, the aircraft having gained a bad name for instability in manoeuvres. It thus may happen that a new pilot is reluctant when he meets defences to manoeuvre his machine sufficiently in combat or that in a sudden emergency he puts his machine into an attitude in which he has had no previous

Chocques power station under attack by 88 Squadron and 126 Squadron, 19 July 1942.

experience of controlling it.' More general handling during training and fighter affiliation sorties were seen as at least partial solutions, although moves were also underway to improve the manoeuvrability of the Halifax.

The ORS had also been looking at the Command's daylight operations in a summary report of the six months to the end of June, the main focus being in the *Circus* operations of No. 2 Group's Boston squadrons. The conclusion was that the tactic's main aim of destroying the *Luftwaffe* was not working. The bombers had flown over 1,000 sorties and had achieved reasonable results for their 3 per cent loss rate; however the fighter combats – the main purpose of the *Circus* – had resulted in 118 victories and 166 losses in 9,486 sorties.

Summer with its shorter nights was normally a time when the bomber's radius of action was reduced and with the exception of another long-range Lancaster raid, to Danzig on 11 July, this pretty much held true.

The summer campaign was, however, not going well and on 10 August an ORS report examined interception rates, with statistics for June of 8.3 per cent of 4,788 sorties being intercepted, with 25 per cent being converted into attacks; the report concluded that: 'Losses have reached a very high level, since they have occurred mostly under conditions of heavy cloud and in the absence of searchlight co-operation it seems likely that effective GCI [Ground Control Interception] must be responsible. The proportion of attacks from below which results in serious damage emphasises the need for more protection from this direction.' One worrying feature was the particularly high loss rates of OTU aircraft, the 31 July raid on Duisburg having cost No. 92 Group eleven of its 105 aircraft. Although Harris was keen to put the maximum number of bombers over the target this use of the training units was counter-productive in operational and morale terms.

The Blenheim made its last Bomber Command *ops* on 17/18 August when 18 Squadron flew intruder sorties over Holland in support of the Main Force attack on Osnabruck.

Pathfinders

In May 1942 the de Havilland Mosquito joined Bomber Command and was soon to prove one of the most effective bomber types for specialist operations and for the pathfinding role with Main Force. Accuracy remained a goal for the bombers and the creation of a target-marking element, the Pathfinder Force (later No. 8 Group), under Air Commodore Don Bennett, was a major development, as was the introduction of new target-marking methods. The first Pathfinder Force (PFF) operation took place on 18/19 August, when the target was Flensburg, and results were poor. The birth of this specialist organisation had not been an easy one. Harris favoured further development of the present tactical use of experienced crews to lead attacks but was against the hiving off of crews to form specialist units. The Air Staff, and bomber leaders such as Group Captain Bufton, Deputy Director of Bomber Operations, favoured the creation of a specialist force. An Air Ministry conference in June came down in favour of the latter idea and on 20 June Harris instructed No. 3 Group to set aside two Wellington and two Stirling squadrons to become the nucleus of the Pathfinder Force (PFF). This was later changed and each operational Group 'donated' a squadron:

> No. 1 Group – 156 Squadron, Wellington.
> No. 3 Group – 7 Squadron, Stirling.
> No. 4 Group – 35 Squadron, Halifax.
> No. 5 Group – 83 Squadron, Lancaster and 109 Squadron, Mosquito.

The PFF was officially formed on 11 August 1942 under Air Commodore (later AVM) Don Bennett), an experienced, determined and effective bomber leader with assets at Graveley, Oakington, Wyton and Warboys.

The first success for the Pathfinders came on 28/29 August when 159 bombers, led by PFF aircraft, attacked Nuremberg. The Pathfinders dropped a new marker, called *Red Blob Fire*, and the results seemed reasonable – although twenty-three bombers failed to return (including four Lancasters). Bomber Command was slowly becoming more effective – but so were the German defences, especially the night fighters. The Command continued to develop new tactics to counter the defences: a tight stream of aircraft to compress the time spent over the target, spoof or decoy raids to confuse and dilute the night fighters, adopting electronic equipment to confuse the enemy, and at the same time it developed improved marking techniques.

With all three heavies in service and with the PFF now leading most attacks, all the major elements of Main Force Bomber Command were in place. In many respects, all that changed between this point and early 1945 was the scale of the offensive and the tactics employed to counter the increasing effectiveness of the German night defences. With the arrival of the Americans in 1942, the bomber offensive became the Strategic Bombing Offensive (SBO) – the Americans bombing by day and the RAF by night. The 97th Bombardment Group's attack on Sotteville-les-Rouen's rail yards on 17 August was the opening shot in the American daylight offensive, an offensive that would assume epic proportions but that is beyond the scope of this account. Oil was to become one of the favoured target systems for the 8th Army Air Force and it was also a regular feature of Bomber Command's operations log. On 3 September Harris was given a directive to concentrate on oil as the Joint Intelligence Committee Technical Sub-Committee had

Lancaster of 83 Squadron; the Squadron flew Hampdens, Manchesters and Lancasters during the war, the latter from May 1942.

determined that the Axis oil situation was critical and that effective attacks on a limited number of targets, Politz being listed as the highest priority, could be decisive. Harris hated such specific instructions, especially from organisations for which he had no respect and as on many other occasions he simply ignored the instruction.

In the remaining months of 1942 the Command turned in mixed results with a number of exceptionally effective raids, including special low level attack on Le Creusot (17 October), and it was evident that the PFF was developing its tactics and equipment with great promise. In November a meeting of the War Cabinet's Chiefs of Staff Committee considered the future of the Anglo-American bomber offensive and concluded that: 'A heavy bomber force rising from 4,000 to 6,000 heavy bombers in 1944 could shatter the industrial and economic structure of Germany to a point where an Anglo-American force of reasonable strength could enter the Continent from the West.' It was predicted that the bomb lift per month would increase from 50,000 tons by the end of 1943 to 90,000 by late 1944. The shattering effect would be used against fifty-eight towns and cities in Germany with populations of 50,000, with the top eighteen targets having populations of 250,000. Each named town also had listed the industries or economic and political rationale for its destruction. The report continued: 'Germany is in no condition to withstand an onslaught of this nature, her strength has passed its peak and is diminishing ... it is difficult to estimate the morale consequences of a scale of bombardment which would far transcend anything within human experience. But I have no doubt that against a background of growing casualties, increasing privations and dying hopes it would be profound indeed. As resources were destroyed the Germans would have three options:

1. Reduce the level of civil resources below that needed to maintain the national economy.
2. Divert effort or armed forces and munitions industry to defensive measures to hold off the bombers.
3. Divert resources into civil industries.'

The report was signed by Portal as CAS but was very much the view of the Combined Chiefs – the bomber war against cities was an approved Allied strategy (despite what some later claimed). The basic points were accurate but the conclusion was false as it was based on the effect such a campaign would have had on Britain; it was still not appreciated that the Nazi regime, and the war footing of its industries, was more resilient. In part this was due to the slow build-up of the bomber offensive which had allowed time for defences, civil and military to develop and adapt.

November also brought new arguments between Harris and the Ministry of Economic Warfare with the latter's call for a renewed offensive against the ball-bearing industry being translated into an Air Ministry directive of 21 November. This stated that: 'The destruction of the Schweinfurt factories would result in a loss to the Germans of considerably more than half their requirements in ball-bearings for the production of armaments …. I require that you [Bomber Command] now reconsider your plans to attack Schweinfurt and the associated ball-bearing factories on the principle that their destruction should be regarded as of critical importance to our strategy, and devastation of the factories and town in one overwhelming operation'. An annex to the directive even gave details of a suggested plan of attack! Harris was not amused and two days later objected to the suggested large-scale attack on a variety of grounds, including the tacit acceptance by the Air Staff of a loss of 200 crews. He queried the overall effect that the successful destruction of the target would have, his aversion to panacea targets being a major factor. Finally, he objected to the type of attack, suggesting that a night low-level pinpoint raid would be more effective. In the event it was irrelevant as he essentially ignored the instruction; it was eventually left to the Americans to mount a daylight raid, with heavy losses and little overall effect.

On 24 November Harris had been sent new instructions, with future policy stated as:

1. Render material support to the Russians.
2. Prepare for the invasion of Europe.
3. Soften-up Europe by bombing.

The latter point was phrased in terms that Harris could relate to: 'From now on we must strike with ever-increasing strength at the German industrial and economic system, submarine construction, sources of air power, and morale of the German people.' Despite this directive the major focus of Bomber Command in autumn 1942 was against Italy. From the operational perspective there were two important developments towards the end of the year; the introduction of a new countermeasures system, *Tinsel*, and the operational trial of *Oboe* when six Mosquitoes of 109 Squadron used this device for an attack on the power station at Lutterade. Further evaluation raids were carried out in December, culminating on the 31 December with two *Oboe* Mosquitoes acting as part of the marker force for an attack on Dusseldorf. These early results looked very promising despite some technical snags with the equipment.

The Air Historical Branch Narrative gave this conclusion for 1942: 'Something had been achieved in terms of material damage and very much more in tactical and technical developments. Even more important, it had been demonstrated to the enemy that nowhere or at any time were they secure from air attack.' Of more import in terms of the effectiveness of attacks was the imminent operational employment of two new aids – H2S and *Oboe* – plus new weapons and a steadily increasing daily bomb lift. In future the Command would wield effective destructive power, but only if it could survive in the face of the German defences. Various tactics had been tried during the latter part of the year, such as concentration over the target, diversionary and spoof raids, deceptive routeing, intruder *ops* against night fighter airfields, and the employment of Radio Counter-measures. This tactical mix would be used for the rest of war as each side tried to gain the

The arrival of the American 8th Army Air Force added a new dimension to the strategic bombing offensive.

upper hand in the cat-and-mouse night war. It would become increasingly important because, although 1942 had been a turning point year, it had also brought deep concern over loss rates. Of the sixty squadrons in the Command, just over half were 'heavies'.

Throughout this book I refer to loss rates and at times it is hard to focus on the fact that these bare statistics refer to people as well as operational capability. In a lecture just after the war, Air Chief Marshal Sir Norman Bottomley had this to say in respect of loss rates: 'The rate of night bomber losses was highest in 1942, before our tactics and counter-measures were properly developed. The loss rate in this year was 4.1 per cent. I often wonder if the significance of a loss rate of 4.1 per cent is generally realised. The normal operational tour of bomber crews was thirty sorties. If they survived, they were then withdrawn for a change of occupation – say for six months – before a second tour. A loss rate of 4 per cent meant therefore that the chances were against completing the first operational tour; and it meant that on an average there was a complete turn-over of aircrews in squadrons in about four months, due to casualties. It is a matter of pride that morale in the heavy bomber forces remained so high in the face of these casualty rates.

'The loss rate fell to 3.7 per cent in 1943 and in 1944 it amounted to 1.7 per cent. In the last months of the war in 1945 it was less than 1 per cent.'

The night war had been hotting up and 1943 was to be a showdown year.

Wielding the weapon

Harris was planning an intensive start to 1943 with a series of major blows against Ruhr targets ('Happy Valley' to Bomber Command aircrews) and other major industrial cities. However, a directive of 14 January called for focused attacks on targets connected with the U-boats, the German Wolfpacks having once more gained the upper hand in the Battle of the Atlantic. However, and with a few named exclusions, the War Cabinet was persuaded that the best way for Bomber Command to achieve this effect was by area attacks on appropriate industrial towns: 'With the object of effectively devastating the whole area in which are located the submarines, their maintenance facilities and the services, power, water, light, communications and other resources upon which their operations depend.' The named exclusions that the Command was required to attack as soon as possible were the U-boat facilities at Lorient, Brest, La Pallice and St Nazaire, the home bases for most of the Atlantic U-boats. Lorient was duly bombed on 14/15 January by 122 aircraft in the first major raid of 1943. Damage was light and, as Harris argued, this type of target was unsuitable as the accuracy of attack and effectiveness of the bombs was such that small, hardened targets such as U-boat pens were almost impossible to damage. This was true – but he was also against the idea on the grounds that it detracted the Command from the main war over Germany. The Bomber Command argument was enumerated as: 'If the number of operational U-boats is to be substantially reduced, the menace must also be powerfully attacked at earlier stages in its career and the continued flow of reinforcements decisively choked. The achievement of a decision is hastened by strategic bombing of the factories employed on the construction of component parts and by the bombing of the U-boat building yards.' The Lorient raid was also the operational debut for No. 6 (RCAF) Group, although some of its squadrons and many of its aircrew were already experienced in the bomber war.

This was to be a year when new equipment and tactics were introduced on a regular basis; the first such event being the use of purpose-built Target Indicators (TIs) by the PFF, the target on 16/17 January being Berlin. A week later another new aircraft started its operational career with No. 2 Group when twelve B-25 Mitchells of 98 and 180 Squadrons joined Bostons and Venturas attacking airfields in France. The light/medium bomber force of this Group was heavily involved with attacks on a variety of targets in Occupied Europe, the *Circus* ops continued to bring mixed results but the intruder work was definitely proving useful. January also saw the Pathfinder Force raised to Group status as No. 8 (Pathfinder) Group on the 25th of the month. At the end of the month another navigation aid went operational when the H2S radar was used during an attack on Hamburg (30/31 January), although only a few aircraft carried the device.

The Allied leaders met at Casablanca to discuss the prosecution of the war, one of the items on the agenda being the Strategic Bombing Offensive. In due course, the Combined Chiefs of Staff issued a new directive (21 January) stating that the 'primary objective will be the progressive destruction of and dislocation of the German military, industrial and economic system, and the undermining of the morale of the German people to a point where their capacity for armed resistance is fatally weakened.' The directive gave five target categories for attack – submarine construction yards, aircraft industry, transportation, oil plants and 'others in the war industry'. It also gave added support to the concept of a 6,000-strong heavy bomber force.

However, in February the Air Staff switched its instruction – an all too frequent occurrence in Harris's view – and ordered attacks on Berlin to emphasise the Allied success of recent weeks, by which they meant the surrender of the German 6th Army at Stalingrad. It was March, however, before the 'Big City' was targeted by Main Force and February saw a wide variety of targets attacked. Overall the scene was now set for the first of a series of 'battles' to be fought between Bomber Command and the *Luftwaffe*. That most desirable but elusive set of targets in the Ruhr was first on the list for what the Command intended, and hoped, would be effective concentrated raids taking advantage

The Lancaster had the lowest loss rates of Bomber Command's operational types, but almost 4,000 were lost on operations.

of the impressive bomb lift and new target-finding aids. This was to be the first real operational test of the appreciable operational capability (at least on paper) of Bomber Command. The Battle of the Ruhr ran from March to July 1943 and at best could be described as a draw in which both sides learnt many lessons and from which both had a momentary rest prior to the next battle.

The Battle of the Ruhr was in full swing when Harris was issued with a new directive on future bombing strategy. This was a result of the Casablanca Conference and under the codename *Pointblank* it gave four main target types for attack by the combined British and American bomber forces:

1. Aircraft industry.
2. Submarine construction yards and U-boat bases.
3. Ball-bearing production.
4. Oil installations.

This was based on a proposal put forward earlier in the year by the American bomber chief, Ira Eaker, and the focus on the enemy aircraft industry was in response to the loss rates the USAAF was suffering in its daylight campaign: 'If the growth of the German fighter strength is not arrested quickly it may become impossible to carry out the destruction planned and thus create the conditions necessary for ultimate decisive action by our combined forces on the Continent.'

There was also much debate at this time as to the future of No. 2 Group, the light bombers no longer fitting the strategic role of Bomber Command but slated to play a major role in a tactical sense with the invasion of Europe. The decision was eventually taken to move the Group to the new Tactical Air Force (TAF) with effect from 1 June 1943, although when this took place the Mosquito-equipped 105 and 139 Squadrons were transferred to No. 8 Group.

Provision of airfields had remained a problem for much of 1942, despite an accelerated building programme, but the rapid expansion of Bomber Command also created difficulties in operational and administrative control of units. To ease the latter problems it was proposed to introduce a base system whereby three airfields would be linked, one as the HQ base and two as satellites, under the command of an Air

Commodore. This concept was finally approved in February 1943 and the first three bases were:

No. 3 Group: Mildenhall with satellites at Lakenheath and Newmarket (although East Wretham was also allocated).
No. 4 Group: Pocklington with satellites at Melbourne and Elvington.
No. 6 Group: Topcliffe with satellites at Dishforth and Dalton.

In addition to operational control, elements of the technical and servicing activities were also centralised and servicing echelons were allocated to squadrons. These were given 9000 numbers, hence that attached to 9 Squadron became 9009 Servicing Echelon.

Overall expansion was progressing at a rapid pace in early 1943 and as part of this process an agreement was reached with the Air Ministry in April to increase the establishment of existing squadrons. Under this agreement, squadrons with two flights had their aircraft UE increased by two (to sixteen IE and four IR), with a corresponding increase in aircrew strength of one crew (from twenty-one to twenty-two crews plus the CO). Squadrons with three flights acquired three extra aircraft (to twenty-four plus six) and one extra crew (to thirty-three plus the CO). There was also a corresponding increase in ground-crew strength. By February 1943 the Command's operational force comprised fifty-one heavy/medium squadrons and eleven light squadrons, made up as follows:

Heavy:	Lancaster	17 squadrons
	Halifax	11 squadrons
	Stirling	7 squadrons
Medium:	Wellington	16 squadrons
Light:	Ventura	3 squadrons
	Boston	3 squadrons
	B-25	2 squadrons
	Mosquito	3 squadrons

This expansion in the first half of 1943 took place as and when aircraft became available as there was, at this time, no significant limitation in terms of aircrew availability. It was

Aircraft, aircrew and airfields - the Command needed all three in increasing numbers as the war progressed; it was an amazing achievement.

then standard policy to add a third flight to an operational squadron and split this flight away to form the nucleus of a new squadron at the same airfield. The splitting of a squadron to form a new unit had been a tried and tested technique since the start of the war and it seemed to create few problems. By May 1943 the following units had been given third flights:

No. 1 Group: 12, 100, 101, 103, 460 Squadrons
No. 3 Group: 75, 90, 149, 214 Squadrons
No. 4 Group: 10, 76, 77, 78, 102 Squadrons
No. 5 Group: 57, 467 Squadrons
No. 8 Group: 97, 156 Squadrons

May brought the award of two Victoria Crosses to Bomber Command pilots; one to Wing Commander Guy Gibson of 617 Squadron for leading the Dams Raid (Operation *Chastise*), and one to Squadron Leader Trent of 487 Squadron in what was one of the final series of raids by No. 2 Group. Neither of these attacks was central to Bomber Command's overall strategy. A further modification of the *Pointblank* directive was issued on 10 June, with four main aims:

1. The destruction of airframe, engine and component factories, and the ball-bearing industry on which the strength of the German fighter force depends.
2. The general disorganisation of those industrial areas associated with the above areas.
3. The destruction of those aircraft repair depots and storage parks within range, and on which the enemy fighter force is largely dependent.
4. The destruction of enemy fighters in the air and on the ground.

The vague wording of much of this enabled Bomber Command to continue its area bombing or industrial centres. Cities such as Dortmund, Dusseldorf, Cologne, Essen, Bochum, Wuppertal, Munster and Oberhausen had all been attacked by Main Force formations of up to 800 aircraft in an intensive series of attacks over four weeks from the last week in May. In this same period the Command also flew a highly successful low-level attack on a factory at Le Creusot (19/20 June) and an accurate long-range attack on the Zeppelin Works at Friedrichshafen (20/21 June). These were still, however, sideshows in the main strategic offensive. In this four-month period Bomber Command had despatched over 23,000 night sorties and lost around 1,000 aircraft; the average loss rate of 4.3 per cent was in line with predictions and was, on paper, 'acceptable' in terms of attrition in terms of maintaining the overall aircraft and aircrew strength of the Command. However, it was becoming increasingly apparent that certain aircraft types were far more vulnerable than others and that the 4 per cent average was being exceeded on a regular basis by the Halifax and the Stirling.

While the reports were still being compiled on the first Battle of the Ruhr, the next Battle was about to begin. Hamburg was designated as the target to receive a concentrated series of attacks over a short period of time, the codename being Operation *Gomorrah*. The first of these, 24/25 July, was also significant as it saw the first operational use of another defensive aid – *Window*. It was an incredibly successful tactic and one that reduced bomber losses for a number of raids, although the Germans soon developed tactics that lessened, though never negated, the use of this simple and cheap counter-measure. The Main Force consisted of 791 bombers, including 354 Lancasters from nineteen squadrons (four of these being Pathfinder units), with 103 Squadron sending no less than twenty-seven aircraft (although three of these returned early and three were

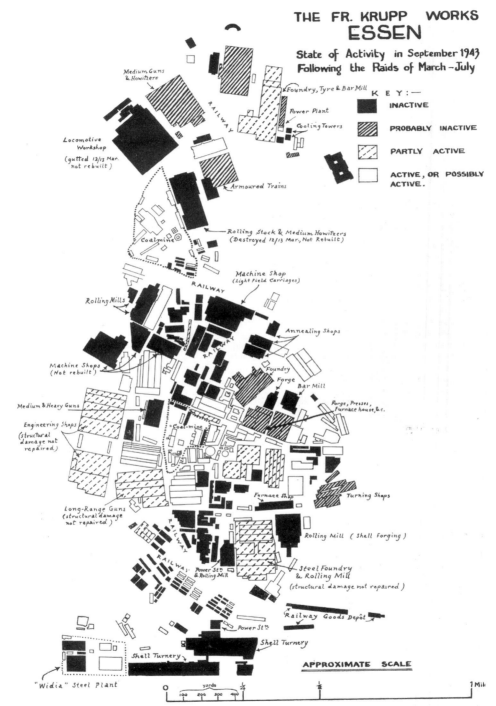

Plan showing Bomber Command summary of the damage caused to the Krupps Works at Essen during 1943.

lost). This series of four Main Force attacks on Hamburg caused major destruction in the city and seriously disrupted its war industries. A German report after the final raid stated: 'The port was severely hit, the damage was gigantic. The failing of the water system, and the fighting of fires which remained from earlier attacks, hampered all work severely. The whole of Hamburg was on fire. Rescue, evacuation, clearing of vital roads, fire fighting, etc, asked the impossible from the available LS forces. Economically, Hamburg was knocked out, as even the undamaged parts had to stop work on account of the destruction of water, gas and electricity supplies.' Propaganda Minister Goebbels in his private diary recorded the damage as a 'catastrophe, the extent of which simply staggers the imagination'; whilst Armaments Minister Speer stated that if another six big German cities were similarly destroyed he would not be able to maintain armaments production. Too many studies of the Battle of Hamburg have focused on the tragic loss of life, and it is true that the firestorm was horrendous, but it is the comments of the likes of Speer that show the strategic value of attacks on German cities.

Hamburg had suffered, but Bomber Command was also suffering. With improvements in the German defences – 'flak' and fighters – the RAF increasingly turned its attention to the provision of Radio Countermeasures, of which *Window* was one example. A range of equipment was developed as either warning aids to show crews that they were being tracked by a fighter (*Monica* and *Fishpond* being two such devices) or as a means of jamming German radar or radio. Jamming systems included specialist operations such as *ABC* (AirBorne Cigar), *Corona* and *Tinsel*. The technical aspects of the night war would play an increasingly important role in the final two years.

Early August brought a large-scale return to Italy and it is accepted that the Bomber Command attacks played a part in the decision by Italy to seek an Armistice in September. In addition to the usual run of Main Force attacks, special *ops* were also flown. Bomber Command launched an effective and important raid against the Germans' main weapons research and testing site at Peenemunde on 17/18 August, the result of which was a significant delay in the development of the V-weapons.

By August 1943 the Command had fifty-seven squadrons operational, of which forty-nine were heavies; however, the actual strength in terms of aircraft in service amounted to the equivalent of sixty-seven standard size squadrons. The limiting factor was still availability of aircraft and this situation was not helped by, as the AHB narrative puts it: 'Changes in operational requirements due to experience and improvements in tactics'. The Lancaster and Mosquito had already proved themselves satisfactory and only minor modifications and additions were made during this period. The only complaint of Bomber Command was that supplies were never sufficient – as a result, the other inferior types had to be accepted.

The Germans realised that the destructive power of the Combined Bomber Offensive was becoming a major factor in the war strategy and that only fighters could provide an effective counter. On 25 August Milch (Nazi chief of aircraft production) declared: '. . . must decide on priorities . . . only the 110 in sufficient numbers can give us the necessary relief at night . . . our fighters have to hit the enemy hard day and night to force him to abandon the policy of destruction of our arms production. Germany is the real front-line and the mass of fighters must go for home defence . . . the only chance to defeat day and night bombers.' It was not a universally shared view; for example Jeschonneck (Chief of General Staff of the *Luftwaffe*) expressed the opinion that: 'Every four-engined bomber the Western Allies build makes me happy, for we will bring these down just as we brought down the two-engined ones, and the destruction of a four-engined bomber constitutes a much greater loss to the enemy.' The *Luftwaffe* was

The German night fighter defences became very potent and included a number of 'experten' pilots, such as Egmont Lippe-Weissenfeld.

certainly doing its best to develop new weapons and tactics; one of the most effective new weapons, in service from August 1943, was the *Schrage musik* upward-firing cannon. This twin-cannon mounting permitted the fighter pilot to fly beneath the bomber and fire upwards into the bomb bay and fuel tanks, the result being critical damage with little risk from the bomber's gunners. The ORS had suspected the presence of such a weapon and evidence mounted that it was being extensively employed; German night fighter *experten* were soon making multiple kills each night, with some claiming six or seven bombers in a single sortie. Once the bomber stream had been found, an experienced crew 'swimming with the stream' was able to pick up bomber after bomber.

On the Berlin raid of 23/24 August the loss rate had been 7.9 per cent (56 of the 727 bombers), with the Halifax units suffering almost 10 per cent casualties, including 6 out of 34 Pathfinder aircraft. The 121 Stirlings of the third wave lost 13 per cent (16 aircraft), the majority to fighter attack. Such loss rates were unsupportable in the long term – and the Battle of Berlin was to throw the whole question into sharp relief. Over the next few months Bomber Command's Main Force would become a Lancaster/Halifax force, the Wellington bowing out of front-line bombing *ops* over Europe after the attack on Hannover of 8/9 October and the Stirling being withdrawn from bombing operations in summer 1944.

Following the Allied Commanders' Quebec conference in August, a new Directive was issued, giving the bombers new priorities in the air build-up for the planned invasion of Europe. Many of the existing industrial targets were still included, but there was to be increasing emphasis on lines of communication and the enemy air assets. However, after the Ruhr and Hamburg 'battles' Harris had already lined up his next target – Berlin. On 3 November he sent a memo to Churchill: 'We can wreck Berlin from end to end if the USAAF will come in on it. It will cost us between 400–500 aircraft. It will cost the Germany the war.' The Americans were not keen as they wanted to maintain their focus on what they believed were key industrial targets and they didn't join the Battle even though they agreed to attack Berlin when it seemed appropriate. This did not deter Harris and from late November Berlin was the preferred target for the Command.

The same day that Harris had sent his memo to Churchill, the Command mounted a very accurate raid on Dusseldorf (3/4 November), with 90 per cent of bombs estimated as falling within the target area even though it was a blind attack. This attack had included the operational debut of another new navigation/bombing aid – *Gee-H* (or *G-H*). The same raid brought the award of the Victoria Cross to Flight Lieutenant Bill Reid of 61 Squadron.

The first raid of the Berlin campaign took place on 18/19 November when 400 Lancasters attacked the 'Big City', with a second force attacking Ludwigshaven to split the night fighter force. A combination of poor weather and poor PFF marking led to a scattered raid, although losses were light. The night of 22/23 November saw the

Command mount a maximum effort against Berlin, 765 aircraft taking part. Marking was accurate and Berlin was hit hard. The Battle of Berlin took place in three phases and lasted to February 1944, by which time the Command had mounted 9,099 sorties against the 'Big City', dropping 29,804 tons of bombs; overall losses were 501 aircraft. Bomber Command was able to reach and hit its targets, but it was paying a high price.

The Bomber Command Quarterly Review summarised the last months of 1943 as: 'The most difficult phase of bombing yet carried out. These three winter months presented the first opportunity of operating large forces over the important but distant targets in Central Germany, including Berlin. Two conditions had essentially to be fulfilled if we were to obtain the desired results. First, it was imperative that the bomb load should be concentrated around the aiming point, and second, the rate of loss had to be maintained at an economic level. These essentials were achieved in the main by constant improvements in aids and counter-measures coupled with improved navigation by crews and a better understanding of the methods involved in marking the target. Tactical surprise was created by diversionary and "spoof" raids in conjunction with carefully planned routeing so that the enemy was kept guessing as to the real target for the night, with the result that he was seldom able to bring his full defences to bear at the crucial moment. In addition, every endeavour was made to jam his air defence communications system.' This was an over-optimistic assessment of the half-way point in the Battle of Berlin; although damage to some parts of Berlin had been extensive the German defences were adapting to the threat and hundreds of night fighters were available to counter the bombers on their flight over German territory. The increased use of Wild Boar and Tame Boar fighters, which gave greater flexibility to pilots in searching out and attacking the bombers had a significant impact on the Battle.

Berlin remained the main target into early 1944 but after an intensive, and expensive, series of attacks in January the Battle petered out and only two more attacks were made before the 'official' ending of this particular campaign. The termination was not primarily brought about by Bomber Command's concern over losses, although there certainly was concern, but rather the pressure being applied for support of the pre-invasion campaign.

The Air Ministry issued a revised directive on 17 February with a change of target priorities; the overall mission stayed the same and the primary objective (Schweinfurt) was also unchanged, but other objectives were listed as *Crossbow*, and 'Berlin and other important industrial areas'. An attack on the ball-bearing factory by the Americans was followed on 24/25 February by a Main Force attack by 734 aircraft. The attack was made in two waves – one hour apart, with the first wave losing twenty-two aircraft, mainly to fighters, and the second wave losing eleven aircraft. The factory reported only slight damage. Berlin and other German cities were attacked during the winter of 1944 but it was spring before *Crossbow* targets became a routine task.

Supporting the invasion

The March 1944 Bomber Command ORB recorded a statement by Lord Portal, Chief of Air Staff in respect of switching production capacity: 'A very careful study has been made of the problems involved in changing Halifax production over to the Lancaster, but the jig and tool capacity of the country was not sufficient to permit changing the Halifax firms to Lancaster production at the same time as changing from the Stirling. Further, that even if it were practicable to make such a switch there would be a prohibitive loss of bombing effort during the vital period between mid 1944 until probably late 1945'. He further stated that: After doing everything practicable to increase Lancaster production,

Bomber Command's 'heavies' played a major role in preparing the D-Day battlefield by cutting German rail links.

including diversion of Halifax resources, delivery will still be at the rate of four Halifaxes to seven Lancasters to the end of this year, although the proportion of Lancasters will continue to increase until the end of 1945.' The final part of his statement is even more telling: 'There is every hope that the German Air Force would be so weakened by the fighting this year that the Halifax can be retained as a front-line bomber in 1945. If this proves false, first-line bomber operations must be limited to Lancasters, delivery of which will rise to 350–450 per month in 1945, and employing the Halifax for mining and other second-line targets and for training.'

The outline overall Air Plan called for four phases of air operation in support of *Overlord*:

1. Preliminary: January–February 1944, but also a continuation of the air offensives of late 1943.
2. Preparatory: March-May 1944, main weight of attacks on invasion targets.
3. Assault: D minus Two to D plus One.
4. Follow-up: D plus Two onwards.

Before we look at the actual elements of the pre-invasion strategy a few general points need to be made: first; an enormous effort had to be expended on convincing the Germans to expect the invasion in the wrong place and as soon as the decision had been taken in favour of Normandy it became vital to make the Germans look to the Pas de Calais. The major aspect of this as far as the air campaign was concerned was to be the policy of attacking two targets outside of the designated invasion area for every one attacked within it. Second, the Allied air forces were by no means a cohesive whole and there were problems both in the command structure and air power doctrine; both of these problems had an effect on the campaign but neither proved to be of a critical nature.

With over 10,000 aircraft the air forces arrayed for the invasion of Europe would be the most powerful ever assembled. However, whilst the number of aircraft was impressive the list of targets prepared by the planning staffs was equally impressive and there was no shortage of experts with opinions as to which targets were the 'war winners' and so merited the greatest weight of air effort.

The preparatory phase

Attacks on enemy lines of communications had been an aspect of the Bomber Command bombing strategy, albeit as a bonus effect of destroying the centres of cities through which such major communications routes passed; however, it was now to be an objective in its own right, a directive to this effect being issued in early March. This is one of the key elements of the pre-invasion bombing strategy and one in which the effective employment of air power was crucial. On 4 March Bomber Command received instructions to carry out a series of trial attacks on French marshalling yards to provide planning data for a series of such attacks planned in support of the *Overlord* Transportation Plan. The targets for the trial were Trappes, Aulnoye, Le Mans, Amiens/Longeau, Courtrai and Laon. The first of these attacks took place on the night of 6/7 March when 261 Halifaxes led by six Mosquito aircraft attacked Trappes; weather conditions were excellent with good visibility and little opposition. The attack was one of the most successful yet undertaken by the Command and there were no losses. Bomber Command analysts enthused over the results concluding that: 'It is appreciated that this new-found ability to saturate with bomb strikes a given area of approx 500 × 1,000 yards square constitutes a weapon of war of enormous power.'

The following night a slightly larger force of Halifax and Lancaster bombers attacked Le Mans, again without loss and, despite cloud cover, with good results, although the number of French civilian casualties did cause concern. At least 300 bombs fell on the rail yards causing several cuts and the destruction of 250 wagons, a number of locomotives and substantial damage to installations.

During the remainder of March several more such raids were carried out against marshalling yards – Le Mans (13/14 March), Amiens (15/16 and 16/17 March), Laon (23/24 March), Aulnoye (25/26 March) and Courtrai (26/27 March). The question of bombing marshalling yards in towns where French civilian casualties might result, as had been the case with the Le Mans attack, continued to trouble some Allied planners and politicians, although many saw such casualties as a price that France would have to pay for liberation.

Harris, however, was determined to maintain his offensive against German cities. On the night of 30/31 March, the major industrial city and communications interchange of Nuremberg was chosen for a Main Force attack and 795 bombers left their bases in England. It was to be a disaster for Bomber Command, with ninety-five aircraft failing to return.

General Eisenhower, the Allied Supreme Commander, held a crucial conference on 25 March to finalise the employment of air power in the two months leading up to the invasion and during the immediate post-invasion period. Much of the discussion centred around items that had already been given tacit approval in the outline air plans, the real arguments started when it came to the employment of the heavy bombers of the US 8th Air Force and RAF Bomber Command. The conference was presented with two very different proposals, from Air Marshal Tedder, the Deputy Supreme Commander, came the 'Transportation Plan' and from Spaatz, commander of the United States Strategic Air Forces (USSTAF) the 'Oil Offensive'. Both had rehearsed their arguments and both held very vehement opinions – it was to be a bitter struggle. Much of the basis of the Transportation Plan came from Tedder's experience in the Italian campaign and he had enlisted the same scientific adviser, Solly Zuckerman. His proposals had been put forward in January in a paper entitled: 'Delay and disorganisation of enemy movement by rail', in which he ventured that if the seventy-six most important rail servicing and repair facilities in North-West Europe were destroyed the effect would be to: 'Paralyse

Amiens marshalling yard a few days after an accurate Bomber Command night raid.

movements in the whole region they serve and render almost impossible the subsequent movement by rail of major reserves into France.'

   The view of the 21st Army was quite similar and concentrated on the need to win the race to build up Allied strength ashore before major German reinforcements could be brought to bear: '... There is little doubt that unless we can disrupt the enemy's communications, the Germans have a 4 to 1 chance of winning the race. It is not too much to say that this would result in the failure of *Overlord* at a very early stage.' As railways were the main military transportation system they were the key to the proposed strategy of isolating the invasion area.

With the tactical and strategic bombers being tasked against railway centres the Allies began a progressive degradation of the French railway network; it must be remembered however that the effort had to be widespread in order to maintain the deception policy of not focusing solely on targets within the proposed invasion area. The allocation of effort to counter the V-weapon threat has been omitted from this article because of space, although they did play a significant part in the overall Allied air strategy.

The pre-invasion bombing strategy was well underway by spring 1944 and in an April 1944 review paper the role of the heavy bombers was discussed: 'A major conclusion emerging from the air operations which have so far been undertaken in preparation for operation *Overlord*, is that outstanding bombing concentrations can now be achieved by RAF Bomber Command upon any given objective of limited size within *Oboe* range, and in certain circumstances outside *Oboe* range. The density of bomb strikes per acre achieved upon, for example, Juvisy and Aulnoye railway centres or Mailly le Camp has much exceeded expectations. The area attacked has been reduced to a wilderness of bomb craters which in many cases are lip to lip, or actually overlapping.'

On 8 April the draft Joint Fire Plan was issued, in essence the 'fire-power' timetable for the assault, and all but one of its schedules concerned air bombardment, such was the importance of this aspect. Operational control of the strategic bomber forces finally passed to SHAEF on 14 April. The most powerful air armada ever assembled was now, in theory at least, under the operational control of the Supreme Commander. All previous restrictions on rail targets were removed on 5 May with the strategic bombers being given clearance to bomb rail yards in densely populated areas, including Paris. Although a huge amount of damage had been inflicted on the rail network it remained a key target category; in the days either side of the invasion even more air effort was tasked to ensure that nothing of any significance was able to move by rail.

One of the major fears of the amphibious operation planners was the destruction that could be wrought by the coastal defence and field artillery batteries located along the stretch of coast selected for the landings. The 155 mm guns in some of the sites had a range of 26,000 yards and with the assault force only able to move at approx 12,000 yards per hour this would mean a period of exposure of two and a half hours. It was considered essential that these sites be destroyed or at least damaged to such an extent as to limit their effectiveness. Early in 1943 discussions and trials took place to consider the best way to attack the coastal batteries, with options ranging from mass bombing to airborne assault. Detonation trials of heavy bombs on the ground close to concrete emplacements proved that only a direct hit would knock out the guns and that the percentage of such hits in even a mass bombing raid would be small. With this type of attack it was considered that the best result would be the effect on crews that might make them incapable of operating the guns. In May trials were carried out with rocket projectiles (RPs) against open emplacements and these showed promise. The studies conclude that the most effective tactic was a three-pronged attack:

1. Heavy blitz bombing and low-flying attack by fighters to soften the defences and cause some damage.
2. Attack by RP aircraft, followed swiftly by
3. Airborne forces to destroy guns not already put out of action.

There was much heated debate as to the employment of bombers against these sites and the bomber chiefs continued to be reluctant to divert effort to what they still considered to be unprofitable targets. One analysis claimed that it would take 420 tons of bombs to ensure damage to a single gun, 2,500 bombs to secure one strike within 5 yards of the aiming point – and that such bomb loads could be more profitably expended elsewhere, the bomber chiefs returning to their favourite argument of bombing the gun before it reached the site (i.e. in the factory or in the rail siding *en route*). Nevertheless, attacks against coastal batteries were considered essential and so they remained on the target list.

By D-Day minus ten, Bomber Command had dropped 3,700 tons and AEAF 5,000 tons of bombs on such installations; the assessment being that eighteen of the fifty-one major guns within the assault area had been damaged. A later report by the Bombing Analysis Unit stated that: 'Bombing both delayed further construction and was very successful in reducing the efficiency of the batteries, not only because of the damage it caused but also because of the threat of further attacks'.

On 2 June Leigh-Mallory outlined to Eisenhower the bombing plan aimed at establishing a belt cutting the major routes through towns and villages to prevent or slow down passage of enemy reinforcements into the assault area. Eisenhower approved the plan and suitable targets joined the list for the medium and heavy bombers, for attack from D minus Two. The air commander saw the transportation campaign as crucial to the Allies in preventing the Germans concentrating in the invasion area once they had identified where the landings had taken place: 'Any large scale reinforcement of his troops near the invasion area could only be made if the railways behind are in good working order. My first object, therefore, in the preparatory stages was to make such a mess of the railway system that the movement of reinforcements would be impossible. The railway experts whom I consulted when considering the programme urged the destruction of railway centres, that is to say, those places where servicing and maintenance shops exist and also where signalling systems are concentrated. Moreover, to clobber junctions with a large number of points would be of immediate assistance, for they are not easily replaced when destroyed. I am quite sure that, speaking at this moment, the potential carrying power of the French and Belgian railways has been very considerably reduced and that there are good prospects of being able to keep them in a state of paralysis.'

The final few days before the invasion brought an intensification of air effort against the three key target systems of transportation, coastal guns and radars. Bomber Command was active in this period against the same type of targets; in the three nights from 2/3 June eleven gun batteries were attacked. In the period 1 April to 5 June, Bomber Command flew 24,629 sorties, dropping 87,238 tons of bombs – and losing 557 aircraft – on targets related to the pre-invasion bombing strategy. The bomb tonnage represented around 40 per cent of the total dropped by all Allied aircraft, whilst the sorties were only 12 per cent of the total – an indication of the impressive bomb lift of the heavy bombers.

The landings went well and, with the exception of Omaha Beach, losses were far lighter than predicted. Nevertheless, victory was by no means certain and everything now rested on who would win the build-up race. Allied air power had been a key factor in ensuring the successful amphibious assault; it would be a key factor in stabilising the lodgement area and the eventual breakout.

During the first week after D-Day the Command flew over 2,500 sorties in support of the landings, attacking road and rail communications and a range of other targets. June 14 marked Bomber Command's return to daylight operations when 200 Lancasters attacked German naval targets threatening the invasion supply lines. A great deal of effort was also being expended against V-weapon targets. The first of the V-1 rockets had fallen on England on 6 June and the destruction of construction, storage and launch sites became a high priority – and yet another diversion from the strategic offensive against the German homeland. Major raids were mounted in July to bomb fortifications around Caen in an effort to break the deadlock that had gripped British ground forces around the city. Operation *Goodwood* saw the employment of massed heavy bombers in a tactical operation dropping thousands of tons of high explosive close to friendly troops. The tactic was used on a number of occasions in this breakout phase.

Throughout 1944 the size of the heavy bomber force continued to increase and by June the Command had almost seventy squadrons with an operational strength of 1,250 Lancasters and 780 Halifaxes, as well as an increasing number of Mosquitoes. By the end of the year the force had grown again, the largest gain being in Mosquito units as this type took on an increasing number of roles, with the Light Night Strike Force (LNSF) adding a new dimension to the overall tactical plan by spreading the air raid warning and strain on the German air defence system.

At its peak strength in the latter part of 1944 and early 1945 the Command could field 3,200 heavy bombers and 400 light bombers, a daily bomb lift of 20,000 tons. It had indeed grown into a powerful and destructive weapon. Target priorities changed from time to time, depending on where the major effort was seen to be required, although Harris was often criticised for sticking with his area bombing to the exclusion of other targets – a broadly unfair assessment but one with some justification.

Between June and August 1944 Bomber Command dropped 180,000 tons of bombs; an indication of the diversion of effort from the main strategic offensive was that only 30,000 tons of this total was dropped on Germany.

Although command of the bomber force reverted to the Air Staff on 14 September, one of the first series of major operations was in support of the airborne landings in Holland as part of Operation *Market Garden*. The striking power of Bomber Command is aptly demonstrated by statistics for October 1944 – 17,000 operational sorties were flown, 13,000 of these to targets in Germany. Over 50,000 tons of bombs fell on German territory: in one twenty-four hour period the Command dropped more tonnage of bombs on Duisburg than the Germans dropped on London in the entire war. By summer 1944 No. 5 Group was operating as a virtually independent organisation. Harris summed this up in his post war diary: 'No. 5 Group operated largely as an independent unit and developed its own techniques, including the original Master Bomber concept as well as offset Skymarking such as the "5 Group Newhaven". This used offset techniques 1,000–2,000 yards from the aiming point, any error in the Red TIs being cancelled by yellows from the Master Bomber. Other techniques were developed, including "sector bombing"

The Mosquito played an important role in the Pathfinder Force for target-marking but its larger contribution to the overall campaign was with the Light Night Strike Force and as a night fighter.

The scale of the support required for one Main Force operation is hard to envisage, so perhaps a few numbers might help put it into perspective. According to a Bomber Command study: 'To prepare for an operation by 1,000 bombers the following material had to be provided: Over 2,000,000 gallons of petrol, 70,000 gallons of oil, and 5,000 gallons of coolant are put into the aircraft. Over 4,500 tons of bombs may be required and 10,000,000 rounds of ammunition for the guns. Some 30,000 bicycles, 3,500 bomb trolleys and 6,000 other vehicles are employed. 15,000,000 litres of oxygen are required, whilst 8,000 pints of coffee and 6,000 lb of food are placed in the aircraft.'

with each aircraft given a heading and overshoot heading. This gave a good bomb distribution but needed very accurate low-level marking.' The latter was a technique for which the Group became well known and from April 1944 it had its own pathfinder element, three experienced Squadrons (83, 97, 627) having been transferred from No. 8 Group.

Winter 1944/45 saw Bomber Command ranging far and wide over Germany attacking cities but also continuing to focus on transportation and, to a lesser extent, oil targets. A number of special missions were flown, such as the various raids against the *Tirpitz* and the No. 5 Group attack on the Dortmund-Ems Canal (23/24 September) to the employment of earthquake bombs by 9 and 617 Squadrons. A new directive was given to Harris on 25 September stating that the first priority, subject to weather and tactical feasibility, was the oil campaign, with equal second priority to target types that included the rail and water transport system, tank production and depots, and motor vehicle production and depots. Direct support of land and naval forces was listed as an 'ongoing commitment' but bombing of important industrial areas was also included. Harris would continue to argue that attacking German cities affected all of these target types. October brought a specific directive that, as Operation *Hurricane*, called for an all-out air offensive by the RAF and USAAF against the Ruhr to demonstrate the Allies overwhelming air superiority and the destruction that could – and would - be wrought unless Germany surrendered. A series of heavy attacks was mounted against Cologne, Essen and Duisburg, with smaller, single raids to Dortmund, Saarbrucken, Stuttgart and Wilhelmshaven.

Only 6 per cent of the Command's effort had been expended against oil targets in September 1944, although this was in part down to the poor wording of directives that allowed Harris to find reasons why he should not be deflected from his own avowed campaign against industrial cities. A new directive of 1 November once more gave oil as the top priority, with transportation targets being the only other option; once again there was 'let-out clause' that stated: 'As far as operational conditions allow, area bombing attacks are to be directed so as to contribute maximum destruction of the petroleum industry and the dislocation of the target systems already indicated.' Despite the seeming clarity of the overall directive, Bomber Command did not focus on individual oil targets, in part arguing that the winter weather made them less suitable, especially when reconnaissance was unable to determine the level of damage already sustained by such targets. The German fighter force was in dire straits due to shortage of pilots and restrictions caused by lack of fuel. However, a German report of 5 November was fairly upbeat: 'As regards our night fighter force, the position is rather more favourable at present. Substantial reinforcements have been received from disbanded bomber and transport units, and striking power has greatly increased. Our total strength of about 1,800 aircraft enabled about 200 fighters to take to the air during each enemy attack. Night fighter crews have achieved considerable success. The present fuel shortage only permits the employment of night fighters for a few days each month. Our forces should carry out operations at full strength on certain days and times based on previous experience. A further solution would be to convert some night fighter units to Me262 as this would enable us to attack and inflict heavy losses on the Mosquito squadrons which are operating in ever-increasing strength over NW Europe.' A number of 262s were converted to the night fighter role but the limited numbers and stage of the war made their contribution negligible.

Final months
With fewer aircrew needed as loss rates reduced and the end of the war in sight, there was a gradual reduction in Bomber Command's training organisation from late 1944. After January 1945 this run-down affected other various elements and so this month can be considered the peak of Bomber Command in terms of its wartime size. The New Year opened with oil and transportation still the main priorities but a new offensive against certain German cities, especially when combined with the Russian advance into Germany, might prove decisive in causing a final collapse of Nazi control. The final months of the war saw the bombers ranging over Germany, flying an increasing number of daylight raids as the German defences finally began to collapse. The four cities considered suitable were Berlin, Chemnitz, Dresden and Leipzig. Berlin, however, was removed from the list following a Joint Intelligence Committee assessment of 25 January: 'The devastation of Berlin, even if it was to coincide with the Russian advance, would be unlikely to break down the German will to continue the war.' The remaining three cities were to be attacked under Operation *Thunderclap*.

The attack on Dresden, which took place on the 13/14 February, has been the subject of much debate and more than any other event in six years of war has been cited in some quarters as proof of the barbaric nature of the bomber war. The *Thunderclap* attacks were intended as joint missions, the USAAF attacking by day and Bomber Command by night; the USAAF was due to attack Dresden on 13 February but because of weather the attack was delayed until the following day. A force of 800 RAF bombers delivered a devastating attack that wrecked Dresden, along with its industry and communications (and it was a key transport node for the Eastern Front) – and caused at least 50,000 civilian casualties. The following night Chemnitz was attacked by 700 heavy bombers but the weather was not clear as it had been the previous night and bombing was scattered and ineffective. This city was attacked again on 5/6 March with a higher level of damage.

The German night fighters were not a totally spent force and in the period 20–22 February Bomber Command lost sixty-two aircraft, mainly to fighters. In a dramatic, but ultimately futile, mission the *Luftwaffe* mounted Operation *Gisella* on 4 March when 100 night fighters followed the bomber stream back to England to attack bases and aircraft when they thought they were safe – it is estimated that twenty RAF aircraft were shot down. March brought heavy attacks, often by over 1,000 bombers, on cities such as Cologne, Essen, Mannheim and Darmstadt. The Dortmund raid of 12 March involved a record 1,108 bombers. Propaganda Minister Goebbels made a number of despondent entries in his diary during March:

1 March: The air war has now turned into a crazy orgy. We are totally defenceless against it. The Reich will be gradually turned into a complete desert.

12 March: The morale of the German people, both at home and at the front, is sinking even lower. The air terror which rages uninterruptedly over German home territory makes people thoroughly despondent.

13 March: When I call to mind that the amount of petrol available to the *Luftwaffe* has fallen from 193,000 tons to 8,000 tons, then I realise what can be expected of the *Luftwaffe* and what cannot. What use is the mass output of new fighters when we have not even the petrol or the crews to put them into action?

Allied ground forces crossed the Rhine at the end of March and the industrial cities of the Ruhr were overrun. Large-scale bombing of cities virtually ceased and the Command focused smaller raids on specific targets, the main exception being Berlin on 10/11 April in support of the Russian advance on the city. Only three more large-scale attacks were made by Bomber Command: on 18 April nearly 1,000 bombers attacked the fortified island of Heligoland in an accurate daylight attack with no bomber losses; on 22 April over 750 bombers attacked the port of Bremen in preparation for the assault on the city by British XXX Corps; and in the final major raid of the war, 375 Lancasters and Mosquitoes attacked Berchtesgaden, the aiming points being Hitler's famed Berghof (Eagles' Nest chalet) and the nearby SS barracks. Bomber Command's final offensive operations of the war took place on 2/3 May, the target being Kiel in an attempt to prevent a supposed attempt by Nazi die-hards to flee Germany for Scandinavia. During this latter series of attacks two Halifaxes and one Mosquito were lost, Bomber Command's last operational casualties of the Second World War.

Bomber Command had three more important operations to complete – all of a peaceful nature: *Manna*, *Exodus* and *Dodge*. The population of The Netherlands was suffering from food shortages in the latter weeks of the war and under an agreement with the local German forces Bomber Command flew low level mercy missions dropping supplies, under the appropriate code name *Manna*. The first drops took place on 28 April with a certain trepidation amongst the aircrew – would the 'free flight' be honoured by the Germans? Over the next two weeks, by which time the unconditional surrender of German forces had been made, the Command flew over 3,000 sorties and dropped 7,000 tons of food, an act that the people of Holland have never forgotten. Operation *Exodus* involved the repatriation of thousands of prisoners of war, mainly by Lancasters with a quick modification to allow them to carry twenty-five passengers. The first flight was made from Brussels on 4 May and by the end of May over 74,000 PoWs had been

A Lancaster dropping supplies to Dutch civilians under Operation Manna *in late April 1945.*

brought home. The final operation, *Dodge*, was similar in that it involved bringing home Allied personnel from Italy and the Mediterranean Theatre.

It had been a long and bitter struggle – a six-year war. Bomber Command had grown from a relatively ineffective force which, despite the courage of its crews, was limited in its ability to find and destroy targets to a weapon of enormous power. With the end of the war, following the unconditional surrender of Japan, the massive firepower that Bomber Command had built up was no longer required and disbandment of units, which had already started in spring 1945, accelerated. Despite the belief in some quarters that now was the time to face up to the Russians, the Cold War was still a few years away. In the immediate post-war period the Command went through a major reorganisation with the disbandment of all operational Groups except No. 1 and No. 3 Groups and a major change-round of airfields. Most of the plans that had been laid for re-equipment and new weapons in the latter part of the war were now cancelled or postponed.

Bomber Command had fought for six years. From the small and ineffective beginnings of the night offensive in 1940 through a period when the entire bomber philosophy was called into question through lack, as some saw it, of tangible results, to an increase in capability but a rising and unsustainable loss rate, to a final period when the destructive power of the Command and the accuracy with which it could deliver attacks was greater than any pre-war bomber exponent could have dreamt. Thousands of aircrew died in combat or in training; countless acts of heroism and devotion to duty went unrecorded or unrewarded. Bomber Command's war was a peoples' war – to friend and foe alike; it is now recorded in stark statistics of tonnage of bombs dropped, aircraft lost, civilians killed, factories put out of action, and a mass of data, much of it debated and disputed. The Victoria Cross is the highest gallantry award in the British military and throughout the war a number of Bomber Command aircrew received this medal (the details of each award are included in the 'Operations' chapter); one award – that to Leonard Cheshire – in many ways encapsulates the bomber war and the contribution made by outstanding individuals, although even then it is mirror for the countless thousands of bomber aircrew and the support personnel. The VC is usually awarded for a single act of gallantry in which there is a high risk of death; the award to Leonard Cheshire was unique in that it was for his overall contribution. The citation read: 'This officer began his operational career in June, 1940. Against strongly-defended targets he soon displayed the courage and determination of an exceptional leader. He was always ready to accept extra risks to ensure success. Defying the formidable Ruhr defences, he frequently released his bombs from below 2,000 feet. Over Cologne in November, 1940, a shell burst inside his aircraft, blowing out one side and starting a fire; undeterred, he went on to bomb his target. About this time, he carried out a number of convoy patrols in addition to his bombing missions.

'At the end of his first tour of operational duty in January, 1941, he immediately volunteered for a second. Again, he pressed home his attacks with the utmost gallantry. Berlin, Bremen, Cologne, Duisburg, Essen and Kiel were among the heavily-defended targets which he attacked. When he was posted for instructional duties in January, 1942, he undertook four more operational missions. He started a third operational tour in August, 1942, when he was given command of a squadron. He led the squadron with outstanding skill on a number of missions before being appointed in March, 1943, as a station commander. In October, 1943, he undertook a fourth operational tour, relinquishing the rank of Group Captain at his own request so that he could again take part in operations. He immediately set to work as the pioneer of a new method of marking enemy targets involving very low flying. In June 1944, when marking a target in the harbour at Le Havre in broad daylight and without cloud cover, he dived well below the range of the light batteries before releasing his marker bombs, and he came very near to being destroyed by the strong barrage which concentrated on him. During his fourth tour which ended in July 1944, Wing Commander Cheshire led his squadron personally on every occasion, always undertaking the most dangerous and difficult task of marking the target alone from a low level in the face of strong defences. Wing Commander Cheshire's cold and calculated acceptance of risks is exemplified by his conduct in an attack on Munich in April 1944. This was an experimental attack to test out the new

Lancasters at peace – aircraft from various squadrons lined-up at an airfield in Italy to take part in Operation Dodge, the repatriation of Allied personnel.

Bomber Command VCs

Recipient	Squadron	Aircraft	Date of action	London Gazette
D. E. Garland	12 Sqn	Battle P2204	12 May 1940	11 Jun 1940
T. Gray	12 Sqn	Battle P2204	12 May 1940	11 Jun 1940
R. A. B. Learoyd	49 Sqn	Hampden P4403	12 Aug 1940	20 Aug 1940
J. Hannah	83 Sqn	Hampden P1355	15/16 Sept 1940	1 Oct 1940
H. I. Edwards	105 Sqn	Blenheim V6028	4 Jul 1941	22 Jul 1941
J. A. Ward	75 Sqn	Wellington L7818	7/8 Jul 1941	5 Aug 1941
J. D. Nettleton	44 Sqn	Lancaster R5508	17 Apr 1942	28 Apr 1942
L. T. Manser	50 Sqn	Manchester L7301	30/31 May 1942	20 Oct 1942
R. H. Middleton	149 Sqn	Stirling BF372	28 Nov 1942	13 Jan 1943
L. H. Trent	487 Sqn	Ventura AJ209	3 May 1943	1 Mar 1946
G. P. Gibson	617 Sqn	Lancaster ED932	16 May 1943	28 May 1943
A. L. Aaron	218 Sqn	Stirling EF452	13 Aug 1943	3 Nov 1943
W. Reid	61 Sqn	Lancaster LM360	3 Nov 1943	14 Dec 1943
C. J. Barton	578 Sqn	Halifax LK797	30/31 Mar 1944	27 Jun 1944
N. C. Jackson	106 Sqn	Lancaster ME669	26/27 Apr 1944	26 Oct 1945
A. C. Mynarski	419 Sqn	Lancaster KB726	12/13 June 1944	11 Oct 1946
I. W. Bazalgette	635 Sqn	Lancaster ND811	4 Aug 1944	17 Aug 1945
G. L. Cheshire	76/617 Sqn	Various	Various	8 Sep 1944
R. A. M. Palmer	109 Sqn	Lancaster PB371	23 Dec 1944	23 Mar 1945
G. Thompson	9 Sqn	Lancaster PD377	1 Jan 1945	20 Feb 1945
E. Swales	582 Sqn	Lancaster PB538	23 Feb 1945	24 Apr 1945

method of target marking at low level against a heavily-defended target situated deep in Reich territory. Munich was selected, at Wing Commander Cheshire's request, because of the formidable nature of its light anti-aircraft and searchlight defences. He was obliged to follow, in bad weather, a direct route which took him over the defences of Augsburg and thereafter he was continuously under fire. As he reached the target, flares were being released by our high-flying aircraft. He was illuminated from above and below. All guns within range opened fire on him. Diving to 700 feet, he dropped his markers with great precision and began to climb away. So blinding were the searchlights that he almost lost control. He then flew over the city at 1,000 feet to assess the accuracy of his work and direct other aircraft. His own was badly hit by shell fragments but he continued to fly over the target area until he was satisfied that he had done all in his power to ensure success.

'Eventually, when he set course for base, the task of disengaging himself from the defences proved even more hazardous than the approach. For a full twelve minutes after leaving the target area he was under withering fire but he came safely through. Wing Commander Cheshire has now completed a total *of over 100 missions*. In four years of fighting against the bitterest opposition he has maintained a record of outstanding personal achievement, placing himself invariably in the forefront of the battle. What he did in the Munich operation was typical of the careful planning, brilliant, execution

Two of Bomber Command's Victoria Cross winners: Leonard Cheshire and Norman Jackson.

and contempt for danger which has established for Wing Commander Cheshire a reputation second to none in Bomber Command.' (Wing Commander Geoffrey Leonard Cheshire DSO DFC, 617 Squadron RAF.)

With the war in Europe over, Bomber Command was tasked to provide squadrons for Tiger Force, a major reinforcement for the war against Japan. Many Canadian squadrons went home to Canada to prepare for this new task whilst RAF squadrons went into a training routine. The dropping of the atom bombs in August 1945 ended the war before Tiger Force deployed.

Cold War

The end of the Second World War brought a massive rebuilding programme throughout Europe and for Britain it was a matter of urgency to return to a peacetime budget as soon as possible. For the military this meant disbandment of units as personnel on 'wartime duration' commitments hastened to return to civilian life – and find a job. Britain attempted to restore its pre-war Empire but the political map had changed, whilst at the same time cutting the military budget, including equipment, as quickly as possible. For Bomber Command this meant a ten-year period of making do with wartime equipment and facilities, not that there was any shortage of aircraft or bombs! In addition to its strategic bombing role from the UK the Command also had a commitment to provide firepower to other theatres to support the resident air assets and this was to become an increasingly important element during the 1950s and 1960s. The period from 1946 to around 1953 is very much one of restructuring and making do, doctrine and tactics remained unchanged although the new 'enemy' was communism and the new Soviet empire in Europe. The Cold War was pretty much in place as soon as the hot war had ended as allies of necessity became enemies of choice.

The striking power of Bomber Command was transformed in the 1950s with the introduction of nuclear weapons and the strategic deterrent became the focus of Bomber Command – and indeed overall British strategy. This was very much an arms race and as with all such arms races one of the main strategies was that of pre-emptive attack; NATO planners believed that the Warsaw Pact would attempt to deliver such an attack against NATO's nuclear assets in an attempt to remove a major threat. The threat of such a pre-emptive attack increased with the introduction of ballistic missiles in the mid 1950s and whilst manned aircraft remained the most numerous and potent nuclear assets for another decade the force mix was starting to change. The best way of protecting aircraft on the ground was to disperse them – and ensure that they could be airborne and out of harm's way as soon as possible. Bomber Command's solution to this was to disperse its V-bombers in groups of four to a number of airfields from Scotland to Cornwall. With the 'accepted wisdom' being that the warning period might be as little as four minutes it was also vital that these dispersed aircraft could be airborne quickly. Each of the dispersal airfields was provided with massive Operational Readiness Platforms (ORPs) at the end of the main runway, each capable of taking four Vulcans or Victors. In times of tension the crews would be on standby and with aircraft having been modified so that all four engines could be started simultaneously, all four bombers could be in the air within two minutes. This reaction time was frequently rehearsed.

The standard organisation for a V-bomber squadron was two Flights, each with an equal number of aircraft; each aircraft had a crew of five – 1st Pilot, 2nd Pilot, Navigator Plotter, Navigator Radar and Signaller (Air Electronics Officer from 1957 onwards). Whilst the allocation of a crew to 'its own' aircraft was not always possible the use of an assigned crew chief and allocated groundcrew to each aircraft worked well.

In its anti-flash white paint this Valiant was part of the trio of nuclear-armed V-bombers with which Bomber Command 'fought' the early years of the Cold War.

In October 1957 the Air Council agreed a new reinforcement plan for the Far East Air Force; this centred on developing Tengah, Singapore as a major base with a 9,000 ft all-weather runway suitable for V-bomber use. The intention was for Tengah to have two resident Canberra units and for an immediate reinforcement capability by two V-bomber squadrons. Squadrons spent most of their time on training exercise or detachments, the latter usually connected with demonstrating – and practising – the global nature of the Command's capability. Participation in exercises, including annual competitions, was vital. The increasingly close relationship between Bomber Command and Strategic Air Command (SAC) was evidenced in 1957 with an invitation to RAF V-bomber crews to participate in the SAC Bombing Competition at Pinecastle. Four Valiants, and six crews, were nominated and under Operation *Longshot* training commenced in January, culminating in a trial bombing competition in June. The four Valiants had been modified by Vickers-Armstrongs with underwing fuel tanks and auto-pilot. Following the competition, held at Marham, a Valiant Competition Flight was formed for the final intensive work-up, flying routes simulating the profiles used in the SAC Competition, the 2,774 mile route included an 800 mile leg using only astro navigation and with three radar attacks. The three chosen Valiants left Wittering on 25 September and after a night stop at Goose Bay, landed at Pinecastle, Florida the following day.

Final training took place hand-in-hand with familiarisation with American procedures. In typical bomber aircrew fashion one of the main comments concerned food: 'The sphere in which the RAF and SAC practice differed most noticeably was in the quality and quantity of flying rations. Five different USAF menus were available, ranging from 'bite-size' steak to fried chicken, complete with milk, fruit, chocolate, cigarettes, condiments and tooth pick; a far cry indeed from lukewarm tomato soup and cheese biscuits.' As to the ground crew: 'A taste for coffee and doughnuts was rapidly acquired by the groundcrew, who, thus fortified, were successfully taking on all comers at soccer.' The competition – Operation *Iron Horse* – began on 30 October, by which time two Valiants (XD859 and XD860) had been chosen as the competition primaries. The Valiants on the ramp at Pinecastle were surrounded by sixty-six B-47s from various SAC units (the B-36 and B-52 competitors operated from Carswell, Texas). It was a detachment from No. 3 Group so the AOC, AVM K. Cross, accompanied by C-in-C Bomber Command, ACM Sir Harry Broadhurst, turned up on the opening day. The Valiant crews had to cope with various equipment problems, especially with the all important Navigation and Bombing System (NBS). Nevertheless the RAF Wing achieved a final placing of twenty-seventh out of forty-five. The SAC Bombing Competition would become a regular feature of the V-force calendar with many crews having fond memories of the social life if not always the flying.

By 1959 the Air Ministry was convinced the future was with ballistic missiles, Thor having entered service and plans being underway for a British system, Blue Streak. In this very confused period of strategy decisions were being taken that simply didn't make sense; the air-launched Blue Steel Mk 1 had not yet entered service (it did so in 1963) but the future ground-based deterrent of Blue Streak was cancelled in 1960. When the Thor squadrons disbanded the AOC issued this message: 'You in the Thor force have maintained a constant vigil day and night for almost four years. You have maintained a higher state of readiness in peace-time than has ever been achieved before in the history of the Armed Forces. I am well aware of the sacrifices, so willingly accepted, that this constant readiness has imposed on the officers and airmen of the force.' It was an accolade designed to sweeten the pill of disbandment but it was also true, and this period of Bomber Command's history deserves more recognition that it usually receives.

With no follow-on for the original Blue Steel and with Thor as only a temporary system, and the next generation of missiles planned as seaborne, a new nuclear weapon was required for the manned aircraft. The search for a weapon led to selection of the Douglas GAM-87A Skybolt stand-off missile that had been designed for SAC's B-52s and B-58s. Political agreement on the acquisition was reached in March 1960 and plans were made to acquire missiles for the Vulcan B.2, with aircraft from airframes on the production line from No. 61 receiving the appropriate installation points and strengthening. The first Vulcan flight with a dummy Skybolt was made in November 1961 and with a British warhead under development the programme appeared to be on course as a Blue Steel replacement.

The Cold War reached one of its coldest periods with the Cuban Missile Crisis of 1962 and Bomber Command came to a high state of readiness at the height of the crisis, although the politicians refused to sanction deployment of the bombers to their UK dispersal airfields. At this time only 617 Squadron was operational with Blue Steel, and even then it was a limited capability, with the other squadrons still carrying free-fall weapons. In the event of the 'scramble' being given, crews would have headed for their pre-planned targets and those that managed to penetrate enemy defences – and remember that with the rest of NATO, and especially Strategic Air Command, in action the skies over Europe would have been crowded with aircraft – would have dropped their weapons and flown on to their sanctuary bases. Most of these bases were in places such as Turkey and RAF bases in the Mediterranean and Middle East, a return to the UK was often out of the question for either radius of action reasons or the expectation that the airfield would no longer be there. This was the period of Mutually Assured Destruction

An RAF crew launch a Thor missile at Vandeburg Air Force Base; the American Thor missile system was part of a NATO nuclear missile shield but the planned British follow-on, Blue Streak, was cancelled.

(MAD), the philosophy being that neither side would gain from conflict therefore peace was the only option.

Setbacks with the Skybolt missile and the pro-ballistic missile lobby in the US, led to Skybolt being cancelled by the Americans in December 1962 – and left the British with no new weapon. It would have been an interesting period if Skybolt had joined the RAF inventory as new tactics were being considered, including keeping aircraft on airborne alert in the same way that SAC did. There was even a new Vulcan, the B.3 in the pipeline (on paper) capable of carrying up to six Skybolts. Sadly, this remained a paper exercise. With the Thor missile system becoming defunct by mid 1963 the British nuclear deterrent still firmly resided with the RAF's bombers despite the fact that the strategic scenario had changed. The previous tactic of high-level penetration of Soviet airspace to deliver nuclear weapons was no longer valid by the early 1960s, a fact aptly demonstrated by the Russian shoot-down with a SAM-2 of a high-flying U-2 spy plane. The increased capability of the defences led the RAF to adopt the tactic of low-level attack for both its nuclear and conventional missions. The Vulcans managed the switch with few problems but it was very much a stop-gap and the time of the large unarmed bombers was reaching its end, although both Bomber Command and SAC would attempt to delay the inevitable.

The 1960s was a decade of appalling political indecision in terms of military capability and Bomber Command was badly affected. If the cancellation of the various weapon upgrades for the V-bombers was a drawback the subsequent decisions on future aircraft programmes was disastrous.

Strategic bombing remained the rationale for Bomber Command with the capability of inflicting 'unacceptable damage' (nuclear attack) on the enemy as the core strategy. Despite the problems outlined above the RAF was looking forward to its new aircraft, a replacement for the Canberra and the Vulcan, and one that promised to introduce a new level of capability. The BAC TSR.2 had its origins in the March 1957 GOR.339 for a tactical strike/reconnaissance aircraft for service entry by 1964 to replace, primarily, the Canberra. Its core design was the ability to deliver a nuclear weapon of Red Beard type (hence 'strike' as this term was applied to nuclear and not conventional operations), day

The TSR.2 was intended as a deep-penetration nuclear bomber and it incorporated a number of new features - but it fell victim to the mid 1960s defence cuts.

and night from low-level and with a radius of action of 1,000 nm. Nine aerospace companies submitted bids, one of which was, ironically, Blackburn with a variant on their NA.39; ironic because the NA.39 became the Buccaneer for the Royal Navy and some years later the RAF was to acquire the 'Bucc' as its 'new' tactical strike aircraft. The politics, civil and military, behind the GOR.339 saga are legendary but despite being fascinating are outside of the scope of this book. Suffice it to say that the decision was taken to proceed with the revolutionary design of the TSR.2 and its systems. The winning design was developed by the newly-created British Aerospace Corporation but a threat to the whole programme was never far away as the Minister of Defence was soon querying the high cost of the aircraft, which was being estimated at £1.7 million per aircraft. This was wrapped up in questions as to capability requirements and the Air Ministry and Admiralty were asked to study the tactical roles of aircraft in both limited and global war. Limited war was used to refer to conventional operations, and later to limited tactical nuclear use, whereas global war was the old MAD idea of an all-out nuclear exchange. Bomber Command was still very much at the cutting edge of these strategies.

The Labour Government of 1965 had made clear its intention of making cuts in defence expenditure and inevitably its axe fell on one of the most expensive programmes then underway. In the Budget speech of April 1965 the announcement was made that the TSR.2 programme was being cancelled on cost grounds. This was a devastating blow both to the British aerospace industry and to Bomber Command. The TSR.2 was the type around which future capability had been based and the Command had expected to acquire around 150 aircraft. To soften the blow the Government announced it had agreed an option with the US to acquire the F-111A, the cost per aircraft being half that of the TSR.2. This would have been an excellent alternative as far as the RAF was concerned but the axe fell again before the ink was dry on the deal. Bomber Command was left with no alternative but to carry on with the aircraft it had, whilst searching for new bombers that could meet the changing operational scenario. Nuclear weapons remained at the heart of the bombing strategy but the doctrine was changing whereby aircraft would carry tactical nuclear bombs, the strategic delivery moving to ballistic-missile submarines.

The 1960s saw a continuation of the run down of the strength of Bomber Command and by the latter part of the decade this had reached the point whereby only one operational Group was under the Command's control. This was illogical and the decision was taken to combine Bomber Command and Fighter Command to form Strike Command: this took effect on 1 May 1968. The role of the bomber element, No. 1 Group, remained unchanged – as did the equipment in the short term – but the change of name brings this overview of RAF Bomber Command to an end.

CHAPTER TWO

Operations

This chapter focuses on the operational career of Bomber Command – the times when it was actively engaged on operations. The six years of almost continuous conflict from late 1939 to 1945 are of course the major period of interest but the Command also saw active employment during the 1950s, albeit on a very small scale in places such as Malaya and Egypt (Suez).

Bomber operations September 1939 to May 1945

In the few years that Bomber Command had to prepare for war from its formation in May 1936 its operational focus remained that of formation daylight attacks on key target systems – the WA (Western Air) list of targets. This 'Planning for a war with Germany' had been instituted in 1937 and in December Bomber Command was ordered to commence detailed planning for WA1 (German Air Force organisation and associated industries), WA4 (German Army concentrations and lines of communication) and WA5 (Manufacturing resources in the Ruhr, inland waterways and ports, and areas outside the Ruhr). The Command was meant to have its plans in place by April 1938, although the large amount of planning effort meant that this date was slipped. However, an internal Bomber Command appraisal stated that the only one of these that was realistically achievable was WA5 as both of the others were inappropriate for strategic bombing.

The concept of the war-winning bomber weapon remained the one with which the Command went to war. From the first operations in September 1939 to the end of the war in Europe in May 1945, Bomber Command fought a six year campaign. The Second World War part of this chapter divides the war into 'campaigns' as fought by the Command in those six years; some are appropriate in military terms in that they relate to a particular set of targets over a short period of time, whilst others fit less well into this formula. There are a number of 'campaigns' that do not fit into this chronological survey but are important in the overall appraisal of the Command's war and include: the Maritime war, U-boat war, Minelaying and Leaflet campaign. The attacks on Italy are covered at the end of the Strategic Bombing Offensive account.

The Strategic Bombing Offensive – early battles

At the outbreak of war Bomber Command's strength, on paper, was around 500 bombers, and despite the fact that some of these were light bombers with small bomb loads it was theoretically a potent force. The departure of the Battles of No. 1 Group to France with the AASF reduced the number of aircraft by 25 per cent but had less effect on the bomb lift. So with the Western Air Plans for destruction of the Ruhr the Groups were ready for action – but it was to be eight months before they were cleared to drop bombs on Germany.

On the first day of war the Command mounted a limited number of sorties: a Blenheim flew a reconnaissance of the north-west coast of Germany, with

Wilhelmshaven and Heligoland as particular points of interest. The Naval Observer on the Blenheim reported that a portion of the German fleet was sighted leaving Wilhelmshaven. With the decision having been taken that attacks on land targets were, for the present, banned, 'fleeting targets at sea' were the main focus of attention. On the evening of 3 September a force of nine Wellingtons from Mildenhall and eighteen Hampdens, nine each from Scampton and Waddington, went in search of the German warships but found nothing. Overnight, ten Whitleys from Linton-on-Ouse dropped propaganda leaflets in Area 1(a) (the Ruhr) with 5.4 million leaflets being dispensed. Whitley K8969 of 58 Squadron had to force-land in a cabbage field at Dormans near the River Marne but Flying Officer O'Neill and his crew were unhurt. The following day, however, Bomber Command suffered its first operational casualties with the loss of two Wellingtons and five Blenheims (four from 107 Squadron) during attacks on shipping. The Operational Order for this raid stated that: 'The greatest care is to be taken not to injure the civilian population. The intention is to destroy the German fleet. There is no alternative target.' At least two major warships, *Admiral Scheer* and *Emden* were in port at Wilhelmshaven and these were the main targets for the fifteen Blenheims; five of each type failed to find the target because of bad weather but the others made a low-level attack. The Blenheim attack was noted in the Bomber Command ORB: 'An eyewitness account obtained from secret sources shows that the action by the Blenheims was a most gallant affair and accorded with the best traditions of the RAF.' Gallantry and high losses were to remain a feature of the Blenheim and No. 2 Group for much of its time with Bomber Command. Fourteen Wellingtons went to Brunsbuttel and five aircraft again failed to find the target because of bad weather.

This remained the pattern of activity for the next few weeks, the Whitleys flying by night over Germany on leaflet-dropping and the other types trying to find and bomb German warships. The Bomber Command ORB for 29 September summarised one such attack: 'Eleven Hampdens from Hemswell carried out a reconnaissance of the Heligoland Bight area with instructions to search for enemy surface craft and if found to attack. One formation of six aircraft returned complete having sighted two destroyers

Wellington Is of 9 Squadron; the tactical concept of daylight formation attacks with their defence provided by the cross-fire from the bombers' guns proved to be a failure.

near Heligoland steaming east at 25–30 kts; the target was attacked and seven 500 lb bombs were dropped by the first three aircraft. The destroyer turned presenting broadside and the second flight did not attack. No results were observed except that large splashes were seen in the water near the destroyers. Heavy anti-aircraft fire was experienced and one aircraft was hit and one of the crew wounded. The other flight of five aircraft failed to return.'

November was a quiet month, with the exception of the decision to cease lone Blenheim reconnaissance flights as losses were outweighing the benefits. The bombers were still a 'force in waiting' and the theories of strategic bombing remained largely untried. There were mixed opinions as to the wisdom of daylight attacks but no conclusive evidence either way. This changed in early December with two Wellington attacks that proved that daylight raids were too costly.

On 14 December twelve Wellingtons from 99 Squadron were sent to patrol the Elbe Estuary and the Frisian Islands to attack shipping. 'At 1425 hours a force of one battleship, one cruiser, three destroyers and one submarine was sighted, but owing to low cloud no attack could be made. Fighter attacks were made by twenty enemy aircraft, Me 109s and Me 110s, two of which were definitely destroyed and two more were probably shot down. Heavy anti-aircraft fire was encountered when the enemy aircraft were clear of our formation. One Wellington was shot down, two collided and fell in flames, two are missing and one, on arriving at Newmarket, collapsed and three of the crew were killed.' On 18 December No. 3 Group sent twenty-four Wellingtons from three squadrons to patrol the Schillig Roads and Wilhelmshaven to report upon any enemy naval forces. 'In Wilhelmshaven a battleship, two cruisers and four destroyers were seen in the harbour and alongside. They were not therefore attacked. There was heavy anti-aircraft fire and some twenty-five Me 109s and Me 40s (sic) attacked – at least twelve of which were shot down. Twelve of our aircraft failed to return; of these two are known to have descended into the North Sea on the way home.'

When the loss rates in daylight raids were compared with those for the Whitleys on their night-time forays (four aircraft in 123 sorties

The powered rear turret was one of the main defensive features of the Wellington and as part of a cone of fire from a formation of aircraft was meant to provide adequate protection against fighter attack.

and many of those over Germany) the message was clear – it was far safer to fly at night. What this simple conclusion failed to address was how to find the target and hit it. This problem was to vex the Command for the next three years.

In January 1940 the Wellingtons and Hampdens joined the nightly leaflet-dropping campaign, not because it was considered to be effective but as a way of giving crews valuable experience in night operations. This routine continued into spring 1940 and the only aggressive actions were those of No. 2 Group who maintained their low-level attacks, with shipping still being the favoured target.

On 16 March Sir Charles Portal had taken over as C-in-C Bomber Command, the appointment being seen by many as political in as much as Portal was seen as less likely to cause waves; when he later became Chief of the Air Staff he and Arthur Harris were frequently in disagreement. Within days of taking command he authorised an attack on a land target – the German seaplane base at Hornum as a reprisal for a German attack on Scapa Flow. A force of thirty Whitleys and twenty Hampdens dropped a mix of incendiaries, 250 lb and 500 lb bombs; although results were hard to determine it had been a significant operation for the Command.

On the night of 13/14 April the Hampdens opened a new campaign for Bomber Command by dropping mines in the sea lanes between Germany and the Norway and Denmark. The minelaying campaign (*Gardening*) is covered in a separate entry in this chapter. The dropping of mines in this particular location was connected with the Allied attempts to disrupt the German invasion of the two Scandinavian countries. The Germans had launched their assault in the early hours of 9 April and Bomber Command Blenheims and Hampdens were airborne on anti-shipping sorties that day, but with little success. On 11 April six Wellingtons of 115 Squadron attacked the airfield at Stavanger/ Sola, Norway in the first planned attack on a mainland target in Europe. The attack was led by Squadron Leader du Boulay to 'bomb runways, aircraft and aerodrome installations', for which task the bombers carried 500 lb SAP bombs and the plan was to attack from 1,000 feet. The first section of three aircraft found and bombed the target with no problems but by the time the second trio arrived the defences were alert and none was able to bomb. Pilot Officer Barber's aircraft was shot down by flak and the other two aircraft were damaged, one having to make a wheels-up landing back at base.

This mini offensive against Norway continued until early May and whilst the number of aircraft involved was small it did represent the bulk of Bomber Command's operational effort. The main targets were airfields, with Stavanger being a favourite as it was being used by the Germans as a main base.

On the night of 1/2 May, 10 Squadron sent a small number of Whitleys to attack Stavanger; 'Larry' Donnelly included an account of this raid in his book *The Whitley Boys*: 'As we were climbing away from Dishforth Bick, our skipper informed us that although we had taken off second with a bit of luck and extra boost we could get there first and surprise them. "We can be in and out before they realise what's hit them." The weather forecast was good for a change and he was determined to take full advantage of it. . . . There was no searchlight or flak activity so it looked as if Bick had achieved his aim of being first to target. Bick throttled back the engines and we commenced our glide from about 4,000 feet. During the descent the bomb doors were opened and the bomb-aimer commenced chanting his directions . . . "Left, Left, Steady" to get the target in his bombsight. He finally called "Bombs Gone" and the Whitley lurched as the bombs fell away. Bick wanged open the throttles and we roared across the airfield at low level going like the clappers. I had an uninterrupted view from the tail and saw the bombs bursting in the hangar and installations area. At the same time the defences opened up. Three

Hampden crews on return from an attack on Bergen; the Command flew a mini-campaign in April and early May against the German invasion of Scandinavia.

searchlights came on attempting to pick us up and flak hosed after us. As we escaped out to sea unscathed and I was able to report that, as a result of our bombing, fires had started in the target area. The crews following us now had something to aim at, but we had also stirred up a hornets nest for them. Highly elated, we made our way home. For a change we felt that we really had achieved something.'

This limited bombing, combined with minelaying and anti-shipping sorties, attempted to delay the German advance but to no avail.

Strategic bombing – round one

May 1940 brought the lifting of the ban on attacking targets in Germany. To use an overused but appropriate phrase, the 'gloves were off' and Bomber Command was given clearance to employ its 'war winning' doctrine of attacks on German industry. The first such attack, by ninety-nine aircraft, took place on the night of 15 May on oil and rail targets in the Ruhr area; the aiming points were industrial sites at places such as Sterkrade and Castrop-Rauxel and eighty-one of the bombers reported attacking their designated targets, although in the light of later evidence of navigation errors and the problems of finding targets, especially in the perennially hazy Ruhr, this seems unlikely. One Wellington (115 Squadron) crashed in France, becoming the first RAF casualty of the strategic bombing offensive, Flight Lieutenant Pringle and his four crew being killed.

Before we get too absorbed in the Strategic Bombing Offensive, which pretty much occupies the rest of this operational history, mention must be made of the valiant but catastrophic employment of light bombers against the advancing German ground force, the Battles of No. 1 Group and the Blenheims of No. 2 Group playing the major part. The 'strategic' bombers were also involved, the Bomber Command directive being to 'attack vital objectives, starting in the Ruhr, to cause maximum dislocation to lines of communication of the German advance through the Low Countries.'

For the deployed squadrons such as the Battles the task was to 'delay and weaken in every way possible the advance of the German mechanized forces and try to relieve the pressure on the Allied armies sufficiently to enable them first to hold the enemy and then to mount an effective counter-attack.' It was a forlorn expectation and over the next few weeks the British light bombers attacked lines of communication, mainly bridges over rivers, and German columns on the march. Seldom having air cover and with strong ground defences the bombers were shot out of the sky. On 12 May two crew of a 12 Squadron Battle were awarded the Victoria Cross, the first such awards to Bomber Command (and the only occasion on which two members of the same crew received this highest gallantry award.) Their aircraft was the only one of five to return. The VC citation read: 'Flying Officer Garland was the pilot and Sergeant Gray the observer of the leading aircraft of a formation of five aircraft that attacked a bridge over the Albert Canal which had not been destroyed and was allowing the enemy to advance into Belgium. All the air crews of the squadron concerned volunteered for the operation and, after five crews had been selected by drawing lots, the attack was delivered at low altitude against this vital target. Orders were issued that this bridge was to be destroyed at all costs. As had been anticipated, (it was) heavily protected by enemy fighters. In spite of this the formation successfully delivered a dive-bombing attack from the lowest practicable altitude and British fighters in the vicinity reported that the target was obscured by the bombs bursting on it and in its vicinity. Only one aircraft returned from this mission out of the five concerned. The pilot of this aircraft reports that in addition to the extremely heavy anti-aircraft fire, through which our aircraft dived to attack the objective, they were also attacked by a large number of enemy fighters after they had released their bombs on the target. Much of the success of this vital operation must be attributed to the formation leader; Flying Officer Garland, and to the coolness and resource of Sergeant Gray, who navigated Flying Officer Garland's aircraft under most difficult conditions in such a manner that the whole formation, was able successfully to attack the target in spite of subsequent heavy losses. Flying Officer Garland and Sergeant Gray unfortunately failed to return from the mission.' (Flying Officer Donald Edward Garland and Sergeant Thomas Gray, 12 Squadron RAF, Battle P2204; awarded for action 12 May 1940, *London Gazette*, 11 June 1940.)

By 21 May the Germans had reached the sea at Le Touquet and although the campaign in the west continued into June, the Armistice with France being signed on 25 June, and included the Allied evacuation from Dunkirk, it was to all intents and purposes over and the next major campaign would be that fought over Britain itself. History has recorded the virtual annihilation of the Battle squadrons but the Blenheims also suffered very heavily in the May–June period, losing over 100 aircraft; the most tragic day being 17 May when 82 Squadron lost eleven out of twelve aircraft that

Battle of 218 Squadron as part of the AASF deployed to France.

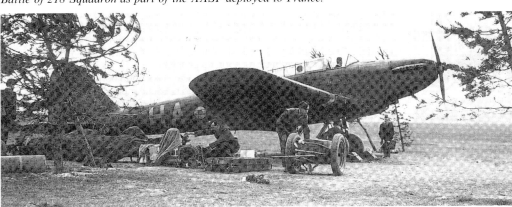

attacked troops near Gembloux – with the twelfth badly damaged and crash-landed in England. Support for the land campaign by attacking communications targets remained important into early June, and there was an intensive period of support during the Dunkirk evacuation.

The strategic bombers spread their attentions over a variety of targets in Germany in the latter part of May, farthest afield being Hamburg, which was attacked on 17/18 May by forty-eight Hampdens. Small scale raids to a variety of targets in the same night remained the pattern of operations, along with minelaying, for the next year or so, although gradually the concept of concentration of effort on a single target became more important. The entry of Italy into the war on 10 June 1940 gave Bomber Command another set of targets to attack, the first such missions being flown the following night; there was never a concentrated campaign by Bomber Command against Italy but industrial cities in the North of the country were frequent targets. The attacks on Italy have been covered in a separate section in this chapter.

Countering the invasion

With the Germans established in the Low Countries and France, the threat of invasion became the highest priority for British military planners. Whilst Fighter Command's role in countering the German plans is well known, the role of other parts of the RAF, especially Bomber Command, has been largely overlooked but the bombing of invasion ports, military camps and airfields was a factor in the German decision to abandon Operation *Sealion*. A Bomber Command summary stated that: 'The invasion ports face us in a crescent, centred on Calais, some of the World's greatest cargo and passenger installations; in fact, if the enemy had built ports himself for the express purpose of invading this country, he could hardly have improved on their actual layout – Amsterdam, Rotterdam, Flushing, Bruges, Zeebrugee, Ostend, Antwerp, Dunkirk, Calais, Boulogne, Dieppe, Le Havre and Cherbourg.' These names would appear on a regular basis in the summary of bomber operations over the next few months.

By the latter part of May 1940 at least 3,000 barges were observed in these ports; enough to transport one million tons of supplies, plus shipping for a further four million tons. More were arriving every day as the German invasion plans progressed. The urgency of attacking this build-up led to an immediate and determined commitment by aircraft of No. 2 Group, the Blenheims bearing the brunt of this work, the main attacks taking place from early July. Even crews still in training were thrown into the battle, some planners seeing these targets as 'nursery slopes' as they were only a matter of minutes flying time away from England. They were, however, heavily defended by anti-aircraft guns. The aircraft of No. 2 Group were also tasked against airfields such as Abbeville, Amiens and Merville; although airfield attacks were little more than nuisance raids at this stage of the campaign. The night bombers were tasked against ports and airfields from time to time but their main emphasis remained that of attacking built-up areas.

Flight Lieutenant R. A. B. Learoyd of 49 Squadron was awarded the Victoria Cross for a low-level attack by two Hampden units, 49 and 83 Squadrons, on the Dortmund-Ems canal on 12 August; this was another of the 'significant' targets identified by the experts in the July directive. Eleven Hampdens attacked this target near Munster; two were shot down by flak but the attack had achieved an element of surprise and the damage to the canal restricted barge traffic on this important waterway for a number of weeks. The VC citation read: 'This officer, as first pilot of a Hampden aircraft, has repeatedly shown the highest conception of his duty and complete indifference to personal danger in making attacks at the lowest altitude objective on the Dortmund-Ems Canal. He had attacked this objective on a previous occasion and was well aware of the risks entailed. To achieve success it was necessary to approach from a direction well known to the enemy, through a lane of especially disposed anti-aircraft defences, and in the face of the most intense point blank fire from guns of all calibres. The reception of the preceding aircraft might well have deterred the stoutest heart, all being hit and two lost. Flight Lieutenant Learoyd nevertheless made his attack at 150 feet, his aircraft being repeatedly hit and large pieces of the main planes torn away. He was almost blinded by the glare of many searchlights at close range but pressed home this attack with the greatest resolution and skill. He subsequently brought his wrecked aircraft home and, as the landing flaps were inoperative and the undercarriage indicators out of action, waited for dawn in the vicinity of his aerodrome before landing, which he accomplished without causing injury to his crew or further damage to the aircraft. The high courage, skill and determination, which this officer has invariably displayed on many occasions in the face of the enemy, sets an example which is unsurpassed.' Acting Flight Lieutenant Roderick Alastair Brook Learoyd, 49 Squadron, Hampden P4403. (Awarded for action 12 August 1940, *London Gazette*, 20 August 1940.) A second Hampden VC was awarded the following month, to Sergeant John Hannah of 83 Squadron during an attack on the invasion barges at Antwerp. His citation read: 'On the night of 15 September 1940, Sergeant Hannah was the wireless operator/air gunner in an aircraft engaged in a successful attack on enemy barge concentrations at Antwerp. It was then subjected to intense anti-aircraft fire and received a direct hit from a projectile of an explosive and incendiary nature, which apparently burst inside the bomb compartment. A fire started which quickly enveloped the wireless operator's and rear gunner's cockpits, and as both the port and starboard petrol tanks had been pierced, there was grave risk of the fire spreading. Sergeant Hannah forced his way through the fire to obtain two extinguishers

and discovered that the rear gunner had had to leave the aircraft. He could have acted likewise, through the bottom escape hatch or forward through the navigator's hatch, but he remained and fought the fire for 10 minutes with the extinguishers, beating the flames with his log book when these were empty. During this time thousands of rounds of ammunition exploded in all directions and he was almost blinded by the intense heat and fumes, but had the presence of mind to obtain relief by turning on his oxygen supply. Air admitted through the large holes caused by the projectile made the bomb compartment an inferno and all the aluminium sheet metal on the floor of this airman's cockpit was melted away, leaving only the cross bearers. Working under these conditions, which

Sergeant John Hannah was awarded the VC for his actions on the night of 15 September 1940.

Distinguished Flying Medal (DFM) to Sgt J. R. Ramshaw of 9 Squadron, May 1940;
Bomber Command aircrew were recipients of thousands of gallantry awards in the Second
World War. The highest number of awards to any RAF Command indicated the intense
nature of the Command's six-year war.

caused burns to his face and eyes Sergeant Hannah succeeded in extinguishing the fire.
He then crawled forward, ascertained that the navigator had left the aircraft, and passed
the latter's log and maps to the pilot. This airman displayed courage, coolness and
devotion to duty of the highest order and, by his action in remaining and successfully
extinguishing the fire under conditions of the greatest danger and difficulty, enabled the
pilot to bring the aircraft safely to its base.' (Sergeant John Hannah, 83 Squadron,
Hampden P1355. Awarded for action 15/16 September 1940, *London Gazette*, 1 October
1940.)

Strategic offensive – round two
The strategic offensive had been continued throughout the anti-invasion period but it
was intensified following the 24 August German attack on London, with Churchill
ordering a raid on Berlin in retaliation. The 'Big City', as Bomber Command crews came
to know Berlin, was attacked by over eighty bombers. Poor weather caused problems,
especially in the target area but some bombs did fall on the Reich capital; Berlin was
attacked twice more before the end of August and Goering's boast that 'no enemy plane
will ever fly over the Reich' was well-and-truly laid to rest; Hitler's response was a speech
declaring that: 'When they declare they will increase the attacks on our cities, then we will
raze their cities to the ground. We will stop the handiwork of these air pirates ....'
Although it would be another two years before the RAF's bombers were capable of
inflicting significant damage, the air war had entered a new phase.
    On the night of 23/24 September the Command made a maximum effort attack on a
single target for the first time; the target was Berlin and 129 bombers took part. Three
aircraft were lost and results were poor, crews being unable to identify their targets
because of a thick haze, made worse by the glare of searchlights. It was, however, a new
tactic.
    Sydney Munn joined 77 Squadron having trained as an Observer (the Flying 'O'
brevet of the Observer was not replaced by the Navigator's 'N' until 1942). 'Our first
operation together took place on 7 November 1940, the target being Wesseling which
we failed to locate owing to complete cloud cover. As an alternative we attacked an

active enemy airfield on the way home. This was clearly visible with blazing runway lights. That sortie lasted eight hours.' The main target that night had been Essen, with sixty-three of the bombers trying to find the Krupps Works. 'Our second sortie was a disaster, and lasted eleven and a half hours – until we ran out of fuel. It took place on 10 November, and the target was one of the most distant, at the extreme end of the Whitley's range, and on the border of Czechoslovakia. We were briefed to bomb an aluminium plant at a place called Rhuland, and on the way home, as a guide to a second wave, we were, if possible, to drop a parachute flare over Dresden. We had a very strong tail wind component on the outbound flight, gale force in fact, and this gave us an exceptionally high groundspeed of over 195 mph. The Whitley V cruised at an Indicated Air Speed of between 125 and 130 mph, which meant that the wind velocity was in the order of 70 mph.

'We seemed to be covering the ground in no time at all and soon found the target, clearly visible in moonlight. I recall that as we completed the bombing run there were greenish flames emanating from the subsequent fire, so someone must have been "on the ball" – whether we were responsible or not I did not know. Having enjoyed a tail wind outbound, I had calculated that the resultant head wind for the homeward flight would give us a ground speed of between 60 and 70 mph – if that! We were in for a long slog! As we approached Dresden the WOp/AG left the radio compartment to prepare to launch the parachute flare down the flare chute. All seemed quiet below, with no light ack-ack tracer to be seen. Suddenly we were hit by a heavy AA shell. Smoke filled the cockpit and the smell of cordite was intense. It was a direct hit on the radio compartment and all our radio equipment was completly wrecked. This meant that I was to get no assistance in the form of radio bearings on the way home, but thank goodness we were still airborne and the engines sounded fine.

'I was now relying on map reading, and began to look out on the starboard side for a checkpoint. After a while I could see flak in the distance which I judged to be about 20 miles north of us, at Hanover and at 90 degrees to our heading. Whitley navigators could use the disc of the starboard propeller as an "on the beam" sighting device, and it confirmed my groundspeed estimate at about 70 mph. It was at this stage that the captain, who had been preoccupied with recent events, began to take an interest in the navigation process, and he challenged my identification of Hanover. He said that in his opinion it was Bremen! I politely pointed out that if this was the case, having enjoyed a tailwind outbound, it had conveniently swung round through 180 degrees and we were making about 200 mph on the way home – hardly a meteorological probability. An argument ensued during which, as a commissioned officer, he pulled rank on me as a humble sergeant and said, "As Captain of this aircraft, I order you to give me an alteration of course from south of Bremen and a revised ETA at the Yorkshire coast". In deference to an experienced navigator I complied, but to protect myself I recorded in my log that it was done on "Captain's orders". At the same time it occurred to me that such an alteration of course from a "false" position would make our landfall on the English coast more likely to be in the Norfolk area and, furthermore, the captain's ETA would surely prove to be over-optimistic in view of the gross error in ground speed. Map reading was now out of the question as we were flying above extensive stratus cloud, and dead reckoning navigation was all we had left to rely on.

'It was normal procedure for us to empty the auxiliary fuel tanks first, and to change over to main tanks when the engines cut out. This enabled the Navigator to calculate accurately the fuel consumption in gallons per hour. Between 60 and 70 gallons per hour was normal. However, it did not occur to me at the time that, since we were operating at extreme range, a major diversion caused by navigation error would make the fuel situation critical. Ten minutes before the questionable ETA at the coast my Skipper began the descent to below cloud, and the white horses showed us that we were indeed still over the sea. After 20 minutes I sensed that it was beginning to dawn on those up front that I had been correct in my original calculation, and ages later we crossed the coast near Yarmouth. An admission of error was immediately forthcoming, and I then gave the pilot a course to steer for base, but we now had a long way to go before reaching Topcliffe.

'At about this time I could hear concern being expressed up front about how much fuel remained in our tanks. It was not long before panic began to set in, and I was told to fire a distress cartridge, using the Very pistol which was situated just above my head. I fired every cartridge we had; with no radio and no R/T it was our only hope. Then luck seemed to be coming our way, and just as both engines began to splutter the pilot called out that he could see a flare path being laid out for us. With undercarriage down we began a glide approach when the engines cut. Ahead could be seen three "gooseneck" flares in line. There was no question of waiting for more to be lit, and we touched down at the first one on what proved to be a very bumpy surface. Seconds later we left both wheels of our undercarriage in a ditch, went through a hedge, and skidded to a halt in a field of turnips. We were near to Barkston Heath airfield in Lincolnshire. The three gooseneck flares turned out to be marking the corner of a triangular cross-country exercise which had been carried out that night by pupil pilots from Cranwell. Within half an hour a rescue team found us and took us to Cranwell, where we had breakfast and waited for another Whitley to come down and collect us. It was then back to Topcliffe for debriefing and a post mortem!' In the interest of crew harmony the Squadron Commander moved him to another crew. Navigation problems, inaccurate Met forecasts and shortage of fuel were frequent occurrences throughout the war, especially prior to the introduction of general aids such as *Gee* and caused the loss of many aircraft and crews.

The bombers operated on most nights in November and December but usually in small numbers; the one significant exception to this was Operation *Abigail Rachel* (16/17 December). This attack on Mannheim was planned to involve over 200 bombers, although only 134 actually took part it was still the largest attack to date. The attack was led by Wellingtons dropping incendiaries but despite good weather and ineffective opposition it was not a success, bombing being scattered and only light damage being caused.

The night bombers continued their attempts to find pinpoint targets, oil targets being the main focus of the directive for the first three months of 1941. However, results against targets such as Gelsenkirchen, Sterkrade and Homberg were generally poor. On 10 January the Blenheims opened a new campaign when six aircraft of 114 Squadron, escorted by seventy-two fighters, flew the first *Circus* operation. The target was an ammunition depot in the Foret de Guines, near Calais and although the bombers found the target, results were indeterminate. Of more importance was the fact that the *Luftwaffe* ignored the bait. This type of operations became the main role for No. 2 Group from spring onwards, although the Group also maintained its commitment to unescorted daylight (cloud cover whenever possible) missions as well as contributing to the night effort.

The Stirling flew its first mission on the night of 10/11 February, 7 Squadron contributing three aircraft to the forty-three bomber force. The ORB recorded the event: 'The Squadron carried out its maiden operational trip, three aircraft successfully bombed the target area at Rotterdam, all returned safely.' Each aircraft carried an 8,000 lb load

The Stirling had a bomb-load twice that of the Wellington but its unusual bomb-bay layout limited the types of weapon it could carry.

(16 × 500 lb bombs) – almost double that of a Wellington. This was followed a few days later, 24 January, by the debut of the Manchester, with six aircraft of 207 Squadron taking part in an attack on a cruiser in Brest harbour. Led by Wing Commander N. C. Hyde the aircraft dropped seventy 500 lb SAP bombs but 'insufficient field of vision for the bomb-aimer to see the bomb bursts' meant that results were not observed. There was no appreciable opposition but one Manchester crashed at Waddington having suffered a hydraulic failure.

A few weeks later, 10 March, it was the turn of the Halifax, with 35 Squadron, led by Wing Commander Collings, sending six aircraft to Le Havre; The AOC had sent the Squadron a goodwill message: 'Good wishes to No. 35 Squadron and the heavyweights on the opening of their Halifax operations tonight. I hope the full weight of the Squadron's blows will soon be felt further afield.' The ORB account for the Wing Commander's aircraft stated: 'Took off from Linton at time stated for target. The weather was excellent to the French coast, where 8/10 cloud was encountered. Le Havre was located first by searchlights and flak, and then seen through a good break in the cloud, the dock area being clearly visible. A level attack was delivered from 13,000 ft in one stick of twelve 500 lb SAP bombs. The bombs were seen to burst along the edge of the main docks. Only slight heavy flak and scattered searchlights were encountered.' One aircraft was damaged by flak but returned safely on three engines; sadly one Halifax was intercepted and shot down by RAF fighters over Surrey, with only two of the crew parachuting to safety. In early March the Command was given targets connected with the U-boat industry as its priority. The primary list comprised aviation and marine targets:

Location	Target
Augsburg	diesel engine factory
Bordeaux	U-boat base, FW Condor base
Bremen	Deschimag and the Focke-Wulf assembly factory
Dessau	Ju 88 factory

Wellington R1379 of 115 Squadron was shot down on 10 May 1941.

Hamburg	Blohm & Voss, Howaldts
Kiel	Germania Werft, Deutsche Werke, Howaldtswerke dockyard
Lorient	U-boat base
Mannheim	diesel engine factory
St Nazaire	U-boat base
Stavanger	FW Condor base
Vegescak	Vulcan Werke

The first of the aircraft targets was attacked on 12/13 March when eighty-eight bombers targeted the Blohm & Voss works at Hamburg and eighty-six bombers went to the Focke-Wulf factory at Bremen; the maritime campaign is covered later in this chapter. As always the target list remained broader than that given in the directives and over the next few weeks a wide variety of targets was attacked.

The Command sent sixty-one Wellingtons and twenty-nine Whitleys to Essen on the night of 3/4 July 1941; Sydney Munns was the Navigator in a 77 Squadron Whitley: 'We took off for Essen at 2300 hours. Of all the targets in the Ruhr Valley's industrial complex of towns, Essen was the most daunting because it lies in the middle of all the others and, no matter from what direction you approached, you had first to run the gauntlet of the other defences before experiencing those at Essen itself – which were considerable. My log shows that a very accurate forecast of wind velocities made navigation easier, and we maintained accurate tracks right through to the target. The D/F station on the island of Texel was transmitting as usual, and I obtained some very accurate loop bearings that put us dead on track. We crossed over Texel on time at 0036 hours, and soon we were weaving through the searchlight belt. We reached the target area at 0130 amid dozens of waving searchlights and very intense flak. The heavy flak bursts were too close for comfort and actually shook the aircraft. I let the bombs go in one stick, and the rear-gunner reported many large fires and heavy explosions on the ground. Twenty minutes later my log records that we were still experiencing continuous flak and searchlights, but finally we escaped on a planned southerly route and set course for Nieuport on the Belgium coast. I did my usual check on the North Star to ensure we were on a westerly and not a "red on blue" heading, and the visibility was so clear that I decided to try my first astro-navigation sight (I had been practising with the sextant on the ground) and took a sight on Polaris, the altitude giving me a reasonably accurate check on our latitude. From Nieuport we set course for Orford Ness, and as we approached the English coast we heard "squeakers": these were transmitted from our own barrage balloon sites on a special frequency to warn us of their proximity. These particular squeakers probably emanated from Norwich and we skirted round them, landing at base at 0535 hours.'

Four German cities were attacked on the first 'back to Germany' night (7/8 July) and the Munster raid brought a VC for Sergeant James Ward of 75 Squadron. His citation read: 'On the night of 7 July 1941, Sergeant Ward was second pilot of a Wellington returning from an attack on Munster. When flying over the Zuider Zee at 13,000 feet, the aircraft was attacked from beneath by a Messerschmitt on which he secured hits with cannon shell and incendiary bullets. The rear gunner was wounded in the foot but delivered a burst of fire which sent the enemy fighter down, apparently out of control. Fire then broke out near the starboard engine and, fed by petrol from a split pipe, quickly gained an alarming hold and threatened to spread to the entire wing. The crew forced a hole in the fuselage and made strenuous efforts to reduce the fire with extinguishers and even the coffee in their vacuum flasks, but without success. They were then warned to be ready to abandon the aircraft. As a last resort, Sergeant Ward volunteered to make an attempt to smother the fire with an engine cover which happened to be in use as a cushion. At first he proposed to discard his parachute, to reduce wind resistance, but was finally persuaded to take it. A rope from the dinghy was tied to him, though this was of little help and might have become a danger had he been blown off the aircraft. With the help of the navigator, he then climbed through the narrow astro-hatch and put on his parachute. The bomber was flying at a reduced speed but the wind pressure must have been sufficient to render the operation one of extreme difficulty. Breaking the fabric to make hand and foot holds where necessary, and also taking advantage of existing holes in the fabric, Sergeant Ward succeeded in descending three

Wellington of 301 Squadron being readied at Hemswell for another mission, July 1941.

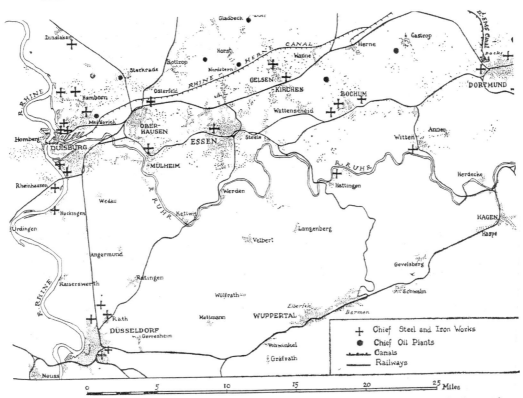

The industrial cities of the Ruhr were a main target area for Bomber Command – but with little success until accurate bombing aids became available.

feet to the wing, and proceeding another three feet to a position behind the engine, despite the slipstream from the airscrew, which nearly blew him off the wing. Lying in this precarious position, he smothered the fire in the wing fabric and tried to push the cover into the hole in the wing and on to the leaking pipe from which the fire came. As soon as he removed his hand, however, the terrific wind blew the cover out and when he tried again it was lost. Tired as he was, he was able with the navigator's assistance, to make successfully the perilous journey back into the aircraft. There was now no danger of the fire spreading from the petrol pipe, as there was no fabric left nearby, and in due course it burnt itself out. When the aircraft was nearly home some petrol which had collected, in the wing blazed up furiously but died down quite suddenly. A safe landing was then made despite the damage sustained by the aircraft. The flight home had been made possible by the gallant action of Sergeant Ward in extinguishing the fire on the wing, in circumstances of the greatest difficulty and at the risk of his life.' (Sergeant John A Ward; 75 Squadron RNZAF, Wellington L7818. Awarded for action 7/8 July 1941, *London Gazette*, 5 August 1941.)

The extension of the bombing directive to include smaller towns had no immediate effect and the bombers were back to their usual haunts of Berlin, Cologne, Essen and Frankfurt for much of August. Other industrial centres were also hit and intelligence reports occasionally provided feedback on results; for example, the 8/9 September attack on Kassel was known to have caused severe damage to a factory making railway rolling stock.

Blenheims at low-level en route *to attack the power station at Knapsack 12 August 1941; two power stations in the Cologne area were attacked, thirty-eight Blenheims going to Knapsack.*

New Brandenburg, Berlin 2/3 September 1941.

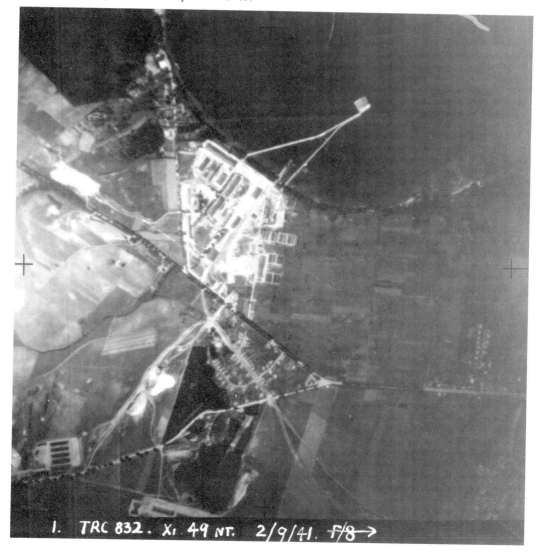

Barrage balloons were a constant threat to all RAF aircraft and from time to time they scored an 'own goal'. On 22 October, the target was Mannheim and Ken Wallis was flying Wellington R1459 of 103 Squadron from Elsham Wolds: 'This was another night with appalling weather and as we struggled back over the North Sea the aircraft was icing up – we had already been hit by lightning on the way out. Navigation was difficult but we fixed our position when we were fired at by the guns at Harwich, it was well known that Harwich always fired at you. We then turned North towards the Humber, turning West for land when the Navigator reckoned it was about time. As we headed west I saw a beacon in the distance and thought it was Elsham Wolds – but by its position I knew we were close to the balloon barrage around Immingham and Grimsby. The next thing I knew we had hit a cable, the impact coming on the port wing about a foot from the fuselage. An impressive shower of sparks as the cable sawed into the wing was followed by a smell of petrol and we were fortunate that the aircraft didn't catch fire. The port engine packed up and the undercarriage dropped. I headed towards the airfield hoping they would switch on the lights but apparently they thought we were Germans and kept themselves blacked out. In the dim glow of the Very lights that we fired I glimpsed a Wellington on the ground but we simply couldn't get down on the airfield. I put the aircraft down in a ploughed field, subsequently discovering that we had narrowly missed a quarry face. If we had landed on the runway we would probably have caught fire so perhaps it is just as well they didn't turn on the lights. Having climbed out of the aircraft we did a head count, and had one too many – the chap with the rifle was one of the guards, we were that close to the airfield.' Inspecting the aircraft they discovered that the cable had cut over four feet into the wing. The balloon barrage personnel at Grimsby were delighted that the aircrew had survived and invited them to a party with the comment 'it's nice to have a live RAF crew'. Ken was recommended for an immediate award of a Distinguished Flying Cross but, 'The paperwork obviously got lost somewhere and nothing happened.'

The main raids on the night of 10/11 October were to Essen (seventy-eight aircraft) and Cologne (sixty-nine aircraft) but smaller forces also attacked a number of other targets, including twenty-two Wellingtons to Bordeaux. Four aircraft from the latter were lost, two of those being from 218 Squadron. Sergeant Haley was 1st Pilot of

Wellington R1459 after its 'engagement' by a friendly barrage balloon cable on 22 October; Ken Wallis managed to put the aircraft down in a field and all the crew escaped unhurt.

Wellington R1511: 'We took off from Marham at 2000 hours on 10 October to bomb oil tanks slightly North of Bordeaux. We reached our objective but shortly after we turned for home the starboard propeller fell off. I turned the aircraft towards the unoccupied zone and gave the order to bale out at approximately 0400 hours.' He was the only one to evade the Germans, arriving in Gibraltar on 4 March 1942; one crewman was killed and the other four became PoWs.

Pilot Officer Groyecki was airborne in Wellington R1705 of 300 Squadron on the evening of 7 November 1941, the target being Mannheim. This was one of seven Wellingtons lost from the fifty-three that attacked Mannheim. He was one of two of the crew who escaped, the others becoming prisoners and his debrief stated: 'Our aircraft took-off from Hemswell about 1720 hours on 7 November to take part in an attack on Mannheim. After leaving the target we found we were short of petrol. The starboard wing tank was leaking and may have been hit by flak splinters. At about 0300, finding we could not get home, we baled out north of Lille. I was first out and came down near Quesnoy. The aircraft dived uncontrolled and came down probably south of Lille.' The main target that night had been Berlin, with 169 bombers attacking the Reich capital; in poor weather only seventy-three claimed to have bombed the target. Losses on the Berlin raid were high at 12.4 per cent (twenty-one aircraft). Cologne was also attacked and the total Command effort for the night was 392 aircraft – the highest number yet despatched in a single night. The loss rate for this night led to a disagreement between Bomber Command and the Air Ministry and led to a conservation policy directive.

The maritime war was once more the focus for the latter weeks of 1941, although for the Blenheims a new task was started on 27/28 December when six aircraft attacked the night fighter airfield at Soesterberg in Holland as part of a new campaign to reduce the effectiveness of the German night defences. These intruder raids became a standard routine for No. 2 Group.

Pinpoint accuracy – and area devastation

Despite the new directive of early 1942 calling for attacks on a limited number of German cities, the first few weeks of the year saw little activity; indeed, the largest raid in January and February was by ninety-eight bombers to Mannheim on 14/15 February. This was largely due to the continued conservation policy plus a reassessment of the Command's tactics. On the night of 3/4 March a modified version of the *Shaker* technique was used against a pinpoint target for the first time. The Renault factory at Billancourt, near Paris, was attacked by 235 aircraft; the three waves making a concentrated and accurate attack. The first wave, experienced crews flying *Gee*-equipped aircraft dropped flares, identified the target and then dropped 1,000 lb bombs. The second wave also dropped 1,000 lb bombs, whilst aircraft of the first wave continued to keep the target illuminated. The third wave carried 4,000 lb bombs as well as 1,000 lb bombs. Defences were light and the bombers flew at 6,000 ft to improve accuracy. Concentration over the target was excellent at 120 aircraft per hour (two per minute) and crews reported good results. For once this assessment was confirmed by post-attack reconnaissance the following day. At least 40 per cent of the factory area had been destroyed and it was estimated that at least 300 bombs had fallen within the factory area. Despite this accuracy, casualties amongst French civilians were heavy.

The same night saw four Lancasters of 44 Squadron laying mines on what was the operational debut of the Avro bomber; recorded in the ORB as: 'It is noteworthy that this is the first occasion that Lancaster aircraft have operated and this squadron is the only one operational with this type.' Each aircraft carried four mines, an early indication of the superior weapon load of the Lancaster. The first true *Shaker* attack was made against Essen on 8/9 March with 211 bombers heading for the Ruhr. The basic concept with *Gee* was for it to be used as a navigation aid to get the bombers in the 'right area' from which a visual acquisition of the target could be made – it was not a blind-bombing aid. Whilst the bombers could be pretty sure they were 'in the area' the usual ground haze prevented accurate identification of the target and bombing results were poor. Essen was attacked four more times in March with equally poor results and with mounting losses; the 26/27 March attack cost 10 per cent of the 115 bombers. There was one other successful *Gee* raid in March when 135 aircraft attacked Cologne, for the loss of a single Manchester. It was estimated that 50 per cent of bombs fell within 5 miles of the aiming point, causing extensive damage to housing and industry.

Harris next chose to try out a true incendiary raid and chose as his target a city that would be easy to find (coastal) and having large areas of wooden structures would be a good incendiary target. Lubeck was attacked on 28/29 March using the now standard *Shaker* technique. Of the 234 bombers despatched, 161 claimed accurate attacks in good weather and with minimal defences – and reports suggested that 62 per cent of the city was burnt out. The British press reported: 'Over 200 aircraft of Bomber Command tonight launched a shattering raid on the Baltic port of Lubeck, a shipbuilding and industrial centre. Hundreds of tons of high explosive were dropped and about half of the built-up area has been destroyed by fire. The RAF has begun a round-the-clock offensive against German arms factories and German-controlled industries in France.' The Lubeck raid was without doubt a success and it provided a nasty shock to the German population and the Nazi leadership; the latter decreed that historic towns in Britain would be flattened by the *Luftwaffe*. Despite some accurate and damaging attacks on British cities the strategic bomber war was now beyond German capabilities and bomber traffic became increasingly one way.

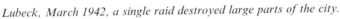
Lubeck, March 1942, a single raid destroyed large parts of the city.

One of the War's most dramatic raids took place on 17 April 1942 when a small force of Lancasters flew deep into Germany – by day – to attack a pinpoint target at Augsburg. The MAN diesel-engine works was a major producer of U-boat engines but would require a low-level daylight attack as it was about the size of a football pitch. Led by Squadron Leader John Nettleton of 44 Squadron, the twelve Lancasters, six each from Waddington's 44 and 96 Squadrons, took-off at 3.00 pm in order to arrive over the target at dusk, which would give them the cover of night for their return flight. Diversionary raids were mounted to cover the period when the Lancasters were entering enemy territory but enemy fighters returning from engaging one of these diversions picked up the second section of 44 Squadron and after a chase shot down all three aircraft. They then picked on the lead section, shooting down another Lancaster before breaking off because they were short of fuel. The two remaining bombers, followed by the still intact 97 Squadron, reached the target and made their attacks, one falling to flak and crashing after releasing its bombs. John Nettleton's was the sole survivor of the 44 Squadron contingent. The second formation lost two aircraft to flak over the target. The target had been bombed but the cost had been high with the loss of seven Lancasters and eighty-five aircrew, only twelve of whom survived to become PoWs. John Nettleton was awarded the Victoria Cross, the citation reading: 'Squadron Leader Nettleton was the leader of one of two formations of six Lancaster heavy bombers detailed to deliver a low-level attack in daylight on the diesel engine factory at Augsburg in Southern Germany on 17 April 1942. The enterprise was daring, the target of high military importance. To reach it and get back, some 1,000 miles had to be flown over hostile territory. Soon after crossing into enemy territory his formation was engaged by twenty-five to thirty fighters. A running fight ensued. His rear guns went out of action. One by one the aircraft of his formation were shot down until in the end only his own and one other remained. The fighters were shaken off but the target was still far distant. There was formidable resistance to be faced. With great spirit and almost defenceless, he held his two remaining aircraft on their perilous course and after a long and arduous flight, mostly at only 50 feet above the ground, he brought them to Augsburg. Here anti-aircraft fire of great intensity and accuracy was encountered. The two aircraft came low over the roof-tops. Though fired at from point blank range, they stayed the course to drop their bombs true on the target. The second aircraft, hit by flak, burst into flames and crash-landed. The leading aircraft, though riddled with holes, flew safely back to base, the only one of the six to return. Squadron Leader Nettleton, who has successfully undertaken many other hazardous operations, displayed unflinching determination as well as leadership and valour of the highest order.' (Acting Squadron Leader John Bering Nettleton, 44 Squadron RAF, Lancaster R5508; awarded for action 17 April 1942, *London Gazette*, 28 April 1942.)

A week later the town of Rostock was subjected to four nights of attacks that caused a great deal of damage and led to Goebbels decrying the British Terror Raid (*Terrorangriff*). The Command attacked a number of cities in May but Harris was already planning a series of spectacular raids.

Thousand bombers

Ever since he took over Bomber Command in February 1942, Arthur Harris was determined to prove that his bomber force could be a decisive weapon if properly equipped and handled the right way. To prove his point and silence the detractors he planned to concentrate 1,000 bombers against a single target in a single night. On the night of 30/31 May 1942 the first of the Thousand Bomber raids took place, a total of 1,047 bombers attacking Cologne.

Wellington crew kit-up: fleece-lined jacket, flying rations and a thermos of soup or coffee, plus a parachute – all essential items of equipment.

On this raid just under 900 bombers reported attacking the target and although forty-one aircraft were lost this was 'acceptable' in percentage terms. The defences had been overwhelmed but there had been no shortage of targets for fighters and flak; of more significance was the fact that the civil defence (ARP) organisation had been overwhelmed. Damage to parts of Cologne, civil and industrial, was heavy; 411 people were killed and over the next few days a large part of the population left the city. This attack was considered a success and combined with the Singleton Report silenced most of the Command's detractors. One Victoria Cross was won this night; the citation for Flying Officer Leslie Manser read: 'Flying Officer Manser was captain and first pilot of a Manchester aircraft which took part in the mass raid on Cologne on the night of 30 May 1942. As the aircraft was approaching its objective it was caught by searchlights and subjected to intense and accurate anti-aircraft fire. Flying Officer Manser held on his dangerous course and bombed the target successfully from a height of 7,000 feet. Then he set course for base. The Manchester had been damaged and was still under heavy fire. Flying Officer Manser took violent evasive action, turning and descending to under 1,000 feet. It was of no avail. The searchlights and flak followed him until the outskirts of the city were passed. The aircraft was hit repeatedly and the rear gunner was wounded. The front cabin filled with smoke; the port engine was over-heating badly.

'Pilot and crew could all have escaped safely by parachute. Nevertheless, Flying Officer Manser, disregarding the obvious hazards, persisted in his attempt to save aircraft and crew from falling into enemy hands. He took the aircraft up to 2,000 feet. Then the port engine burst into flames. It was ten minutes before the fire was mastered, but then the engine went out of action for good, part of one wing was burnt, and the air-speed of the aircraft became dangerously low. Despite all the efforts of pilot and crew, the Manchester began to lose height. At this critical moment, Flying Officer Manser once more disdained the alternative of parachuting to safety with his crew. Instead, with grim determination, he set a new course for the nearest base, accepting for himself the prospect of almost certain death in a firm resolve to carry on to the end. Soon, the aircraft became extremely difficult to handle and, when a crash was inevitable, Flying Officer Manser ordered the crew to bale out. A sergeant handed him a parachute but he waved it away, telling the non-commissioned officer to jump at once as he could only hold the aircraft steady for a few seconds more. While the crew were descending to safety they saw the aircraft, still carrying their gallant captain, plunge to earth and burst into flames.

'In pressing home his attack in the face of strong opposition, in striving, against heavy odds, to bring back his aircraft and crew and, finally, when in extreme peril, thinking only of the safety of his comrades, Flying Officer Manser displayed determination and valour of the highest order.' (Flying Officer Leslie Thomas Manser, 50 Squadron, Manchester L7301; awarded for action 30/31 May 1942, *London Gazette*, 20 October 1942.)

Five Mosquitoes of 105 Squadron made that type's operational debut with Bomber Command on 31 May, flying as single aircraft their task was to fly over Cologne for post-attack assessment – and also drop bombs to keep the defences on alert. The weather was too poor for photographs and one aircraft (W4064, Pilot Officer Kennard) failed to return.

Two nights later the second mass raid took place, Essen being attacked by 956 bombers. This Ruhr target proved as elusive as ever and identification was impossible because of industrial haze. The loss of 31 bombers for no appreciable result was not a good result. The final raid in this series did not take place until 25/26 June, when 1,067 bombers attacked Bremen using three aiming points; aircraft of No. 5 Group went for the Focke-Wulf factory, the 102 aircraft of Coastal Command attacked the docks area (the Deschimag shipyard) and the Main Force targeted the centre of the city. It appeared to be a reasonable attack, although German records suggested a small force of around 80 bombers! However, at a cost of 48 bombers it was the most expensive of the thousand-bomber raids.

The operational pace slackened after the effort of May and June and the bombers went to nearer targets in the short summer nights, although on 11 July a force of forty-four Lancasters flew a 1,500-mile round-trip to attack U-boat construction yards at Danzig. The outbound leg was in daylight and the bombers were routed over the sea towards Denmark where they split to make individual 'cloud cover' attacks on the target. The tactic was successful in that only two Lancasters were shot down, both by flak over the target. Major night raids were flown during the summer against Duisburg, Dusseldorf, Hamburg, Saarbrucken, Vegesack and Wilhelmshaven but loss rates were once more causing concern.

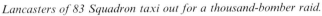

Lancasters of 83 Squadron taxi out for a thousand-bomber raid.

Thousand bomber raids: summary of operations

30/31 May, Cologne

Group	Wellington	Whitley	Hampden	Lancaster	Manchester	Stirling	Halifax
1 Gp	156	0	0	0	0	0	0
3 Gp	134	0	0	0	0	88	0
4 Gp	9	7	0	0	0	0	131
5 Gp	0	0	34	73	46	0	0
91 Gp	236	21	0	0	0	0	0
92 Gp	63	0	45	0	0	0	0
Totals	598 (29)	28 (1)	79 (1)	73 (1)	46 (4)	88 (2)	131 (3)

Note: In addition, 56 aircraft, including Blenheims of No. 2 Group and Army Co-operation Command, plus a small number of Fighter Command Havocs, flew intruder *ops*.

1/2 June, Essen

Wellington	Whitley	Hampden	Lancaster	Manchester	Stirling	Halifax
545	29	71	74	33	77	127

In addition, 48 Blenheims flew intruder *ops* against German airfields.

25/26 June, Bremen

Wellington	Whitley	Hampden	Lancaster	Manchester	Stirling	Halifax
472	50	50	96	20	69	124

Note: This third raid included 51 Blenheims, 24 Bostons and 4 Mosquitoes as part of Main Force plus 56 aircraft of No. 2 Group on intruder *ops* against night fighter airfields.

Flensburg was the target on the night of 18/19 August and for the first time the Main Force (of 118 aircraft) was led by a Pathfinder force of thirty-one aircraft. It was not an auspicious start as poor weather led to misidentification of the target, some bombers actually dropping their loads over Denmark. Cloud obscured the next attack, Frankfurt on 24/25 August and although the weather over Kassel three nights later was much better the attack was still poor. The fourth attack was more successful, the marking and bombing of Nuremberg on 28/29 August being accurate, although losses (twenty-three aircraft) to the small force of 159 bombers were very high, including 25 per cent of the Wellingtons. Of most significance on this raid was the first use of a specialist target-marker – Red Blob Fire.

For much of the rest of the year Italy was the focus of the Command's attention although German cities and a number of special targets were also 'visited'.

Attacks on targets in France had always raised the spectre of French casualties and whilst such casualties were generally seen as the 'fortunes of war', every effort was made to keep them to a minimum. It was for this reason that the important Schneider armament works at Le Creusot was attacked in daylight on 17 October. Lancasters of No. 5 Group were allocated the task and carried out low-level formation flying practice. The target was 300 miles inside France and it was certainly a risky target as previous daylight ventures had met with heavy losses. On the afternoon of 17 October, ninety-four Lancasters left their bases in England and led by Wing Commander L. C. Slee of

Lancasters of 50 Squadron at Swinderby August 1942.

Flares, searchlights and flak over Dusseldorf in the early morning of 1 August 1942; 630 bombers, almost half of which were Wellingtons, dropped nearly 900 tons of bombs.

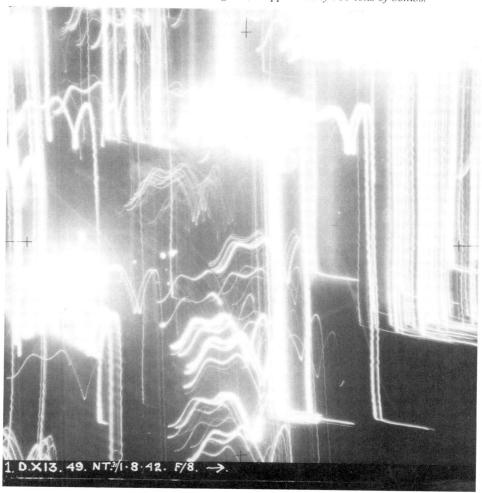

The Krupps Works at Essen was the target on the night of 16/17 September 1942; 369 bombers made the most successful attack on this important but elusive target. Losses were high at thirty-nine aircraft (10.6 per cent of the attackers).

49 Squadron, set course to coast in between La Rochelle and St Nazaire. 'At the height we were flying we disturbed the cattle in the fields and numbers of them stampeded. At one place we saw oxen bolt, dragging their plough after them. Many of the French peasants in the fields waved to us as we swept over.' No fighters appeared and other than a few bird strikes the bombers had a clear run to the target. They climbed to bomb from between 2,500 and 7,500 ft and crews reported an accurate attack with only light flak. The 140 tons of bombs dropped were spread over the factory area but some also fell within the workers housing area. A small formation of Lancasters also attacked the nearby power station, one crashing into the buildings during its low-level attack. On the return flight a 207 Squadron aircraft was attacked by three Arado Ar196 seaplanes; two Ar196s were shot down but the Flight Engineer was killed by return fire.

One of the most spectacular special raids was that of 6 December against the Philips Works at Eindhoven, a target that had been slated for attack some months before. This raid was carried out by 93 Bostons, Mosquitoes and Venturas of No. 2 Group. The low-level attack in good weather caused serious damage to the Works and was considered a great success, although at the cost of fourteen aircraft. The Italian campaign came to an end in late December and the Command returned to Germany on the night of 20/21 December with an attack on Duisburg by 232 bombers.

Operationally, 1943 opened slowly with the main target in January being the U-boat facility at Lorient, which was attacked four times without much success. A few Main Force raids went to Germany, such as Dusseldorf on the night of the 27th, which included *Oboe* Mosquitoes using a ground-marking technique.

Battle of the Ruhr: March to July 1943

'The intensity of effort expended against the Ruhr and Rhineland industrial area in the second quarter of 1943 is entirely without precedent in air warfare. The scope of it can best be gauged by comparison with the corresponding quarter of 1942:

    Apr–Jun 1942   9,751 sorties   14,057 tons dropped.
    Apr–Jun 1943   14,723 sorties   39,113 tons dropped.

'The increase in sorties is less striking than that in bomb tonnage, because of the very different proportion which heavy bombers bear in the force as a whole in 1943. The average strength of heavies in the second quarter of 1942 was about 40 per cent of the total. In 1943, this figure has risen to about 70 per cent.' These comments appeared in *Bomber Command Quarterly Review* No. 5, which went on to point out that loss rates had decreased from 3.5 to 2.0 aircraft per 100 tons of bombs dropped. This was a significant figure but meant little if the increased weight of bombs was not being delivered accurately. The Review, however, determined that accuracy had indeed improved: 'This is largely attributable to the efficiency of the new navigational aids which render our bombing to a great extent independent of weather conditions over the target, and to the evolution of the Pathfinder technique. We are thus able not only to hit objectives under weather conditions which would have previously made night bombing a fruitless task, but we are able to operate on nights when night fighters find it difficult to leave and return to their aerodromes, and are otherwise impeded by the weather conditions.' The introduction to the Review's summary of the Battle of the Ruhr concluded: 'It has thus been true to say that 1943 has so far been the year of achievement for Bomber Command.'

To what extent was this positive picture justified? The Battle of the Ruhr was very much a test of what Harris believed to be the new potential of his Command and he was determined to prove that the important but previously hard to hit industrial heartland of the Reich was now vulnerable. What the Review did not mention was that during the complete period of the Battle of the Ruhr, which opened with the attack on Essen on 5/6 March and ended with the attack on Aachen on 13/14 July, the offensive had cost the Command almost 1,000 bombers. This four-month period was the first of the great trials of strength between the night bombers and the German defences; the bomber weapon had developed the potential to be a major factor – it was now time to see if it could achieve what its supporters claimed. On the evening of 5 March a force of eight Pathfinder Mosquitoes equipped with the *Oboe* navigation system led a Main Force of 434 bombers to the industrial city of Essen, most famed as home to the extensive Krupps Works. Three of the *Mossies* had to turn back with technical problems (as did over fifty of the Main Force aircraft) but the remainder used the *Oboe* beams to drop their markers on target and on time. The initial markers were backed-up by the next wave of Pathfinders and by the time the Main Force arrived the target area was well lit and easily distinguishable despite the inevitable ground haze that had effectively shielded Ruhr targets on previous occasions. The first wave of Halifaxes was followed by a wave made up of Stirlings and Wellingtons, and a final wave of Lancasters concluded an attack that had taken around 40 minutes. The principle of concentration of effort and time had the dual tactic of causing greater destruction on the ground (and preventing effective fire-fighting) and less time for the defences to engage the attackers. In what had become a standard tactic, two-thirds of the bomb load comprised incendiaries in order to cause extensive fires after HE bombs had destroyed walls and broken gas pipes, and a percentage of the HE bombs had long delay fuses. The attack cost fourteen aircraft (3.2 per cent) but had been a major success after a winter of little activity. It is estimated that 160 acres of Essen, including parts of the Krupps Works, were destroyed or heavily damaged. The destruction included over 3,000 houses – and de-housing 'industrial workers' was one of the avowed aims of this type of attack. Harris summarised the importance of the Essen attack: 'Years of endeavour, of experiment, and of training in new methods have at last provided the weapons and the force capable of destroying the heart of the enemy's armament industry.' The bomber strategy expounded before the war, and incorporated in the WA Plans, now appeared to hold real promise. As the events of winter 1943 were to show, the situation was by no means this straightforward.

Nevertheless, the promise of Essen led to a new offensive aimed at destroying the vital war industries of the Ruhr.

On the night of 11/12 March 1943 the target for the bombers was Stuttgart, the fourth night of attacks in the Battle of the Ruhr. Of the 314 aircraft, 109 were Halifaxes and of those six were lost. Four of these losses were from 405 Squadron, a particularly bad night for the Canadians operating out of Leeming. Halifax II BB250 was flown by Pilot Officer Dennison on his twenty-first operation and in the early hours of 12 March they were picked out by a German fighter. At 0100 they saw a red flare which the crew decided was a fighter flare ... the Wireless Operator advised the Captain to start weaving as he had picked up a German conversation on the *Tinsel* frequency he was searching. The Pilot began weaving and the Bomb Aimer reported a searchlight astern of the aircraft. Five minutes later cannon tracer hit the aircraft and fire broke out between the Starboard Inner and the fuselage. It was not long before it was obvious that the Halifax was doomed and Captain ordered the crew to bale out. Pilot Officer Dennison's debrief, he was one of five of the crew to evade capture, continued the story: 'When the Pilot's turn came to leave the machine was diving fast and he was pressed up against his Perspex canopy so he could not manoeuvre to get down onto the floor. He held on to the control column and managed to get his feet onto the dash. The elevators still seemed to be working as he was suddenly thrown to the floor and he then managed to crawl to the exit. He was hampered by either his oxygen tube or his intercom lead, which he had not been able to disconnect owing to his parachute having been put on over them. After getting through the hatch he was unable to get away from the aircraft and he accordingly pulled his ripcord and was jerked away when the aircraft was at a height of 5,000 to 6,000 feet. He sustained two broken ribs while in the aircraft.' Of the three crew that did not manage to escape, two had been killed and one taken prisoner.

The overall losses had been eleven aircraft and the attack had not been a success as the marking had been inaccurate, perhaps in part because of the reported first use by the Germans of dummy Target Indicators (TIs). The main weight of the attack fell to the South-West of the city, although some suburb areas were hit. With Bomber Command becoming increasingly effective the Germans had been expending a great deal of effort on increasing both the physical defences of night fighters and anti-aircraft guns and the 'spoof' defences of decoy fires and, now, dummy Target Indicators.

Stirling III BK653 of 214 Squadron was shot down by fighters on the Mannheim raid of 16/17 April 1943; four of the crew managed to escape and return to England, three were taken prisoner and one, the Rear Gunner Sergeant E. Lee was killed. The aircraft, Captained by Flying Officer D James had taken off from Chedburgh at 2150 and two hours later was cruising at 9,000 ft in bright moonlight and good visibility just South of St Quentin. The debrief of the escapees gave details of the attack by three Bf 109s: 'An Me 109 was seen approaching on the starboard beam at the same level as the Stirling at a range of 800 to 1,000 yards. The Stirling immediately began corkscrewing, starting with a diving turn to starboard and shortly afterwards the Rear Gunner reported a second Me 109 coming in to attack from astern. Almost at once a third Me 109 was seen attacking from the port beam and level. The first 109 opened fire and hit the wings of the Stirling, apparently with no serious effects but it seems probable that the turret hydraulics may have been damaged as the rear turret became unserviceable after a 2–3 second burst had been fired.

'The Stirling jettisoned its bombs and continued its evasive action, picking up speed by diving, and at times reached a speed of 300 mph. The 109 on the starboard side opened fire at 800 yards and then came in very close, almost colliding with the Stirling. A stream of bullets passed through the window between the Pilot and the Navigator; the mid-upper turret was damaged and the centre section and rest position riddled. The intercom and all electrical services failed. The Mid-Upper Gunner fired all his ammunition in two or three long bursts.

'All three 109s pressed home their attacks and fired many bursts of tracer and HE shells at the Stirling. It is thought by the crew that the enemy aircraft broke off the combat because they had fired all their ammunition. The Stirling set course for home.'

In this incredible – and one-sided combat – none of the crew had been injured but it was soon evident that the aircraft had been seriously damaged. The No. 5 and No. 6 starboard wing tanks had been holed and petrol was leaking out and there was a fire beyond the starboard outer engine with burning petrol coming from the trailing edge of the wing. Some 8 or 9 minutes later the Captain gave the order to abandon the aircraft.

Bomber Command had sent 271 aircraft to Mannheim, comprising 159 Wellingtons, 95 Stirlings and 17 Halifaxes. The target was effectively marked by the Pathfinders and bombing was reasonably concentrated causing extensive damage. The bombers lost eighteen of their number (6.6 per cent of their total) – nine Wellingtons, seven Stirlings and two Halifaxes, the majority of these falling to fighters. With clear conditions it was in ideal night for the single-engined fighters but the difficulty that the three Bf 109s had in bringing down the Stirling emphasised the problems faced by these fighter pilots who were not used to the size of an aircraft such as the Stirling, which presented problems of estimating range and of combat at night. The overall losses had been high – but not as high as for the other raid mounted that night. The Command despatched 327 bombers to attack Pilsen, the aiming point being the important Skoda armaments factory. Thirty-six of the 197 Lancasters and 130 Halifaxes (eighteen of each) were lost on this raid and despite bright moonlight the attack was poor as the target was misidentified.

Halifax HR663 of 102 Squadron was one of the aircraft that didn't make it back, although the pilot, Squadron Leader Lashbrook DFC DFM (on his thirty-sixth operation) and three other members of the crew managed to evade capture (two crew were taken prisoner and the Rear Gunner, Flying Officer G Williams was killed). Debrief of the evaders summarised the fate of the aircraft: 'After having bombed the target the aircraft flew into the Mannheim region at 9,000 feet and experienced very severe icing. After climbing to 14,000 feet the ice began to evaporate and as the height of the cloud tops became les the aircraft reduced height to 9,000 feet.

'In the Ardennes region an aircraft was seen going down in flames on the starboard side – tracer was seen and it was assumed to be a fighter attack. Approximately 3 minutes later another aircraft was seen going down in flames on the port side. The Pilot told the Mid-Upper Gunner to keep a sharp lookout and almost immediately bullets hit the aircraft. The fighter was not seen but was apparently attacking from astern and below. All members of the crew said they were OK. The Pilot put the aircraft into a steep dive to port and at once saw there was a very fierce fire between the Port Inner engine and the fuselage. ... After 3,000 feet loss of height the Pilot found that he could not pull the aircraft out of the dive as the controls were not working properly, nor could he throttle back the port engines as the throttle control rods were loose or severed. The Pilot gave the order to bale out. The Pilot left, he believes, last and as he was trying to leave, the aircraft went into a spin. Eventually he got free at less than 1,000 feet and made a heavy landing.'

With total losses for the night of fifty-four aircraft (8.8 per cent of the force) this was the highest number of losses in a single night to date, although fourteen of the aircraft managed to ditch in the sea on the way home and a number of aircrew were rescued.

Halifax JB873 of 78 Squadron was fitted with the mid-upper turret and the poorer performance of the aircraft with this turret was cited as a contributing factor to its loss on the Bochum attack of 13/14 May. The aircraft had departed Linton-on-Ouse at 2339 and was to be one of the three of the Squadron's aircraft to fail to return that night. One of the crew, Sergeant R. Goddard, the Navigator, evaded capture and his account of the mission was recorded by the RAF interrogators. 'The aircraft was slow on this trip, only 145 IAS, possibly because this was the first trip with the mid-upper turret. When 5–10 miles South of Cologne at 20,000 ft the revs on the Starboard engine dropped and it cut out. The Pilot feathered the propeller. It was not possible to maintain height on three engines and after a 5,000 ft height loss the bombs were jettisoned live. It was decided to make for the nearest point on the English coast by a route that missed enemy defences. Some time later a jar was felt in the aircraft and the Pilot said the Port Outer engine was on fire. The Pilot ordered the crew to prepare to abandon and pressed the Graviner switch. The fire went out and the Pilot said that there might not be a need to bale out. Two or three minutes later the engine caught fire again and the Pilot ordered the crew to abandon the aircraft. From the Bomber Aimer's position the fire appeared to be coming from around the engine and the flames, which were a reddish colour, were licking back to about half chord of the mainplane. The Navigator was first to abandon the aircraft, the Bomb Aimer and Wireless Operator were preparing to follow. At the time he (the Navigator) jumped the aircraft was at a height of 10,000 feet and was diving steeply but still just about under control. The fire was spreading fast towards the centre of the aircraft.' The Pilot, Sergeant G. Dane, was one of the two crew to be killed, the others, with the exception of Sergeant Goddard, escaped the aircraft but were taken prisoner. Subsequent investigation has attributed this loss to a night fighter flown by Lieutenant Heinz Wolfgang Schnaufer of II/NJG1. One of the other 78 Squadron Halifaxes also fell to a night fighter *experten*, JB924 being credited to Hpt Helmut Lent of IV/NJG1.

The Bochum raid had involved 442 aircraft, 135 of which were Halifaxes; of the latter thirteen were shot down out of total loss for the raid of twenty-four bombers. The Command lost a further nine aircraft on the raid to Pilsen mounted by 167 aircraft.

On the night of 23/24 May 1943 Dortmund was attacked by a force of 826 aircraft: In cloudless conditions an exceptionally accurate ground marking attack was delivered, virtually devastating the town and causing severe industrial damage. Ground defences in the target area and night fighters on the return route put up a strong opposition and thirty-eight aircraft failed to return. German records agree that the attack was accurate and in addition to extensive damage to houses a large number of industrial premises were destroyed or damaged. Zero hour was timed for 0100 with the attack to take place between 0058 and 0200. As an aid to navigation eleven *Oboe* Mosquitoes dropped yellow TIs at a key turning point. They then went on to drop three red TIs in salvo on the aiming point, with thirty-three backers-up dropping green TIs on the centre of the reds. The first wave of 250 aircraft comprised the best crews from all Groups, with all remaining non Lancasters in the second wave and the Lancasters in the final wave, with PFF aircraft at the head of each wave.

Dams raid

The most famous Bomber Command attack of the Second World War took place in May 1943 under the codename Operation *Chastise*, and its participants, Wing Commander Guy Gibson and 617 Squadron earned themselves a place in the RAF's operational annals. The concept of attacking dams believed to be critical to war industries had been part of the original Western Air Plans, although it was not until late 1942 that the subject was raised again. One of the many weapons being developed by Dr Barnes Wallis was a 'bouncing bomb' (mine) specifically designed for attacking the German dams and despite early official indifference to the idea he was at last successful in persuading the Air Staff to take the idea seriously. The other essential part of the plan was an aircraft capable of delivering the weapon and aircrew able to fly the accurate attack profile that would be required. The former was achieved by modifying the bomb doors of the Lancaster; the solution to the latter was the creation of a special squadron. As an experienced bomber pilot (174 missions) Guy Gibson had just completed a tour with 106 Squadron but was asked by AOC No. 5 Group to form a special squadron and undertake one more operation. With selected crews 617 Squadron formed and started training. By May the aircraft, the crews and, after initial problems, the 'bouncing bomb', were ready. Time was tight as the attack relied on the water level in the dams being correct. At 2130 on 16 May the first wave of Lancasters took-off from Scampton, followed by two further waves for a total of nineteen aircraft. The first wave, of nine aircraft, was led by Gibson and was destined for the Mohne Dam, with the Eder Dam as their second target; the second wave, of five aircraft, was destined for the Sorpe Dam and the third wave, of five aircraft, was an airborne reserve for attack on any of the three dams not breached by the first attackers.

One aircraft of the first wave was shot down on the outbound route but overall it was a fairly easy run. The Lancasters arrived over the Mohne Dam around midnight and Gibson made an accurate attack with his bomb. He was followed by Flight Lieutenant Hopgood but by this time the flak gunners were fully alert and the Lancaster was hit on the run in. The bomb was dropped late, missing the target, and the aircraft crashed, with only two survivors. The third Lancaster, flown by Flight Lieutenant Martin, ran in – with Gibson flying alongside to distract the flak gunners. Despite this the bomb went short. Squadron Leader Young was next in and this time both Gibson and Martin flew escort. The bomb was accurate and the dam was drenched in the plume of water; two good hits had been made but Barnes Wallis had predicted that three would be needed to cause fatal damage. It was an accurate prediction for when Flight Lieutenant Maltby's mine hit the dam, the plume of water was followed by the collapse of the dam wall and a flood down the river valley. It must have been an amazing sight for the circling Lancasters. Gibson took the remaining bombed-up Lancasters on to the Eder Dam whilst the others returned home (Squadron Leader Young was shot down by coastal flak over Holland).

Modified Lancaster of 617 Squadron; the Lancaster bomb bay has the distinctive cut-out for the 'bouncing bomb'.

The Eder Dam was breached after two 'bouncing bombs' had been accurately dropped.

There were no defences at this dam and the Lancasters could make their runs with no distractions other than the terrain. The first run, by Flight Lieutenant Shannon, was accurate and actually caused a small breach. The second bomb, dropped by Squadron Leader Maudslay, was dropped late and caused no damage to the target, although it did damage the Lancaster (this aircraft was shot down during the return flight). Pilot Officer Knight made a good run and after the plume had subsided the dam gave way. Two targets had been destroyed but at a cost of nearly 50 per cent of the attackers (four aircraft).

The second wave was not so lucky; two aircraft turned back with technical problems, two were shot down on the outbound route and only Flight Lieutenant McCarthy made it to the target. His bomb hit the dam but caused no appreciable damage. The third wave also lost two aircraft on the way to the target area, with a third returning to base with technical problems. Of the remaining two, Flight Sergeant Ken Brown attacked the Sorpe Dam and Flight Sergeant Townsend attacked the Ennepe Dam. No appreciable damage was caused. Overall it had been a highly successful raid despite the loss of eight aircraft (with fifty-three aircrew killed); two of the main targets had been destroyed and whilst the military value of the attack has been questioned there can be no doubt of the good effect on morale of the attack. It was heralded in the British press: 'Tonight, walls of water swept down the Ruhr and Eder valleys in Germany, destroying everything before them, after the RAF had attacked two dams. The raids, by specially fitted Lancaster bombers using new "bouncing bombs" were planned to cripple Germany's vital industrial heartland.'

The citation of the award of a VC for Guy Gibson, said: 'This officer served as a night bomber pilot at the beginning of the war and quickly established a reputation as an outstanding operational pilot. In addition to taking the fullest possible share in all normal operations, he made single-handed attacks during his 'rest' nights on such highly defended objectives as the German battleship *Tirpitz*, then completing a refit in Wilhelmshaven. When his tour of operational duty was concluded, he asked for a further operational posting and went to a night-fighter unit instead of being posted for instructional duties. In the course of his second operational tour, he destroyed at least three enemy bombers and contributed much to the raising and development of new night-fighter formations. After a short period in a training unit, he again volunteered for operational duties and returned to night bombers. Both as an operational pilot and as leader of his squadron, he achieved outstandingly successful results and his personal courage knew no bounds. Berlin, Cologne, Danzig, Gdynia, Genoa, Le Creusot, Milan, Nuremberg and Stuttgart were among the targets he attacked by day and by night. On the conclusion of his third operational tour, Wing Commander Gibson pressed strongly to be allowed to remain on operations and he was selected to command a squadron then forming for special tasks. Under his inspiring leadership, this squadron has now executed one of the most devastating attacks of the war – the breaching of the Mohne and Eder dams. The task was fraught with danger and difficulty. Wing Commander Gibson personally made the initial attack on the Mohne dam. Descending to within a few feet of the water and taking the full brunt of the anti-aircraft defences, he delivered his attack with great accuracy. Afterwards he circled very low for 30 minutes, drawing the enemy fire on himself in order to leave as free a run as possible to the following aircraft which were attacking the dam in turn. Wing Commander Gibson then led the remainder of his force to the Eder dam where, with complete disregard for his own safety, he repeated his tactics and once more drew on himself the enemy fire so that the attack could be successfully developed. Wing Commander Gibson has completed over 170 sorties, involving more than 600 hours operational flying. Throughout his operational career, prolonged exceptionally at his own request, he has shown leadership, determination and valour of the highest order.' (Acting Wing Commander Guy Penrose Gibson DSO DFC, 617 Squadron RAF, Lancaster ED932; awarded for action 16 May 1943, *London Gazette*, 28 May 1943.)

Another Bomber Command pilot was awarded the Victoria Cross for an action in May 1943, although it would be nearly three years before the award was announced. This raid had none of the glamour, or success, of the Dams Raid and was recorded in the diary of 487 Squadron in sad terms: 'A very black day in the history of the Squadron ... a better set of boys could not be met in 30 years, everybody is dazed by the news.' On 3 May the Squadron sent eleven Venturas to attack a power station near Amsterdam. Unfortunately the formation was bounced by fighters; nine bombers were shot down and a tenth limped home to crash at Feltwell. The sole survivor, Squadron Leader Leonard Trent, pressed on to the target – but was shot down, only Trent and one other member of the crew surviving. The *London Gazette* again: 'On the 3 May 1943, Squadron Leader Trent was detailed to lead a formation of Ventura aircraft in a daylight attack on the power station at Amsterdam. This operation was intended to encourage the Dutch workmen in their resistance to enemy pressure. The target was known to be heavily defended. The importance of bombing it, regardless of enemy fighters or anti-aircraft fire, was strongly impressed on the air crews taking part in the operation. Before taking off, Squadron Leader Trent told the deputy leader that he was going over the target, whatever happened. All went well until the Venturas and their fighter escort were nearing the Dutch coast. Then one bomber was hit and had to turn back. Suddenly, large numbers of enemy fighters appeared. Our escorting fighters were hotly engaged and lost touch with the bombing force. The Venturas closed up for mutual protection and commenced their run up to the target. Unfortunately, the fighters detailed to support them over the target had reached the area too early and had been recalled. Soon the bombers were attacked. They were at the mercy of fifteen to twenty Messerschmitts which dived on them incessantly. Within four minutes six Venturas were destroyed. Squadron Leader Trent continued on his course with the three remaining aircraft. In a short time two more Venturas went down in flames. Heedless of the murderous attacks and of the heavy anti-aircraft fire which was now encountered, Squadron Leader Trent completed an accurate bombing run and even shot down a Messerschmitt at point-blank range. Dropping his bombs in the target area, he turned away. The aircraft following him was shot down on reaching the target. Immediately afterwards his own aircraft was hit, went into a spin and broke up. Squadron Leader Trent and his navigator were thrown clear and became prisoners of war. The other two members of the crew perished. On this, his twenty-fourth sortie, Squadron Leader Trent showed outstanding leadership. Such was the trust placed in this gallant officer that the other pilots followed him un- waveringly. His cool, unflinching courage and devotion to duty in the face of over- whelming odds rank with the finest examples of these virtues.' (Squadron Leader Leonard Henry Trent DFC, 487 Squadron RNZAF, Ventura AJ209; awarded for action 3 May 1943, *London Gazette*, 1 March 1946.)

It was unusual for a Mosquito to fall victim to the German defences, as evidenced by the low level of losses in the Summary of Operations table. On 14 June Mosquito IX LR501 of No. 1409 Met Flight was airborne out of Oakington for a 'routine' daylight reconnaissance over Germany – and just after midday became the first Mosquito IX lost on operations (LR501 had only flown 10 hours 45 minutes total time when it was lost). The crew were flying at 28,000 feet in clear skies and the Navigator, Pilot Officer R. Taylor (on his twenty-first *op*) was making an entry in his Navigation Log when he felt the impact of cannon shells on the aircraft and looking up he saw pieces flying off the tail unit. The intelligence report of his subsequent debrief stated that he 'saw an Fw 190 below and shouted to the pilot; he then pulled up the collapsible bullet proof shield and started giving evasive directions to the Pilot. A second Focke Wulfe made an attack but no hits were apparent. The Mosquito corkscrewed and performed skid turns but the controls finally disabled and broke. One shell went through the fuselage and the Navigator was thrown forward; his left hand became full of blood and he received cuts to his eyes and neck. The Pilot told the Navigator to bale out as the aircraft went into a spin. The Navigator, who was of stout build, was jammed in the entrance and could not move. The Pilot then left the aircraft by the top escape hatch. The Navigator fumbled for his parachute and after some time got hold of one of the carrying handles and succeeded with the greatest difficulty in attaching the parachute to his harness. He does not really know how he left the aircraft but is convinced he came out through the nose of the machine and believes the Perspex must have been blown away. He landed in a wheat field after a 2 or 3 minute descent and saw the aircraft on fire three-quarters of a mile away. He saw the Pilot coming down by parachute.' The pilot made a safe landing but was taken prisoner. The report concluded: 'the greater part of the damage was done in the first attack. If warning had been given it is likely that the Mosquito would have been saved. It is recommended that *Monica* be fitted to all Met Reconnaissance aircraft and that consideration be given to fitting it to PRU aircraft.' Whilst the loss rate for the Mosquito remained remarkably low, for other aircraft in the latter half of 1943 it was far too high.

Summer 1943 saw two particularly significant attacks by Bomber Command:

1. 19/20 June, Schneider factory and Breuil Steelworks, Le Creusot.
2. 20/21 June, Zeppelin Works, Friedrichshafen.

The Le Creusot attack was made from low-level at night and was one of the most successful of the war so far.

The attack on the Zeppelin Works, an important manufacturer of Wurzburg radars and not an airship manufacturer, was the first of its type in that the extreme range meant that the bombers would not return to England but would fly on to bases in North Africa. The sixty Lancasters on this *Shuttle* raid were mainly from No. 5 Group and the flight to Lake Constance and on to Africa was expected to take over 10 hours, much of this being over enemy territory. A small Pathfinder force dropped TIs and the Main Force made a timed run from a good visual point on the lake shore. In another first this was a 'directed attack' with Wing Commander G. L. Gomm controlling the bombing – a technique that was later formalised as the Master Bomber technique – although Gibson had effectively done the same thing on a smaller scale during the Dams Raid. The target was effectively bombed and no aircraft were lost. One crew described the scene in the target area: 'We stayed over Lake Constance for 13 minutes and had an excellent view of the attack. There were approximately sixteen to twenty heavy flak guns and eighteen to twenty

Damage to the Krupps Works, Essen, June 1943.

light flak guns, and twenty-five searchlights, within a radius of 6–8 miles of the target. Several aircraft were coned but not for any length of time. Heavy guns were firing both predictor-control and unseen. As the defences were heavier than expected, the Deputy Leader [Gomm had taken over from Group Captain Slee] gave the order for all aircraft to increase height by 5,000 feet, so that the attack was actually delivered from 10,000 to 15,000 feet.'

Three nights later, 23/24 June, 52 of the *Shuttle* Lancasters returned to England – bombing La Spezia on the return route. Despite the special attacks detailed above, the main focus of the Command in early summer 1943 remained the Battle of the Ruhr. In the last weeks of the battle targets included Cologne, Gelsenkirchen, Krefeld, Aachen and Wuppertal. However, with the nights becoming shorter and the loss rate increasing Harris finally drew this campaign to a halt and took stock of the results.

Friedrichshafen Zeppelin Works after the attack of 20/21 June 1943.

Battle of the Ruhr: summary of operations

Date	Target	Halifax	Lancaster	Mosquito	Stirling	Wellington
5/6 Mar	Essen	94 (3)	157 (4)	8	52 (3)	131 (4)
8/9 Mar	Nuremberg	103 (2)	170 (2)	0	62 (4)	0
9/10 Mar	Munich	81 (2)	142 (5)	0	41 (1)	0
11/12 Mar	Stuttgart	109 (6)	152 (2)	0	53 (3)	0
12/13 Mar	Essen	91 (7)	156 (8)	10	42 (2)	158 (6)
26/27 Mar	Duisburg	114 (1)	157 (1)	9 (1)	2	173 (3)
27/28 Mar	Berlin	124 (4)	191 (3)	0	81 (2)	0
29/30 Mar	Berlin	103 (7)	162 (11)	0	64 (3)	0
	Bochum	0	0	8	0	149 (12)
3/4 Apr	Essen	113 (12)	225 (9)	10	0	0
4/5 Apr	Kiel	116 (4)	203 (5)	0	90 (2)	168 (1)
8/9 Apr	Duisburg	73 (3)	156 (6)	10	56 (3)	97 (7)
9/10 Apr	Duisburg	104 (8)	0	5	0	0
10/11 Apr	Frankfurt	124 (3)	136 (5)	0	98 (5)	144 (8)
13/14 Apr	La Spezia	3	208 (4)	0	0	0
14/15 Apr	Stuttgart	135 (4)	98 (3)	0	83 (8)	146 (8)
16/17 Apr	Pilsen	130 (18)	197 (18)	0	0	0
	Mannheim	17 (2)	0	0	95 (7)	159 (9)
18/19 Apr	La Spezia	5	181 (1)	0	0	0
20/21 Apr	Stettin	134 (7)	194 (13)	0	11 (1)	0
	Rostock	0	0	0	86 (8)	0
	Berlin	0	0	11 (1)	0	0
26/27 Apr	Duisburg	119 (7)	215 (3)	14	78 (2)	135 (5)
30/1 May	Essen	105 (6)	190 (6)	10	0	0
4/5 May	Dortmund	141 (12)	255 (6)	10	80 (7)	110 (6)
12/13 May	Duisburg	142 (9)	238 (10)	10	70 (5)	112 (10)
13/14 May	Bochum	135 (13)	98 (1)	0	95 (4)	104 (6)
	Pilsen	12 (?)	156 (?)	0	0	0
	Berlin	0	0	12 (1)	0	0
16/17 May	DAMS	0	19 (8)	0	0	0
23/24 May	Dortmund	199 (18)	343 (8)	13	120 (6)	151 (6)
25/26 May	Dusseldorf	169 (4)	323 (9)	12	113 (8)	142 (6)
27/28 May	Essen	151 (11)	274 (6)	12 (1)	0	81 (5)
29/30 May	Wuppertal	185 (10)	292 (7)	11	118 (8)	113 (8)
11/12 Jun	Dusseldorf	202 (12)	326 (14)	13	99 (2)	143 (10)
	Munster	22 (2)	29 (2)	0	21 (1)	0
12/13 Jun	Bochum	167 (10)	323 (14)	11	0	0
14/15 Jun	Oberhausen	0	197 (17)	6	0	0
16/17 Jun	Cologne	10	202 (14)	0	0	0
19/20 Jun	Le Creusot	181 (2)	2	0	107	0
	Montchain	0	26	0	0	0
20/21 Jun	Friedrichshafen	0	60	0	0	0
21/22 Jun	Krefeld	209 (17)	262 (9)	12	117 (9)	105 (9)
22/23 Jun	Mulheim	155 (12)	242 (8)	12	93 (11)	55 (4)
23/24 Jun	La Spezia	0	52	0	0	0
24/25 Jun	Wuppertal	171 (10)	251 (8)	9	98 (10)	101 (6)
25/26 Jun	Gelsenkirchen	134 (7)	214 (13)	12	73 (6)	40 (4)
28/29 Jun	Cologne	169 (10)	267 (8)	12	75 (5)	85 (2)
3/4 Jul	Cologne	182 (9)	293 (8)	13	76 (5)	89 (8)
8/9 Jul	Cologne	0	282 (7)	6	0	0
9/10 Jul	Gelsenkirchen	190 (7)	218 (5)	10	0	0
12/13 Jul	Turin	0	295 (13)	0	0	0
13/14 Jul	Aachen	214 (15)	18 (2)	11	55 (1)	76 (2)
15/16 Jul	Montbeliard	165 (5)	0	0	0	0

Notes

1. Italy: 13/14 April, 18/19 April attacks on the dock area at La Spezia, Italy.

2. This is not a complete list of all Bomber Command operations during this period as it does not include minor operations, minelaying or leaflet dropping sorties. It is worth mentioning the minelaying effort of 27/28 April when the Command sent out 160 aircraft to lay mines; 123 reported successful planting of their vegetables and a total of 458 mines were laid for the loss of one Lancaster. This record number of aircraft was exceeded the following night when 207 aircraft were sent out, with 593 mines being laid by the 167 successful aircraft – but for the loss of 22 aircraft, a very high percentage for this type of operation. Indeed, the record losses – and record number of mines – were not exceeded for the rest of the war.

3. Aircraft details show number despatched and (in brackets) number lost.

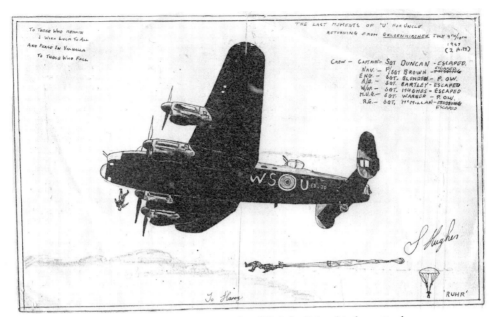

Cartoon of a 9 Squadron Lancaster lost on the 9/10 July Gelsenkirchen attack.

Battle of Hamburg: 24 July 1943 to 3 August 1943

The city of Hamburg had been on Bomber Command's target list almost 100 times before this short but intense series of attacks in summer 1943, during which just over 3,000 sorties were made in four major night attacks. One of the reasons that Hamburg was chosen for destruction, under the codename Operation *Gomorrah*, was its role as a major shipbuilding port and especially its involvement with U-boat construction. Also, its location meant that it should be easy to locate using H2S. The Battle of Hamburg was intended as a two-pronged campaign with the bombers of the USAAF hitting the city by day thus giving no respite to the defenders and making any repair work even more difficult. In the event this proved to be unworkable as the effect, primarily the pall of smoke, caused by the first Bomber Command attacks meant that the Americans could not see their targets and blind bombing was not an option.

However, the more important innovation was the first use of *Window* in an attempt to reduce loss rates of bombers, and with a loss rate of only 1.5 per cent on this first attack the tactic certainly worked. Of the 791 bombers on the first night, 728 claim to have attacked the target and in a well concentrated raid of only 50 minutes dropped 2,284 tons of bombs, the aiming point being the centre of the city. The bombing was somewhat scattered but three nights later a more effective attack was made, with 729 bombers of the 787 despatched claiming to have bombed the target. The Pathfinders used H2S to mark the aiming point near the centre of the city and in good conditions the Main Force dropped 2,326 tons into the area in one of the most concentrated attacks of the war. It also proved devastating to the inhabitants of Hamburg with an estimated 40,000 dying in the firestorm that raged through the city. Following this raid almost two-thirds of the population, over 1,000,000 people, fled the city to escape future raids. This was one of the strategic aims of area bombing – to de-house workers and disrupt war industry.

The Bomber Command ORS analysed the Hamburg raids: 'The very low casualties incurred on the first two raids were largely due to the temporary disorganisation of the

Battle of Hamburg: summary of operations

Date	Target	Halifax	Lancaster	Mosquito	Stirling	Wellington
24/25 Jul	Hamburg	246 (4)	347 (4)	0	125 (3)	73 (1)
25/26 Jul	Essen	221 (10)	294 (5)	19	104 (7)	67 (4)
27/28 Jul	Hamburg	244 (4)	353 (11)	0	116 (1)	74 (1)
29/30 Jul	Hamburg	244 (11)	340 (11)	0	119 (4)	70 (2)
30/31 Jul	Remscheid	95 (5)	82 (2)	9	87 (8)	0
2/3 Aug	Hamburg	235 (10)	329 (13)	5	105 (3)	66 (3)

Note: Aircraft details show number despatched and (in brackets) number lost.

German fighter defences by a new countermeasure which precluded the vectoring of controlled night fighters. The final attack was ruined by unexpected deterioration of weather conditions over the target. Eighty-seven aircraft is a high price in itself, but in comparison with the loss suffered by Germany in the almost complete annihilation of her second city, it can only be regarded as minute. The 'Hafen' with its imposing array of shipbuilding yards, docks, warehouses and administrative buildings was the basis of Hamburg's contribution to German economic life.

'The destruction of Hamburg by bombing was thus far the stiffest task yet undertaken in air warfare. It was not until 1 August that smoke from the conflagrations cleared sufficiently to make reconnaissance possible. The heavily damaged areas covered 6,200 acres out of the 8,380 acres which comprise Hamburg's closely built-up residential area. All parts of the city and dock were shattered – all four main shipbuilding yards were hit, five floating docks were sunk or badly damaged, 150 industrial plants were destroyed or badly damaged, plus massive disruption of communications and power.'

Italy was the main focus of attention in August but the Command also mounted Operation *Hydra*, an attack on the research installation a Peenemunde on the Baltic coast. The Allies had been acquiring evidence that this was the site of advanced weapon research, especially rocket technology and by late June 1943 the War Cabinet had scheduled Peenemunde as a high priority target for Bomber Command. Harris requested a delay until the longer nights of late summer would make his aircraft less vulnerable and on the night of 17/18 August a force of 596 bombers converged on the target. The initial markers were slightly off the aiming points but the Master Bomber, Group Captain John Searby was able to call on the backer-up markers to re-mark the target and to pass bombing instructions to the Main Force. It was a clear moonlit night and the target was well and truly plastered, although the moonlight was also perfect for the night fighters. Fortunately they were late arriving and only caught the last wave. Bomber losses of forty were considered acceptable for the level of destruction on such a vital target.

Battle of Berlin: August 1943 to March 1944

Harris had already decided that his next major campaign would be against the 'Big City' and the Battle opened on the night of 23/24 August when 727 bombers, almost half of which were Lancasters, took part in a Master Bomber attack. The results were disappointing with scattered bombing, the markers having fallen on the southern part of the city. The defenders took a heavy toll with fifty-six aircraft (7.9 per cent loss rate) being lost, the highest number in a single raid so far; it was a particularly bad night for the Stirlings with sixteen of the 124 aircraft involved being lost.

The Battle of Berlin took place in a number of phases and lasted to March 1944, by which time the Command had mounted 9,099 sorties against the 'Big City', dropping 29,804 tons of bombs; overall losses were 501 aircraft. Bomber Command was able to reach and hit its targets, albeit with mixed results, but it was paying a high price.

The second attack of the introductory phase took place on the last night of August 1943 and once again the bombers failed to do much damage and suffered high casualties with the loss of 47 of the 622 aircraft, with the Stirlings once more having the highest losses relative to aircraft dispatched (17 of 106 aircraft). The next raid, 3/4 September, was an all Lancaster affair, along with four *Mossies* whose task was to drop spoof route flares in an attempt to decoy German fighters. Accuracy was again poor and with 7 per cent of the Lancasters failing to return, a high rate for the Lancaster, it proved what a tough nut Berlin was. Some damage had been caused and after the bombing of Hamburg the Germans were wary of concerted offensives against a single city and a partial evacuation of the city was ordered. However, Bomber Command was also taking stock of the results with a view that the high loss rates, particularly those of the Stirling and Halifax, for low levels of damage could not be justified. For the next few weeks the bombers turned to other targets but it was only a short respite for Berlin and Harris was determined to launch an all-out offensive against this heartland of Nazi power.

One of the 'other' targets attacked in this period was Dusseldorf. The raid of 3/4 November was notable for two reasons: the operational debut of G-H, which in part explained the accuracy of the attack, and the award of a Victoria Cross to Bill Reid. His citation read: 'On the night of 3 November 1943, Flight Lieutenant Reid was pilot and captain of a Lancaster aircraft detailed to attack Dusseldorf. Shortly after crossing the Dutch coast, the pilot's windscreen was shattered by fire from a Messerschmitt 110. Owing to a failure in the heating circuit, the rear gunner's hands were too cold for him to open fire immediately or to operate his microphone and so give warning of danger; but after a brief delay he managed to return the Messerschmitt's fire and it was driven off.

'During the fight with the Messerschmitt, Flight Lieutenant Reid was wounded in the head, shoulders and hands. The elevator trimming tabs of the aircraft were damaged and it became difficult to control. The rear turret, too, was badly damaged and the communications system and compasses were put out of action. Flight Lieutenant Reid ascertained that his crew were unscathed and, saying nothing about his own injuries, he continued his mission. Soon afterwards, the Lancaster was attacked by a Focke Wulfe 190. This time, the enemy's fire raked the bomber from stem to stern. The rear gunner replied with his only serviceable gun but the state of his turret made accurate aiming impossible. The navigator was killed and the wireless operator fatally injured. The mid-upper turret was hit and the oxygen system put out of action. Flight Lieutenant Reid was again wounded and the flight engineer, though hit in the forearm, supplied him with oxygen from a portable supply. Flight Lieutenant Reid refused to be turned from his objective and Dusseldorf was reached some 50 minutes later. He had memorised his course to the target and had continued in such a normal manner that the bomb-aimer, who was cut off by the failure of the communications system, knew nothing of his captain's injuries or of the casualties to his comrades.

'Photographs show that, when the bombs were released, the aircraft was right over the centre of the target. Steering by the pole star and the moon, Flight Lieutenant Reid then set course for home. He was growing weak from loss of blood. The emergency oxygen supply had given out. With the windscreen shattered, the cold was intense. He lapsed into semi-consciousness. The flight engineer, with some help from the bomb-aimer, kept the Lancaster in the air despite heavy anti-aircraft fire over the Dutch coast.

The North Sea crossing was accomplished. An airfield was sighted. The captain revived, resumed control and made ready to land. Ground mist partially obscured the runway lights. The captain was also much bothered by blood from his head wound getting into his eyes. But he made a safe landing although one leg of the damaged undercarriage collapsed when the load came on. Wounded in two attacks, without oxygen, suffering severely from cold, his navigator dead, his wireless operator fatally wounded, his aircraft crippled and defenceless, Flight Lieutenant Reid showed superb courage and leadership in penetrating a further 200 miles into enemy territory, to attack one of the most strongly defended targets in Germany, every additional mile increasing the hazards of the long and perilous journey home. His tenacity and devotion to duty were beyond praise.' (Acting Flight Lieutenant William Reid, 61 Squadron RAF, Lancaster LM360; awarded for action 3/4 November 1943, *London Gazette*, 14 December 1943.)

The initial raid in the first real phase of the Battle of Berlin took place on 18/19 November when 440 Lancasters attacked the 'Big City', with a second force attacking Ludwigshaven to split the night fighter force. A combination of poor weather and poor PFF marking led to a scattered raid, although this time losses were light. Four nights later the weather forecast was near perfect and the Command mounted a maximum effort raid against Berlin, 765 aircraft taking part. The outbound route was near direct, which meant an increased bomb load. However, the weather was worse than forecast but this was an advantage as it proved more of a problem for the defenders than the attackers and marking was accurate with Berlin being hit hard. The Stirlings suffered a high loss rate again (10 per cent) and Harris reluctantly ordered their withdrawal from this target. Indeed, this was very much a Lancaster battle as the Halifax too had to be withdrawn from the Battle as their loss rates increased. The Halifax squadrons took a greater part in the latter phases when more of the improved Mk III became available. Although the cloud cover over the target meant that the attackers could not determine the accuracy of the raid it was, according to German sources, one of the most successful attacks made on Berlin with extensive damage over a wide area.

The bombers returned the following night but back-to-back *ops* meant fewer aircraft were available and less than 400 Lancasters took part, although with accurate blind marking through cloud, combined with fires still burning from the previous raid, it was considered successful. Berlin had a few nights of respite before almost 700 bombers left England on the evening of 26 November; near Frankfurt the bomber stream split to divide the German fighter force with one force heading for Stuttgart and the other carrying on to Berlin. Over Berlin clear weather meant a reasonable concentration for the attack and although the Lancaster loss rate was 6 per cent the raid was a success. Unfortunately the weather in England had deteriorated with fog covering the area South of the Humber; bombers were diverted to airfields in Yorkshire but thirty Lancasters crashed or crash-landed, resulting in several crews being killed. A maximum effort raid was planned for 2/3 December but the Halifax squadrons were grounded by fog and only 458 bombers took part and some of those turned back over the North Sea having encountered severe icing. Bad weather and inaccurate forecast winds meant that the Main Force was scattered by the time it arrived over Berlin, where German fighters had gathered having had a reasonable warning of the approach of the bombers. Most of the forty bombers that failed to return were lost over and near the target; this was one of the few occasions when Lancaster loss rates neared 10 per cent. It was two weeks before Berlin was targeted again. With fog forecast for the areas in which German night fighter airfields were concentrated Harris ordered another attack on Berlin on 16/17 December. Unfortunately the fog didn't ground all the fighters and combat was joined as soon as the

The Junkers factory in Leipzig showing heavy damage after the attack of 3/4 December 1943.

bombers crossed the Dutch coast, and continued all the way to Berlin and back. Bad weather was a problem for the Lancasters on their return to England and once more a number of aircraft and crews were lost in the futile search for a safe place to land. For 97 Squadron it was a particularly bad night with seven aircraft lost; Arthur Tindall was a WOP/AG on the raid: 'I can still recall the Met Officer saying that the weather would close in by the early hours of the following morning and he anticipated the raid being cancelled. In the event it wasn't with disastrous results. Our squadron lost seven aircraft that night. We were airborne for 7 hours 45 minutes compared with usual Berlin raids of 6 to 6½ hours. The following morning our ground crew said we had less than 50 gallons of petrol. In other words we were very lucky to have made it.' Arthur was also on the next Berlin raid, 23/24 December: 'Another early take-off – 0020 to Berlin. On the return we were attacked eight times by fighters, all of our guns were frozen. We landed on three engines and one tyre had burst – unknown to us until touchdown. The aircraft was written off.' The final raid in December was a maximum effort with the Halifax units joining in to send 712 bombers and with a longer outbound route, combined with poor weather, the German controllers failed to bring many fighters into contact with the bomber stream and only twenty bombers were lost. It was a relief to the planners that the loss rate had dropped but they could take little comfort from the course of the Battle of Berlin to date.

Harris continued the Battle into 1944 and Berlin was attacked six times in January, twice early in the month and four times late in the month – with nearly three weeks respite in the middle. The two attacks in the first few days of January brought another increase in loss rates, both being around 7 per cent, and disappointing results as the bombing was poorly concentrated. The two attacks on consecutive nights were different in that most losses on 1/2 January were outside the area of Berlin whereas the following night the controllers had mad an early prediction that Berlin was the target and they had 40 minutes to collect fighters at appropriate beacons. One of the effects of this was that the first aircraft over the target – the Pathfinders – were hit hard, losing ten aircraft. Bomber Command paused for a few weeks with very few operations of any type being flown; the 'Big City' was still the favoured target but Bomber Command assessment was that less than 25 per cent of the city had been destroyed, an underestimate if German records are taken into account, a disappointing result when lesser campaigns had resulted in destruction levels on other cities of 50–70 per cent.

When the briefing curtains were drawn back on 20 January crews groaned as they saw the tape leading once more to Berlin, although the direct route had been changed in favour of a more diverse approach. This was another maximum effort with 769 bombers, 264 of which were Halifaxes but it followed the same pattern as previous raids with fighters getting in amongst the bombers and with a cloud-covered Berlin proving hard to hit. It was not a promising return for the Halifax, with twenty-two of the 264 aircraft being lost. It was 102 Squadron's 'turn' to suffer and the Pocklington-based squadron lost five of its sixteen Halifaxes over enemy territory plus another two that crashed in England (it lost a further four aircraft the following night).

The Halifaxes were once more taken off the Berlin roster for the next raid and it was 515 Lancasters and fifteen Mosquitoes that returned to the city on 27/28 January. The bombers had a reasonable run to the target and bombed on sky markers as the aiming point was cloud covered; fighter combats took place on the return route and overall losses remained at over 6 per cent. It was back to a maximum effort the next night and a route via Denmark to try and throw off the fighters. The tactic was only partly successful and when the bombers arrived over Berlin the fighters were waiting and most of the forty-six losses occurred in the vicinity of the target. It was however the most accurate raid for a while as cloud was broken and the Pathfinders were able to lay ground markers. The planning for both of these raids had included diversionary operations to divert German defensives as well as offensive support operations against night fighter airfields and with an increasing number of *Serrate*-equipped Mosquito night fighters flying with the bomber stream. Two nights later 534 bombers were *en route* for the final attack in January. The northern route via Denmark once more prevented combats until the Berlin area but several bombers were shot down in the target area. Cloud was thick over Berlin but bombing was reasonably effective.

There were only two more attacks on the city during the Battle of Berlin: the first of these came after a respite due to the phase of the moon making bomber operations unwise; on 15/16 February nearly 900 bombers, the largest force yet to attack Berlin, left England for the northern route. With a near direct route home bomb loads were high and the total dropped this night was a record 2,642 tons. The German

Berlin, Siemens Electrical plant March 1944.

fighters were out in force and combats began over Southern Denmark; of the forty-three bombers that failed to return most fell to fighters. Despite cloud cover the city was hit hard and in general this was a successful raid. It was another month before Berlin was targeted again, the main reason being the new directive issued to Harris for attacks on the German aircraft industry. It could be argued that the February raid was the end of the Battle of Berlin but it is worth including the 24/25 March attack as after this Berlin was never again subjected to a Main Force attack – and the March raid was little short of a disaster for Bomber Command.

The raid of 24/25 March was a maximum effort with 811 bombers taking part; seventy-two (8.9 per cent) of these aircraft failed to return – the highest single loss to date. The main cause of the disaster was weather and in particular an inaccurate wind forecast with stronger than expected winds scattering the bombers. Whilst this made them less vulnerable to fighters it meant that they strayed over flak defences, including those of the Ruhr, and it is estimated that fifty of the losses were caused by flak. The strong winds also meant that marking was poor and bombing was not concentrated, although large parts of the city were damaged.

The Battle of Berlin was over; Harris's prediction of 500 bomber losses was correct – and that was only RAF losses – but his hope that Berlin would be destroyed from end to end was not fulfilled, despite the fact that almost 30,000 tons of bombs had been dropped. Nevertheless, the effect on the extensive industrial, economic and adminis-

Berlin 24/25 March 1944.

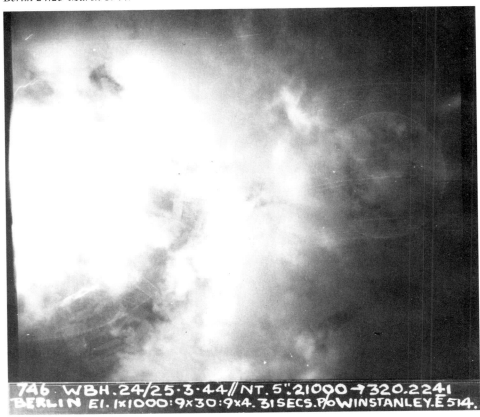

Lancaster LL704 of 115 Squadron, complete with German guard. The aircraft was shot down on the night of 30/31 March 1944 and was one of sixty-four bombers lost that night – the highest loss of the war.

trative activities of the Reich capital was significant both in direct (destruction) and indirect (evacuation or personnel, resources spent on repairs, and so on) results.

The latter part of March brought an increase in the number of attacks on targets in France as the pre-invasion bombing campaign got into its stride, although the largest individual raids were still those against German cities; for example 863 bombers to Stuttgart on 15/16 March and 846 bombers to Frankfurt three nights later. The latter city was hit hard in this accurate attack despite the usual creepback in the latter stages of the attack. The city was targeted again on 22/23 March as part of the policy of hitting the

Battle of Berlin: summary of operations

Date	Target	Halifax	Lancaster	Mosquito	Stirling
23/24 Aug	Berlin	251 (23)	335 (17)	17	124 (16)
31 Aug/1 Sep	Berlin	176 (20)	331 (10)	9	106 (17)
3/4 Sep	Berlin	0	316 (22)	4	0
18/19 Nov	Berlin	0	440 (9)	4	0
22/23 Nov	Berlin	234 (10)	469 (11)	1	50 (5)
23/24 Nov	Berlin	10	365 (20)	8	0
26/27 Nov	Berlin	0	443 (28)	7	0
2/3 Dec	Berlin	15 (2)	425 (37)	18 (1)	0
16/17 Dec	Berlin	0	483 (25)	10	0
23/24 Dec	Berlin	0?	364 (16)	8	0
29/30 Dec	Berlin	252 (9)	457 (11)	3	0
1/2 Jan	Berlin	0	421 (28)	0	0
2/3 Jan	Berlin	9	362 (27)	12	0
20/21 Jan	Berlin	264 (22)	495 (13)	10	0
27/28 Jan	Berlin	0	515 (33)	15	0
28/29 Jan	Berlin	241 (26)	432 (20)	4	0
30/31 Jan	Berlin	82 (1)	440 (32)	12	0
15/16 Feb	Berlin	314 (17)	561 (26)	16	0
24/25 Mar	Berlin	216 (28)	577 (44)	16	0

Note: Aircraft details show number despatched and (in brackets) number lost. Other targets were also attacked in this period.

same target in quick succession, adding to the destruction that essentially finished Frankfurt as a working city.

Whilst Main Force raids continued during this period there was an increasing number of smaller operations against specific, and often pinpoint, targets, with No. 5 Group increasingly operating as an independent force. In a typical night three or four targets might be attacked, in addition to the usual selection of minor operations such as intruder or minelaying. On the night of the Stuttgart raid (15/16 March) for example, two other targets were attacked: 140 bombers went to Amiens and a small force of Lancasters (twenty-two aircraft) attacked an aircraft-engine factory at Woippy. However, one of the most successful nights in this period was that of 10/11 March when No. 5 Group sent 102 Lancasters on moonlight raids to four factories in France; thirty-three went to Clermont-Ferrand – one failed to return. As the photographs of two of the targets (below) illustrate, the attacks were accurate and caused extensive damage. The attack on La Ricamerie was made by sixteen Lancasters of 617 Squadron. Both these photographs appeared in the *Bomber Command Quarterly Review* and were used to illustrate the accuracy that the Command was achieving.

The night of 30/31 March 1944 was one of the worst of the war for Bomber Command. A force of 795 bombers was sent to Nuremberg and ninety-five failed to return (sixty-four Lancasters and thirty-one Halifaxes). A further ten were written-off in landing accidents and fifty-nine were recorded as having significant damage. The loss rate of 12.1 per cent to the Lancasters and 16.8 per cent to the Halifaxes, and the loss of 535 aircrew, with 180 others wounded or taken prisoner, was a major blow for the Command and if it had been repeated then Bomber Command would have ceased functioning. Les Bartlett flew on the raid as a rear gunner with 50 Squadron from Skellingthorpe and his diary entry recorded the events. 'At 2200 we taxied out and were first airborne. We crossed the enemy coast and it was eyes wide open. As we drew level with the south of the Ruhr valley, things began to happen. Enemy night fighters were all around us and, in no time at all, combats were taking place and aircraft were going down in flames on all sides. So serious was the situation that I remember looking at the other poor blighters going down and thinking to myself that it must be our turn next, just a question of time. A Lancaster appeared on our port beam converging, so we dropped 100 feet or so to let him cross. He was only about 200 yards or so away on our starboard beam when a string of cannon shells hit him and down he went.

'We altered course for Nuremberg, and I looked down at the area over which we had just passed. It looked like a battlefield. There were kites burning on the deck all over the

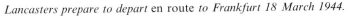

Lancasters prepare to depart en route *to Frankfurt 18 March 1944.*

The Michelin Works at Clermont-Ferrand; reconnaissance photograph showing the damage caused by the attack on the night of 10/11 March 1944.

place, bombs going off where they had been jettisoned by bombers damaged in combat, and fires from their incendiaries across the whole area. Such a picture of aerial disaster I had never seen before and hope never to see again.

'On the way to the target the winds became changeable and we almost ran into the defences of Schweinfurt, but we altered course just in time. The defences of Nuremberg were nothing to speak of, a modest amount of heavy flak which did not prevent us doing our normal approach, and we were able to get the Target Indicators dropped by the Pathfinder Force in our bombsight to score hits with our 4,000 lb 'Cookie' and our 1,000 lb bombs. To reach the coast was a binding two-hour stooge. The varying winds were leading us a dance and we found ourselves approaching Calais instead of being 80 miles further south, so we had a slight detour to avoid their defences. Once near the enemy coast it was nose down for home at 300 kts. Even then we saw some poor blokes 'buy it' over the Channel. What a relief it was to be flying over Lincoln cathedral once more. Back in debriefing we heard the full story of the Squadron's effort. It was the worst night for the Squadron.'

Pilot Officer Cyril Barton was awarded the Victoria Cross for his actions during this attack; his citation read: 'On the night of 30 March 1944, Pilot Officer Barton was captain and pilot of a Halifax aircraft detailed to attack Nuremberg when, some 70 miles short of the target, the aircraft was attacked by a Junkers 88. The first burst of fire from the enemy made the intercommunication system useless. One engine was damaged when a Messerschmitt 210 joined the fight. The bomber's machine guns were out of action and the gunners were unable to return the fire. The two fighters continued to attack the aircraft as it approached the target area and, in the confusion caused by the failure of the communications system at the height of the battle, a signal was misinterpreted and the navigator, air bomber and wireless operator left the aircraft by parachute. Pilot Officer Barton now faced a situation of dire peril. His aircraft was damaged, his navigational team had gone and he could not communicate with the remainder of the crew. If he continued his mission, he would be at the mercy of hostile fighters when silhouetted against the fires in the target area and if he survived, he would have to make a 4 hour journey home on three engines across heavily-defended territory Determined to press home his attack at all costs, he flew on and, reaching the target, released the bombs himself. As Pilot Officer Barton turned for home the propeller of the damaged engine, which was vibrating badly, flew off. It was also discovered that two of the petrol tanks had suffered damage and were leaking. Pilot Officer Barton held to his course and, without navigational aids and in spite of strong head winds, successfully avoided the most dangerous defence areas on his route. Eventually he crossed the English coast only 90 miles north of his base. By this time the petrol supply was nearly exhausted. Before a suitable landing place could be found, the port engines stopped. The aircraft was now too low to be abandoned successfully and Pilot Officer Barton therefore ordered the three remaining members of his crew to take up their crash stations. Then, with only one

Another accurate pinpoint attack on 10/11 March 1944 destroyed the needle-bearing plant at La Ricamerie.

Bombing up a Mosquito of 692 Squadron with a 4,000 lb 'Cookie'.

engine working, he made a gallant attempt to land clear of the houses over which he was flying. The aircraft finally crashed and Pilot Officer Barton lost his life, but his three comrades survived. Pilot Officer Barton had previously taken part in four attacks on Berlin and fourteen other operational missions. On one of these, two members of his crew were wounded during a determined effort to locate the target despite appalling weather conditions. In gallantly completing his last mission in the face of almost impossible odds, this officer displayed unsurpassed courage and devotion to duty.' (Pilot Officer Cyril Joe Barton, 578 Squadron, Halifax LK797; awarded for action 30/31 March 1944, *London Gazette*, 27 June 1944.)

An ORS report agreed with the comments regarding the wind and suggested that most problems were caused by the bombers becoming scattered and flying over heavily defended areas, although most losses were to night fighters. It was estimated that eighty bombers had been shot down *en route* to the target and that very few bombs actually fell on Nuremberg. In many respects it was just as well that the main focus of the Command for the next few months would be support of the invasion – and by the time they returned in strength to Germany the overall war situation, and the capabilities of the *Luftwaffe*, had changed.

Although pre-invasion targets were the main priority from March 1944 the Command continued to attack targets in Germany, including yet another attack on Schweinfurt. This raid took place on the night of 26/27 April and was primarily a No. 5 Group affair by 206 Lancasters supported by eleven Mosquitoes, along with nine specialist Lancasters from No. 1 Group. The low-level marking that had been proving so successful was for once inaccurate and the attack was scattered. Once again the high-level winds were stronger than forecast and the delay *en route* meant that the German night fighter force was able to take a heavy toll of the attackers; twenty-one Lancasters (9.3 per cent) were lost. The Schweinfurt attack saw the award of a VC to Sergeant Norman Jackson, although this was not promulgated until after the war; his citation read: 'This airman was the flight engineer in a Lancaster detailed to attack Schweinfurt on the night of 26 April 1944. Bombs were dropped successfully and the aircraft was climbing out of the target area. Suddenly it was attacked by a fighter at about 20,000 feet.

The captain took evading action at once, but the enemy secured many hits. A fire started near a petrol tank on the upper surface of the starboard wing, between the fuselage and the inner engine. Sergeant Jackson was thrown to the floor during the engagement. Wounds which he received from shell splinters in the right leg and shoulder were probably sustained at that time. Recovering himself, he remarked that he could deal with the fire on the wing and obtained his captain's permission to try to put out the flames. Pushing a hand fire-extinguisher into the top of his life-saving jacket and clipping on his parachute pack, Sergeant Jackson jettisoned the escape hatch above the pilot's head. He then started to climb out of the cockpit and back along the top of the fuselage to the starboard wing. Before he could leave the fuselage his parachute pack opened and the whole canopy and rigging lines spilled into the cockpit. Undeterred, Sergeant Jackson continued. The pilot, bomb aimer and navigator gathered the parachute together and held on to the rigging lines, paying them out as the airman crawled aft. Eventually he slipped and, falling from the fuselage to the starboard wing, grasped an air intake on the leading edge of the wing. He succeeded in clinging on but lost the extinguisher, which was blown away.

By this time, the fire had spread rapidly and Sergeant Jackson was injured. His face, hands and clothing were severely burnt. Unable to retain his hold, he was swept through the flames and over the trailing edge of the wing, dragging his parachute behind. When last seen it was only partly inflated and was burning in a number of places. Realising that the fire could not be controlled, the captain gave the order to abandon aircraft. Four of the remaining members of the crew landed safely. The captain and rear gunner have not been accounted for. Sergeant Jackson was unable to control his descent and landed heavily. He sustained a broken ankle, his right eye was closed through burns and his hands were useless. These injuries, together with the wounds received earlier, reduced him to a pitiable state. At daybreak he crawled to the nearest village, where he was taken prisoner. He bore the intense pain and discomfort of the journey to Dulag Luft with magnificent fortitude. After 10 months in hospital he made a good recovery, though his hands require further treatment and are only of limited use. This airman's attempt to extinguish the fire and save the aircraft and crew from falling into enemy hands was an act of outstanding gallantry. To venture outside, when travelling at 200 miles an hour, at a great height and in intense cold, was an almost incredible feat. Had he succeeded in subduing the flames, there was little or no prospect of his regaining the cockpit. The spilling of his parachute and the risk of grave damage to its canopy reduced his chances of survival to a minimum. By his ready willingness to face these dangers he set an example of self sacrifice which will ever be remembered.' (Sergeant Norman Cyril Jackson, 106 Squadron RAF, Lancaster ME669; awarded for action 26/27 April 1944, *London Gazette*, 26 October 1945.)

Normandy Campaign: April 1944 to August 1944

As highlighted in the overview chapter the employment of the heavy bombers of Bomber Command and the US 8th Air Force was crucial to the Allied pre-invasion strategy in order to prepare the battlefield. The major problems were that of ensuring a successful initial landing on the heavily fortified Atlantic Wall and, even more crucially, ensuring that once ashore the troops would not be pushed back into the sea. The heavy bombers were involved in both parts of this strategy. One of the main elements of this as far as Bomber Command was concerned was attacks on lines of communication, especially the railway network. The first of the series of attacks on key French rail centres took place on 6/7 March, the target being Trappes. The 261 Halifaxes and six Mosquitoes attacked in

The Aulnoye Railway Centre before the attack by Bomber Command on 27/28 April 1944.

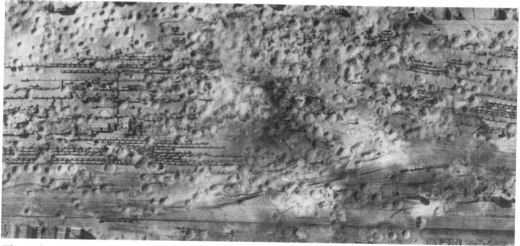

The Aulnoye Railway Centre after Bomber Command had dropped 931 tons on the yard on 27/28 April 1944. The area depicted is approximately 1,000 yards by 600 yards. Notice the elimination of the main road across the top of the picture and the appearance of a rough winding track in its place: also the disappearance of the branch railway line, passing under the road, and the road junction (top right).

good weather and delivered an accurate attack that proved the viability of night attacks on this type of target. Over the next few weeks Bomber Command caused heavy damage to a number of rail yards and, whilst the Germans proved adept at repairing through lines, the overall effect of the attacks caused massive disruption to rail traffic, especially where follow-up attacks were made on key nodes such as Amiens.

On the night of 3/4 May 1944 the Command suffered one of its most disastrous nights when forty-two bombers were lost on what should have been as 'easy' target in support of the forthcoming invasion. The target was the large military camp at Mailly-le-Camp and 362 bombers took part. The Bomber Command ORS report stated that the target was 'attacked by Lancasters with devastating effect in bright moonlight. Extremely heavy and widespread damage was caused, but forty-two aircraft (11.6 per cent) were lost. The high losses were associated with the delay in the issuing of instructions by the Master Bomber due to communications difficulties; this resulted in aircraft concentrating over the datum point in ideal weather conditions for fighters.

'The first intercepts occurred on the south-east leg beyond Compiegne, and at first the enemy lost more heavily than did the bombers, losing three, probably four, fighters before we turned south. Then the unfortunate delay before the Main Force received their instructions resulted in concentration of our aircraft over the datum point in bright moonlight, presenting fighters with great opportunities for wholesale interceptions. The attack lasted 19 minutes longer than had been planned and it was during this period that most of the losses occurred. At least twenty-five aircraft fell in combat and nine were lost to flak, mostly over the target.' The 1,500 tons of bombs caused massive damage and destroyed large numbers of vehicles, including thirty-seven tanks.

Whilst rail targets remained the most important target category for Bomber Command's support of the invasion preparations, other targets were also hit, some with no great expectation of results but considered important as part of the overall preparation. This included the fixed coastal gun batteries that dominated the approach routes and from April onwards, and particularly from late May, this type of target became a regular feature, with some key batteries such as that at Boulogne being attacked a

30/31 May 1944; Bombs going down onto a coastal gun battery at Boulogne as part of the softening-up of enemy defences before the invasion.

Bomber Command Operations, 1–7 June 1944

Date	Main target	Aircraft	Date	Main target	Aircraft
1/2 June	Ferme D'Urville	109	5/6 June	Ouistreham	116
	Saumur	58		Maisy	116
2/3 June	Trappes	128		Houlgate	116
	Dieppe	107		Merville-Franceville	109
	Neufchatel	74		Crisbecq	101
	Haringzelles	67		St Martin de Varreville	100
	Calais	67		Longues	99
	Wimereux	65		Osnabruck	31
	Wissant	63	6/7 June	Coutances	139
	Leverkusen	23		Caen	129
3/4 June	Ferme D'Urville	100		Argentan	128
	Calais	70		Conde sur Noireau	122
	Wimereux	65		St Lo	115
	Argentan	5		Chateaudun	112
	Ludwigshaven	20		Vire	112
4/5 June	Calais	79		Lisieux	104
	Swingatte	57		Acheres	104
	Maisy	56		Ludwigshaven	32
	Boulogne	67	7/8 June	Foret de Cerisy	212
	Argentan	6		Acheres	108
	Cologne	20		Versailles/Matelots	83
5/6 June	La Pernelle	131		Massy	75
	Mont Fleury	124		Juvisy	71
	St Pierre du-mont	124		Cologne	32

Note: Highest number of sorties despatched in one night = 1,333 (5/6 June). Highest bomb tonnage dropped in one night = 5,316 tons (5/6 June).

number of times. Typical of these attacks was that of the night of 30/31 May when fifty Lancasters and four Mosquitoes attacked the batteries at Boulogne.

The lines of communication campaign remained crucial in the weeks after the invasion. The rail yards at Cambrai were the target on the night of 12/13 June and Pilot Officer Andrew Mynarski of 419 Squadron was awarded a posthumous VC for his action that night. His citation read: 'Pilot Officer Mynarski was the mid-upper gunner of a Lancaster aircraft, detailed to attack a target at Cambrai in France, on the night of 12 June, 1944. The aircraft was attacked from below and astern by an enemy fighter and ultimately came down in flames.

'As an immediate result of the attack, both port engines failed. Fire broke out between the mid-upper turret and the rear turret, as well as in the port wing. The flames soon became fierce and the captain ordered the crew to abandon the aircraft. Pilot Officer Mynarski left his turret and went towards the escape hatch. He then saw that the rear gunner was still in his turret and apparently unable to leave it. The turret was, in fact, immovable, since the hydraulic gear had been put out of action when the port engines failed, and the manual gear had been broken by the gunner in his attempts to escape. Without hesitation, Pilot Officer Mynarski made his way through the flames in an endeavour to reach the rear turret and release the gunner. Whilst so doing, his parachute and his clothing, up to the waist, were set on fire. All his efforts to move the turret and free the gunner were in vain. Eventually the rear gunner clearly indicated to him that there was nothing more he could do and that he should try to save his own life. Pilot Officer Mynarski reluctantly went back through the flames to the escape hatch. There, as a last gesture to the trapped gunner, he turned towards him, stood to attention in his flaming clothing and saluted, before he jumped out of the aircraft. Pilot Officer Mynarski's descent was seen by French people on the ground. Both his parachute and clothing were on fire. He was found eventually by the French, but was so severely burnt that he died from his injuries. The rear gunner had a miraculous escape when the aircraft crashed. He subsequently testified that, had Pilot Officer Mynarski not attempted to save his comrade's life, he could have left the aircraft in safety and would, doubtless, have escaped death. Pilot Officer Mynarski must have been fully aware that in trying to free the rear gunner he was almost certain to lose his own life. Despite this, with outstanding courage and complete disregard for his own safety, he went to the rescue. Willingly accepting the danger, Pilot Officer Mynarski lost his life by a most conspicuous act of heroism which called for valour of the highest order.' (Pilot Officer Andrew Charles Mynarski, RCAF, 419 (RCAF) Squadron, Lancaster KB726; awarded for action 12/13 June 1944, *London Gazette*, 11 October 1946.)

Len Manning's crew joined 57 Squadron at East Kirkby in Lincolnshire at the end of June 1944: 'We did several training flights on Lancasters before our first *op* on the 15 July. This was a raid on the railway goods yards at Nevers in the south of France, which was spectacular but uneventful.' On 18 July the crew was scheduled for the massed daylight bombing raid on the area around Caen … 'We dropped our bombs and as we turned for home I had a Grandstand view from the rear turret, the whole area was covered in smoke and dust to about 5,000 feet. It was also an amazing sight to see so many planes in the sky at one time, something that we never saw during our usual night time activities. We took off for this raid at 4.00 am and on our return, straight after debriefing we were told that we were 'On' again that night. This was to prove to be our third and last *op* with 57 Squadron.

'On the evening of 18 July, we took off for Revigny in northern France. After crossing the coast. We were coned by searchlights and during our evasive action we lost the protection of the 'Bomber Stream' and became vulnerable to attack by enemy fighters. Having lost the searchlights, we set a new course for the target. Shortly after this there was an enormous explosion in the port wing, we had been hit by cannon fire. Immediately flames were streaming past my turret, which had stopped working as the pumps for the turrets were operated by the port engine. I centralized the turret by hand and opened the door into the fuselage and climbed in. Fred Taylor our mid-upper gunner was already out of his turret and was clipping his chute onto his harness, he struggled to open the rear door, having done this he leapt into the night. By this time the fuselage was a mass of flame and molten metal, the aircraft was now in a steep dive. My chute, which was stowed on the port side had started to smoulder. I pulled it from the stowage and struggled to clip it onto my harness, this was difficult due, to the 'G' force. I managed to clip the chute onto one of the clips but the other was impossible. With every- thing burning, I thought 'It's now or never' and leapt through the door into the night. As I fell, I pulled the rip-cord and hoped that it would open. And as you can see, it did!

'I was hanging to one side, I felt something brush my face, it was the intercom cord which was attached to my helmet and had been whipped off when the chute opened and had become entangled in the silk shrouds. I grabbed the cord and hung on. This probably saved my life, as it helped to take my weight. My helmet should have been removed before I jumped. I looked up and saw that the chute was burning and hoped that I would get down before it fell apart. On the way down there was a terrific explosion, this was the

Massed heavy bombers used in support of the ground offensive near Caen in an attempt to break the deadlock.

Lancaster exploding as it hit the ground at Bassevelle, which is about 60 miles east of Paris.

'I hit the ground flat on my back, which winded me. My chute had started to burn – I quickly smothered the flames, bundled the chute and pushed it into a hedge and headed off into the darkness. I staggered on for about 8 miles before collapsing on the step of a farmhouse. The farmer must have heard me moaning, as the burns to my face and arms were giving me great pain. He took me in and with his wife put me to bed. The following day I was given civilian clothes to replace my burned uniform and boots. The Germans came looking for me at the farm but the farmer convinced them that I had not been seen. But in view of this, it was decided to move me on again. A member of the resistance, who's codename was "Lulu" came for me and we travelled across country to avoid German patrols. At one stage my guide indicated that he was lost and would have to call at a house to ask the way! He handed me a Luger pistol, hid me in the hedge and told me to shoot if he ran into trouble. We eventually arrived at a small cafe in the village of La Tretois, which was owned by two elderly ladies, Louise Beaujard and her mother. Although they didn't speak English they made me very welcome and I was given a room in their hotel across the courtyard.

'I had the run of the orchard behind the hotel, but the cafe was out of bounds except at meal times. One morning some jubilant young resistance men arrived and told us that the Americans had arrived outside the village and were setting up a field hospital. The following day I went down and found an officer who said that he would take me to Paris the following day. That night there was a large party in the village to celebrate their liberation; all the good wines came out of hiding, for the wining and dining. My charred battle dress also appeared, having been darned and pressed. A good night was had by one and all!'

Only three of the crew escaped the Lancaster; the mid-upper gunner, Fred Taylor, was another escaper whilst the Navigator, Rusty Ruston, was taken prisoner. The aircraft had been shot down by Herbert Altner, a night fighter *experten* flying a Bf 110, who claimed five bombers in the space of 30 minutes. The attack on the railway junction at Revigny was made by a force of Lancasters from No. 5 Group – they were caught by fighters and lost twenty-four aircraft (a 22 per cent loss rate), with 619 Squadron losing five of its thirteen aircraft.

Operation *Goodwood* called on Bomber Command to bomb defensive positions around Caen to support the British 2nd Army break-out attempt. Two major raids, 7 and 18 July, attacked fortified villages; the first attack was by 450 bombers and although it turned some strongpoints into rubble it did not achieve any significant military advantage. The second attack, by twice as many aircraft, was more successful, although the Germans were able to retreat in good order. A third raid, 30 July by 700 bombers, attacked targets in the Normandy area to support American operations. Harris reckoned that a Main Force attack was the equivalent of a 4,000 gun barrage and this flying artillery was employed again in August with attacks on the 7/8th and 14th of the month. The first of these was by over 1,000 bombers and was remembered as an awesome sight by air and ground observers. The second was slightly smaller, 800 aircraft, and was in support of the 3rd Canadian Division attack on Falaise.

Crossbow and *Noball*

Tied in with the Normandy campaign was the offensive against the V-weapon sites and under the code names of *Crossbow* and *Noball* Bomber Command expended a large number of sorties against launch sites and storage facilities. This campaign also involved the USAAF's 8th and 9th Air Forces as well as the Tactical Air Force and Air Defence of Great Britain (ADGB being a short-lived designation for Fighter Command.)

The V-weapon storage site at Trossy St Maximin was the target for a major attack on 4 August, during which Squadron Leader Ian Bazalgette acted as Master Bomber and for which he was awarded a posthumous Victoria Cross. His citation read: 'On 4 August 1944, Squadron Leader Bazalgette was "master bomber" of a Pathfinder squadron detailed to mark an important target at Trossy St Maximin for the main bomber force. When nearing the target his Lancaster came under heavy anti-aircraft fire. Both starboard engines were put out of action and serious fires broke out in the fuselage and the starboard main-plane. The bomb aimer was badly wounded. As the deputy "master bomber" had already been shot down, the success of the attack depended on Squadron Leader Bazalgette and this he knew. Despite the appalling conditions in his burning aircraft, he pressed on gallantly to the target, marking and bombing it accurately. That the attack was successful was due to his magnificent effort. After the bombs had been dropped the Lancaster dived, practically out of control. By expert airmanship and great exertion Squadron Leader Bazalgette regained control. But the port inner engine then failed and the whole of the starboard main-plane became a mass of flames. Squadron Leader Bazalgette fought bravely to bring his aircraft and crew to safety. The mid-upper gunner was overcome by fumes. Squadron Leader Bazalgette then ordered those of his crew who were able to leave by parachute to do so. He remained at the controls and attempted the almost hopeless task of

Crossbow **raids 16 June–31 August 1944**

Date	Total aircraft	Lancaster	Halifax	Mosquito
16/17 Jun	405	236	149	20
23/24 Jun	412 (5)	226 (5)	164	22
24/25 Jun	739 (22)	535 (22)	165	39
27/28 Jun	721 (3)	477 (3)	207	37
2 Jul	384	374	0	10
5/6 Jul	542 (4)	321 (4)	201	20
6 Jul	551 (1)	210	314 (1)	26
20 Jul	369 (1)	174 (1)	165	30
1 Aug	777	385	324	67
2 Aug	394 (2)	234 (2)	99	40
3 Aug	1,114 (6)	601 (6)	492	21
5 Aug	742 (1)	257	469 (1)	16
31 Aug	601 (6)	418 (6)	147	36

1798 WBH. 3/8/44. // 8′ 15000′ ← 130° 1404.
BOIS DE CASSAN. U. 11x1000 4x500. C 33SECS. F/S LAWRIE. U514

No. 514 Squadron attack a V-weapon site in the Bois de Cassan, 3 August 1944. Bomber Command sent 1,114 aircraft to attack three V-weapon storage sites on this day.

landing the crippled and blazing aircraft in a last effort to save the wounded bomb aimer and helpless air gunner. With superb skill, and taking great care to avoid a small French village nearby, he brought the aircraft down safely. Unfortunately, it then exploded and this gallant officer and his two comrades perished. His heroic sacrifice marked the climax of a long career of operations against the enemy. He always chose the more dangerous and exacting roles. His courage and devotion to duty were beyond praise.' (Acting Squadron Leader Ian Willoughby Bazalgette, DFC, 635 Squadron RAF, Lancaster ND811; awarded for action 4 August 1944, *London Gazette*, 17 August 1945.)

Germany: the final offensive – August 1944 to May 1945

In the middle of August, Harris was given clearance to return to his major effort of the strategic campaign, although the bombers continued to provide assistance to the ground troops from time to time.

On the night of 25/26 August a force of 190 Lancasters and six Mosquitoes of No. 5 Group attacked Darmstadt in what was an unsuccessful attack due to the fact that the Master Bomber had to return early and his two deputies were shot down; target marking was poor and bombing was scattered. Bill Carmen was in one of the seven Lancasters lost that night – it was the thirty-third mission for this 83 Squadron crew and only two of them survived. 'Our participation in this sortie was as part of the flare force, backing up the Bombing Leader and his deputy. Our route to the target was along the track of a raid up ahead of us heading for Russelheim [comprising 412 Lancasters], but falling short and attacking Darmstadt. All part of the cunning plans to confuse the enemy defences.

'Just before we turned to line up on our approach to the target our air gunners had briefly caught a glimpse of a twin-engine night fighter but he moved away. I was busy with my radio equipment when without warning there was a tremendous explosion somewhere behind me in the rear of the aircraft. The bulkhead door just behind my right shoulder burst open and I looked back into a raging, menacing inferno of flames. We were carrying fifteen bundles of flares, each one constituting 1,000,000 candle-power. The intercom was dead and I knew I had no time to lose. I ripped off my helmet and oxygen mask, clipped my parachute pack onto the front of my harness and headed for the nose of the aircraft and the escape hatch in the floor of the bomb aimer's compartment. My navigator was kneeling down on the floor groping for his parachute pack and he waved me forward. The noise from the screaming engines was deafening. I reached the skipper, who was still trying to regain control of the aircraft, and slapped his knee to let him know I was there. He pointed towards the front escape hatch. Our Flight Engineer and Bomb Aimer were crouched either side of the now open escape hatch and as far as I could see neither had his parachute on. Both of them indicated that I should jump.

'I remember turning over and over; my parachute pack, attached to the harness clips, had pulled off my chest and was somewhere above my head. I had the presence of mind to pull on the harness webbing straps until my fingers found the chute release handle on the pack and pulled it.' Bill Carmen landed in a forest and managed to evade capture for 30 hours before being spotted by a railway worker and arrested by the police. Bill was uncertain at the time if they had been hit by a fighter or by flak but the chances are that it was the former, and Hauptmann Tino Becker was credited with three Lancasters in the Darmstadt area that night.

Allen Clifford recalled the attack on Homberg 8 November 1944: 'If ever there was a low point in anybody's life this was it – to be woken at 0400 hours knowing that you were going to war. I crawled out of a warm bed into a frozen Nissen hut at Methwold,

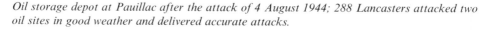

Oil storage depot at Pauillac after the attack of 4 August 1944; 288 Lancasters attacked two oil sites in good weather and delivered accurate attacks.

Darmstadt September 1944.

gathered up towel and soap and shivered miserably in the wintry gap between the hut and the ablutions blocks to splash water over my face – but no time to shave. The breakfast of bacon and egg, and a mug of hot sweet tea preceded the briefing. The red tape, which slithered disconcertingly across the map like a long trail of blood, led from Norfolk to a suburb of the huge German inland river port and industrial city of Duisberg. "It's bloody Homberg again" we all thought.'

This attack on 8 November consisted of 136 Lancasters from No. 3 Group and only one aircraft was lost, a Lancaster of 218 Squadron. This was the twenty-first operation for Allen. The crew was skippered by an Australian, Flying Officer Les Hough, and having been dropped at dispersal they climbed aboard Lancaster HA-C. According to the briefing the weather would be clear as far as the German border and then the aircraft would enter a bank of cloud to the target area. It turned out to be the reverse. 'Over France we flew into heavy cloud and the tail wind was much higher than predicted and we were ahead of ETA as we broke into clear sunshine near the Rhine. The bombers were scattered having split up because of the cloud and so we were a straggling group of aircraft rather than a neat formation. We were at the front at 18,000 ft so had no protection from window; one minute the sky was clear and the next it was full of bursting shells. The bomb doors were open on the long approach to the target when we were hit

Lancasters of 428 Squadron, Middleton St George November 1944.

by a savage burst of flak. A fearsome clatter was followed by smoke swirling into the fuselage.' When the smoke cleared there was a 4-foot hole by the rear door and the starboard inner engine was on fire. Despite the best efforts of Flight Engineer Jack Tales the fire could not be extinguished and he began pumping fuel from tanks near the fire across to those in the port wing. Les Hough had maintained course to the target and just after the bombs were released the starboard outer engine failed. 'There was a torrent of flames over the starboard wing as the Skipper turned west to try and make the Allied lines. We were now clawing our way against the wind and our ground speed dropped to 80 mph. The wing was burning fiercely and had begun to "flop" so Les ordered everyone out.' The Engineer found the pilot's parachute and clipped it on him before heading for the escape hatch. Allen exchanged waves with the grim-faced pilot, still at the controls, and dropped headfirst through the hatch. He was dragged out like a leaf by the

Duisburg October 1944.

slipstream, which whipped his helmet away. As he fell on his back another figure exited the aircraft. They were still in the area where flak was exploding and no-one had thought to explain the advantage of getting away as quickly as possible from this area. Indeed, the only 'how to parachute' drill had been a few landing rolls on a mat in the gym. As Allen pulled his ripcord 300 feet below the blazing Lancaster the starboard wing broke off and he watched the remains of his aircraft fall past and explode on the ground. He looked up again and saw the remaining Lancasters heading home. 'Suddenly it was all quiet, you could hear the swishing of the wind and it seemed a very long way to the ground. I was being blown over Duisburg and at less than 3,000 feet I could hear the phhht phhht of rifle and machine gun bullets as people on the ground were firing at me. You don't realise until you are near the ground how fast you are falling, and I shot past a big town-clock as all-clear sirens were wailing. My flying boots hit the roof of an old three-storey house and I went through to my waist and was jammed and unable to move. I saw a dozen men of the *Volksturm* in the garden shooting at me with rifles, bullets hitting the roof all around me. I undid my parachute harness, wriggled like mad and fell through into the attic.' He was picked up and roughly treated by a group of men. Fortunately he was rescued by a *Luftwaffe Feldwebel* who told him he would be ok if he avoided the SS; he was delivered to a police station and was soon joined by Stan Lee. That afternoon they were paraded by armed soldiers through Duisberg with people shouting '*terrorflieger*' and throwing stones at them. They were put up against a wall and were about to be shot when a woman intervened and saved their lives. Others of the crew had not been so lucky. Three had died in the aircraft and at least one had been murdered by the SS. Allen and Stan ended up in Stalag Luft IIIA at Luckenwalde, near Potsdam.

Oil targets featured a number of times in subsequent weeks, although German cities, especially those with major rail yards, were still very much on the list, including a number of daylight attacks. On 23 December the Command sent 153 aircraft, all from No. 3 Group, to attack rail yards at Trier in support of US Army operations, whilst a smaller force of twenty-seven Lancasters and three Mosquitoes from No. 8 Group attacked the rail yards of Gremberg at Cologne. The lead Lancaster was flown by Squadron Leader R. A. Palmer (a 109 Squadron pilot but flying with 582 Squadron) and despite the weather conditions being unfavourable he made an *Oboe* run that exposed the aircraft to Cologne's heavy flak. He was awarded a posthumous VC for this attack, the citation reading: 'This officer has completed numerous bombing missions [this was his 110th *op*]. Most of them involved deep penetration of heavily defended territory; many were low-level 'marking' operations against vital targets; all were executed with tenacity, high courage and great accuracy. He first went on operations in January 1941. He took part in the first thousand bomber raid against Cologne in 1942. He was one of the first pilots to drop a 4,000 lb bomb on the Reich. It was known that he could be relied on to press home his attack whatever the opposition and to bomb with great accuracy. He was always selected, therefore, to take part in special operations against vital targets. The finest example of his courage and determination was on 23 December 1944, when he led a formation of Lancasters to attack the marshalling yards at Cologne in daylight. He had the task of marking the target and his formation had been ordered to bomb as soon as the bombs had gone from his, the leading aircraft. The leader's duties during the final bombing run were exacting and demanded coolness and resolution. To achieve accuracy he would have to fly at an exact height and air speed on a steady course, regardless of opposition. Some minutes before the target was reached, his aircraft came under heavy anti-aircraft fire, shells burst all around, two engines were set on fire and there were

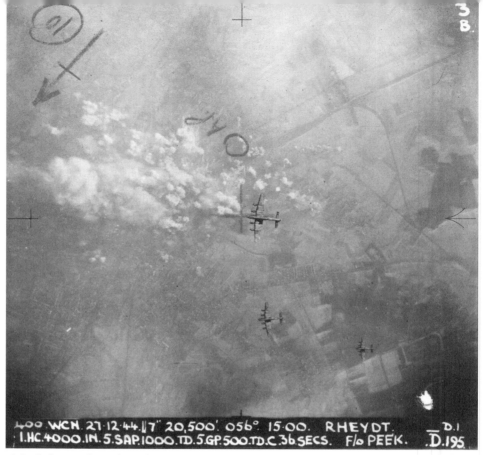

A daylight attack on the rail yards at Rheydt by 200 Lancasters and eleven Mosquitoes on 27 December 1944.

flames and smoke in the nose and in the bomb bay. Enemy fighters now attacked in force. Squadron Leader Palmer disdained the possibility of taking avoiding action. He knew that if he diverged the least bit from his course, he would be unable to utilise the special equipment to the best advantage. He was determined to complete the run and provide an accurate and easily seen aiming-point for the other bombers. He ignored the double risk of fire and explosion in his aircraft and kept on. With its engines developing unequal power, an immense effort was needed to keep the damaged aircraft on a straight course. Nevertheless, he made a perfect approach and his bombs hit the target. His aircraft was last seen spiralling to earth in flames. Such was the strength of the opposition that more than half of his formation failed to return. Squadron Leader Palmer was an outstanding pilot. He displayed conspicuous bravery. His record of prolonged and heroic endeavour is beyond praise.' (Acting Squadron Leader Robert Anthony Maurice Palmer, DFC, 109 Squadron RAF, Lancaster PB371; awarded for action 23 December 1944, *London Gazette*, 23 March 1945.)

The campaign against rail and oil installations continued into early 1945, although the New Year opened with yet another special raid when No. 5 Group sent 102 Lancasters and two Mosquitoes to attack the Dortmund-Ems canal, a target that Bomber Command had visited a number of times since 1940. The canal was breached near Ladbergen and only two Lancasters were lost, although a number of others were damaged by flak. One of these was a 9 Squadron aircraft – and Flight Sergeant George Thompson's gallant aid to injured comrades earned him a VC. His citation read: 'This airman was the wireless operator in a Lancaster aircraft which attacked the Dortmund-

Ems Canal in daylight on the 1 January 1945. The bombs had just been released when a heavy shell hit the aircraft in front of the mid-upper turret. Fire broke out and dense smoke filled the fuselage. The nose of the aircraft was then hit and an inrush of air, clearing the smoke, revealed a scene of utter devastation. Most of the Perspex screen of the nose compartment had been shot away, gaping holes had been torn in the canopy above the pilot's head, the inter-communication wiring was severed, and there was a large hole in the floor of the aircraft. Bedding and other equipment were badly damaged or alight; one engine was on fire.

'Flight Sergeant Thompson saw that the gunner was unconscious in the blazing mid-upper turret. Without hesitation he went down the fuselage into the fire and the exploding ammunition. He pulled the gunner from his turret and, edging his way round the hole in the floor, carried him away from the flames. With his bare hands, he extinguished the gunner's burning clothing. He himself sustained serious burns on his face, hands and legs. Flight Sergeant Thompson then noticed that the rear gun turret was also on fire. Despite his own severe injuries he moved painfully to the rear of the fuselage where he found the rear gunner with his clothing alight, overcome by flames and fumes. A second time Flight Sergeant Thompson braved the flames. With great difficulty he extricated the helpless gunner and carried him clear. Again, he used his bare hands, already burnt, to beat out flames on a comrade's clothing.

'Flight Sergeant Thompson, by now almost exhausted, felt that his duty was yet not done. He must report the fate of the crew to the captain. He made the perilous journey back through the burning fuselage, clinging to the sides with his burnt hands to get across the hole in the floor. The flow of cold air caused him intense pain and frost-bite developed. So pitiful was his condition that his captain failed to recognise him. Still, his only concern was for the two gunners he had left in the rear of the aircraft. He was given such attention as was possible until a crash-landing was made some 40 minutes later.

'When the aircraft was hit, Flight Sergeant Thompson might have devoted his efforts to quelling the fire and so have contributed to his own safety. He preferred to go through the fire to succour his comrades. He knew that he would then be in no position to hear or heed any order which might be given to abandon aircraft. He hazarded his own life in order to save the lives of others. Young in years and experience, his actions were those of a veteran. Three weeks later Flight Sergeant Thompson died of his injuries. One of the gunners unfortunately also died, but the other owes his life to the superb gallantry of Flight Sergeant Thompson, whose signal courage and self-sacrifice will ever be an inspiration to the Service.' (Flight Sergeant George Thompson, 9 Squadron RAF, Lancaster PD377; awarded for action 1 January 1945, *London Gazette*, 20 February 1945.)

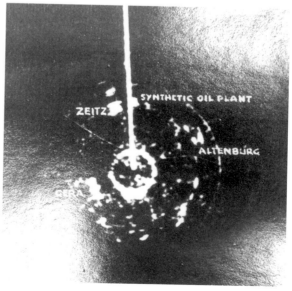

H2S radar picture of attack on Zeitz oil facility 16/17 January 1945.

Bomber Command was now ranging across Germany attacking a variety of targets, some in support of land operations as Allied forces closed in from west and east, and others in a more strategic sense. The most infamous of Bomber Command raids in the eyes of some post-war commentators was the attack on Dresden as part of Operation *Thunderclap*. On the night of 13/14 February the Command sent two waves of bombers, three hours apart, to attack Dresden. The first wave consisted of 244 Lancasters from No. 5 Group and although the accuracy of the attack was hampered by cloud the city was hit. The second wave comprised over 500 bombers and a further 1,800 tons of bombs were dropped in clear weather. Six Lancasters failed to return but Dresden was devastated and as the city's population has been boosted by refugees there was heavy loss of life. The Bomber Command attack was followed the next day by 311 USAAF B-17s, adding to the destruction and confusion.

Bomber Command's last Victoria Cross was won on the night of 23/24 February, the award going to Captain Edwin Swales of 582 Squadron, a South African operating as Master Bomber for the attack on Pforzheim. His citation read: 'Captain Swales was "master bomber" of a force of aircraft which attacked Pforzheim on the night of 23 February 1945. As "master bomber" he had the task of locating the target area with precision and of giving aiming instructions to the main force of bombers following in his wake. Soon after he had reached the target area he was engaged by an enemy fighter and one of his engines was put out of action. His rear guns failed. His crippled aircraft was an easy prey to further attacks. Unperturbed, he carried on with his allotted task; clearly and precisely he issued aiming instructions to the Main Force. Meanwhile the enemy fighter closed the range and fired again. A second engine of Captain Swales' aircraft was put out of action. Almost defenceless, he stayed over the target area issuing his aiming instructions until he was satisfied that the attack had achieved its purpose. It is now known that the attack was one of the most concentrated and successful of the war.

'Captain Swales did not, however, regard his mission as completed. His aircraft was damaged. Its speed had been so much reduced that it could only with difficulty be kept in the air. The blind-flying instruments were no longer working. Determined at all costs to prevent his aircraft and crew from falling into enemy hands, he set course for home. After an hour he flew into thin-layered cloud. He kept his course by skilful flying between the layers, but later heavy cloud and turbulent air conditions were met. The aircraft, by now over friendly territory, became more and more difficult to control; it was losing height steadily. Realising that the situation was desperate Captain Swales ordered his crew to bale out. Time was very short and it required all his exertions to keep the aircraft steady while each of his crew moved in turn to the escape hatch and parachuted to safety. Hardly had the last crew-member jumped when the aircraft plunged to earth. Captain Swales was found dead at the controls. Intrepid in the attack, courageous in the face of danger, he did his duty to the last, giving his life that his comrades might live.' (Captain Edwin Swales, DFC, SAAF, 582 Squadron RAF, Lancaster PB538. Awarded for action 23 February 1945, *London Gazette*, 24 April 1945.) The attack had been made by 367 Lancasters and thirteen Mosquitoes, with ten Lancasters being lost (plus two others that crash-landed in France).

During March and April the mix of target types continued, with Main Force raids comprising anything from 300 to 1,100 bombers. Cities that had previously only received light damage were now devastated by Bomber Command's accurate delivery of heavy bomb loads. The final Main Force operations against Germany took place by day on 25 April 1945, the targets being Wangerooge and Berchtesgaden. The attack on Wangarooge was made by 482 bombers, over 300 of which were Halifaxes, for the loss of

One of the last major bombing targets Heligoland, 18 April 1945.

seven aircraft (six of these in mid-air collisions). The aim of the attack was to destroy coastal gun batteries that controlled the approaches to the ports of Bremen and Wilhelmshaven and to prepare the way for a possible amphibious assault. The attack was made in good weather and was a success, although as usual with established fortified gun emplacements direct damage was fairly light. The attack on Berchtesgaden was highly popular with the crews that took part as it struck at Hitler's famous Eagles Nest chalet – and the associated SS barracks. The 359 Lancasters and sixteen Mosquitoes made an accurate attack and the bomb load included the last operational drop of the *Tallboy*.

The Command's final operational bombing mission took place on 2/3 May after a break without *ops* of almost a week. This was an all Mosquito affair against Kiel to destroy shipping in the harbour. A total of 126 Mosquitoes attacked in two waves, with a further fifty-three Mosquitoes flying support, primarily airfield intruder, in the Kiel area. Only one Mosquito, from 169 Squadron, was lost. The only heavies airborne were eighty-nine aircraft from No. 100 Group flying Radio Countermeasures (RCM) support and tragically two of these were lost, probably in a mid-air collision. These three aircraft, from which only three of the Halifax crewmen survived, were the last operational losses suffered by Bomber Command.

A force of forty-six Lancasters (twelve from No. 3 Group, thirty-four from No. 6 Group) were airborne on the evening of 3 May to drop mines in the Kattegat, Laeso Rende and Aalborg areas as part of the campaign aimed at preventing Nazi die-hards escaping. However, the mission was cancelled and the bombers were recalled shortly after take-off: thus ended the last offensive sortie that Bomber Command despatched in the Second World War. This brought to a close nearly six years of war for Bomber Command.

Operations *Exodus, Manna* and *Dodge*

By the time these final operational mission were being flown, Bomber Command had turned most of its effort to more peaceful pursuits under Operations *Exodus* and *Manna*. Operation *Exodus*, the repatriation of British PoWs from Europe, commenced on

26 April and in the period to 7 May Lancasters flew 469 sorties bringing home 75,000 personnel. On 29 April the Command flew the first of almost 3,000 sorties under Operation *Manna* to air-drop food to the starving Dutch population in that area of the country still occupied by the Germans. The final *Manna* sortie on 7 May involved 561 aircraft comprising 299 Lancasters of No. 1 Group, 217 Lancasters of No. 3 Group and twenty-seven Lancasters plus eighteen Mosquitoes from No. 8 Group. The main food drops took place at Kralingsche Plas (Rotterdam), Valkenburg airfield, Ypenburg airfield, the racecourse at the Hague and Gouda. The final part of this trio of humanitarian operations, *Dodge*, involved flying British personnel from Italy.

Before looking at Bomber Command's post-1945 operations, there are a number of specific Second World War 'campaigns' to review.

THE MARITIME WAR

Although in September 1939 the Command's first operational bombing missions were flown against German warships this was not from any strategic desire to attack these targets but was down to political constraints that prevented attacks on 'real' strategic targets such as German industry. These early anti-shipping operations by the medium bombers, and the light bombers of No. 2 Group, were covered above. However, as the maritime war progressed, and with the German capital ships and U-boats creating havoc in Britain's vital sea lanes, maritime targets became far more important and Bomber Command expended a great deal of effort against such targets. There were three aspects to this:

1. Attacks on U-boat facilities.
2. Attacks on capital ships in harbour.
3. Attacks on industry associated with U-boat construction.

Of the capital ships there were three that appeared frequently in Bomber Command records: *Gniesenau*, *Scharnhorst*, and *Tirpitz*, and the Command expended a great deal of effort in trying to destroy these warships. Attacks on docks and maritime cities, such as Kiel and Hamburg, and other maritime installations, combined with the minelaying campaign, were aimed at German military and commercial shipping and without doubt had a major effect on the enemy's capability. The anti-shipping campaign involved the medium and heavy bombers as well as the light bombers of No. 2 Group; the latter flew thousands of anti-shipping sorties, with the Blenheims continuing to shoulder the bulk of this work. On 28 April 1941 Blenheims of 101 Squadron, with fighter escort, flew the first Channel Stop, an attempt to close the English Channel to daylight German shipping. With the Germans employing flak ships and providing fighter escort this coastal shipping was by no means an easy target. However, the focus here will be on the three ships mentioned by name.

Salmon and *Gluckstein*

The warships *Scharnhorst* and *Gneisenau,* often referred to as 'Salmon' and 'Gluckstein' by RAF crews, were high on the target list whenever they appeared in Brest, the major naval base in France for the German capital ships. On one Atlantic foray they had sunk twenty-two Allied ships and when Bomber Command's main priority was switched to the maritime war in March 1941 these two ships were attacked a number of times in the following weeks.

After the 4/5 April attack on Brest, the *Gneisenau* was moved out of her dry dock because of the threat posed by unexploded bombs – and whilst in clear water she was

Halifax over Brest docks; this naval target – home to major German warships – was a frequent target in the Command's contribution to the maritime war.

damaged by a torpedo attack by Coastal Command Beauforts. Back in dry dock she was hit by at least four bombs on the night of 10/11 April. Brest was 'visited' a number of times day and night over the next few months and although the current range of bombs was not capable of destroying these armoured vessels they caused damage to the ships, the dock facilities and the capability of the repair teams. The arrival of the cruiser *Prinz Eugen* in Brest in late May added even more interest in attacking this port.

One final daylight raid is worthy of mention. Bremen harbour was attacked on 4 July by 112 Blenheims of 105 Squadron led by Wing Commander Hughie Edwards and despite the lack of cloud cover the bombers pressed home their attack in the face of heavy flak, with four aircraft being shot down. For his tenacious leadership of this raid Hugh Edwards was awarded the VC, his citation reading: 'Wing Commander Edwards, although handicapped by a physical disability resulting from a flying accident, has repeatedly displayed gallantry of the highest order in pressing home bombing attacks from very low heights against strongly defended objectives. On 4 July 1941, he led an important attack on the Port of Bremen, one of the most heavily defended towns in Germany. This attack had to be made in daylight and there were no clouds to afford concealment. During the approach to the German coast several enemy ships were sighted and Wing Commander Edwards knew that his aircraft would be reported and that the defences would be in a state of readiness. Undaunted by this misfortune he brought his formation 50 miles overland to the target, flying at a height of little more than 50 feet, passing under high-tension cables, carrying away telegraph wires and finally passing through a formidable balloon barrage. On reaching Bremen he was met with a hail of fire, all his aircraft being hit and four of them being destroyed. Nevertheless he made a most successful attack, and then with the greatest skill and coolness withdrew the surviving aircraft without further loss. Throughout the execution of this operation which he had planned personally with knowledge of the risks entailed, Wing Commander Edwards displayed the highest possible standard of gallantry and determination.' (Acting Wing Commander Hugh Idwal Edwards, 105 Squadron, Blenheim V6028. Awarded for action 4 July 1941, *London Gazette*, 22 July 1941.)

With the termination of the main four-month anti-naval effort in early July 1941 the bombers returned their focus on Germany. The net effect of the attacks, including twenty-four major raids on Brest, was one of negating, for a period of time, the operational capability of these major German naval assets. It was not quite the end because a special raid was called on 23/24 July when *Scharnhorst* moved from Brest to La Pallice; a raid by thirty Whitleys overnight was followed by a fighter-escorted daytime attack on Brest, La Pallice and Cherbourg. Brest was targeted by 100 bombers, including the operational debut of the Boeing B-17 Fortress with Bomber Command, three aircraft of 90 Squadron taking part. The attack was reasonably accurate and the defences caused little damage. It was a different story at La Pallice where the unescorted Halifaxes of 35 and 76 Squadrons lost five of their number to fighters and had to face heavy flak over the target. Despite this, the bombers scored five direct hits and *Scharnhorst* had to return to the dry dock in Brest.

A final burst of activity occurred in December with an Air Ministry signal of 10 December instructing Bomber Command to give 'highest priority to the destruction of enemy capital ships' with a 'suggestion' for a series of daylight attacks on Brest. This target was attacked a number of times in December, the largest raid being 121 bombers on 17/18th of the month.

Before closing the story for 1941 it is worth highlighting the statistics from a report into the anti-shipping activities of No. 2 Group. In the period March to October 1941 the Group had flown 2,320 such sorties, during which it lost 126 aircraft. As with all statistics the picture is somewhat skewed as on only 30 per cent of occasions were targets found, which meant an actual loss rate of 18 per cent, with a further 7 per cent seriously

Daylight attack by Venturas on a whaling ship in Cherbourg docks, 15 April 1943.

Camouflaged ships at Dunkirk under attack by twelve Bostons on 23 June 1942.

damaged. Of those losses it was estimated that 51 per cent were caused by anti-aircraft fire from the ships, 18 per cent to enemy aircraft, 5 per cent from colliding with ships, and 25 per cent to unknown causes. Of the 456 ships attacked it was estimated that seventy-two had been sunk and a further sixty-five seriously damaged. As with every other aspect of Bomber Command's activities at this time, one of the main problems was lack of effective weapons – the 250 lb GP and SAP bombs were simply inadequate.

Brest had become such a hot spot for the warships that in February 1942 the Germans decided to move them to safer havens in Germany; the Channel Dash, as it became known was a risky venture and once it was learnt that the warships were loose – and in theory vulnerable – the RAF and Fleet Air Arm mounted an intensive search. Bomber Command was part of this, flying 242 sorties, none of which scored any hits. This also brought the operational debut of one of No. 2 Group's new aircraft, the Bostons of 88 Squadron. It was an embarrassing period for the RAF in that the only damage caused to the warships was by mines, both *Gneisenau* and *Scharnhorst* hitting mines that were believed to have been laid by Hampdens of No. 5 Group. All the major vessels reached port safely.

Tirpitz

There was one German capital ship that occupied a great amount of Bomber Command effort, primarily because of Churchill's determination to see it destroyed – the *Tirpitz*. John Morrison was a W/Op Air Gunner with 35 Squadron during the series of raids on the *Tirpitz* in April 1942. The crew of Halifax TL-G (W1053) took-off from Kinloss at 2021 on 27 April destined for Faettenfjord as part of a force of thirty-one Halifaxes and twelve Lancasters. By the time they reached the target area the ship's smoke screen was in full force and an accurate attack was impossible: the crew dropped their load of mines in the general area. They landed back at Kinloss at 0455 and after debrief and breakfast retired to bed as the crew was on the roster for a repeat attack. Halifax W1053 left Kinloss at 2035 was part of a force of thirty-one Halifaxes and twelve Lancasters. Two of the Squadron's aircraft failed to return, as did two other Halifaxes and a Lancaster. John Morrison recalled what happened. 'The outbound journey was uneventful and as we flew up Trondheim fjord Johnny Roe descended to 150 feet and before long it looked like we were entering hell. The aircraft was in the smoke screen and was being fired at by every gun in the area; the noise of the bullets and shrapnel hitting the aircraft was unbelievable and there were flashes of light and tracer in all directions. Reg Williams [the Navigator] shouted that the *Tirpitz* had swung round through 90 degrees and Johnny said we were going round again. However, the aircraft was hit badly and he told us to take up crash positions, at which point Reg went and jettisoned the mines.' Halifax W1048 of 35 Squadron is now on show at the RAF Museum having been recovered in 1973 from Lake Hammer Vand (Hoklingen); Pilot Officer Macintyre's (*sic*) subsequent debrief noted: 'While over Trondheim at about 300 feet we were hit by light flak and set on fire. We crash-landed on Lake Hammer Vand at 0050. We left the aircraft burning furiously and later I heard that it sank through the ice in the morning.' The crew escaped the crash and all managed to evade capture with the exception of Sergeant Stevens who had broken his leg and was taken prisoner. Wing Commander Don Bennett (later to be commander of the Pathfinder Force) was also shot down and managed to escape. The second attack, the following day, was equally without result, although hits were claimed, and cost another two Halifaxes.

In July a Russian submarine damaged the warship and put it in dry dock for six months, after which she was damaged again by a Royal Navy midget submarine.

The next air attacks were naval affairs in April, July and August 1944 – but all with no appreciable result. By this time Bomber Command had very large bombs and two special squadrons to drop them.

In early September 1944 it was rumoured that *Tirpitz* was about to leave its anchorage in Kaa Fjord, Norway and Operation *Paravane* was mounted in yet another attempt to destroy the ship. The attack was to be made by 9 and 617 Squadrons using *Tallboy* bombs; which meant that they had to deploy to Yagodnik in Russia in order to have sufficient range. A detachment of thirty-eight Lancasters was led to Russia by OC 617 Squadron, Wing Commander 'Willie' Tait. The flight to Russia was fraught with

Aircrew discuss bomb plots following the final attack on the Tirpitz.

problems because of poor weather and six Lancasters crashed; Flying Officer Ross, 'Selected a long stretch of wooden road void of telegraph poles' on which to land but had to abort his approach and put the aircraft down in nearby marshy land – with all crew surviving the crash. At 0630 on 15 September a force of twenty-eight Lancasters left Yagodnik at low level; twenty-one were armed with *Tallboys* and seven with *Johnny Walker* mines. There was no significant opposition and weather over the target was good – until the very effective smokescreen was put into action; seventeen *Tallboys* and all the mines were dropped but results were not observed. All the aircraft returned to Yagodnik and flew back to England a few days later. Subsequent reconnaissance showed that *Tirpitz* was damaged but still afloat. Further raids were planned but the Germans had already decided that damage was too severe to make the ship operationally seaworthy. *Tirpitz* was moved to Trondheim Fjord to be used as a floating gun battery; a move that brought it into the range of bombers from Scotland.

'Willie' Tait led forty Lancasters from 9 and 617 Squadrons out of Lossiemouth on 29 October but when they arrived the target was obscured by cloud; most of the *Tallboys* were dropped blind but with no result. On 12 November it was a different story and Tait's thirty-one bombers found clear skies and having achieved complete surprise there was no opposition and no smokescreen. Bombing was accurate with a number of direct hits and near misses; at 0927 the battleship rolled over and sank. There was immediate debate, which has continued ever since, as which of the two squadrons delivered the crucial blows to *Tirpitz*; 617 Squadron claiming that with their SABS bombsight they were more accurate – as an ex 9 Squadron Navigator (Tornado period) this author refuses to accept this assertion!

Anti-shipping operations continued to the end of the war; indeed in the last few weeks of the war ships became prime targets with Allied fears that hard-core Nazis would try to escape to Norway.

U-boats

Whilst the capital ships might have made headlines it was the U-boat war that was far more important in strategic terms. German submarines had been operating in the sea lanes since the first days of the war but by mid 1940 they were proving increasingly effective and Bomber Command was asked to join in the battle against this threat. The first specific attack was made on the night of 2/3 September when thirty-nine Hampdens attacked the submarine base at Lorient. A new directive of 21 September had instructed the Command to allocate three squadrons for this campaign, with attacks on U-boat bases, crew training and rest centres, and manufacturing centres, including construction yards and component manufacturers.

For the remainder of the war Bomber Command played a direct part in countering this most effective of German threats, with

U-boat pens at Brest under attack 15 April 1943; target photo by 21 Squadron.

attacks on U-boat construction facilities and component factories, including special attacks such as that against the MAN engine works at Augsburg, and U-boat bases, especially those in France. The minelaying campaign and, in Harris's view, the general strategic offensive, also contributed to the overall campaign against the U-boats. The effect of attacks increased in the latter part of the war as accuracy improved and weapons became more effective, although the massive concrete U-boat pens were not seriously affected until the advent of the super-heavy bombs such as *Grand Slam*.

Minelaying (*Gardening*)

'It is not unusual for the mine-laying aircraft to fly round and round for a considerable time in order to make quite sure that the mine is laid exactly in the correct place. It calls for great skill and resolution. Moreover, the crew does not have the satisfaction of seeing even the partial results of their work. There is no coloured explosion, no burgeoning of fire to report on their return home. At best all they see is a splash on the surface of a darkened and inhospitable sea.' With these words, a Bomber Command report of 1941 summarised the minelaying role. I have covered this role in some detail as it is one of the most oft-ignored, yet vital contributions made by Bomber Command.

It had long been realised that two of the most effective weapons against shipping – merchant and military – were the torpedo and the mine; the latter being of particular value if it could be laid in sufficient quantity and with an element of secrecy. Air delivery was an obvious option and enabled the sea-mining campaign to be extended in range. However, the Admiralty, who held responsibility for naval warfare of this nature, did not place an order for air-dropped mines until July 1939 – and then only for thirty mines as a trial. These trials were completed in March the following year and production of the 1,500 lb (680 kg) A (for airborne) Mk 1 mine commenced.

On the night of 13/14 April 1940, a number of Hampdens flew to the Danish coast to lay the first mines in what was to develop into a major Bomber Command offensive. This campaign has remained one of the least recognised aspects of the Bomber Command story; yet, it occupied a huge slice of the overall Command effort – especially in the critical period of 1942–1943. As with so much of military history, the main reason that this campaign has been 'sidelined' is that it lacks 'glamour'. It was lonely, it was dangerous, but it was rarely spectacular.

Minelaying, or *Gardening* as it was called involved the aircraft laying a mine (planting a *vegetable*) in a specific location. All of these locations were given suitable agricultural names (flowers and vegetables) in line with the general terminology implied by *Gardening*, although some areas were, for no particular reason given the names of sea-creatures. Amongst the most frequented areas were: *Eglantine* (the approach to Heligoland), *Nectarines* (Frisian Islands), *Artichokes* (Lorient) and *Forget-Me-Not* (Kiel Canal). There were just under 130 code names in total and some target areas were given more than one. Likewise, the mines themselves were often referred to by a suitable code-name rather than the somewhat more boring technical description such as a 1,000 lb AI Mk V. Without knowing the relevant codes for mine and area the recorded details in Operations Record Books (ORBs) appear very cryptic.

Bomber Command involvement in minelaying stemmed from a meeting held at the Air Ministry in early April 1940 at which representatives from Bomber Command, Coastal Command, and the Admiralty examined ways in which to execute the requirements of Western Air Plan 15 (WA15). Arthur Harris, as AOC of No. 5 Group, was confident that his crews would have no major problem in accurately dropping mines. It was his aircraft that would have to carry out this task, the Hampden being the only

Bomber Command type at that time capable of carrying the existing generation of mines. The initial plan was for each Station with No. 5 Group to cover specific targets for the first series of drops, as follows:

Hemswell (61 and 144 Squadrons) – sixty mines to Kiel and Warnemunde.
Waddington (44 and 50 Squadrons) – sixty mines to Elbe and Swinemunde.
Scampton (49 and 83 Squadrons) – forty-two mines to Neustadt, Travemunde and Swinemunde.

The plan called for three sorties by each Station, of twenty aircraft per sortie, to be flown over a seven-day period on moonlit nights. It was a new role but crews were given no specific training; parameters were set as delivery height of 400–1,000 feet (122 to 305 m), speed below 200 mph (322 km/h), and the drop was to be carried out away from ships, lighthouses or likely places of observation – secrecy being the aim of the game.

In the event, the target areas were changed to reflect the operational requirements, hence the early missions went to Danish and Norwegian waters in an attempt to disrupt the German invasion of Scandinavia. The fifteen Hampdens (from all of the nominated units except 83 Squadron) which took part in the first operation of the night of 13/14 April 1940, laid their mines in Danish and southern Norwegian waters – one aircraft was lost (L4605 of 50 Squadron, Flight Lieutenant Cosgrove and crew). On the following night, twenty-eight Hampdens went out minelaying, with the loss of two aircraft.

During the following four weeks (up to 9/10 May) the Hampdens were minelaying on ten nights – a further 218 sorties, for the loss of four more aircraft. It had been an intensive period and lessons were quickly learnt and applied. Post-war research reveals it was also a successful start; at least three vessels (*Nyborg*, *Odin* and *Christian IX*) were damaged in the Great Belt, between Denmark and Sweden, in the latter part of April.

Each aircraft could carry only a single 1,500 lb (680 kg) A Mk I mine. As with so many other aspects of Bomber Command's operations in the first half of the war, the major problem was one of navigation – how to get to the target area and then plant the *vegetable* in exactly the right spot. Navigation relied on Deduced Reckoning (DR) and whatever fixes, astro or visual, were available; the actual drop was usually carried out by timed run from a visual fixpoint in the area of the target. This was one of the most dangerous periods of the operation as it was quite likely that the area where the landfall was made would be defended, or at the very least that the aircraft would be spotted and reported upon.

The converse of this was that defended areas were often an aid to navigation! The Germans realised the dangers from an effective mining campaign and so the coastal defences were strengthened on land and sea. A number of old warships were converted into flak ships, with a formidable array of weapons – a 'typical' arrangement being five 105 mm, four 20 mm and one 30 mm, plus one or more searchlights. Later in the war, gun-laying radars were added to the ships to make them even more effective. New light flak positions sprang up in all the known mining areas and RDF (radar) stations were established to give early warning and fighter control.

After the early burst of activity in conjunction with the Norwegian campaign the minelaying impetus decreased. However, it remained a regular element of the Bomber Command task; with, on average, three Hampden squadrons on stand-by for minelaying duties (they were tasked on normal bomber *ops* as well).

At first the Command was given five general areas for its minelaying operations, part of a coordinated campaign being run by the Admiralty through Coastal Command;

the areas being Norwegian waters, Danish waters, the Baltic, Kiel Canal and the Elbe estuary, and the Bay of Biscay. As the campaign progressed, and especially following the 1942 offer, by the new commander of Bomber Command – Arthur Harris, to drop 1,000 mines a month, the areas were extended so that in effect Bomber Command was *gardening* from the extreme north of Norway right down to the Spanish border. The overall mining campaign was under the control of the Admiralty Directorate of Minelaying Operations; within the constraints of the broad directives it issued, the Air Ministry and Bomber Command had considerable flexibility regarding the actual targets and percentage of effort in a given period.

In consultation with naval advisers, and with consideration of the prevailing strategic situation (i.e. U-boat waters became a key target area during the intensive periods of anti-U-boat *ops*), operations were planned and the Groups were notified of their required effort. The planning procedure then followed that of a normal bombing mission. This 'political' aspect of the minelaying campaign is an important factor towards understanding the position of Bomber Command (and Harris in particular), and the pleas of the Admiralty for a diversion of resources away from the Strategic Bombing Offensive and into more critical areas such as the battle against the U-boats. The Bomber Command answer was the classic one given by all supporters of strategic air power – that it is better to destroy the target system (in this case the U-boats) at its place of origin, the centres of production, than it is to try to hunt them down later; hence the strategic bombing of construction yards and component factories. One important aspect of the overall strategy was the minelaying campaign in areas used by the U-boats for training (the Baltic) and transit (Bay of Biscay). These two operational areas saw a large percentage of the total minelaying effort – and the highest percentage of losses amongst the minelaying aircraft. Two periods that saw particular attention being paid to the U-boat areas were November 1942, in connection with Operation Torch, the landings in North Africa; and June 1944, in connection with Operation Overlord, the landings in Normandy. One senior German naval officer was to comment, 'without training in the Baltic, and safe escort through coastal waters and the routes to and from the operation area in mid-ocean, there can be no U-boat war.'

In June 1943 Bomber Command summarised the general purposes of the large-scale minelaying campaign as:

1. To cause serious embarrassment and dislocation to the enemy's vital sea-borne traffic, especially in regard to raw materials for the Ruhr and military supplies for the Russian Front or for the Norwegian theatre of operations.
2. To assist the Battle of the Atlantic by interrupting the passages of U-boats leaving or entering the French West Coast bases, and by rendering the U-boat training areas unsafe.
3. To interfere with the arrivals and departures of blockade runners, armed merchant raiders, iron ore ships and sundry traffic using the Gironde River and other Atlantic ports.
4. To force the enemy to maintain numbers of experienced personnel and much valuable material for the purpose of sweeping his widely-spread harbours and channels.

The Hampdens of 5 Group had shouldered the task and achieved reasonable results at an acceptably low loss rate; however, being able to carry only one mine meant that the overall impact of the Hampden campaign was limited. With the decision that all medium and heavy bombers should be equipped for carrying out minelaying tasks, the scene was set for a rapid expansion of capability. When the Wellingtons joined in the campaign they doubled the capability as they could carry two mines; likewise, the overall Bomber Command capability was increased by the decision to employ training units on the mine-laying task. It now became a routine element for the various OTUs – with mixed feelings from those involved. To some it was seen as an 'easy' introduction to planning and executing an operational mission; to others, it was a risk taken by a partly-trained crew before they were ready.

When the warships *Scharnhorst*, *Gneisenau*, and *Prinz Eugen* broke out of Brest and made the so-called Channel Dash to the safety of ports in Germany the RAF was caught off guard. After months of trying to destroy these important vessels at Brest, the opportunity of catching them in open waters was lost. The only consolation for the RAF was that the two battle cruisers (*Scharnhorst* and *Gneisenau*) hit mines that had almost certainly been laid a few days earlier by aircraft from 5 Group. Although both ships were damaged they still managed to reach port before any effective air attacks could be mounted. (Hampdens and Manchesters had been flying day and night sorties laying mines during the previous ten days.)

Heavy bombers, such as the Manchester and Halifax, were equipped to carry four mines, the redoubtable Lancaster could take six, as could the Stirling. Even the Mosquito was given the capability of carrying two mines, albeit over a much shorter range.

Stirlings joined in the minelaying campaign on the night of 23/24 March 1942, with three aircraft (N3669, N3674 and R9303) from 15 Squadron laying mines off Lorient. For the Lancaster, minelaying was to be the type's first operational outing – L7549 of 44 Squadron, pilot W/O Crum, dropping four mines in the Heligoland area on 3 March 1942. The sortie was recorded thus in the Operations Record Book:

> TASK GARDENING ROSEMARY. Vegetables (2 Assembly 22, 1 Ordinary and 1 PDM No. 2) dropped in allotted position. Height 600 ft. Time 2046 hrs. Heading 288 at 180 mph. Visibility bright moonlight. Slight haze. Pinpoint on Trischen from which a careful timed run was made. Uneventful. Surprising lack of flak. Crew cooperated well.

It was important to record details of the accurate laying of the mines as this information would be sought in the debrief by the naval armaments officer (who had also been at the briefing), in order that he could transfer the details to an Admiralty Chart.

The employment of the heavy bomber force was essential as in February 1942, Harris had made an offer to the Admiralty to lay an average of 1,000 mines a month – a ten-fold increase! However, he did stress that this was not to have a detrimental effect on the main bomber offensive. What it gave Harris was a political lever to use on the Admiralty, and Churchill, whenever the cry went up for Bomber Command to help out in the naval war.

The Air Staff agreed the commitment on 25 March 1942, and the policy was implemented. During 1942 the minelaying effort absorbed some 14.7 per cent of the total Bomber Command operational effort, with 4,743 sorties, during which 9,574 mines were laid (1941 figures had been 1,250 sorties and 1,055 mines). There had also been an increase in the loss rate, up from 1 per cent to nearly 4 per cent, although with marked variation depending upon the operational area – Kiel had the lowest rate and the Weser estuary the highest. Throughout 1942 and 1943 the squadrons sent crews to find nominated stretches of water in which to place their cargo. It was certainly looked on by most crews as a bit of light relief after the hazards of 'Happy Valley' (the Ruhr) or Berlin. Ken Pincott was with 15 Squadron: 'These were looked on as an easy operation because most often the main attack that night would be against a mainland target by the bomber force. Apart from a little flak and occasional fighter, the odds of survival were much higher.'

Tom Wingham was operating with 102 Squadron on the night of 28 April 1943 in Halifax JB894/X: 'Kattegat, two 1,500 lb mines. Good visibility although 7/10 cloud base 2,000 feet. Mines laid as ordered from 1,500 feet heading 156 at 176 TAS, after timed run. Avoided flak ships but saw some light flak. Easy run. Surprised to hear later of the heavy losses suffered that night.'

No less than 207 aircraft had been tasked with minelaying that night, 167 reported successful missions (a total of 593 mines), but twenty-two aircraft were lost (seven Lancasters, seven Stirlings, six Wellingtons and two Hampdens) – at over 10 per cent, by far the most costly night of minelaying recorded by the Command. This large-scale effort broke the previous sortie record, set only the night before, of 160 sorties.

Not all minelaying sorties were straightforward, Harry Hull was air gunner in a Halifax of 10 Squadron: 'We were briefed for a minelaying trip and, full of confidence that there could not be many more, set off, but barely half an hour from base I felt a thump, thump, thump from under the aircraft which just did not sound normal. The skipper sent the bomb aimer down to inspect the bomb bay for the vibration. Upon opening the inspection hatch he found a mine had broken free from one of the holding straps and was swinging backwards and forwards with the movement of the aircraft. After waiting for the end of the radio silence period we contacted base and they gave us a jettison area – they certainly did not want an unexploded mine rolling down the runway when we landed!'

On rare occasions aircraft witnessed the results of the minelaying effort; the *Bomber Command Quarterly Review* carried this account from a 305 Squadron Wellington. 'At about 2100 on 16 February 1943, this aircraft was laying mines in the Bay of Biscay. The night was extremely clear, there was bright moonlight and the sea was calm. The aircraft was making a run-up at a height of 500 feet when she saw a U-boat crash-dive ahead.

'It took her less than a minute to reach the position and she had just passed over it when there was a violent explosion which shook her considerably. The bomb aimer and rear gunner both saw a big column of spray and the latter saw what he took to be the tail of the U-boat standing almost vertically out of the water. It disappeared after a short while and nothing more was seen. Mines had also been laid on previous sorties in this area.'

It was not only the estuary and open sea areas that were attacked with mines, the campaign also targeted inland waterways and canals. A very successful example of this was the raid by twenty-two Mosquitoes of No. 8 Group against the Kiel Canal on the night of 12/13 May 1944. All but two of the aircraft made attacks on the target and the canal was closed for seven days. One Mosquito was lost.

The mines themselves were robust and reliable devices, fitted with a drogue parachute to slow them down for water entry. Prior to 1943 all delivery was low level, usually 600–800 feet (180–240 m); the main requirement being accurate delivery and the need to reduce entry shock. Improvements in mine technology and delivery systems meant that by March 1943 aircraft were cleared to drop their mines from 3,000 feet (920 m), an improvement but still not ideal as it still required the aircraft to loiter at heights where light flak was effective. However, later in the year, the Stirlings carried out trials dropping mines from 12,000 feet (3,658 m) and before long the cleared height was up to 15,000 feet (4,572 m). This became the standard technique.

The task of accurate navigation was aided by the use of the radio nav aid *Gee*, although the accuracy and reliability decreased close to the enemy coastline because of

Loading mines into a Stirling, March 1944.

jamming. However, trials were later carried out using the H2S radar system, including its employment by one aircraft acting as a 'minelaying pathfinder' for other aircraft. Eventually mines were being laid blind from 15,000 ft using the H2S information.

This tactical change was highlighted in a Bomber Command report of March 1944. 'Since the beginning of the year, a new technique which enables mines to be dropped accurately from high altitudes has been developed and put into operation. In conjunction with H2S and the Mark XIV bombsight, it is now possible for mines to be laid successfully over heavily defended areas either visually or through 10/10ths cloud. Kiel Bay, the Belts, the Heligoland Bight, the Sound, the Kattegat, Oslo Harbour, the Rade de Brest, and the Gironde, have all been mined by the new method. The exercising areas and swept channels in the vicinity of Kiel alone have received 1,111 mines.'

At around the same time, Bomber Command received a most welcome testimony from the First Sea Lord: 'The extensive and deep penetration into enemy waters made on the night of 9/10 April is typical of the skill and determination shown by the aircraft that take part in minelaying operations. The work of the minelaying aircraft of Bomber Command during the past four years has paid rich dividends. Shipping losses have been inflicted on the enemy and the sea traffic has been impeded and delayed to an extent which has seriously dislocated their general communications. I should be grateful if you would convey to those concerned the Navy's appreciation of their fine work.' (103 Lancasters of No. 1 Group and No. 5 Group laid mines in the Baltic off Danzig, Gdynia and Pillau – for the loss of nine aircraft.)

Throughout the war improvements were made in the mines, including the use of acoustic mines from September 1942. A variety of mines of between 1,000 lb (454 kg) and 2,000 lb (907 kg) were used during the campaign. The primary weapons were:

1. 1,500 lb (680 kg) A Mk I with about 750 lb (340 kg) High Explosive. Modifications led to others, up to Mk IV. Acoustic or combination mine.
2. 1,000 lb A Mk V with about 650 lb (295 kg) HE. Magnetic mine.
3. 2,000 lb A Mk VI, more HE and greater sophistication of fusing.
4. 1,000 lb A Mk VII with greater sophistication all round.

In the period 1 February 1942 to 8 May 1945, Bomber Command flew 16,240 mining sorties, dropping a total of 45,428 mines (statistics do vary between sources). Statistics as to the losses of enemy shipping are hard to determine, and often show great variance. One Bomber Command analysis (post-war) claimed 491 ships sunk and 410 damaged – an average of one ship per 50 mines dropped. The total effort by the Command from April 1940 onwards was 47,152 mines, for a loss of 467 aircraft.

There was always a degree of argument as to what effect this campaign had, and thus if the effort expended was worth the result. Whilst the actual sinkings do not always look particularly impressive it is essential to remember other equally important factors. A great quantity of shipping was damaged and this had a direct impact on the construction yards – effort, including resources and manpower, had to be expended in repairing these vessels.

In order to reduce the danger, the Germans conducted an intensive mine-sweeping programme, again involving resources and manpower that could have been employed elsewhere. Every ship sunk or damaged caused disruption in the communications of military and civil, often industrial, material. Losses, or the threat of losses, eventually became so severe that neutral countries, the most important being Sweden with the supply of raw materials such as iron ore, were reluctant to ship goods to Germany. Any one of these elements was important, taken together they are very significant. Harris summed it up, '... could put a large part of the German navy on the work of mine sweeping, and many workers on to the repair of ships.'

Operation *Thunderbolt*, the RAF's post-war analysis of Bomber Command's efforts, had this to say: 'The main contribution which the strategic air forces made in the conduct of sea warfare was in the minelaying campaign. During the war Bomber Command laid 47,000 mines, which were responsible for sinking or damaging over 900 enemy ships. The Command was in fact responsible for over 30 per cent of sinkings inflicted on enemy merchant shipping in north-western waters.'

The inevitable conclusion must be that the *gardening* carried out by Bomber Command between 1940 and 1945 deserves to be recognised as an important facet of the air power story of the Second World War.

Stirling crew de-briefing after a minelaying operation, 17 March 1944, a night when three Stirlings were out gardening.

Propaganda leaflets (*Nickelling*)

Although in the early months of the war aircraft flew pure leaflet-dropping missions as soon as the Strategic Bombing commenced in May 1940 it was more usual for leaflets to be dropped as part of a bombing mission.

On the first night of war ten Whitleys from Linton-on-Ouse dropped propaganda leaflets in Area 1(a) (the Ruhr) with 5.4 million leaflets being dispensed. By the end of the war the Command had dropped billions of leaflets over Germany and Occupied Europe, greatly assisting the enemy, the cynics said, by providing them with good quality toilet paper! The first method was that of stuffing leaflets down the flare chute of the aircraft, not an easy task in the confines of the Whitley when the crew had to unwrap the bundles of leaflets to ensure that they would disperse in the slipstream of the aircraft and float to earth. The leaflets were in bundles of 1,500, in packs containing twelve bundles and the task was to

If the recipient pulled on the tag (Ziehen) the picture changed to a sinking U-boat and a drowning sailor.

Many of the propaganda leaflets were aimed at Occupied Europe and were in the appropriate language, with French and Dutch being the two most common.

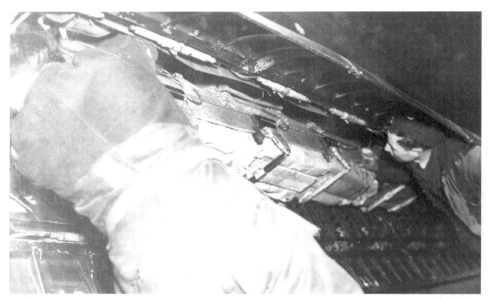

Wellington bomb bay with containers of leaflets being attached to the bomb beam, May 1944.

slit open the packs and drop them down the chute attached to the training flare opening. A normal load was 1,200–1,800 lb of leaflets. Automatic systems were subsequently developed whereby leaflets were containerised and could be carried in the bomb bay.

Sydney Munns's 77 Squadron Whitley was typical with its 'mixed load' on the night of 14 November 1940: 'On this particular raid on Berlin, apart from HE bombs and incendiaries we carried leaflets to drop over the target – what we called the "newspaper delivery" – and also over Holland we dropped hundreds of bags of tea, sealed in strong canvas, which we delivered "courtesy" of the RAF. The tea came from the Dutch East Indies, and this we called the "grocery run". I cannot remember whether on this occasion we dropped forged ration books, but sometimes we did so – anything to upset the economy!' Nearly five years later Bomber Command would have a serious purpose with its food drops over Holland as it took much-needed supplies to the Dutch people under Operation *Manna*.

In December 1940 the Air Ministry was urging Bomber Command to drop more leaflets as the improvement in material deserved greater effort. However, with the launch of the bombing offensive the leaflet campaign was seen as secondary. The same complaint was made again in March 1941 and that leaflets were becoming obsolete before they were dropped and were having to be pulped. The following month the Command was told that the Prime Minister would like to see as many leaflets dropped as possible! March 1941 saw another propaganda food drop to Holland; a gift of 4,000 lb of tea had been made by the Dutch in Batavia and this was dropped in $^2/_3$ oz bags over Holland with a label saying 'Holland will rise again, Greetings from the Free Netherlands Indies. Keep a good heart.' According to a Dutch naval attaché the reaction from the people was that it would be better to bomb the Germans!

The psychological warfare experts were forever designing new messages to drop on the enemy in an effort to destabilise the morale of the German people and make them lose confidence in the Nazi regime. Favourite topics included depicting the Nazi leadership as the wreckers of Europe, including Germany, and as caricature figures; from mid-1942 when the war began to turn against Germany it was common for leaflets to run headlines of Allied victories and the progress of the war.

The leaflet campaign continued to the end of the war but it tends to be ignored in the RAF records after it was no longer a specific mission but was combined with a normal bombing mission, although the training units continued to fly *nickel* sorties into 1944.

THE OFFENSIVE AGAINST ITALY

Italy joined the war on 10 June 1940 and Bomber Command made an immediate response by launching 36 Whitleys to attack the Turin area on the night of 11/12 April. Having refuelled in the Channel Islands the aircraft proceeded on their long flight to Italy only to encounter bad weather that made twenty-three of them turn back before crossing the Alps. Nine aircraft claimed to have bombed Turin, where the lights were on until the bombs began to fall, and two claimed to have bombed Genoa. A Whitley of 77 Squadron crashed near Le Mans with the loss of its crew, the first Bomber Command losses in action against Italy.

The blurred nature of this night-target photo of Genoa docks was caused by the low level attack by this 49 Squadron crew on 7/8 November 1942.

Haddock Force Wellingtons from Salon attacked Genoa on the night of 15/16 June but only one of the eight aircraft claimed to have reached the target. Genoa and Milan were attacked the following night and Italy was left alone for a while as other priorities required attention.

Autumn 1942 brought a concerted series of attacks against the industrial centres of Northern Italy. This new offensive was launched with a raid on Genoa on 22/23 October. Italy remained a high priority for the rest of year, with November being a particularly busy month.

The Turin raid of 28/29 November saw another Bomber Command VC awarded: 'Flight Sergeant Middleton was captain and first pilot of a Stirling aircraft detailed to attack the Fiat Works at Turin one night in November, 1942. Great difficulty was experienced in climbing to 12,000 feet to cross the Alps, which led to excessive consumption of fuel. So dark was the night that the mountain peaks were almost invisible. During the crossing Flight Sergeant Middleton had to decide whether to proceed or turn back, there being barely sufficient fuel for the return journey. Flares were sighted ahead and he continued the mission and even dived to 2,000 feet to identify the target, despite the difficulty of regaining height. Three flights were made over Turin at this low altitude before the target was identified. The aircraft was then subjected to fire from light anti-aircraft guns. A large hole appeared in the port main plane which made it difficult to maintain lateral control. A shell then burst in the cockpit, shattering the windscreen and wounding both pilots. A piece of shell splinter tore into the side of Flight Sergeant Middleton's face, destroying his right eye and exposing the bone over the eye. He was probably wounded also in the body or legs. The second pilot received wounds in the head and both legs which bled profusely. The wireless operator was also wounded in the leg.

Lancasters of 9 Squadron were part of the force that bombed Genoa on 22/23 October 1942; mission certificate for Squadron Leader Fry and crew.

GENOA
9 SQUADRON
22/23 OCTOBER 1942

S/LDR FRY, SGT RITCHIE, W/O WILLAN,
F/SGT PERKINS, SGT CLARKSON, SGT DULLMAN,
SGT HALL.

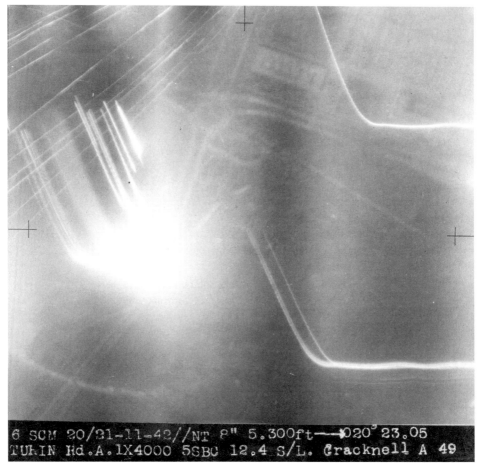

6 SCM 20/21-11-42//NT 8" 5.300ft——020° 23.05
TURIN Hd.A.1X4000 5SBC 12.4 S/L. Cracknell A 49

Turin 20/21 November 1942 from a 49 Squadron aircraft.

'Flight Sergeant Middleton became unconscious and the aircraft dived to 800 feet before control was regained by the second pilot, who took the aircraft up to 1,500 feet and released the bombs. There was still light flak, some very intense, and the aircraft was hit many times. The three gunners replied continuously until the rear turret was put out of action. Flight Sergeant Middleton had now recovered consciousness and, when clear of the target, ordered the second pilot back to receive first aid. Before this was completed the latter insisted on returning to the cockpit, as the captain could see very little and could only speak with loss of blood and great pain. Course was set for base and the crew now faced an Alpine crossing and a homeward flight in a damaged aircraft, with insufficient fuel. The possibilities of abandoning the aircraft or landing in Northern France were discussed but Flight Sergeant Middleton expressed the intention of trying to make the English coast, so that his crew could leave the aircraft by parachute. Owing to his wounds and diminishing strength, he knew that, by then, he would have little or no chance of saving himself. After four hours, the French coast was reached and here the aircraft, flying at 6,000 feet, was once more engaged and hit by intense light anti-aircraft fire. Flight Sergeant Middleton was still at the controls and mustered sufficient strength to take evasive action.

The offensive against Italy: summary of operations Autumn 1942 campaign					
Date	Target	Halifax	Lancaster	Stirling	Wellington
22/23 Oct 1942	Genoa	0	112	0	0
23/24 Oct	Genoa	53 (2)	0	51 (1)	18
24 Oct	Milan	88 (3)	0	0	0
24/25 Oct	Milan	25	0	23 (2)	23 (4)
6/7 Nov	Genoa	72 (2)	0	0	0
7/8 Nov	Genoa	45 (4)	85 (1)	39	6 (1)
13/14 Nov	Genoa	0	67	9	0
15/16 Nov	Genoa	40	27	11	0
18/19 Nov	Turin	Total 77 aircraft			
20/21 Nov	Turin	47 (1)	86	45 (1)	54 (1)
28/29 Nov	Turin	45	117	47 (2)	19 (1)
29/30 Nov	Turin	0	7	29 (2)	0
8/9 Dec	Turin	9	108 (1)	7	9
9/10 Dec	Turin	47	115 (1)	25	40 (2)
11/12 Dec	Turin	48 (3)	20	8 (1)	6

Note: Aircraft details show number despatched and (in brackets) number lost.

'After crossing the Channel there was only sufficient fuel for 6 minutes flying. Flight Sergeant Middleton ordered the crew to abandon the aircraft while he flew parallel with the coast for a few miles, after which he intended to head out to sea. Five of the crew left the aircraft safely, while two remained to assist Flight Sergeant Middleton. The aircraft crashed in the sea and the bodies of the front gunner and flight engineer were recovered the following day. Their gallant captain was apparently unable to leave the aircraft and his body has not been traced.

'Flight Sergeant Middleton was determined to attack the target regardless of the consequences and not to allow his crew to fall into enemy hands. While all the crew displayed heroism of a high order, the urge to do so came from Flight Sergeant Middleton, whose fortitude and strength of will made possible the completion of the mission. His devotion to duty in the face of overwhelming odds is unsurpassed in the annals of the Royal Air Force.' (Flight Sergeant Rawdon Hume Middleton, No. 149 Squadron; awarded for action 28 November 1942, *London Gazette*, 13 January 1943.)

Turin was the target for the night of 8/9 December 1942 and according to the ORS report (Night Raid Report No. 216) '89 per cent of the force despatched report having reached the target, where weak defences and clear skies enabled pilots to bomb with deliberation. Serious damage was caused to industry, municipal and residential property at a very low cost to our forces.' The attack involved 133 aircraft from No. 5 Group but 10 per cent of the force turned back early with technical problems. The attack was led by a Pathfinder force that accurately marked the target from 2 minutes before Zero Hour (2100) to 18 minutes after Zero Hour. The initial wave of Pathfinders comprised ten aircraft as 'finders' dropping a long stick of flares at 8-second intervals across the target area so that the aiming point could be identified. The 'illuminators' then released flares in an arc east and south of the city centre, this illumination being maintained until Zero+18. The Main Force was thus able to bomb in near ideal conditions. The ORS Report stated that 'the heavy gun defences appear to have been increased, but there was no improvement in accuracy. The light guns were also more numerous than before and were fairly accurate at times. They appeared to be firing barrage. Night fighter activity on the route to Turin was negligible.' The attackers dropped 121 tons of HE and 151 tons of incendiaries, with forty-six bombers carrying a full load of 4 lb incendiaries whilst most of the rest carried a mixed load of HE and incendiaries. Only one Lancaster was lost on this raid – targets in Italy were invariably thought of as 'soft' because of weak defences and low loss rates.

Although Italy remained on the target list there were few major attacks until late summer 1943 when a concerted series of attacks was part of Allied pressure designed to persuade the Italian Government to sign an Armistice (and in due course to change sides). Genoa, Milan and Turin were attacked a number of times; Flight Sergeant Arthur Aaron was awarded the VC for his actions on the Turin raid of 12/13 August, his citation read: 'On the night of 12 August 1943, Flight Sergeant Aaron was captain and pilot of a Stirling aircraft detailed to attack Turin. When approaching to attack, the bomber received devastating bursts of fire from an enemy fighter. Three engines were hit, the windscreen shattered, the front and rear turrets put out of action and the elevator control damaged, causing the aircraft to become unstable and difficult to control. The navigator was killed and other members of the crew were wounded.

'A bullet struck Flight Sergeant Aaron in the face, breaking his jaw and tearing away part of his face. He was also wounded in the lung and his right arm was rendered useless. As he fell forward over the control column, the aircraft dived several thousand feet. Control was regained by the flight engineer at 3,000 feet. Unable to speak, Flight Sergeant Aaron urged the bomb aimer by signs to take over the controls. Course was then set southwards in an endeavour to fly the crippled bomber, with one engine out of action, to Sicily or North Africa. Flight Sergeant Aaron was assisted to the rear of the aircraft and treated with morphine. After resting for some time he rallied and, mindful of his responsibility as captain of the aircraft, insisted on returning to the pilot's cockpit, where he was lifted into his seat and had his feet placed on the rudder-bar.

'Twice he made determined attempts to take control and hold the aircraft to its course but his weakness was evident and with difficulty he was persuaded to desist. Though in great pain and suffering from exhaustion he continued to help by writing directions with his left hand. Five hours after leaving the target the petrol began to run low, but soon afterwards the flare path at Bone airfield was sighted. Flight Sergeant Aaron summoned his failing strength to direct the bomb aimer in the hazardous task of landing the damaged aircraft in the darkness with undercarriage retracted. Four attempts were made under his direction; at the fifth Flight Sergeant Aaron was so near to collapsing that he had to be restrained by the crew and the landing was completed by the bomb aimer.

'Nine hours after landing, Flight Sergeant Aaron died from exhaustion. Had he been content, when grievously wounded, to lie still and conserve his failing strength, he would probably have recovered, but he saw it as his duty to exert himself to the utmost, if necessary with his last breath, to ensure that his aircraft and crew did not fall into enemy hands. In appalling conditions he showed the greatest qualities of courage, determination and leadership and, though wounded and dying, he set an example of devotion to duty which has seldom been equalled and never surpassed.' (Acting Flight Sergeant Arthur Louis Aaron DFM, 218 Squadron, Stirling EF452; awarded for action 13 August 1943, *London Gazette*, 3 November 1943.)

The Italians changed sides in September but the Germans maintained a tight grip on Italy to the end of the war, the Allies having to fight hard for every mile – but this was not Bomber Command's war.

BOMBER OPERATIONS 1946–1968

There can be no doubt of Bomber Command's intense operational activity during the Second World War – but what about the 20 years following the war? For most of that period the Command's main concern was the Cold War and, from the mid-1950s, its role in the nuclear deterrence of NATO against the Warsaw Pact. This general situation is covered in the overview history of Bomber Command but there were periods in the 1950s when the Command, or parts of it, was back in combat. As part of the global nature of British commitments, and the post-war problem of anti-colonialism, the British military became involved in a number of conflicts. Of these conflicts two involved small-scale Bomber Command detachments – the Malayan Emergency (1948–1960) and the Mau Mau campaign in Kenya (1952–1956), whilst the third was on a large scale but short duration, Suez 1956.

Malayan Emergency (1948–1956)

A State of Emergency had been declared in Malaya on 16 June 1948 as communist guerrillas attempted to seize control of the country. It was not until March 1950, under Operation *Musgrave*, that Bomber Command became involved in supporting the RAF units based in the Far East Air Force (FEAF). The first bomber detachment was by eight Lincolns of 57 Squadron, which deployed from the UK to Tengah, Singapore, being joined in June by an RAAF Lincoln detachment. The overall British strategy was to cut-off the communists from their sources of supply and to destroy the active terrorist bands in the jungle. It was with the latter that the Bomber Command detachments became involved.

The Lincolns were replaced from February 1955 by detachments of Canberras, under Operation *Mileage*, as Bomber Command retained its commitment to the Malayan Emergency to the end of the operational period of the conflict in 1956, although it did not officially end until July 1960. Air strength was at its height in the mid 1950s but Bomber Command's commitment was normally restricted to six or eight aircraft from a single squadron, the units deploying in rotation from the Binbrook Wing. The first Canberra unit, 101 Squadron was in theatre from February to June 1955 and in that

Lincoln of 100 Squadron over Malaya.

Canberras bomb jungle targets.

period flew thirty missions, the majority by three or four aircraft, with a standard weapon load of six 1,000 lb bombs. The Canberra rotation continued to August 1956:

101 Squadron	Feb–Jun 1955
617 Squadron	Jun–Oct 1955
12 Squadron	Oct 1955–Mar 1956
9 Squadron	Mar–Jun 1956
101 Squadron	Jun–Aug 1956

Crews from 101 Squadron had been training for Operation *Mileage* since January, the focus being on low level navigation and bombing. Departing Binbrook on 7 February they arrived at Changi on 11 February. After a few days local flying and bombing on China Rock range the detachment flew a simulated attack a week later. The first operational flight took place on 23 February when Squadron Leader Robertson led three Canberras to attack a terrorist camp. Over the next few weeks the detachment was kept busy with day and night attacks in 'static', i.e. known, targets. Initially the Canberras flew similar tactics to those developed by the Lincolns but two main techniques soon became standard: Auster Mark and Datum Point. Pinpoint targets were usually attacked by a vic of three aircraft to ensure a good distribution of bombs over the target area, the six bombs (1,000 lb or 500 lb) being dropped in sequenced pairs or a single stick of six. Having been given the target map reference this was plotted on a one million scale map and a circle of 10 minutes flight time (at 200 kts groundspeed) drawn around it. The area was then examined for the best run-in taking into account such factors as terrain and navigation features (always tricky in the jungle). The formation would set up for the pre-briefed run and check in with the Auster Mark aircraft. At the 10-minute point the formation leader would call 'bombing in 10'. The bombers would navigate visually from the run-in point and call every one minute down to 'bombing in 90 seconds', at which point the Auster would drop his marker flare on the target and call 'target marked'. The Datum Point technique involved a timed run from a distinctive Initial Point and as it was less accurate was used for 'area attack'. Various other techniques, some of which used ground radar, were also employed from time to time.

The break of deployment in mid 1956 was caused by the Suez Crisis but also coincided with a reduction in terrorist activity. Canberras were back in action in 1958 but with the resident FEAF bomber unit, 45 Squadron, being employed. Whilst the Bomber

Command detachments had played a role in the overall Malayan Emergency campaign it is only right to state that the work of FEAF units, from Hornets and Venoms to Dakotas and Pembrokes, and even Dragonfly helicopters developing the role of Casualty Evacuation (CASEVAC), was far more significant in the overall air and land campaign.

Mau Mau (1952–1956)

The Mau Mau uprising in Kenya was a vicious 'post Colonial' struggle and trouble had been brewing since the late 1940s, the heartland of the rebels being the Kikuyu tribe. Although a State of Emergency was not declared until October 1952, Bomber Command had sent aircraft to Eastleigh, the main airfield at Nairobi, since March 1947 (Lancasters of 82 Squadron). However, it was not until the main offensive against the terrorists, from 1953 and particularly in 1955, that the Lincolns of Bomber Command flew offensive operations in support of ground forces, the main operational area being the Aberdare region. The combined air and ground assault soon broke the back of the rebellion and by mid 1956 the crisis was over.

Suez (1956)

The British presence in Egypt had been under pressure since the end of the Second World War and by the early 1950s the main military presence had been confined to the Canal Zone, including a number of RAF Stations. Under an Anglo-Egyptian agreement the British finally withdraw in June 1956 but the following month the Egyptian leader, Nasser, nationalised the Suez Canal. This action was used by Britain and France as a rationale for intervention, although this was masked in the excuse of protecting the Canal from an Israeli–Egyptian conflict. As far as our Bomber Command story is concerned the British air plan, Operation *Musketeer*, involved a major deployment of Canberras to Malta and Cyprus, and of Valiants to Malta. The main strategic air campaign had two elements:

1. Neutralise the Egyptian Air Force (which on paper was quite potent).
2. A psychological warfare campaign to disrupt the Egyptian economy, morale and armed forces.

Both of these strategic aims would have been instantly recognisable to air planners of 1942! Indeed, the tactics employed would also have been recognisable. The primary role of the Air Task Force, under Air Marshal Barnett, was the neutralisation phase and the main targets for the bombers were Egyptian airfields. Bombing was planned as selective in order to avoid civilian casualties or excessive material damage and so the second element of the bombing campaign was abandoned and the bomber effort was concentrated on military installations. In terms of technique it was back to the old Pathfinder concept with marker Canberras dropping Target Indicators for the Main Force.

In August 1956 six Bomber Command Canberra squadrons – 9, 12, 15, 101, 109 and 139, the latter two as marker units, had been ordered to restrict training and prepare for deployment to the Middle East. This was a surprise for one of the Binbrook units, 101 Squadron, as it had only recently sent a detachment to Malaya. Binbrook was a hive of activity as aircraft and personnel prepared; the former having extra equipment fitted and the latter having inoculations. It was a similar story for the two marker squadrons at Hemswell, although they also flew visual aiming sorties as there would be no radio aids (*Gee-H*) where they were going. Other Bomber Squadrons were tasked with ferrying bombs out to Malta as this would be the main base for the longer-range B.6 Canberras and stocks of 1,000 lb bombs at that base were low. The overall work-up concluded with a Command Exercise on 28 August when the 'target' was marked by Valiants dropping green proximity markers, which were then 'centred' with red TIs for the Main Force to bomb on. The exercise went well and the marker Canberras were amongst the first to deploy, a joint 109/139 detachment moving to Malta towards the end of September, although the latter was later concentred with 109 Squadron as 139 Squadron became part of the Cyprus force. At Binbrook, 101 Squadron was ordered to, 'Deploy to Luqa as the vanguard of any air action which might be required in connection with the Suez crisis.' The Squadron duly moved to Luqa, being joined on 22 September by 12 Squadron, the latter moving to Hal Far. Strength at Malta was subsequently boosted by the arrival of 9 Squadron on 30 October. The main Canberra force was based at Nicosia, Cyprus under Group Captain Key and comprised seven squadrons: 10, 15, 18, 27, 44, 61 and 139). All aircraft were painted with recognition stripes on wings and fuselage, just like those used for D-Day but this time being yellow and black for most aircraft rather than white and black. On 30 October the BBC broadcast a warning to Egyptian civilians to keep away from military targets as these were now under threat of bombing.

The Canberras and Valiants went into action on the night of 30 October, the targets being Almaza, Kabrit, Abu Sueir, Inchas and Cairo West airfields. Most of the bombers

Cairo West, 5 November 1956.

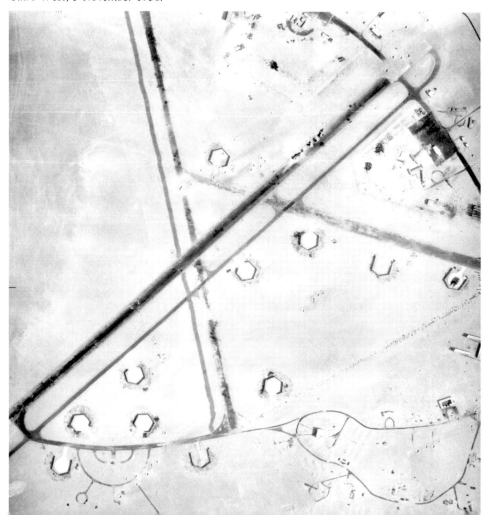

were recalled *en route* as there was uncertainty as to the clearance to bomb certain targets, in part generated by worry over causing American casualties – it was though they were evacuating from one of the Cairo airfields.

One of the main targets for the following night was Almaza airfield and 139 Squadron was tasked with marking the target. The standard technique of Marker 1 and Marker 2 (each with eight 4.5 inch flares and two 1,000 lb TIs) and Flare 1 and Flare 2 (each with twelve 4.5 inch flares) was used. Taking off at 1715 the aircraft flew out at 30,000 feet aiming for a distinctive bend on the Nile and from there to the IP for a timed run and descent to 8,000 feet and final run to the target. With the target identified in the light of the flares the TIs were dropped on the east and west hardstands of the airfield. As soon as the flares ignited the ground defences opened fire with continuous but ineffective anti-aircraft fire. Mike Heather was a Navigator on this mission: 'Strict R/T silence was maintained during start-up, taxi and take-off. We got airborne in WT369 at 1715 and set course. We crossed the Egyptian coast as it was getting dark and when we arrived over Cairo all the lights were still on. We had little difficulty in finding Almaza but in spite of this we went through the full procedure of dropping flares over the target and then into a shallow dive to place the TIs. The Egyptian AA gunners seemed to shoot at the flares rather than us so marking the target was easy, although by the time we had finished all the lights had been turned off.'

By 6 November the military campaign was progressing well, including airborne and seaborne landings, but the political situation was a mess and under American pressure a cease-fire was brought into force at 1700 GMT. The Bomber Command detachments had flown their final sorties the day before. Operations had lasted less than a week but it was Bomber Command's largest operational involvement since the end of the Second World War. The Canberras had flown seventy-two operational sorties from Malta and 206 from Cyprus, with the Valiants from Malta flying a further forty-nine sorties. The Canberras dropped 1,439 bombs, the standard Canberra load being four 1,000 lb bombs from Malta and six 1,000 lb bombs from Cyprus. It had not been a great success and the Bomber Command report stated that visual bombing standards were low because of lack of practice following prolonged grounding for aircraft modifications and a concentration of effort on flypasts and VIP visits! By December all but one squadron had returned to the UK.

CHAPTER THREE

Operational Groups

The RAF's command structure is organised into Commands, Groups, Wings and Squadrons. Within Bomber Command the Wing structure was rarely used, the main exception being within No. 1 Group's Battle squadrons. The main functional command organisation was the Group, each of which was responsible for a number of airfields and squadrons or other units. With the formation of Bomber Command in May 1936 a new series of Groups was created, the first three being Nos. 1, 2 and 3 Groups; as the Command continued to expand so new Groups were formed. During this period of rapid expansion various rationalisation schemes were put in place and eventually the decision was taken to concentrate a particular aircraft type within a single Group. This led to No. 1 Group (Battles), No. 2 Group (Blenheims), No. 3 Group (Wellingtons), No. 4 Group (Whitleys) and No. 5 Group (Hampdens), with No. 6 Group having a training role. It was rarely quite as clear cut as this, as a glance at the Orders of Battle will show.

As the war progressed this basic principle was maintained, although as a particular aircraft type came to dominate, the Wellington in the early years and the Lancaster in the later years, it was usual for more than one Group to operate the same type; indeed by the latter months of the war Bomber Command comprised almost solely Lancaster-equipped Groups. The politics between Groups and between the Groups and Bomber Command is touched on in the chapter on Bomber Command development.

With the decline of operational strength in 1945 the number of Groups was reduced and by the end of that year four Groups (5, 6, 8, and 100) had disbanded. It was a difficult period for the surviving Groups as they came to terms with peacetime routines – and lack of new aircraft. The disbandment of No. 4 Group in February 1945 left the Command with just two operational Groups and over the next 20 years these remained the RAF's main strategic force, at first with increasingly antiquated types but gradually re-equipping with jets (Canberras and V-bombers), plus a 'flirtation' with ballistic missiles, that put them at the forefront of the Cold War.

The end came in the late 1960s with the disbandment of No. 3 Group in 1967 and the decision to amalgamate Bomber Command and Strike Command.

No. 1 GROUP

Badge: A Panther's head erased sable.
Motto: Swift to Attack.
The Group badge was authorised in June 1941 and the selection of a Black Panther head reflected the fact that the Group used the callsign *Panther* in the early part of the Second World War.

No. 1 Group formed at Abingdon on 1 May 1936 with an initial establishment of three stations – Abingdon (four squadrons), Bircham Newton (four squadrons) and Upper

Heyford (two squadrons). All the squadrons were equipped with Hawker Hinds. By the end of 1938 strength had grown to seventeen squadrons equipped with either the Bristol Blenheim or Fairey Battle.

The ten Battle squadrons of the Advanced Air Striking Force (AASF) deployed to airfields in France on 2 September 1939 to support the British Expeditionary Force (BEF). The Battles were organised in five Wings and the AASF had its HQ at Rheims under the command of AVM Sir P. Playfair. Initial operations consisted of leaflet dropping and daylight reconnaissance as part of the 'Phoney War' of late 1939 and early 1940. When the Germans launched their offensive in May 1940 the Battles were committed to attacks on lines of communication, especially bridges. In the absence of fighter escort and facing heavy opposition in the air and on the ground they were literally shot out of the sky.

What was left of the squadrons was withdrawn to the UK in June 1940 and No. 1 Group was re-established with a Headquarters at Hucknall and a clutch of airfields in Lincolnshire and the Midlands. The obsolete light bombers gave way to Vickers Wellingtons and the Group was soon taking part in operations against targets in Germany and Occupied Europe as part of Main Force, Bomber Command. Four Polish bomber squadrons joined the Group (two in September 1940 and two in March 1941) to bring it up to eight operational squadrons, two each at Binbrook, Newton, Swinderby and Syerston. However, the Polish squadrons operated at reduced strength for some time and were amongst the last to convert from Wellingtons.

As part of a general reorganisation of Bomber Command the Group moved to a new HQ at Bawtry Hall on 20 July 1941. By the end of the year changes in the allocation of airfields meant that the Group was using Binbrook, Elsham Wolds, Snaith, Holme, Hemswell and Lindholme. The first Australian unit became operational in mid-1942, 460 Squadron taking up residence at Breighton.

No. 1 Group remained a Wellington-equipped Group into 1942 when a number of squadrons acquired Halifaxes, the first such unit being 103 Squadron in August. This however was short-lived with the decision to re-equip with Lancasters, the first of which had entered service with the Group by the end of the year.

The scale of operations, or at least the weight of bombs, continued to increase and whereas in early 1943 it was considered noteworthy that, 'The Group reached the record

Wellington of 12 Squadron at Binbrook.

Lancaster crews of 576 Squadron, Fiskerton, May 1945.

of 1,000 tons of bombs in one month.' In August it was noted that of the 5,000 tons of bombs that month 460 Squadron 'made 271 sorties and dropped 1,110 tons.'

Summer 1943 had brought other changes with Holme and Breighton being handed to No. 4 Group whilst 101 Squadron moved to Ludford Magna. Summer 1943 was an intensive period of operations with the Battle of the Ruhr giving way to the Battle of Hamburg.

Autumn 1943 brought another reorganisation of airfields with the establishment of the Base system, No. 12 Base (Binbrook) being the first within this Group, with its satellite stations at Grimsby and Kelstern. Although Lancasters had formed the backbone of the Group for some while, it was not until March 1944 that 300 Squadron flew its last Wellington operation. The same month saw the heavy losses of the Nuremburg attack on the night of 30/31 March, No. 1 Group alone losing twenty-one aircraft.

In May and June 1944 the Group was part of the heavy effort made against the German V-weapon sites. These Crossbow missions and attacks on targets in connection with the build-up to D-Day, and subsequent support of the ground offensive, occupied much of the Command's effort during the summer of 1944. On 3 May the military centre at Mailly-le-Camp was attacked and in bright moonlight the bombers were attacked by German fighters, the Group losing twenty-eight aircraft, a disastrous night. However, the following month brought another record bomb tonnage with 15,062 tons dropped – and the lowest loss rate (1.9 per cent) for almost two years.

June was also noteworthy for thirty-six operations being flown in twenty-two days, including daylight missions with fighter escort as part of the D-Day support. It had been a hectic and costly year and in the three months ending 15 December the Group's aircrew had been awarded 200 DFCs, sixty-two DFMs, five DSOs, thirteen bars to DFCs, and one CGM. A number of aircraft also achieved milestones. In January Lancaster M2 of

No. 1 Group Operations 1939–1945			
Aircraft	*Total sorties*	*Aircraft losses*	*% loss rate*
Battle	287	6	2.1
Wellington	12,170	395	3.2
Halifax	137	12	8.8
Lancaster	43,836	1,016	2.3
Total	56,430	1,429	

Note: Battle losses do not include the period with the AASF in France.

Lincoln of 44 Squadron at Wyton.

103 Squadron was taken off operations having achieved the remarkable total of 140 missions, including ninety-eight to Germany, fifteen of which were to Berlin. The pace of operations continued into 1945 but with an increased number of daylight missions as the German defences crumbled. By the end of the war the total weight of bombs and mines dropped by No. 1 Group was 238,356 tons – and 8,577 aircrew had lost their lives.

Post 1945

In the post-war period the Group remained part of Bomber Command and re-equipped with Lincolns, with which it saw operational service in Malaya 1950–1954. Jet bombers entered service in 1951 in the shape of the English Electric Canberra, the first to re-equip being 101 Squadron as part of the Binbrook Wing. Other Wings followed as No. 1 Group became the primary offensive force for the Command. As the Order of Battle for April 1953 shows, the Group's Canberra strength was increasing, with two main Wings complete, Binbrook and Hemswell but with Lincolns and Washingtons still in service

AVM P. H. Dunn takes the salute at an AOC's parade.

No. 1 Group Order of Battle, Aug 1939–Jan 1945

	Aug 39	Nov 40	Feb 42	Feb 43	Nov 43	Jan 45
Abingdon	15, 40, 52, 63	–	–	–	–	–
Benson	103, 150		–	–	–	–
Bicester	12, 142	–	–	–	–	–
Binbrook	-	12, 142	12	–	460	300, 460
Boscombe Down	88, 218	–	–	–	–	–
Breighton	–	–	460	460	–	–
Cranfield	35, 207	–	–	–	–	–
Elsham Wolds	–	–	103	103	103, 576	100, 103
Fiskerton	–	–	–	–	–	576
Grimsby	–	–	142	100	100, 550	–
Harwell	105, 226	–	–	–	–	–
Hemswell	–	–	300, 301	300, 301, 305	150, 170	
Holme	–	–	–	101	–	–
Hucknall	98	–	–	–	–	–
Ingham	–	–	–	199	–	–
Kelstern	–	–	–	–	625	625
Kirmington	–	–	–	166	166	166
Lindholme	–	–	304, 305	–	–	–
Ludford Magna	–	–	–	–	101	101
Newton	–	103, 150	–	–	–	–
N. Killingholme	–	–	–	–	–	550
Scampton	–	–	–	–	–	153
Snaith	–	–	150	–	–	–
Swinderby	–	300, 301	–	–	–	–
Syerston	–	304, 305	–	–	–	–
Wickenby	–	–	–	12	12, 626	12, 626

with other Wings – as were the Lancaster and the Mosquito. This situation changed over the next few years as the Canberra replaced most of the other types. The Group maintained its pre-eminent position throughout the rest of Bomber Command's period of existence, at the forefront of the nuclear capability with Vulcans and, for a short period of time, Thor missiles.

In November 1967 it had become the Command's sole Group, which spelled the death-knell for Bomber Command as it made no sense having a Command with only one Group. The inevitable happened when on 1 May 1968 Bomber Command was amalgamated with Fighter Command to form RAF Strike Command – taking No. 1 Group with it. The Group continued to operate as the main offensive force for its new Command, but that part of the story falls outside the scope of this book.

Air Officers Commanding No. 1 Group
Command from:

3 Sep 1939	AVM A. C. Wright
27 Jun 1940	A/C J. J. Breen
27 Nov 1940	AVM R. D. Oxland
24 Feb 1943	AVM E. A. B. Rice
5 Feb 1945	AVM R. S. Blucke
15 Jan 1947	AVM C. E. N. Guest CB CBE
24 Jan 1949	AVM G. H. Mills CB DFC
8 Aug 1950	AVM E. C. Huddlestone CB CBE

No. 1 Group Order of Battle, Post 1945

	Apr 1953		Apr 1962	
Bardney	–	–	106 Sqn	Thor SSM
Bassingbourn	231 OCU	Meteor, Canberra	231 OCU	Canberra
Breighton	–	–	240 Sqn	Thor SSM
Binbrook	9 Sqn	Canberra	–	–
	12 Sqn	Canberra	–	–
	50/103 Sqn	Canberra	–	–
	101 Sqn	Canberra	–	–
	617 Sqn	Canberra	–	–
Caister	–	–	269 Sqn	Thor SSM
Carnaby	–	–	150 Sqn	Thor SSM
Catfoss	–	–	226 Sqn	Thor SSM
Coleby Grange	–	–	142 Sqn	Thor SSM
Coningsby	–	–	9 Sqn	Vulcan
Driffield	–	–	98 Sqn	Thor SSM
Finningley	–	–	18 Sqn	Valiant, Canberra
	–	–	230 OCU	Vulcan
Full Sutton	–	–	102 Sqn	Thor SSM
Hemswell	83/150 Sqn	Lincoln	97 Sqn	Thor SSM
	97 Sqn	Lincoln	–	–
	105/109 Sqn	Canberra	–	–
	139 Sqn	Canberra	–	–
	199 Sqn	Lincoln, Mosquito	–	–
	JCF	Meteor, Canberra	–	–
Lindholme	–	–	CBS	Hastings, Varsity
Ludford Magna	–	–	104 Sqn	Thor SSM
Scampton	10 Sqn	Canberra	27 Sqn	Vulcan
	–	–	83 Sqn	Vulcan
	–	–	617 Sqn Vulcan	
Waddington	49/102 Sqn	Lincoln	44 Sqn	Vulcan
	61/44 Sqn	Lincoln	50 Sqn	Vulcan
	100 Sqn	Lincoln	101 Sqn Vulcan	

5 Apr 1951	AVM D. A. Boyle CB CBE AFC
27 Apr 1953	AVM J. R. Whitley CB CBE DSO AFC
3 Oct 1956	AVM G. A. Walker CBE DSO DFC AFC
14 Jun 1959	AVM J. G. Davis CB OBE
1 Dec 1961	AVM P. H. Dunn CB CBE
1 May 1964	AVM D. C. Stapleton CB CBE DFC AFC
1 Jun 1966	AVM M. H. Le Bas CBE DSO

No. 2 GROUP

Badge: Perched on a helmet an eagle wings elevated Sable.

Motto: *Vincimus* – We Will Conquer.

The helmet represents the army with which the Group, represented by the eagle, was closely connected. The badge was issued in May 1952.

No. 2 Group was formed on 20 March 1936 with a Headquarters at Abingdon but with a diverse collection of airfields, two of the earliest being Abbotsinch and Turnhouse, both in Scotland. The Group's squadrons were equipped with Hawker Hinds in the light day-bomber role. On 26 January 1937 the HQ moved to Andover, by which time Air Commodore S. J. Goble had become its Air Officer Commanding (AOC). In these early months of Bomber Command's existence there was much exchanging of airfields and squadrons (see the tables in the various Group entries) as well as a major re-equipment programme. The Hinds were being replaced by Fairey Battles, the first of which went to 63 Squadron at Upwood in May 1937. At the time this seemed an advanced aircraft, as indeed it was against some other service types, but within three years the crucible of war changed this view. Other Group units were receiving Bristol Blenheims (114 Squadron at Wyton being the first operator, March 1937) and one unit, 207 Squadron, was given the Vickers Wellesley although this was short-lived.

As war approached the Group was primarily equipped with Blenheims and as part of the mobilisation plan a number of squadrons were allocated to the 2nd Echelon of the Advanced Air Striking Force (AASF) to deploy to France 'when required'. This element comprised No. 79 Wing (Watton – 21 and 82 Squadrons), No. 81 Wing (West Raynham – 90 and 101 Squadrons), No. 82 Wing (Wyton – 114 and 139 Squadrons), No. 83 Wing (Wattisham – 107 and 110 Squadrons) and No. 70 Wing (Upper Heyford – 18 and 57 Squadrons).

On the first day of the war a lone Blenheim of 139 Squadron undertook a photographic reconnaissance of the German Fleet in the Schillig Roads – No. 2 Group's war had begun. The following day a Blenheim force was tasked to attack the same ships from low-level; of the ten Blenheims that made attacks five failed to return to base, including four out of five from 107 Squadron. News was subsequently received that two crew-members had survived and were prisoners – the RAF's first PoWs of the war.

Attempts were made to improve the armour plating of the Blenheim, along with its defensive armament, as it was realised just how vulnerable the aircraft were when attacking heavily-defended targets at low level; however, with the Blenheims specialising in low-level attacks the loss rate remained high. With the German attack in the West the Blenheims were thrown into the battle against the rapidly advancing enemy ground forces. Whilst the Battle squadrons of the AASF (from No. 1 Group) are usually remembered for the part they played in the attacks on the advancing German forces the Blenheims of No. 2 Group were also involved. Attacks on columns of troops, bridges and airfields became the routine and losses began to mount – on 12 May ten Blenheims from two squadrons were lost when attacking enemy columns. Operations intensified in support of the Allied evacuation from Dunkirk and the mistaken belief that the RAF played little part in this battle is one of the errors of history.

With France fallen and Britain next in line much of the bomber effort was expended in attacking concentrations of invasion barges and other related targets, the Blenheims daring low-level attacks proving particularly effective. In July, for example, the Blenheims were active on all but one day and flew 304 daylight sorties for the loss of eight aircraft. It is worth noting that the squadrons also participated in the night bombing offensive, the Bomber Command strategy at the time being to attack a wide range of targets each night. Photographic Reconnaissance (PR) sorties flown by Blenheims were equally hazardous but in the absence of other aircraft types this type of tasking remained important into late 1941 when specialist types such as PR Spitfires became available.

During 1941 there was an increasing emphasis on offensive operations. When fighter sweeps over Northern France failed to bring the *Luftwaffe* to battle it was decided to use the light and medium bombers to attack targets and force the German fighters to engage

– at which point the fighter escort would intervene. The theory behind these *Circus* operations was good but in practice the *Luftwaffe* tended to ignore the attacks. Nevertheless, this type of operation increased in importance and by 1942 was occupying a good percentage of the Group's sorties. However, anti-shipping work plus attacks on key installations in Occupied Europe by small formations of Blenheims remained the core activities of the Group and between March and October 1941 2,320 such sorties were flown – for the loss of 126 aircraft. All of these were day low-level missions and most were tasked against known targets rather than being free-ranging sweeps. Fighter escort was sometimes available but often the Blenheims went alone. It is estimated that 51 per cent of losses were to anti-aircraft fire from the ships and 18 per cent to enemy aircraft. Of the 456 ships attacked in this period, seventy-two were estimated as having been sunk and a further sixty-five seriously damaged.

Overall much of the work undertaken by the Group's aircraft was 'routine' but occasionally there was a more dramatic mission. One such was the attack on Bremen on 4 July 1941 when Wing Commander Hughie Edwards won a VC.

With the arrival of 90 Squadron's B-17 Fortresses the Group possessed a single 'heavy' squadron, although this was very much in the way of a trial of the American bomber. Sadly the performance proved disappointing and the RAF never adopted the aircraft as a Main Force bomber, although this decision was also in part due to American reluctance to supply such aircraft. The Group was also detaching squadrons to operate from Malta against shipping in the Mediterranean, as well as detachments to Scotland and Northern Ireland, also on anti-shipping work.

A new type of mission was introduced at the end of the year when six aircraft were tasked on 27/28 December for a night attack on the fighter airfield at Soesterberg in Holland. Intruder raids such as this in support of the night bombers were to become a standard Bomber Command tactic and became an increasing focus for No. 2 Group.

New aircraft
New aircraft types were introduced in 1942, the Blenheims having reached the end of their operational suitability; indeed there had been calls for some months for the Blenheims to be withdrawn as loss rates had remained prohibitive. The last Blenheim *op* in Bomber Command was flown on 17/18 August by aircraft of 18 Squadron, by which time a number of new aircraft, primarily American types, had joined the Group.

The first few weeks of the year saw little activity but on 12 February this lull was broken by the frenzy of the 'Channel Dash' when the RAF attempted to intercept three German capital ships, *Gneisenau*, *Scharnhorst*, and *Prinz Eugen* as they tried to move from Brest to safer points in Germany. Of significance to No. 2 Group was the first outing by ten of 88 Squadron's Douglas Bostons.

Mosquito IVs had replaced Blenheims with 105 Squadron in November 1941, this unit becoming the first Bomber Command squadron to operate this superlative aircraft. In what was in many ways a confirmation that the type of operation undertaken by the Group was not really part of the main activities of Bomber Command the May/June 1942 thousand-bomber raids saw the aircraft of No. 2 Group flying intruding and harassing raids in support of the main attacks.

The year continued to be busy both with operations and expansion/re-equipment. Two more aircraft types joined the Group; Lockeed Venturas entered service with 487 Squadron at Feltwell (August 1942) and North American B-25 Mitchells with 98 Squadron at West Raynham (September 1942). The first Ventura operation was 3 September 1942 with aircraft of 21 Squadron attacking Hengelo.

Blenheims of 82 Squadron at Watton, May 1940.

Special operations became a regular feature of the Group's monthly diary. These included small-scale *ops* such as that by four Mosquitoes of 105 Squadron against the Gestapo HQ in Oslo, to major raids such as the 6 December attack on the Philips works at Eindhoven. This latter was one of the classic missions of the Second World War in the courageous way in which the aircrew attacked this important and heavily-defended location – losing sixteen aircraft in the process but causing heavy damage. Overall loss rates in the Group had decreased by 1943 and at 2–3 per cent was now lower than that of the Main Force but there were exceptions. However, one of the last operations by the Group within Bomber Command ended in disaster and a VC for one of the pilots. On 3 May eleven Venturas of 487 Squadron attacked a power station near Amsterdam. They were bounced by fighters and nine were shot down, one limped home to England and one, piloted by Squadron Leader Trent carried on to the target but was shot down. The Squadron diary recorded, 'A very black day in the Squadron history ... a better set of boys could not be met in 30 years, everybody is feeling dazed by the news.'

With the nature of the Group's operations now including an increasing emphasis on support of ground forces, and with the Allies looking towards the invasion of Europe in 1944 the decision was taken to transfer the Group from Bomber Command to the new Tactical Air Force. The final sortie within Bomber Command was flown on 31 May when fifty-four aircraft attacked five different targets.

This change became effective at the end of May 1943, when the HQ moved to Dereham, and Bomber Command lost its light bomber force – albeit a new light bomber force was reborn the following year. The Group went on to have a distinguished wartime career as 2nd Tactical

No. 2 Group Operations 1939–1945			
Aircraft	*Total sorties*	*Aircraft losses*	*% loss rate*
Blenheim	11,311	421	3.7
Boston	1,215	41	3.4
Fortress	52	3	4.0
Mosquito	793	40	5.0
Ventura	868	31	3.6
Mitchell	221	6	2.7
Total	14,460	542	

No. 2 Group Order of Battle, Aug 1939–Feb 1943				
	Aug 39	*Nov 40*	*Feb 42*	*Feb 43*
Attlebridge	–	–	88	–
Bodney	–	–	82	–
Feltwell	–	–	–	464, 487
Foulsham	–	–	–	98, 180
Gt Massingham	–	–	107	107
Horsham St Faith	–	114, 139, 105	–	–
Marham	–	–	–	105, 139
Methwold	–	–	–	21
Oulton	–	–	–	88
Swanton Morley	–	105	88, 226	226
Upper Heyford	18, 57, 104, 108	–	–	–
Watton	21, 82	21, 82	21	–
Wattisham	107, 110	107, 110	18, 110	–
West Raynham	90, 101	18, 101	114	–
Wyton	114, 139	–	–	–

Air Force, and indeed into the post-war period but that part of its story is outside of the scope of this book.

Air Officers Commanding No. 2 Group
Command from:

1 Sep 1936	A/Cdr S. J. Goble (RAAF)
15 May 1938	AVM C. T. Maclean
17 Apr 1940	AVM J. M. Robb
12 Feb 1941	AVM D. F. Stevenson
17 Dec 1941	AVM A. Lees
29 Dec 1942	AVM J. H. D'Albiac to May 1943 (No. 2 Group transferred to Tactical Air Force)

No. 3 GROUP

Badge: Three Astral Crowns pierced by three swords.
Motto: *Niet Zonder Arbyt* (Dutch) – Nothing without Labour.
The badge comprises three 'astral crowns' and three swords. The crowns symbolise the first three Royal Abbesses of Ely, the three daughters of King Anna of Exning who gave his life fighting the pagan hordes. As the Group was located near Exning, with airfields around Ely, this seemed appropriate. The three swords denote the warlike activity of the Group. The motto is Old Dutch and was taken from the house of Cornelius Vermuyden, a Dutch engineer who reclaimed 40,000 acres of the fens around Ely. The Dutch motto was adopted to commemorate the fact that most of the Group's operations took its aircraft over Holland on their way to Germany, and also in gratitude for the help given to British aircrew who landed in that country.

No. 3 Group was formed at Andover on 1 May 1936, by the renaming of the old Western Area, although the following January it moved to Mildenhall to be nearer its clutch of operational airfields in East Anglia. In common with the other Groups of Bomber Command it was equipped with obsolete aircraft such as the Heyford, Overstrand and Virginia, all lumbering biplanes. In October 1938 the first Vickers Wellington entered service with 99 Squadron and by the outbreak of war the Group's re-equipment with the type was virtually complete. With ten squadrons at five airfields – Feltwell, Harwell, Honington, Marham and Mildenhall – the Group had a paper establishment of around 140 aircraft, although the Bomber Command return of 'aircraft available with crews' showed a daily average of seventy-seven aircraft with crews, this being average over the month.

With the decision to concentrate aircraft types within a single Group, No. 3 became the Wellington Group and as such became responsible for developing the tactical employment of the aircraft. The Wellington concept of operations was for daylight formation attacks, in the belief that the mutual firepower of the aircraft's turrets would be more than a match for enemy fighters. With a political constraint that attacks could only be made on targets at sea, the Wellingtons went in search of German shipping and although few attacks were made in 1939 the bombers suffered heavy losses. However, a series of daylight attacks on shipping in December revealed that the tactical doctrine was unworkable; in the 18 December attack German fighters claimed twelve out of the twenty-two Wellingtons. This led to a radical rethink of tactics and in 1940 the bombers were switched to night operations, the Wellingtons joining the Whitleys of No. 4 Group in dropping leaflets. However, from May 1940 the main task became attacks on German industry as Churchill had agreed to the bombing of land targets.

In the early months of the night war against targets in Germany and Occupied Europe, one of the major threats to the bombers came from the weather as German night defences had yet to develop. Stories of aircraft icing up and falling thousands of feet, or crews listening to ice thrown off the propellers and thumping against the sides of the aircraft, put into some perspective what it was like to fly these aircraft in the winter of 1940-41. For the rear gunner in his cold and isolated position at the back of the aircraft it must have been a strange world.

As part of Bomber Command's expansion plan the first of the four-engined bombers, the Short Stirling, entered service with No. 3 Group, with 7 Squadron receiving aircraft from August 1940. The Squadron re-formed at Leeming but moved to Oakington

Wellington of 101 Squadron at Bourn, 1942.

to join its operational Group and it was from there that the first operation was flown on 10/11 February 1941, when the target was oil storage tanks at Rotterdam. However, re-equipment with the type was slow and there were great difficulties not only in the production of the aircraft, but also in its operational performance. At one stage in mid-1941 only eight Stirlings were considered 'operationally fit', and continued problems with the Hercules II powered aircraft, with a service ceiling of only 10,000 feet, led to them being taken off operations. Whilst this problem lessened with the introduction of the Hercules X, the Stirling remained a cause for concern. In December 1942 the Group AOC wrote that he was, 'Lucky if the Group was able to raise thirty aircraft for an operation on a single night – even after a week of inactivity. The aircraft had made no worthwhile contribution to the bomber effort for some time'.

Throughout 1941 the Group had developed its tactics in the face of increased opposition, having flown thousands of sorties to targets throughout Europe, including Berlin, and lost hundreds of aircraft and crews. The Wellington was, without doubt, the mainstay of Bomber Command's offensive effort at this time, having re-equipped other Groups. Generally it performed very well – the nature of its construction meant that it was a very robust aircraft and there were numerous instances of aircraft returning with substantial parts of the airframe shot away or with the fabric covering burnt away. In July 1941, the Group's first VC was awarded to Sergeant Ward, a New Zealander with 75 Squadron. By the end of the war a further two VCs had been won by Group personnel, along with an impressive total of other gallantry awards.

The milestone attack mounted on Cologne on the night of 30/31 May 1942, saw No. 3 Group contribute 134 Wellingtons and 88 Stirlings to the great thousand bomber raid. This total of 222 aircraft was the highest for an operational Group but was exceeded by the 257 sent by No. 91 (OTU) Group.

Tactical developments to improve the accuracy of attacks and to reduce loss rates were introduced on a regular basis, often from suggestions made at Group level. Following trials in early 1942, a target marking concept was introduced whereby selected aircraft of No. 3 Group, equipped with the navigation aid *Gee*, would be first over the target area and would drop flares to mark the target for the main force of bombers. This Flare Force was the forerunner of the later Pathfinder Force and the *Shaker* technique was first used against Essen on the night of 8/9 March. However, results were poor as the

Stirling N6103 of 149 Squadron.

industrial haze over the Ruhr meant that despite the illumination from flares, the aiming point – the Krupps Works – could not be picked out.

When the specialist Pathfinder Force (PFF) was formed in August 1942 it was initially under the administrative control of No. 3 Group, although its squadrons had been provided by all the operational Groups in Bomber Command. It became an independent Group the following January.

No. 3 Group Operations 1939–1945			
Aircraft	Total sorties	Aircraft losses	% loss rate
Wellington	20,584	608	3.0
Stirling	15,895	577	3.6
Lancaster	26,462	380	1.4
Various types	3,672	103	2.8
Total	66,613	1,668	

The other major development for Bomber Command in 1942 was the introduction of the Avro Lancaster, though it was not until the following year that Lancasters joined No. 3 Group. With the Stirlings remaining operational despite growing concern over their loss rates, there was debate over the introduction of the Halifax, although the first two such units were both part of the Special Duties element within the Group. However, it was decided that No. 3 Group would become the focus for all Stirling operations and so the Halifaxes went to No. 4 Group instead. The February 1943 Group Order of Battle comprised seven Stirling squadrons and two Halifax squadrons, along with a single Wellington unit.

Main Force attacks during 1943 ranged far and wide over Germany, culminating at the end of the year in the 'Battle of Berlin', the first phase of which commenced on 18 November. This campaign, which comprised four phases, ran to March 1944 and by

No. 3 Group Order of Battle, August 1939–January 1945						
	Aug 39	Nov 40	Feb 42	Feb 43	Nov 43	Jan 45
Alconbury	–	–	156	–	–	–
Bourn	–	–	101	15	–	–
Chedburgh	–	–	–	214	214, 620	218
Downham Market	–	–	–	218	218, 623	–
East Wretham	–	–	311	115	–	–
Feltwell	37, 214	75	57, 75	–	–	–
Gransden Lodge	–	–	–	192	–	–
Harwell	75, 148	–	–	–	–	–
Honington	9, 215	9, 311	9, 214	–	–	–
Lakenheath	–	–	–	149	149, 199	–
Little Snoring	–	–	–	–	115	–
Marham	38, 115	115	115, 218	–	–	–
Mepal	–	–	–	–	75	75
Methwold	–	–	–	–	–	149
Mildenhall	99, 149	99, 149	149, 419	15, 622	–	15, 622
Newmarket	–	–	–	75	–	–
Oakington	–	7, 218	7	–	–	–
Ridgewell	–	–	–	90	–	–
Stradishall	–	214	214	–	–	186
Tempsford	–	–	–	138, 161	138, 161	
Tuddenham	–	–	–	–	–	90
Waterbeach	–	–	–	–	–	514
Witchford	–	–	–	–	196	115
Wratting Common	–	–	–	–	90	195
Wyton	–	15, 40, 57	15	–	–	–

the time it ended, the Command had flown over 9,000 sorties for the loss of 501 aircraft. The Stirlings of No. 3 Group operated on only one night in November – and lost five of the fifty aircraft. With the exception of special duties operations the Stirling was effectively withdrawn from Bomber Command's Main Force. Until enough Lancasters became available to re-equip the Group it was essentially 'relegated' to second-line tasks, although the three existing Lancaster units continued to participate in Main Force attacks. By spring 1944 most squadrons had converted to Lancasters and the Group was back as a fully active part of Bomber Command, just in time to take part in operations connected with D-Day and the anti V-weapon campaign.

Over the winter of 1944/45 all the Command's Groups were involved in a concerted offensive against industrial cities, especially in the Ruhr, including daylight operations. In March 1945 the Group despatched a record 2,791 sorties. During Operation *Manna*, the dropping of food supplies to the Dutch population, the Group flew ninety-four sorties on 29 April – with some trepidation on the part of the aircrew as to whether the German truce would be adhered to.

AVM Smallwood, AOC No. 3 Group from 28 November 1965.

Post 1945

In the immediate post-war period the Avro Lincoln replaced the Lancaster and in 1950 the Group was chosen to operate the B-29 Washington, with 115 Squadron at Marham being the first unit to re-equip. By April 1953 two Washington Wings were operational, Coningsby and Marham. The Group was also responsible for strategic reconnaissance, with Wyton becoming the centre of this activity. Offensive power was increased with the arrival Valiants and Victors, along with Thor missiles from 1958 to 1963. The Group was eventually disbanded on 31 October 1967, when it was amalgamated with No. 1 Group.

207 Squadron pose with Valiant and trophy, June 1960.

Air Officers Commanding No. 3 Group
Command from:

29 Aug 1939	AVM J. E. A. Baldwin
14 Sep 1942	AVM R. A. Cochrane
27 Feb 1943	AVM R. Harrison
9 Jul 1946	AVM R. M. Foster
14 Dec 1948	AVM A. Hesketh
15 Sep 1951	AVM W. A. D. Brook
1 Sep 1953	AVM E. C. Hudlestone
2 Feb 1956	AVM K. B. B. Cross
4 May 1959	AVM M. H. Dwyer
9 Oct 1961	AVM B. K. Burnett
5 Aug 1964	AVM D. F. Spotswood
28 Nov 1965	AVM D. G. Smallwood
15 Feb 1967	Air Cdre J. T. Lawrence

No. 3 Group Order of Battle, Post 1945

	Apr 1953		Apr 1962	
Coningsby	5/21 Sqn	Washington	–	–
	149 Sqn	Washington	–	–
	57/104 Sqn	Washington	–	–
	44/55 Sqn	Canberra	–	–
Cottesmore	–	–	10 Sqn	Victor
	–	–	15 Sqn	Victor
Feltwell	–	–	77 Sqn	Thor SSM
Folkingham	–	–	223 Sqn	Thor SSM
Gaydon	–	–	232 OCU	Valiant, Canberra
Harrington	–	–	218 Sqn	Thor SSM
Honington	–	–	55 Sqn	Victor
	–	–	57 Sqn	Victor
	–	–	90 Sqn	Valiant
Marham	35 Sqn	Washington	49 Sqn	Valiant
	90 Sqn	Washington	148 Sqn	Valiant
	115/218 Sqn	Washington	207 Sqn	Valiant
	207 Sqn	Washington	214 Sqn	Valiant
Melton Mowbray	–	–	254 Sqn	Thor SSM
Mepal	–	–	113 Sqn	Thor SSM
North Luffenham	–	–	144 Sqn	Thor SSM
North Pickenham	–	–	220 Sqn	Thor SSM
Polebrook	–	–	130 Sqn	Thor SSM
Shepherds Grove	–	–	82 Sqn	Thor SSM
Tuddenham	–	–	107 Sqn	Thor SSM
Upwood	7/76 Sqn	Lincoln	–	–
	148 Sqn	Lincoln	–	–
	214 Sqn	Lincoln	–	–
Wittering	–	–	7 Sqn	Valiant
	–	–	138 Sqn	Valiant
	–	–	139 Sqn	Victor
Wyton	58 Sqn	Mosquito	58 Sqn	Canberra
	82 Sqn	Lancaster	543 Sqn	Valiant
	540 Sqn	Canberra	–	–

No. 4 GROUP

Formed: 1 April 1937.
Disbanded: 7 May 1945 to Transport Command.
Badge: No official badge awarded: the badge shown here is not official.

No. 4 Group was formed on 1 April 1937, with its HQ at Mildenhall, as part of the new Bomber Command organisation. It was designated for night bombing and its equipment types included Wellesleys and Hendons.

At the outbreak of war the Group comprised eight squadrons of Whitleys in pairs at four airfields, the HQ being at Linton-on-Ouse. During the course of the war, and in common with most other Groups, various re-organisations took place, and all but two of its pre-war airfields (Driffield and Leconfield) changed hands.

The Group's first operational mission was flown on the night of 3 September when ten Whitleys took off to drop leaflets over the Ruhr, Hamburg and Bremen. These nocturnal forays on leaflet dropping, or *nickelling* as it was known, were the bread-and-butter operations of the Group for the first nine months of the war. During this period the Group also flew anti-shipping sorties and reconnaissance, though leaflet-dropping was what it specialised in. Over this first winter of the war, the experiences of the Whitleys were to prove invaluable for Bomber Command as it struggled to find a new tactical doctrine to replace daylight formation attacks. With low loss rates on night operations, and most of those due to weather or navigation error, the concept of night bombing was developed – along with the need for improved training in night operations and navigation.

On 19 March 1940, the seaplane base at Hornum was bombed by aircraft from four of the Group's squadrons – the first attack on a land target in Germany, although this was seen as a retaliation attack. With bombing of German targets authorised from May 1940, the experiences gained on the night leaflet missions were now used in anger as

Whitley of 10 Squadron at Leeming 1941; No. 4 Group pioneered Bomber Command night operations (Peter Green Collection).

The later Halifax variants were on a par with the Lancaster in terms of general performance.

the Whitleys were tasked to attack industrial targets in the Ruhr. In August and September Berlin was attacked eight times, although the effort was small compared to what was to come a few years later. For each of these attacks the Group could muster no more than twelve aircraft. Re-equipment with the Halifax began towards the end of 1940, with 35 Squadron being the first such unit. The Squadron flew its first operation, to Le Havre, on the night of 10/11 March 1941. Over the next 12 months more squadrons in the Group exchanged Whitleys for Halifaxes but it was a slow process and there were problems with the Handley Page 'heavy'. By February 1942 only three squadrons had been fully converted, with two others operating as joint Halifax/Whitley units. The Group also had two squadrons with Wellingtons. A year later, the Whitleys had all but gone but there were four Wellington squadrons. It was not until mid-1943 that the Group was completely equipped with Halifaxes, a type it retained to the end of the war. Nevertheless, the Halifax had provided the major operational contribution since mid-1942.

For the first thousand bomber raid (Cologne, 30 May 1942) the Group contributed 147 aircraft, of which 131 were Halifaxes – three of these failed to return. From this point onwards, the offensive grew in scale and effect – as well as losses.

Creation of the Canadian No. 6 Group in Yorkshire meant a loss of airfields as a general reshuffle took place, No. 4 Group concentrating in the southern and eastern parts of North Yorkshire. However, new airfields were becoming available, and by late 1943 the Group was established at the airfields at which it would remain for the last two years of the war.

In April 1944, the Group acquired two French-manned bomber squadrons, 346 and 347 at Elvington. By late summer, the Station was almost entirely French and had a French CO, a unique arrangement within Bomber Command.

Support for the D-Day landings occupied much of the Group's effort in the weeks either side of 6 June, as it did the rest of the Command. The Halifax was an adaptable aircraft and in one critical week of the Allied advance towards Arnhem, the Group's aircraft were used to transport 432,840 gallons of much-needed petrol from the UK to Brussels. However, from autumn 1944, Bomber Command was released to what it considered to be its primary task, the destruction of German industry. The primary targets were oil and

No. 4 Group Operations 1939–1945			
Aircraft	*Total sorties*	*Aircraft losses*	*% loss rate*
Whitley	9,169	288	3.1
Wellington	2,901	97	3.3
Halifax	45,337	1,124	2.5
Total	57,407	1,509	

No. 4 Group Order of Battle, August 1939–January 1945

	Aug 39	*Nov 40*	*Feb 42*	*Feb 43*	*Nov 43*	*Jan 45*
Andover	–	–	51	–	–	–
Breighton	–	–	–	–	78	78
Burn	–	–	–	431	578	578
Croft	–	–	78	–	–	–
Dalton	–	–	102	–	–	–
Dishforth	10, 78	51, 78	–	–	–	–
Driffield	77, 102	C&M	158	–	–	466
East Moor	–	–	–	429	–	–
Elvington	–	–	–	77	77	346, 347
Foulsham	–	–	–	–	–	462
Full Sutton	–	–	–	–	–	77
Holme	–	–	–	–	76	76
Leconfield	97, 166	–	–	196, 466	466, 640	640
Leeming	–	10, 35	10, 77	–	–	–
Linton-on-Ouse	51, 58	58, 102	35, 58	76, 78	–	–
Lisset	–	–	–	–	158	158
Melbourne	–	–	–	10	10	10
Middleton	–	–	76	–	–	–
Newmarket	–	–	138	–	–	–
Pocklington	–	–	405	102	102	102
Rufforth	–	–	–	158	–	–
Snaith	–	–	–	51	51	51
Topcliffe	–	77	–	–	–	–

transportation and over the next few months the destruction of these vital assets played a major part in the final collapse of the German military, especially the *Luftwaffe*.

During the final months of the war the Lancaster arrived in the Group and squadrons began to re-equip, though it had been the Whitley and Halifax with which No. 4 Group had fought its war. By early 1945 thoughts had turned to the post-war requirements and it was decided that the Group would adopt a transport role. On 7 May the organisation was redesignated as No. 4 (Transport) Group and was transferred to Transport Command.

Air Officers Commanding No. 4 Group
Command from:

3 Jul 1939	AVM A. Coningham
26 Jul 1941	AVM C. R. Carr
12 Feb 1945	AVM J. R. Whitley

No 5 GROUP

Badge: A Lion rampant Azure.
Motto: Undaunted.
The blue Lion facing left in an attacking pose is symbolic of the qualities to which the Group aspired.

'No. 5 Group not only contributed to the general heavy bomber offensive but was responsible for many of the most dramatic and specialised attacks of the war.' These words are contained in a summary of the Group's activities written in May 1945 but even accepting some bias the basic point being made is accurate – in the latter years of the war the Group was to all intents and purposes 'independent' within Bomber Command.

The Group was formed on 1 September 1937 out of No. 3 Group and had its first HQ at St Vincents, Grantham and prior to its take-over of its initial clutch of airfields it remained affiliated to this Group. The first four Stations allocated were Hemswell, Waddington, Grantham and Scampton – only one of these was still operational with the Group at the end of the Second World War.

On the outbreak of war the Group comprised ten Hampden squadrons at five stations (Cottesmore, Finningley, Hemswell, Scampton and Waddington). The Group ended the war with eighteen Lancaster squadrons and was able to field a force of around 400 bombers – a massive increase in numbers, bomb lift and capability from September 1939. Later the same month AVM Arthur Harris assumed command of No. 5 Group, a post he held until November 1940. This was the second operational bomber Group he commanded and his time here helped frame a number of his later ideas of bomber employment. For the first six months of the war the Group's Hampdens were engaged on anti-shipping sweeps over the North Sea, security patrols and leaflet dropping. Most of the latter were over Germany and in a typical 'raid' two Hamdpens dropped 324,000 leaflets on Hamburg and Bremen.

The first bombs dropped on an enemy land target fell on the island of Sylt on the night of 19 March 1940, a small force of Hampdens and Whitleys dropped bombs and incendiaries as a 'reprisal' for German bombs that had fallen on Orkney. Losses had been light during the first winter of the war but with the German invasion of Denmark and Norway in April 1940 the pace of operations for the bomber units was increased – as were the risks. Anti-shipping remained a major task and one such mission five Hampdens

The Hampden was the Group's operational type well into 1942 and flew almost 16,000 sorties; bombing-up Hampden of 49 Squadron.

Hampden crew of 50 Squadron; the Squadron flew 2,300 Hampden sorties for the loss of 57 aircraft.

from Waddington were tasked to attack shipping in Kristiansand Harbour; only one aircraft returned to base and that was due to the actions of the WOP, Corporal Wallace who shot down two of the attacking fighters. He removed the forward-firing gun and used it from the beam position, for his initiative and courage he was awarded a DFM for his actions, the first such award to an NCO in No. 5 Group.

With the start of the Strategic Bombing Offensive in May 1940 the Hampdens joined the nightly attacks on targets in Germany, as well as taking an increasing part in the naval war by dropping mines in sea lanes and harbour entrances. The variety of target types increased when bombers were sent to attack the ports in which the German invasion barges were gathering. At the same time communications targets, such as canals and railway yards, attracted the attention of the planners.

On the night of 12/13 August Flight Lieutenant Learoyd of 49 Squadron was awarded the Victoria Cross for his attack on the Dortmund–Ems canal, the first VC to this Group.

In November 1940 the first Manchesters entered service with 207 Squadron at Waddington but it was not to be a happy association despite the initial promise of the type. Nevertheless the overall growth of the Group's offensive power continued and by spring 1941 it was able to launch 100 bombers on each major mission.

On 3 March 1942 the first operational sortie by the Avro Lancasters of 44 Squadron took place, a date of major significance to No. 5 Group and Bomber Command. This first mission was by four aircraft on minelaying in the Heligoland Bight. On the same night other aircraft of the Group undertook one of the Command's most successful and accurate attacks to date when they caused heavy destruction to the Renault works at Billancourt, Paris.

Pinpoint attacks
However, the most sensational raid took place on 17 April when twelve Lancasters made a daring daylight attack on the MAN diesel engine factory at Augsburg. Only five of

the twelve Lancasters returned but in some respects this daring raid set a tone of determination that became a hallmark of the Group on many other occasions.

Main Force attacks were the primary task of all the bomber Groups and the Lincolnshire airfields of No. 5 Group were kept busy with the nightly offensive over Germany. The Group contributed 162 aircraft to the first of the 1,000 bomber raids, comprising seventy-three Lancasters, forty-six Manchesters and thirty-four Hampdens. It was during this raid that Flying Officer Leslie Manser of 50 Squadron won the Victoria Cross.

By September the Group was recording monthly bomb tonnages of 2,000 tons. The following month saw three more dramatic raids. The daylight attack on the Schneider works at Le Creusot on 17 October followed by two attacks on targets in Italy: Genoa on the night of 22/23 October and Milan by day on 24

The charismatic AOC of No. 5 Group during the latter years of the war, Ralph Cochrane.

October. All three missions were flown by Lancaster-only formations. Although the Group continued its role as part of Main Force, Bomber Command it was developing a reputation for skill and determination, and the arrival of Ralph Cochrane as AOC in February 1943 brought a dynamic and effective 'bomber leader' to the helm.

In the early hours of 17 May 1943 the Lancasters of 617 Squadron succeeded in breaching two dams and an RAF legend was born: Guy Gibson's Dambusters squadron. This squadron, later joined by 9 Squadron, flew specialist missions often using very heavy special bombs, culminating in the 22,000 lb Grand Slam.

The potential of the Lancaster meant that the Group could undertake attacks that were impossible for the other 'heavies'. The 'shuttle raid' that attacked the Zeppelin

Lancasters of 106 Squadron were based at Metheringham as part of No. 5 Group.

works at Friedrichshafen and then flew on to North Africa is a case in point. Targets such as this had previously been out of range of Allied bombers.

By early 1944 the Group had proven its abilities and from April it was officially recognised that it should be used as a separate force whenever this seemed appropriate. The first significant attack using this new policy took place on 22/23 April when Brunswick was attacked by 235 aircraft of No. 5 Group, although for protection they were accompanied by ten ABC Lancasters from No 1 Group. This decision was in part due to the views of the AOC, who had been unhappy with the employment of the Pathfinder Force. For some time the Group had been developing its own techniques – in large measure prompted and led by distinguished bomber figures such as Guy Gibson and Leonard Cheshire. No. 5 Group had been the first of the all-Lancaster Groups and as such had developed the tactical employment of the type on both special and Main Force operations. Harris later summed up the situation as it stood in mid 1944: 'No. 5 Group operated largely as an independent unit and developed its own techniques, including the original Master Bomber concept, also offset skymarking continued to be developed e.g. '5 Group Newhaven' using offset techniques 1,000–2,000 yards from the aiming point, any error in the Red TIs being cancelled by yellows from the Master Bomber. Two squadrons, 83 and 97, were allocated for pathfinder work having

No. 5 Group Operations 1939–1945

Aircraft	Total sorties	Aircraft losses	% loss rate
Hampden	15,771	417	2.6
Manchester	1,185	69	5.8
Lancaster	52,262	1,389	2.7
Mosquito	1,133	13	1.1
Total	70,351	1,888	

No. 5 Group Order of Battle, Aug 1939-Jan 1945

	Aug 39	Nov 40	Feb 42	Feb 43	Nov 43	Jan 45
Balderton	–	–	408	–	–	–
Bardney	–	–	–	–	9	9, 227
Bottesford	–	–	207	467	–	–
Coningsby	–	–	97, 106	–	–	83, 97
Cottesmore	106, 185	–	–	–	–	–
Doncaster	–	271	–	–	–	–
Dunholme Lodge	–	–	–	–	44	–
East Kirkby	–	–	–	–	630	57, 630
Finningley	7, 76	106	–	–	–	–
Fiskerton	–	–	–	49	49	–
Fulbeck	–	–	–	–	–	49, 189
Hemswell	61, 144	61, 144	–	–	–	–
Langar	–	–	–	207	207	–
Lindholme	–	50	–	–	–	–
Metheringham	–	–	–	–	–	106
N. Luffenham	–	–	144	–	–	–
Scampton	49, 83	49, 83	49, 83	57	57	–
Skellingthorpe	–	–	50, 455	50	50, 61	50, 61
Spilsby	–	–	–	–	–	44, 207
Strubby	–	–	–	–	–	619
Syerston	–	–	–	61, 106	106	–
Waddington	44, 50	44, 207	44, 420	9, 44	463, 467	463, 467
Woodhall Spa	–	–	–	97	619	627
Woolfax Lodge	–	–	61	–	–	

been transferred from the PFF in April, and these two units also received other modifications, such as the *Carpet Jammer*, approved for the PFF.

D-Day preparation and support occupied much of the period from April to August 1944 but the naval war was not forgotten and the Group's Lancasters attacked German warships, such as the *Tirpitz*, and key points such as ship canals. The *Tirpitz* was eventually sunk by the two specialist squadrons, 9 and 617. It was not only the Lancasters that undertook daring roles, one of the most dramatic was flown by Mosquitoes to attack, with pinpoint accuracy, the Gestapo HQ in Oslo.

In the remaining months of the war the Lancasters of No. 5 Group attacked a wide range of targets throughout Germany and in support of the advancing ground forces, invariably independent organisation from Main Force.

A number of the Group's squadrons were earmarked for Tiger Force and training and preparation for a move to the Far East began in late spring 1945, although the deployment was subsequently cancelled. At the end of the war in Europe, and in common with most units of Bomber Command, the Group flew hundreds of sorties bringing back Allied prisoners. However, the Group also undertook a number of interesting weapon trials.

Despite its fine wartime record No. 5 Group was one of those chosen to disband as Bomber Command's strength was reduced, the axe falling on 15 December 1945.

Air Officers Commanding No. 5 Group
Command from:

11 Sep 1939	AVM A. T. Harris
22 Nov 1940	AVM N. H. Bottomley
12 May 1941	AVM J. C. Slessor
25 Apr 1942	AVM W. A. Coryton
28 Feb 1943	AVM R. A. Cochrane
16 Jan 1945	AVM H. A. Constantine

No. 6 (RCAF) GROUP

Formed: 1 January 1939.
Disbanded: 17 July 1945.
Badge: In front of a York rose a Maple Leaf proper.
Motto: *Sollertia et Ingenium* (Latin) – Initiative and Skill.
An autumnal Maple leaf, the symbol of Canada, superimposed on the white rose of York, the symbol of Yorkshire, to show the association of the Canadian Group with Yorkshire.

No. 6 (Bomber) Group was not originally a Canadian Group, having formed on 1 January 1939 with its HQ at Norwich. With the outbreak of war the Group took on the administrative control of the Group Pool (training) squadrons within the other operational Groups. This was very much an *ad hoc* arrangement as the Bomber Command training organisation evolved.

The Group was renumbered on 11 May 1942 becoming No. 91 (Operational Training) Group. However, on 25 October the same year No. 6 Group was reborn as the operational Group for the Royal Canadian Air Force bomber squadrons, with its Headquarters at Linton-on-Ouse. This latter was a temporary arrangement and the HQ had moved to its permanent location at Allerton Park, near Knaresborough by

1 December. This '75-room Victorian castle' had been requisitioned from Lord Mowbray and a collection of Nissen huts soon sprang up in its grounds.

The creation of this Group was part of an agreement with Commonwealth and Dominion governments, especially Canada and Australia, to group their nationals into squadrons rather than divide them up amongst the RAF units. Whilst the Australians were formed into a number of Australian squadrons, in the 400 series of RAF numbering, there were not enough squadrons to form a distinctive Group, whereas in the case of the Canadians the numbers were far larger. Of equal significance was the fact that the costs of No. 6 (RCAF) Group were borne by the Canadian Government. However, they would still fall under the overall operational control of HQ Bomber Command. The Group was given operational status on 1 January 1943 and its squadrons were based at six airfields – Croft, Dalton, Dishforth, Leeming, Middleton St George and Skipton-on-Swale. There were eight operational squadrons at this time, equipped with Wellingtons or Halifaxes. The first mission as part of No 6 Group was flown on the night of 3/4 January 1943 when six Wellingtons of 427 Squadron, from Croft, dropped mines off the Frisian Isles. The first true bombing raid was to Lorient on 14 January.

The airfield situation remained fairly stable as the main period of Bomber Command reorganisation was over; however, new airfields were added as the Group continued to expand. This was in part a reflection of the adoption of the Base system,

Lancaster DS778 of 408 Squadron.

and amongst the gains made by the Canadians were newly built airfields such as Wombleton, used primarily by No. 1666 HCU, and well-established airfields such as Linton-on-Ouse.

In addition to the operational bases the Group controlled its own training and four airfields became No. 61 Base, the main training unit being No. 1659 HCU This situation changed in November 1944 when the training element was absorbed by the RAF Training Group and became No. 76 Base, although this was effectively only an admin move and the Canadian connection in terms of personnel was maintained. Three new squadrons were formed in the Group during 1943 and as the Group's strength stabilised it was reorganised into three operational Bases: No. 62 (Beaver) Base – Linton-on-Ouse, No. 63 Base – Leeming and No. 64 Base – Middleton St George.

No. 6 (RCAF) Group Operations 1939–1945

Aircraft	Total sorties	Aircraft losses	% loss rate
Wellington	3,287	127	3.9
Halifax	28,126	508	1.8
Lancaster	8,171	149	1.8
Total	39,584	784	

No. 6 (RCAF) Group Order of Battle, Feb 1943–Jan 1945

	Feb 43	Nov 43	Jan 45
Beaulieu	405	–	–
Croft	427	–	431, 434
Dalton	428	–	–
Dishforth	425, 426	–	–
East Moor	–	–	415, 432
Leeming	408	427, 429	427, 429
Linton-on-Ouse	–	408, 426	408, 426
Middleton	419, 420	419, 428	419, 428
Skipton-on-Swale	–	424, 432, 433	424, 433
Tholthorpe	–	420, 425, 434	420, 425
Topcliffe	424	–	–

Halifax specialists

However, from May to November 1943 three squadrons had been detached from the Group to serve in North Africa as No. 331 Medium Bomber Wing. The Halifax gradually replaced the Wellington but a number of units also received Lancasters. The decision was taken to make No. 6 Group an all-Halifax command and so the Lancasters were transferred out. Throughout 1944 the Canadians participated in Main Force attacks throughout Europe, the later marks of Halifax proving as operationally effective in the hands of their Canadian crews as the much vaunted Lancaster.

The final bombing mission by No. 6 (RCAF) Group was to Wangarooge on 25 April. However, the Group's war planning did not come to an end with victory in Europe and eight squadrons were earmarked to train as part of Tiger Force, the massive reinforcement planned for the war against Japan. Training and reorganisation for this took place from mid-May and on 17 July 1945 the Group was transferred to the RCAF. In the event Tiger Force did not need to deploy as the atom bomb attacks on Japan brought the Second World War to an end. The Canadian contribution to the RAF's war effort was enormous and it is fitting that one operational Group carried the RCAF banner for much of the campaign. The connection made between the Canadians and Yorkshire survived into the post war years and it will be a shame if with the passing of generations this is lost.

Air Officers Commanding No. 6 (RCAF) Group
Command from:

25 Oct 1942	AVM G. E. Brookes
29 Feb 1944	AVM C. M. McEwen

No. 8 (Pathfinder) GROUP

Formed: 15 August 1942.

Disbanded: 15 December 1945.

Badge: A Mullet of eight points Azure surmounted by an Arrow Or enflamed proper point downwards in bend sinister.

Motto: We Guide to Strike.

The long and complex heraldic description means a blue eight-pointed star with a gold flaming arrow zooming across it from left to right, with point down to the left. The eight points represent No. 8 Group and the astro-navigation used by its navigators whilst the flaming arrow symbolises the Group's Pathfinder role.

By the middle of 1941 it had become obvious that Bomber Command's inability to find its night targets meant that the strategic bombing offensive was having limited effect. Amongst the debates that came from this realisation was the creation of a specialist 'target finding' force that could lead the bombers to the targets. Some bomber leaders such as Group Captain S. Bufton, ex bomber squadron and Station CO and latterly Deputy Director of Bomber Operations, were great supporters of such a force – others, including Harris, were less keen. In the latter's view it was better to have such a specialist force within each Group rather than rob the best crews from each Group. However, in April 1942 the Air Staff decided in favour of creating a target finding force and instructed Harris that this should be done as soon as possible. Despite his opposition to the idea his choice of leader for the new organisation was inspired. Wing Commander Don Bennett was an experienced pilot and aviation pioneer with exceptional navigational skills.

The Pathfinder Force (PFF) was formed on 15 August 1942, under the command of the newly-promoted Group Captain D. C. T. Bennett. At this time it was under the administrative control of No. 3 Group, although its squadrons had been provided from across the operational groups of Bomber Command. The PFF's HQ was at Wyton, and operational squadrons were based at Graveley, Oakington and Warboys. Founder squadrons of the Pathfinder Force were 7 Squadron (No. 3 Group), 35 Squadron (No. 4 Group), 83 Squadron (No. 5 Group), 109 Squadron (Wireless Intelligence Development Unit) and 156 Squadron (No. 1 Group). The initial problem lay in persuading Group commanders to release their best crews, and in the early days a number of crews were returned as not being up to the required standard.

All applicants for the PFF were volunteers and had to have been assessed as above

average in their specific trade, although in practice Captains tended to take their crews with them. Tour length was set at fifty operations and as the PFF aircraft were always first over the target the risks were even greater than for Main Force crews. A PFF badge, an eagle, was awarded to aircrew once they were signed off as proficient and this helped develop the elite nature of the new force. It had been agreed from the start that the aircraft of No. 8 Group would be equipped with the latest navigational aids. However, in the early months no such equipment was available and the PFF concentrated on training and the development of tactics. An important tactical element was the introduction of Target Indicators (TI), the first of which were improvised from 250 lb and 4,000 lb bombs. These were filled with an incendiary charge of benzole, rubber and phosphorous, the idea being for the TI to provide a distinctive and visible aiming point for the main force of bombers. The first successful attack led by the Group, using 'Red Blob Fires', was to Nuremberg on 28/29 August and by the end of the month, 175 sorties had been flown for the loss of sixteen aircraft.

Tactics continued to develop with the use of flares and sky or ground markers. Different tactical combinations were employed depending on the conditions and type of target. In general terms the basic tactic involved a wave of illuminators dropping flares, followed by a wave of primary visual markers dropping coloured flares or TIs. Next came the 'backers up' to drop incendiaries on the coloured TIs in order to start a fire that the Main Force could bomb on. This basic technique, with variations on flare and TI type, remained in use for the rest of the war, with the subsequent addition the following August of the Master Bomber concept. By the end of 1942, the Pathfinders had flown 1,091 sorties for the loss of fifty aircraft.

AVM Don Bennett.

The PFF became No. 8 (PFF) Group on 13 January 1943 and Don Bennett, now an Air Commodore, remained its commander. With the introduction of *Oboe*-equipped Mosquitoes, the accuracy of navigation and target-finding increased and as the value of the PFF was recognised by the Group commanders there was less resistance to releasing the 'best crews'. Three significant developments took place in January. The PFF led a raid to Berlin on 16/17 January using the first purpose-designed TIs, and despite haze cover the glow from the TIs was strong enough to permit bombing. On 27/28 January the first *Oboe* ground marking took place at Dusseldorf, with 109 Squadron's Mosquitoes leading the attack. Three nights later H2S radar was used for the first time by the PFF and the route to the target was marked with red and green flares.

In June 1943, the Group gained two Mosquito squadrons, 105 and 139 Squadrons, from No. 2 Group, one of which joined the marker force while the other became part of the Light Night-Strike Force (LNSF).

The vital attack on the research installation at Peenemunde on 17 August 1943, involved two 'firsts' – the use of Red Spot Fires and the Master Bomber. The former was one of a number of new markers whilst the latter was a tactical development of great significance. It is worth noting that the German night fighters were also developing, and August saw the introduction of the *schrage musik* cannon system which subsequently claimed many Allied bombers. The Germans increasingly used decoy flares, TIs and ground fires and it was estimated that in October 1943 up to 30 per cent of the bomb effort was diverted by such decoys. This made the role of the Master Bomber even more crucial as it was his task to direct the bombers to the correct target and aiming point and to adjust either the marking or the bombing effort as required. It was without doubt the single most dangerous role in Bomber Command.

No. 8 Group continued to expand, acquiring new squadrons and airfields throughout 1943 and early 1944. There was a continued revision of techniques and new equipment entered service. Bennett was against letting Main Force squadrons have specialist equipment such as H2S as he feared they would misuse it, but by mid-1944 some Group

No. 8 (PFF) Group Operations 1942–1945

Aircraft	Total sorties	Aircraft losses	% loss rate
Wellington	305	17	5.6
Halifax	2,106	77	3.7
Stirling	826	37	4.5
Lancaster	19,601	444	2.3
Total	22,838	575	

Note: Mosquito statistics not available.

No. 8 (PFF) Group Order of Battle, Feb 1943–Jan 1945

	Feb 43	Nov 43	Jan 45
Bourn	–	97	105
Downham Market	–	635	608
Gransden Lodge	–	405	142, 405
Graveley	35	35, 692	35, 692
Little Staughton	–	–	582
Oakington	7	7, 627	7, 571
Upwood	–	–	139, 156
Warboys	156	156	–
Woodhall Spa	–	–	109
Wyton	83, 109	83, 139	128

commanders were pressing for more independence. Tactics continued to develop throughout 1944, including splitting the PFF effort on more than one target or simulating a PFF attack on a spoof target. Lancasters became the main 'heavy' with No. 8 Group and more airfields were taken over. The Pathfinders led many raids in support of the D-Day landings and in addition to leading Main Force attacks they also marked and bombed their own targets.

The Mosquito had established an excellent reputation and Bennett decided to build up a Mosquito bombing force within the Group: 139 Squadron commenced operations in this role in August 1943. High-flying Mosquitoes were ideal for small-scale attacks on a wide range of German cities as a way of splitting the defences and affecting the morale of citizens. By early 1944 the LNSF had increased to three squadrons and whilst Main Force marking remained an important role, the aircraft were also carrying 4,000 lb bombs. Losses amongst the LNSF were low – in April only one aircraft was lost in over 550 sorties. By the end of the year the seven-squadron force was flying over 1,000 sorties a month.

The final year of the war saw the Pathfinders still at the forefront of operations, though with the lower threat from German defences and the increase in daylight operations more sorties were flown by individual Groups, No. 5 Group in particular acting as an independent force. No. 8 (PFF) Group disbanded 15 December 1945.

No. 100 (Bomber Support) GROUP

Formed: 25 November 1943
Disbanded: 17 December 1945
Badge: The head of Medusa Azure/Or/Sable.
Motto: Confound and Destroy.
The Group, responsible for electronic countermeasures, considered the head of Medusa suitable as a badge, as the severed head of that Goddess not only confounded her enemies but also turned all who saw her to stone.

The creation towards the end of 1943 of a specialist Group for Radio Counter Measures (RCM) was recognition of the growing importance of the 'electronic war' as part of Bomber Command's offensive and it brought together both offensive and defensive units. Under the command of AVM E. B. Addison, No. 100 (Bomber Support) Group was formed at West Raynham on 25 November 1943. Up until 1941 most British use of RCM had been connected with researching and jamming equipment used by the German bombers operating over England. The capture of a German *Freya* radar in the daring

February 1942 raid on Bruneval gave the scientists more solid evidence on which to work. As bomber losses continued to rise in 1942, with radar-laid searchlights and guns and radar-equipped night fighters taking an increasing toll, Bomber Command needed to redress the balance – and jamming enemy systems seemed one of the best solutions.

Early equipment such as *Tinsel* and *Mandrel* was fitted to selected aircraft in Main Force squadrons and most aircraft also received warning receivers that told the crew when an enemy radar was looking in their direction. A refinement of the system was to introduce a transmitter, *Monica*, at the back of the aircraft that gave an audio or visual indication of any aircraft in its beam (maximum range of 4 miles). The downside

of the latter system was that Germans developed a homing device that locked on to the transmission. It was never a popular device and by mid-1944 had been taken out of the Main Force aircraft – but was retained by No. 100 Group as a lure for the enemy.

The basic elements of the radio war were spoofing and jamming using 'noise' to blot out a signal or by decoying the enemy through false radio messages. Much of the early jamming and spoofing was undertaken by ground-based units of No. 80 Wing in England, although they were subsequently incorporated into No. 100 Group.

Voice spoofing was one of the most effective methods and involved fluent German speakers, either on the ground or in an aircraft, 'taking control' of the enemy night fighter and sending him to the wrong place. Noise jamming was also effective and in its simplest form used a transmitter that picked up engine noise from the bomber and blasted it out on the German frequency.

Perhaps the most surprising omission in the Group's Order of Battle was the ABC Lancasters operated by 101 Squadron as these remained with No. 1 Group. Extensive use of *window*, strips of aluminium foil, to blank out radar screens had been a standard tactic for some time and the Group's roles eventually included the special window force (SWF).

However, as can be seen from a glance at the Group's Order of Battle, there was also a strong offensive element to its squadrons and the *Serrate*-equipped Beaufighters of 141 Squadron were amongst the first units to join the new Group. The task for night fighters equipped with this homing system was either to freelance and lurk over German night fighter airfields looking for targets or to fly with the bomber

No. 100 (BS) Group Operations 1943–1945

Aircraft	Total sorties	Aircraft losses	% loss rate
Halifax	3,383	23	0.7
Fortress	1,465	4	0.3
Stirling	1,235	13	1.1
Wellington	589	1	0.2
Mosquito	544	1	0.2
Total	7,216	42	

Note: Statistics do not include night-fighter operations.

No. 100 (Bomber Support) Group Order of Battle, January 1945

Foulsham	192 Sqn	Halifax/Mosquito
Great Massingham	169 Sqn	Mosquito
Little Snoring	23 Sqn	Mosquito
North Creake	171 Sqn	Halifax
	199 Sqn	Stirling
Oulton	214 Sqn	Fortress
Swannington	157 Sqn	Mosquito
	85 Sqn	Mosquito
West Raynham	141 Sqn	Mosquito
	239 Sqn	Mosquito

stream. In the latter instance the ability of the German fighter to home on its target would turn to a disadvantage as the 'bomber prey' would suddenly manoeuvre and become the hunter. Indeed, this type of operation, with the Mosquito taking over from the Beaufighter, was one of the most effective undertaken by the Group. Intruder operations over night fighter airfields and concentration areas proved remarkably effective.

During its time with the Group the Mosquitoes flew some 8,000 offensive sorties during which they claimed 267 enemy aircraft for the loss of sixty-nine of their own number. The psychological effect on the enemy night fighters and the improved morale amongst Bomber Command crews far outweighed these simple statistics.

The organisation was redesignated as No. 100 (Bomber) Group on 25 March 1944, by which time it was established at Bylaugh Hall, East Dereham. With an Order of Battle that included Mosquito and Halifax squadrons, along with a single Fortress unit, all based in Norfolk, the Group remained a key element of Bomber Command for the rest of the war. New equipment and tactics were introduced as part of the on-going 'cat and mouse' game of the electronic war but by late 1944 it was the Mosquito intruders that dominated in terms of aircraft numbers. The Group disbanded on 17 December 1945 – a short period of existence but one that played a major part in the bomber war.

CHAPTER FOUR

Aircrew Training

Without the training machine, the front-line could not exist. This was admirably expressed by Harris in his Despatch on Bomber Operations: 'It can be justly asserted that the success of the Bomber Offensive depended ultimately on the standard of training which could be maintained. It would have been easy to improve training at the expense of the front line by increasing the length of the courses given; by training Lancaster crews on Lancasters only; by ensuring that all the best aircrews were taken off operations early in order to fill the pressing need for instructor posts, and by introducing new equipment into the training units first, so that crews could have been provided fully trained in all new devices. It is believed that the best all-round result was obtained.'

In this chapter the focus will be on the later stages of bomber aircrew training, from the Operational Training Unit onwards, with little mention of selection or early stages of training such as Elementary Flying Training School (EFTS) and Service Flying Training School (SFTS) that all pilots underwent. By the time that aircrew had reached OTU they were already trained in their specialisation and the aim of the subsequent stages was to provide them with training on more appropriate types and with an emphasis on operationally-related activities – and the building of the crew co-operation that was vital to a multi-crew bomber.

The early years
In 1938 Air Chief Marshal (ACM) Ludlow-Hewitt, AOC-in-C Bomber Command, pointed out that, 'One of the chief results of this year's experience is that the work of the members of a modern bomber [by which he meant the Wellington] requires a very much higher standard of training and specialisation than has hitherto been contemplated.'

This was followed up by a proposal from one of his staff, Air Marshal Welsh in November for the establishment of one Advanced Flying Training Centre for each operational Group to, 'Provide each one with a reservoir or pool from which replacement crews can be drawn and to train the output of the Flying Training Schools up to an operational standard before it passes to the operational squadrons.'

Thus was born the idea of additional training for qualified aircrew to make them better suited for front-line duties. In this chapter we are going to focus on this stage of training, from the arrival of the aircrew member into the Bomber Command training machine until his departure to join a squadron.

It was considered that six of the new Group Pool Squadrons would be able to feed the seventy-three operational squadrons, and as an interim measure a number of the non-mobilisable squadrons from the Bomber Command Order of Battle would take on this role. From these simple beginnings, the training machine would grow to one employing over 2,000 aircraft and thousands of personnel. First to take on the role was 75 Squadron at Honington, which was still equipped with Harrows in March when it adopted the new role, although these gave way to Wellingtons in July. Indeed it was to be

Crew of a 115 Squadron Wellington arrive at their aircraft.

the Vickers-Armstrongs Wellington that became the workhorse of the majority of the later Operational Training Units (OTUs).

By June 1939 there were nine Group Pool Squadrons, but this interim measure had its detractors. Ludlow-Hewitt commented: 'It is most uneconomical in practice, even in peacetime, to make operational squadrons undertake the initial operational training of pilots and crews coming direct from the flying schools, and it would be quite impossible in wartime. It is necessary, therefore, to consider the extent of the training organisation required to undertake the whole of this initial operational training.'

At this stage the pre-squadron training course was notionally fourteen weeks long and included sixty-two flying hours, and it was suggested that a twenty-four-aircraft unit would be able to train twenty-two pilots per course. On 16 September 1939, it was agreed that the Group Pool squadrons would be concentrated into a separate training group, No. 6 Group, under Air Commodore Macneece-Foster.

Bomber Command had decided to allocate one operational type to each operational Group, the Wellingtons being concentrated in No. 3 Group and this was reflected in the establishment and syllabus of the appropriate training unit(s). In the case of the Wellington units, three squadrons had been transferred to No. 6 Group – 75 and 148 Squadrons at Harwell and 215 Squadron at Bassingbourn. Each unit was given an establishment of twelve aircraft, half of which were Ansons, although the latter were in short supply at this time and it was more usual for only three or four to be on strength per unit. The course included fifty-five flying hours and there were eleven crews per course. In the light of early operational experience a major change was proposed at the end of 1939 and this led to the creation of the Operational Training Unit. The initial part of the process was to bring together two squadrons at each of the training airfields, although this ideal was not always achieved. The final part of the process was implemented in spring 1940 by the simple expedient of combining Pool Squadrons and re-designating them as Operational Training Units within a new numbering system.

In February Ludlow-Hewitt had defined the role of the new training units: 'The proper role of the OTU is to convert otherwise fully-trained pilots, air observers and air gunners to the type of aircraft in which they will be required to operate and to give them sufficient operational training to fit them to take their place in operational squadrons. Obviously the first essential is to teach the new pilots how to fly a service type by day and night, which entails a considerable amount of local flying. Once a pilot has mastered the new type, he has to be trained in advanced instrument flying, and long-distance flying by day and night, but to enable him to do this the rest of the crew must have reached a satisfactory standard in wireless and navigation. Finally, the complete crew must be taught bombing and air firing.'

By April three of the eight OTUs had Wellingtons, two had Blenheims and one each had Battles, Whitleys or Hampdens. Standard aircraft establishment was seventy aircraft, 25 per cent of which should be Ansons, and the courses were set at six weeks to include fifty-five flying hours. Courses comprised 180 pupils: sixty pilots, thirty observers and ninety air gunners (i.e. thirty crews). Each OTU was meant to have one parent and one satellite airfield. Inevitably these paper numbers were not always adhered to in the real world and numbers and split of aircraft would vary, as would the number of pupils and airfield availability.

At full output, the OTU organisation was able to provide 930 pilots a year, but Bomber Command was already predicting a need for 1,350 pilots. It is worth remembering that at this time each operational bomber had two pilots, and when OTU output is discussed it is usually crews rather than pilots that are referred to. However, it proved constantly difficult for the training units to match crew output to the requirements of the front-line – a problem that was affected by a great many factors, not least of which was the loss rate of crews on operations. The flow of crews could only be increased by either

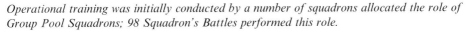

Operational training was initially conducted by a number of squadrons allocated the role of Group Pool Squadrons; 98 Squadron's Battles performed this role.

The length of time that aircrew spent in training varied throughout the war because of the pressing need to keep front-line units at full strength.

cutting the length of the course, with a consequent reduction in quality, or increasing the size/number of OTUs. Whilst the latter might appear an obvious choice, it was a struggle to find aircraft, airfields and manpower for any expansion – at a time when the front-line was also expanding. Two more OTUs were formed in June and the following month a new training Group, No. 7 Group, was formed.

On 16 July 1940, Bomber Command approved the employment of OTU aircraft on leaflet-dropping missions, although this was restricted to a limited area in France. Three aircraft took part in the first such 'attack' on the night of 18/19 July. The employment of OTU aircraft on operations became standard policy, the theory being that sending student crews to 'easy' targets was a means of increasing their experience and confidence. It was a philosophy that was to cause much argument and dissent, but one that appears to have been generally supported by the student crews, all of whom were keen to join in the offensive as soon as possible. The first loss occurred on 27/28 July when Wellington N3002 of No. 11 OTU crashed at Clophill when returning from a leaflet raid; four of the crew were injured.

Shortage of crews

By November, the OTU course had been lengthened to ten weeks with ninety flying hours, primarily because of a reduction in flying hours at the Service Flying Training School (SFTS) stage of pilot training. This had an immediate impact on output and it was decided that four more OTUs would be needed.

The changes made in the latter part of 1940 had the net effect that the training units were not able to produce enough crews for the planned expansion of the operational squadrons. Input of pilots was not expected to be a problem as the first pilots from the

Hampden gunners with a gun rig used either for ground training or airfield defence. There is not sufficient space in this chapter to look at individual aircrew trades, such as Air Gunner, in any detail.

By the latter part of 1940 the training organisation was unable to produce enough crews for the planned expansion of Bomber Command – a situation that would become worse as loss rates increased. Whitley aircrew of 58 Squadron at Linton-on-Ouse 1940.

overseas SFTSs were starting to arrive. What was needed was an expansion of the OTU organisation itself. It was predicted that twenty such units would be required (there were ten at the end of 1940), along with 600 instructor pilots – at a time when there were only 1,120 pilots in the front-line. There was no simple solution to this apparent dichotomy of interests, other than to reduce the amount of training and thus speed up the flow of crews.

In March 1941 it was decided that as an interim measure the course would be reduced to eight weeks, with fifty-five flying hours. According to ACM Sir Charles Portal, AOC-in-C Bomber Command: 'It is of vital importance to obtain a greater output from the OTUs, since if we do not do so, I do not see how we are to produce the crews for our expansion and at the same time keep up our pressure on Germany.'

The reduced course would mean that a pilot would arrive on his squadron having flown 177 hours, comprising fifty hours at EFTS, probably on Tiger Moths, seventy-two hours at SFTS, probably on Ansons, and fifty-five hours at the OTU.

Although two more OTUs were formed in March, in the following month Portal agreed to further cuts in training with the proposal that ... 'The course should be radically cut and that trainees should go to squadrons for a short period as second pilots'. On 12 April the length of the course was set at thirty-two flying hours over six weeks, although this experimental system was to be trialled at a selection of OTUs before being universally adopted. Meanwhile three further units were formed, bringing the total to sixteen – nine were equipped with Wellingtons (which took up 40 per cent of the Wellington strength in the UK!), whilst the others had Whitleys or Blenheims, along with training types such as Ansons.

John Gee was introduced to the Wellington at No. 11 OTU Bassingbourn in April 1941. 'In the early months of 1941 the system of training was not the scientific procedure of the later war years and many of the instructors had not taken a flying instructors' course. In addition, the aircraft were not fitted with a full set of dual controls; all of this made the first few hours rather tricky and a bit frightening. After five hours dual instruction I was allowed to go solo; I remember taxiing around the perimeter and praying that I had completed all the cockpit checks in the correct sequence. ... On the approach I must have been a bit high or my speed too low, for suddenly we dropped, hit the runway and bounced back high into the air, then fell back to the runway with a resounding bang. The Wellington had clearly been built to withstand the efforts of heavy-handed sprog pilots!'

Philip Dawson was at Wellesbourne Mountford (No. 22 OTU) in May. 'The aircraft were generally pretty clapped out having been taken from operational units. The first part of the course was general flying, circuits and bumps and familiarisation with the aircraft. The second phase was the more 'advanced' elements with navigation and bombing; the longest sorties were about five hours and often included visits to the ranges on the Isle of Man to bomb smoke floats. A crew on the course in front of us was killed in an accident and we were 'accelerated' to join this course, this meant flying eight trips day and night in one twenty-four-hour period!'

The shortened course was not proving a success, especially as the front-line squadrons were unable to provide the promised 'top-up' training. In October the old eight-week course was re-introduced for all OTUs, although the Command was requesting a twelve-week duration for the winter courses to allow for poor weather. In December the effects of the short course caused AOC Bomber Command to state: 'I am under the impression that when it was agreed to reduce the OTU course, it was agreed by all concerned that the reduced course would be adequate to produce the necessary training. I understand that the course is being lengthened once more and I fully support this, but there arises out of these ideas a point upon which we must insist most firmly. It is the responsibility of Bomber Command, its Group and Station commanders to ensure that no crew is normally sent out on an operation if they are considered to be insufficiently trained ... it is vitally important that the Command should not relax this standard simply because the Air Ministry have cut down the training course.'

The sentiments expressed by the Commander were all very well but the practicalities meant that the requirements for numbers invariably outweighed other considerations. After two full years of bombing attacks there was strong evidence that Bomber Command had reached a crisis point. However, 1942 was to see a major change in the Command's fortunes and this was reflected in the training organisation.

In February 1942 Air Vice Marshal Arthur Harris had taken over as AOC-in-C and the following month the Command undertook a number of studies into aircraft crewing, the motivation for this being the continued high loss rate. Bomber Command had lost ninety aircraft and crews in the six-week period to the end of March, which had including a number of attacks where the loss rate was around 10 per cent. Inevitably there was a direct correlation between losses, the rate of expansion of the Command and the require-ments from the training organisation. The studies focused on crew roles and the options for streamlining the system – in other words saving time and thus increasing the output.

However, the most significant decision was the removal of the two-pilot system that had hitherto been standard for medium/heavy bombers. Harris was also keen to maximise employment of his trained crews and overall expected two operational tours and two training tours before they could be released to any other jobs.

The change in crewing had a fundamental effect on the training syllabus, the core decisions being:

1. Only one pilot per crew to be trained.
2. Air Bomber added to crew, allowing navigator to concentrate on navigation – part of this decision was the problem of the bomb aimer keeping good night vision. The air bomber would also receive some air gunner training to man the front guns.
3. Only one Wireless Operator/Air Gunner per crew, the other being replaced by an Air Gunner with no wireless training. In the four-engined bomber two air gunners were added.

Staff of 21 OTU at Enstone (Ken Wallis).

Finningley was home at various times to 18 (Polish) OTU and 25 OTU.

According to Harris in his Despatch on War Operations: 'These changes made it possible to give each member of the crew a full course on his own subjects, and, particularly in the case of the pilot, enabled a very much better course to be given, as it was no longer necessary to give a double number of circuits and bumps to each crew. This in turn relieved both the strain on the pilot instructors and the congestion around the OTU airfields.'

The lack of a second pilot was addressed by giving one of the crew members rudimentary training on the Link Trainer and in the aircraft to act as a Pilot's Assistant (PA). This role was allocated to the Air Bomber, although with the later introduction of a Flight Engineer to the heavies, he took on the PA task.

It is worth noting that the Whitley flew its last operational bombing raid on 27/28 April 1942, although OTU Whitleys continued to fly leaflet-dropping missions for some time, so the type did not vanish completely from operations.

Choosing a crew

It was whilst at the OTU that crews were formed: 'Then they go to the OTU where they are formed into a crew and begin to learn team work. The duties of all members of the crew are carefully defined as far as the principal tasks are concerned, but the captain of each aircraft is responsible for arranging the duties of his crew and for seeing that they carry them out punctually and efficiently.'

A new pilot would start the trawl to find the rest of a crew, the decision being left to the individuals as far as possible rather than the 'system' just putting names together. It worked remarkably well and gradually the crew would come together.

This was outlined in the August 1944 Aircrew Training Bulletin: 'The aircrew meet for the first time at the OTU and during the first two weeks of the ground course are given certain discretion in sorting themselves out into complete crews (with the exception of the Flight Engineer who does not arrive until later.)'

John Long went through the crewing up 'process' at Moreton-in-the-Marsh (No. 21 OTU): 'On arrival we were directed to one of the hangars where the completely un-directed process of crewing up took place. Pilots, Navigators, Wireless Operators, Bomb Aimers and Gunners all milled around, making their categories and names known to each other as the random selection went on. Having crewed up, through the rest of July and on into September we became a 'unit'. We were learning not only how to operate our war machine but also about each other.'

Crew of 83 Squadron; bomber crews 'assembled' during the OTU phase – by mutual consent whenever possible.

Bomber Command Training Organisation 1939–1942

Unit	Aircraft	Airfield	Unit	Aircraft	Airfield
November 1939: No. 6 Group (Abingdon)					
97, 166 Sqns	Whitley	Abingdon	207 Sqn	Battle, Blenheim	Cranfield
215 Sqn	Wellington	Bassingbourn	98 Sqn	Battle	Hucknall
35 Sqn	Blenheim	Bassingbourn	7 Sqn	Hampden	Upper Heyford
52, 63 Sqns	Battle	Benson	76 Sqn	Anson	Upper Heyford
104, 108 Sqns	Blenheim	Bicester	90 Sqn	Blenheim	Upwood
185 Sqn	Hampden	Cottesmore			
May 1941: No. 6 Group (Abingdon)					
10 OTU	Whitley	Abingdon	19 OTU	Whitley	Kinloss
11 OTU	Wellington	Bassingbourn	20 OTU	Wellington	Lossiemouth
12 OTU	Wellington	Benson	21 OTU	Wellington	Moreton-in-the-Marsh
15 OTU	Wellington	Harwell	23 OTU	Wellington	Pershore
18 OTU	Wellington	Bramcote			
May 1941: No. 7 Group (Brampton)					
13 OTU	Blenheim	Bicester	17 OTU	Blenheim	Upwood
14 OTU	Hampden	Cottesmore	25 OTU	Hampden	Finningley
16 OTU	Hampden	Upper Heyford			
April 1942: No. 6 Group (Abingdon)					
10 OTU	Whitley	Abingdon	19 OTU	Whitley	Kinloss
11 OTU	Wellington	Bassingbourn	20 OTU	Wellington	Lossiemouth
12 OTU	Wellington	Chipping Warden	21 OTU	Wellington	Moreton-in-the-Marsh
15 OTU	Wellington	Harwell	23 OTU	Wellington	Pershore
18 OTU	Wellington	Bramcote	27 OTU	Wellington	Lichfield
April 1942: No. 7 Group (Winslow)					
13 OTU	Blenheim	Bicester	25 OTU	Hampden,	
14 OTU	Hampden	Cottesmore		Wellington,	
16 OTU	Wellington	Upper Heyford		Manchester	Finningley
17 OTU	Wellington	Upwood	26 OTU	Wellington	Wing

Hampden and Hereford of 14 OTU, Cottesmore.

Reorganisation, growth – and operations

May 1942 saw a reorganisation of the training system with No. 6 Group becoming No. 91 Group, and No. 7 Group becoming No. 92 Group, the main reason being that the lower numbers were being allocated to new operational Groups, although in the event only No. 6 (RCAF) Group formed. This was to be a difficult year for the Command but also one in which it 'turned the corner' in terms of operational effectiveness; however, overall the Command contracted in size – with exception of the formation, in June, of a third OTU Group, No. 93 Group with its HQ at Burton-on-Trent.

At this stage of the war, it was taking an average of eighteen months for a trainee to get from 'civvy street' to a front-line squadron. After selection, the route started with three days at the local Aircrew Reception Centre (ACRC) where the main task was getting kitted out. Then came what many thought was the worst part, twelve weeks at an Initial Training Wing (ITW) which included intensive classroom work on technical and air-related subjects, but also far too much 'bull'. This was followed by flying training through elementary/basic, advanced and finally operational phases.

From 1941 the training units had been participating in operational sorties, albeit only leaflet dropping over notionally easy targets. However, the Thousand-Bomber raids of early summer 1942 would not have been possible without the widespread use of aircraft and crews from the training units. Of the 1,047 bombers tasked to attack Cologne on the night of 30/31 May the two training Groups provided 365 aircraft. No. 91 Group sent 236 Wellingtons and twenty-one Whitleys, whilst No. 92 Group sent sixty-three Wellingtons and forty-five Hampdens. Two further raids followed whilst this massive force was available, Essen (1/2 June) and Bremen (25/26 June). The latter was a disaster for the OTU crews, with the force of around 200 Wellingtons and Whitleys suffering almost thirty losses, with 10, 11 and 12 OTUs each losing four aircraft. Regardless of such losses, it was not practical to keep the training units away from their primary task any longer and besides, Harris felt that he had proved the point that used *en masse*, the bomber weapon could be decisive. Despite the fact that the units were released from operational standby they were still liable to be called on whenever a Maximum Effort was planned. However, as losses began to mount – for example, No. 92 Group lost eleven of the 105 aircraft it sent to Duisburg on the night of 31 July – there was increased pressure to remove the OTUs from operations. Again there was no immediate change of policy and the records show heavy losses on other raids in 1942, one of the worst being five out of thirteen Wellingtons from No. 16 OTU over Düsseldorf on 10/11 September.

With the entry to service of the trio of 'heavy' bombers, the existing training organisation of the OTUs had to be modified in the light of experience. The comments that had been made when the Wellington was introduced of needing appropriate training for advanced aircraft, was even more appropriate for the four-engined types.

Heavy Conversion Units
When the Lancaster entered service in early 1942 the initial task of converting crews to the aircraft was undertaken by small Conversion Flights, usually two or three aircraft, within the individual squadrons. This is why you will see in the records reference, for example, to No. 106 CU – this being the conversion flight within 106 Squadron. A similar policy had been used for the other heavies. The decision was taken in September 1942 to combine the on-squadron Conversion Flights into special training units as Heavy Conversion Units (HCUs) equipped with Manchesters and Lancasters. Using the Lancaster example, by the end of October the following units had formed:

No. 1654 HCU at Wiglsey (ex 50 and 83 Squadron CFs)
No. 1656 HCU at Breighton (ex 103 and 460 Squadrons)
No. 1660 HCU at Swinderby (ex 61, 97, 106 and 207 Squadrons)
No. 1661 HCU at Skellingthorpe (ex 9, 44 and 49 Squadrons)

Of these, all except No. 1656 HCU, which was for No. 1 Group, were part of No. 5 Group. The initial establishment of sixteen Lancasters and sixteen Manchesters was almost immediately changed to twelve Lancasters plus twenty Manchesters of Halifaxes. With a desire to put as many Lancasters as possible into the operational squadrons even this ratio was soon changed.

The basic HCU course was conducted in a similar format to that of the OTU, albeit over a shorter time frame, and at this point the Flight Engineer was added to the crew. Eventually each of the three operational heavy Groups controlled its own HCUs, with an allocation of three such units per Group – a notional total of fifteen HCUs. By January 1943, with the formation of No. 1662 HCU at Blyton, the total number of units had reached eleven, with the plan being to increase this to sixteen by November. This policy of keeping the HCUs under the Groups for which they provided crews, gradually became more unworkable as the front-line expanded and the training organisation grew but it was not until September 1944 that their admin and control was brought together under No. 7 (HCU) Group, headquartered at Grantham.

By April 1943 Bomber Command was over 100 crews short of establishment and as a short-term fix it was decided to increase the intake of each OTU course from sixteen to eighteen crews every two weeks. The overall output requirement was set at 383 crews a month (from March) rising to 622 crews by December. The number of bomber OTUs peaked in December 1943 with a total of twenty-two and a half units, with a strength of around 1,300 aircraft, and thousands of air and ground personnel.

Lancaster crew, June 1943; it was essential for a crew to have confidence in its 'skipper' and to work as a team to operate the aircraft in the most effective manner. Initial crewing-up usually took place at the OTUs.

Bill Carmen arrived at Upper Heyford (No. 16 OTU) in July 1943: 'Here at the OTU the aircrew came together to get to know each other and choose whom they would be happy to fly with, eventually being formed into a crew. The Wellington became our "chariot" and we realised that from now on we were at the start of a serious business. On one occasion our crew were grouped outside the Control Tower waiting our turn to take over a *Wimpey* from another crew. It pulled up by the Tower and suddenly its starboard engine burst into flames. The occupying aircrew evacuated at maximum speed out of the front hatch – they were like rabbits coming out of a rabbit hole ahead of a ferret. My crew were by then pelting around to the far side of the Tower out of harms way. The Station fire-engine leapt into action but for some reason couldn't raise any pressure in their hose and the nozzle hung limp at the business end. This situation provoked some explicit ribald remarks from the aircrews. With bullets flying about in all directions as the ammunition belts "cooked" in the heat, the poor old *Wimpey*, its geodetic skeleton now exposed, sank to its knees. By this time we had all taken cover inside the Control Tower.'

Arthur Harris in his post-war Despatch on War Operations highlighted the problem of finding instructors: '. . . It was quickly found that only aircrew with operational experience could successfully train crews from the OTU stage onwards, but owing to the constant expansion of the front line, and the rate of casualties at the height of the war, which did not allow for a large number of tour-expired aircrew becoming available as instructors, there was always a lag in the number of pilot instructors. For a considerable period there was also a deficiency in the number of navigators and air bombers. In

Gunnery Flight 21 OTU, 1943 (Ken Wallis).

consequence of this, until well into 1944, training units had to struggle along with their strength of instructors well below establishment.'

Reg White trained with 30 OTU at Seighford in mid-1943 and recalled one particular 'hairy moment': 'We were stooging along over Dorset when the port engine failed (this supplied all the hydraulics for the wheels and flaps) so the pilot decided to lob down at an airfield whose Drem lights we could see below us – "Hello Darky – hello Darky this is E-Edward" – and all the bloody lights went out. We were still flying quite happily on one engine so the pilot decided to return to our own airfield at Seighford. Entering the circuit he called up and told them our problem and was asked whether he was going to land or bale out; he decided to land and the rest of us didn't fancy jumping into the darkness either so the bomb aimer used the emergency reserve to pump the wheels down whilst the pilot took us well out to line up with the runway.

'Sitting in the rear turret I could feel him literally lifting the aircraft over hedges as we came in on the long runway; as soon as we over the boundary he cut the starboard engine and we dropped onto the runway and ran and ran and ran until we rolled to stop. Looking out of the rear turret all I could see was trees on either side and as the pilot gunned the good engine the tail went onto rough grass – we had used the whole length of the 2,200 yards but we were alive. On reaching the crew room the tannoy was calling for F.S. McLachlan to report to the control tower. Someone left the switch down and we heard the pilot climbing the stairs and all the ensuing conversation. "Flight Sergeant what is the landing speed of a Wellington." ... "90 mph Sir." ... "What was your speed when you came over the hedge?" ... "110 mph Sir." ... "What do you think you were doing at that speed." ... "Sir the aircraft was E-Edward, I have flown it several times and even with two engines the port wing tends to drop at the correct landing speed; if you think you can land it any better without the port engine then I am prepared to come up with you but I won't take my crew." ... "Hand in your log book." Two days later it was returned with a Green Endorsement.'

By 1943 a full-size OTU had an establishment of fifty-four aircraft and was capable of producing thirty-two crews a month in summer and twenty-two a month in winter. November brought another request for a slowing down of output as OTU crews were 'clogging up' the training system further down stream at the HCU stage. In general each unit now had seven courses at any one time, five in training, one on leave and one awaiting posting.

Wellington of 27 OTU airborne out of Lichfield on a practice bombing sortie.

Based at Wellesbourne Mountford, No. 22 OTU was typical of a bomber training unit in early 1944. Its aircraft strength comprised eighty aircraft, primarily Wellington IIIs and Xs, but with a number of Martinet Is for target towing (gunnery practice). The course size averaged twenty-eight to thirty crews, a total of 654 students, the majority of them Canadian. In a typical summer month, an OTU of standard size would expect to fly around 5,000 hours, just under half of which would be at night.

Lancaster Finishing Schools

With the Lancaster having proved the most effective of the Command's bombers it had been decided towards the end of 1943 to equip as many operational Groups as possible with the Avro heavy. No. 3 Group was earmarked to join No. 1 and No. 5 Group as Lancaster operators and the only way to provide enough aircraft was to remove them from the HCUs.

The plan was to equip the HCUs within No. 3 and No. 5 Group with Stirlings and to give the other HCUs Halifaxes. However, it was recognised that crews would need some degree of Lancaster orientation and whilst at first it was believed that this could be done at squadron level, it was eventually decided to form specialist training units to carry out a short orientation course. Three Lancaster Finishing Schools (LFS) were formed, one for each of the Lancaster-equipped operational Groups and numbered appropriately – No. 1 LFS at Lindholme/Hemswell, No. 3 LFS at Feltwell and No. 5 LFS at Syerston, although 1678 and 1679 HCUs also kept Lancaster elements. The initial intention was that each LFS would train thirty-six crews per fortnight; thus the student pilot would have a four-week course, of forty flying hours, at the HCU followed by two weeks, with ten flying hours, at the LFS. John Gee, having completed a tour on the Halifax, was sent to No. 1 LFS in mid-1944, 'As soon as one got into the seat one could feel that there was something different about this aeroplane. All the controls were easily to hand and the Perspex cover over the cockpit was slightly higher than the top of the fuselage, giving the pilot a commanding view. As soon as I took my first flight I could feel the difference, it was wonderfully balanced and light on the controls, it handled more like a fighter than a bomber.'

Bomb Aimer Don Clay was at the same LFS in August: 'The ground work consisted mainly of getting to know our various stations and equipment as well as escape procedures for baling out and dinghy drill. One of our final sorties at the LFS was fighter affiliation and by the end of the exercise our 'lad' left us in no doubt that, given the correct 'gen' by the gunners, no Jerry fighters would ever mark us down as a kill. With our last exercise at LFS we were sent home on leave for a week and told to report back before being posted to an operational squadron.'

As an example of how variable the training requirement was, there were three major changes in 1944. In April the Command was seeking to increase the supply of crews, primarily due to a period of heavier than expected losses. However, by July the War Cabinet was worried about an overall manpower shortage and was looking for reductions in the training system. The decision was taken to stop expansion of the bomber training organisation and to reverse the trend in order to have fifteen OTUs at the end of the year, further reducing to six by March 1945.

The August 1944 Aircrew Training Bulletin included an article entitled 'Bomber Command Training' and this provides a neat overview of the training system: 'The training organisation is divided into five stages:

1. Operational Training Unit – ten weeks with forty day and forty night hours.
2. Air Crew School – two weeks with no flying.
3. Conversion Unit – four weeks with twenty day and twenty night hours.
4. Lancaster Finishing School – two weeks with five day and five night hours.
5. Squadron conversion – one with five hours day and five hours night.

The Bulletin went on to address the OTU phase in more detail:

The flying course starts with conversion to the Wellington aircraft, gradually progresses through various stages and ends up with a leaflet raid in a Wellington over enemy-occupied Europe. The syllabus includes the following exercises:
1. Synthetic training. Link trainer, AM Bombing Teacher, clay pigeon shooting, turret training.
2. Gunnery. Combat manoeuvres, air-to-sea firing, air-to-air firing, fighter affiliation exercise day and night.
3. Bombing. High-level bombing by day and night, bombing on cross-countries, infra-red bombing, demonstration of pathfinder technique and target indicators.
4. Navigation. DR navigation, cross-countries, radar training.
5. Operational training. Night exercises with night fighters, searchlight and anti-aircraft organisation in this country, leaflet raid over enemy territory.
6. Drills. Dinghy, parachute, fire, oxygen, crash drills.
7. Operational procedures. *Darky,* searchlight homing, SOS.

June 1944 was the highpoint of the training machine in terms of aircraft numbers, with a strength of 2,018 aircraft at forty-four units, comprising twenty-two OTUs, fifteen HCUs, three LFSs and four 'miscellaneous training units' such as the Pathfinder Navigation Training Unit (PFNTU). These aircraft were housed at fifty-nine airfields and employed thousands of air and ground personnel.

One final training role has yet to be mentioned: No. 8 Group's specific requirement for Mosquito training. Initially this task was carried out by the Mosquito Training Unit (MTU) but as the number of squadrons increased (eventually reaching twelve

Gunners played a key role in the survivability of a bomber – they needed to be alert to warn of enemy fighters, call for evasive manoeuvres and engage the enemy.

squadrons) the MTU was incorporated into No. 16 OTU when this was re-equipped from Wellingtons to Mosquitoes.

The final months and rundown of strength

Accident rates at OTUs were always a problem, as evidenced by the fact that over 8,000 Bomber Command aircrew lost their lives in training. Air Vice-Marshal J. Gray, AOC No. 91 Group, sent the following message to No. 22 OTU: 'Congratulations on October's 3,600 flying hours without accident, and this after four months of over 1,000 hours per accident.' Sadly, the following month had its share of tragedy with two fatal Wellington accidents on 20 November with LN460 exploding in mid-air and MF509 crashing in Wales, both with the loss of their crews.

However, the predicted loss rates, and thus the expansion plans for the training machine, were amended during the latter part of 1944 as losses were generally lower than expected. On 29 September 1944, the War Cabinet had instructed that overall strength was not to exceed eighty-five heavy bomber squadrons by the end of the year and the number of training establishments should be reduced. It was proposed to run an establishment of seventeen OTUs, seventeen HCUs and four LFS but almost as soon as soon as the ink was dry on a plan it was amended both in terms of the number and strength of units and the aircraft types allocated to each. The peak was achieved in December with eighty-five

Pilots and Navigators for the Command's Mosquito units went through a different training routine, culminating for most with time at the Mosquito Training Unit.

Bomber Command Training Organisation 1943–1945

Unit	Aircraft	Airfield	Unit	Aircraft	Airfield

April 1943

No. 91 Group

Unit	Aircraft	Airfield	Unit	Aircraft	Airfield
10 OTU	Whitley	Abingdon	21 OTU	Wellington	Moreton-in-the-Marsh
15 OTU	Wellington	Harwell	22 OTU	Wellington	Wellesbourne Mountford
19 OTU	Whitley	Kinloss	23 OTU	Wellington	Pershore
20 OTU	Wellington	Lossiemouth	24 OTU	Whitley	Honeybourne

No. 92 Group

Unit	Aircraft	Airfield	Unit	Aircraft	Airfield
11 OTU	Wellington	Westcott	16 OTU	Wellington	Upper Heyford
12 OTU	Wellington	Chipping Warden	17 OTU	Blenheim	Upwood
13 OTU	Blenheim	Bicester	26 OTU	Wellington	Wing
14 OTU	Wellington	Cottesmore	29 OTU	Wellington	North Luffenham

No. 93 Group

Unit	Aircraft	Airfield	Unit	Aircraft	Airfield
18 OTU	Wellington	Bramcote	28 OTU	Wellington	Wymeswold
25 OTU	(disbanding)	Finningley	30 OTU	Wellington	Hixon
27 OTU	Wellington	Lichfield	81 OTU	Whitley	Whitchurch Heath

Conversion Units*

Unit	Aircraft	Airfield	Unit	Aircraft	Airfield
1662 CU	Halifax/Manchester	Blyton (No. 1 Gp)	1654 CU	Lancaster/Halifax	Swinderby (No. 5 Gp)
1657 CU	Stirling	Ridgewell (No. 3 G)	1661 CU	Lancaster/Manchester	Winthorpe (No. 5 Gp)
1651 CU	Stirling	Waterbeach (No. 3 Gp)			
1652 CU	Halifax	Marston Moor (No. 4 Gp)	1660 CU	Lancaster/Manchester	Wigsley (No. 5 Gp)
1663 CU	Halifax	Rufforth (No. 4 Gp)			
1658 CU	Halifax	Riccall (No. 4 Gp)	1659 CU	Halifax	Dishforth (No. 6 Gp)

July 1944

No. 91 Group (Abingdon)

Unit	Aircraft	Airfield	Unit	Aircraft	Airfield
10 OTU	Whitley	Abingdon	21 OTU	Wellington	Moreton-in-the-Marsh
19 OTU	Whitley	Kinloss	22 OTU	Wellington	Wellesbourne Mountford
20 OTU	Wellington	Lossiemouth	24 OTU	Wellington	Honeybourne

No. 92 Group

Unit	Aircraft	Airfield	Unit	Aircraft	Airfield
11 OTU	Wellington	Westcott	26 OTU	Wellington	Wing
12 OTU	Wellington	Chipping Warden	29 OTU	Wellington	Bruntington
14 OTU	Wellington	Market Harborough	84 OTU	Wellington	Desborough
16 OTU	Wellington	Upper Heyford	85 OTU	Wellington	Husbands Bosworth
17 OTU	Wellington	Silverstone			

No. 93 Group

Unit	Aircraft	Airfield	Unit	Aircraft	Airfield
18 OTU	Wellington	Finningley	82 OTU	Wellington	Ossington
27 OTU	Wellington	Lichfield	83 OTU	Wellington	Peplow
28 OTU	Wellington	Wymeswold	86 OTU	Wellington	Finningley
30 OTU	Wellington	Finningley			

Conversion Units*

Unit	Aircraft	Airfield	Unit	Aircraft	Airfield
1656 CU	Lancaster	Lindholme (No. 1 Gp)	1658 CU	Halifax	Riccall (No. 4 Gp)
1662 CU	Halifax/Lancaster	Lindholme (No. 1 Gp)	1654 CU	Stirling	Swinderby (No. 5 Gp)
1667 CU	Halifax	Lindholme (No. 1 Gp)	1661 CU	Stirling	Winthorpe (No. 5 Gp)
1653 CU	Stirling	Stradishall (No. 3 Gp)	1660 CU	Stirling	Wigsley (No. 5 Gp)
1657 CU	Stirling	Stradishall (No. 3 G)	1659 CU	Halifax	Dishforth (No. 6 Gp)
1651 CU	Stirling	Stradishall (No. 3 Gp)	1664 CU	Halifax	(No. 6 Gp)
1652 CU	Halifax	Marston Moor (No. 4 Gp)	1666 CU	Halifax	(No. 6 Gp)
1663 CU	Halifax	Rufforth (No. 4 Gp)			

Notes

* The Conversion Units were allocated to the operational Groups (Group number in brackets after the airfield).

(1) Specialist flights such as BATF, TGF, BDTF, etc have been omitted from these lists for the sake of clarity.

(2) Most OTUs had other types on charge, in addition to the main operational type; for example, in the May 1943 organisation it is recorded that every OTU had Ansons.

Engine change on a 58 Squadron Halifax. This chapter has concentrated on aircrew training but they were only a small percentage of the total personnel on an airfield of Bomber Command.

heavy bombers squadrons and seventeen Mosquito squadrons; falling loss rates and reduced aircrew wastage in training and through accidents brought about a rapid rundown of training units and a re-equipment programme.

Having been taken out of Main Force, the Stirling had been a key part of the HCU operation, but with an increasing number of Lancasters becoming available in the latter part of 1944 it was decided to re-equip each Stirling HCU with an establishment of thirty-two Lancasters and to incorporate within them the role performed by the LFSs. First to undergo this transformation was No. 3 Groups' 1651 and 1653 HCUs, although three more Stirling HCUs had acquired Lancasters by January 1945. A similar re-equipment programme was also instituted for the Halifax-equipped training units.

The Operational Training Units were also undergoing change during this period and by the end of 1944, five OTUs had been disbanded – but four new ones had been created or re-equipped and expanded! This was, however, a short-lived 'expansion' and the overall trend was one of reduction – with spare aircrew looking for employment.

The final operational losses of OTU aircraft occurred on the night of 14/15 January 1945 when three out of a force of 126 aircraft never made it back to their bases (one from 27 OTU at Lichfield and two from 30 OTU at Hixon); the mission was an Operation *Sweepstake*, a diversionary flight over the North Sea that did not penetrate enemy territory but was classed as an operational mission.

By 1945 courses were being cancelled all the way through the

Summary of Bomber Command OTUs with Operational Losses			
OTU	*Formed*	*Disbanded*	*Op Loss*
10 OTU	8 Apr 1940	10 Sep 1946	63 Whitley
11 OTU	8 Apr 1940	18 Sep 1945	16 Wellington
12 OTU	8 Apr 1940	22 Jun 1945	14 Wellington
13 OTU	8 Apr 1940		Nil
14 OTU	8 Apr 1940	24 Jun 1945	11 Hampden
15 OTU	8 Apr 1940	15 Mar 1944	9 Wellington
16 OTU	8 Apr 1940	15 Mar 1947	17 Wellington
17 OTU	8 Apr 1940	15 Mar 1947	Nil
18 OTU	15 Jun 1940	30 Jan 1945	6 Wellington
19 OTU	27 May 1940	26 Jun 1945	1 Whitley
20 OTU	27 May 1940	17 Jul 1945	3 Wellington
21 OTU	21 Jan 1941	15 Mar 1947	11 Wellington
22 OTU	14 Apr 1941	24 Jul 1945	16 Wellington
23 OTU	1 Apr 1941	15 Mar 1944	10 Wellington
24 OTU	15 Mar 1942	24 Jul 1945	10 Whitley
25 OTU	1 Mar 1941	1 Feb 1943	10 Wellington
26 OTU	15 Jan 1942	4 Mar 1946	12 Wellington
27 OTU	23 Apr 1941	22 Jun 1945	12 Wellington
28 OTU	16 May 1942	15 Oct 1944	8 Wellington
29 OTU	21 Apr 1942	27 May 1945	5 Wellington
30 OTU	28 Jun 1942	12 Jun 1945	10 Wellington
81 OTU	10 Jul 1942		1 Whitley
82 OTU	1 Jun 1943	9 Jan 1945	6 Wellington
83 OTU	1 Aug 1943	28 Oct 1944	3 Wellington
84 OTU	1 Sep 1943	14 Jun 1945	1 Wellington
85 OTU	15 Jan 1944	14 Jun 1945	Nil
86 OTU	15 Jun 1944	15 Oct 1944	Nil

Armourers bombing up a Mosquito, 25 February 1944.

training system, from basic pilot training onwards, and trained aircrew were being sent to holding units pending decisions on where they would end up. Many never made it to a squadron. The final fatalities during the wartime period occurred on 20 April 1945 when Wellington LP760 of 19 OTU took-off from Kinloss at 11.52 and appeared to explode in mid-air; all six on board were killed.

By May 1945 the rundown of operational squadrons had commenced and towards the end of the year Bomber Command was already a shadow of its former self.

Cold War

Specialist training units remained the primary training organisations for Bomber Command for the rest of its history; in the immediate post war period the OTUs and HCUs continued to operate, albeit a drastically reduced number of them and with far less aircraft – and students. With the Lancaster as the main equipment, rapidly being replaced by the Lincoln, the basic training changed little. On 15 March 1947 a wholesale change of designations took place with training units becoming Operational Conversion Units (OCUs), a designation still used by the RAF (although all now carry Shadow Squadron numbers).

There is not enough space to do more than touch on Bomber Command training during the Cold War and so three short examples will have to suffice: the B-29, Canberra and Valiant; plus a reference or two to other significant developments such as the demise of aircrew trades such as Air Gunner and Signaller and the creation of a new trade of Air Electronics Operator. Air Gunners had been a critical element of Bomber Command throughout the Second World War but with the plan for unarmed jet bombers to enter service from the early 1950s they had a final few years with the Lincoln and B-29 Washington before there was no longer a role for them within the Command. The AG brevet was still to be seen at bomber stations well after there were no longer any turrets to man.

On 4 September 1957 the last RAF Signallers course graduated from Swanton Morley bringing to an end the training of some 30,000 aircrew who had worn the WOP/AG, WOP or S aircrew brevet. The last course had only comprised six students and the trade had been in decline since before the end of the war, the need for air gunners vanishing overnight with the introduction of unarmed jet bombers. However, the previous year had seen the introduction, in March, of a new aircrew category of Air

Bomber Command OCUs

OCU	Formed	Previously	Main aircraft	Disband
230 OCU	15 Mar 1947	1653 HCU	Lancaster, Lincoln, Vulcan	(31 Aug 1981)
231 OCU	15 Mar 1947	16 OTU	Mosquito, Meteor, Canberra	(23 Apr 1993)
232 OCU	21 Feb 1955		Canberra, Valiant	(4 Apr 1986)
237 OCU	31 Jul 1947	8 OTU	Mosquito, Canberra	(1 Oct 1991)

Note: Aircraft do not include those used after the Bomber Command period.

Electronics Operator (AE). The main reason for the new category was the increasing importance of electronic devices, especially counter-measures for the V-bomber force. The first of the new courses commenced in July.

The arrival of the first four B-29 Washingtons at Marham in March 1950 led to the creation of the Washington Conversion Unit (WCU) under Squadron Leader F. R. Flynn, with 115 Squadron being the first 'customers'. The WCU ran courses for aircrew and groundcrew and also provided a 'road show' to visit units as required for further training or evaluation. The courses were typical of RAF courses with a ground school phase followed by flying, at first with an instructor and gradually as a crew. By the time that Ken White attended the course in December it was well established: 'First flight as Radar Navigator was 13 December 1950 and we flew our first 'crew solo' on 22 January, with a final check ride a week later before we moved to our squadron, 15 Squadron, at Coningsby. The conversion course had included six flights totalling twenty-four hours thirty minutes.'

The introduction in the 1950s of a new range of jet types meant a major change of focus for the training organisation; each OCU specialised in one type and during this period of Bomber Command's history the main types were Canberra (231 OCU), Valiant and Victor (232 OCU) and Vulcan (230 OCU).

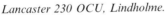

Lancaster 230 OCU, Lindholme.

Students admire their new mount – Canberra conversion at No.231 OCU, Bassingbourn.

Conversion for the first few Canberra units was courtesy of the Jet Conversion Flight (JCF), which arrived at Binbrook to work initially with 101 Squadron. Most flying was done on the Meteor F.4 and T.7 to familiarise pilots as with jet engines – and the asymmetric thrust from having widely-spaced engines. The JCF later acquired a Canberra B.2, with the student pilot occupying the rumble seat to observe the instructor before places were changed. However, later in 1951 No. 231 (Mosquito) OCU and No. 237 (Meteor) OCU were in residence at Bassingbourn as the Canberra conversion units, although No. 237 OCU was absorbed into No. 231 OCU in December. Bassingbourn became the home of the Canberra, eventually operating a large number of aircraft of different variants and in its heyday flying up to 1,500 hours a month. The first student course arrived on 27 May 1952 – the Canberra era was about to be well and truly launched. Meteors continued to be used until the dual-control Canberra T.4 became available; over the next four decades the OCU turned out thousands of Canberra aircrew for the RAF and overseas air forces. Over that period of time there was no standard course as such, the course the author attended with No. 231 OCU at Marham in 1977 was very different to that of the early 1950s – although the ground-training aids, which might have seemed 'state of the art' in 1952 were decidedly antiquated. In the early 1950s the OCU ran three main course: the Light Bomber course, the 'long' course of conversion to type and weaponry, and the photo-recce course. An article in the RAF magazine *Air Clues* gave an overview of the training at the OCU and its comments on the Navigator training included: 'The navs will probably be found either navigating an aircraft on a 1,000-mile cross-country while firmly rooted to the earth in a cubicle in the DRI or lying full length on a mock-up bombing platform aiming imaginary bombs at a projected picture on the Earth's surface which moves sedately beneath them. They may be in the radar demonstration room learning the art of manipulating radar devices; at the same time the PR navs, who, at heart, are quite snooty about this bombing business, will be learning about cameras and how to take pictures, and having taken them, how to interpret them.' Bassingbourn remained at the heart of Bomber Command training throughout the type's service with the Command.

A short article appeared in *Air Clues* in April 1958 entitled 'Salute the Victor' with the comment that, 'The first real course has just started and the staff are just managing to keep ahead or our eager students.' No. 232 OCU at Gaydon had formed on 21 February 1955 to train Valiant and Victor air and ground crew; it received its first Victors on 28 November 1957. Initial training of staff had taken place with Handley Page at Radlett and selection of aircrew for V-bombers was rigorous. The basic selection criteria for a Valiant 1st Pilot, for example, was a total of 2,000 flying hours as 1st Pilot, including 200 hours 1st Pilot on four-engined bombers and current flying experience on the Canberra. Before being posted to the OCU at Gaydon they had to attend a three-week ground school with Vickers-Armstrongs. Navigator plotters were selected mainly from Canberra squadrons on the basis of their results in their crew classification schemes. Navigator radars came from Canberra and Lincoln squadrons. Before joining the OCU course they went on a bomb-aiming course at the Bomber Command Bombing School (BCBS), Lindholme for a forty-two-week course in H2S and NBS equipment. Signallers came from a variety of backgrounds but required a minimum of 500 flying hours; the introduction of the AEO category provided trained AEs via the new sixty-week course run by Flying Training Command. It would be some time, however, before the 'S' brevet vanished from the squadrons.

No. 1 Vulcan course at 230 Operational Conversion Unit.

It was a similar picture for the other V-bombers, with the OCUs initially converting staff, often with the assistance of the manufacturer, before turning their attention to the first 'real' students. The OCU syllabi were designed to convert aircrew to the new type, the length of the course and its content varying depending on the aircrew trade, the longest courses being those for the pilots. After the basic conversion the students would progress to learning how to operate the aircraft systems in an operational scenario, including weapons and electronic warfare. The syllabus content and length also varied during the life of the aircraft within Bomber Command to reflect new roles, equipment and doctrine. Specialist training courses, from the radar bombing at Lindholme to Special Weapons (nuclear bombs) training, also varied during this period and there is not enough space in this short account to mention this aspect.

As can be seen from the OCU table above the arrangement outlined here remained in place beyond the end of the Bomber Command period.

CHAPTER FIVE

Aircraft of Bomber Command

omber Command's rationale throughout its thirty years of existence was to provide an offensive bombing force to take any war to the enemy's homeland: the doctrine of strategic bombing. The striking power of the Command's aircraft rose from the virtually insignificant with slow biplanes, whose bomb load in some cases was as low as 500 lb, through the massive wartime armada of heavy bombers, each capable of carrying 10,000 lb or more of bombs and whose total bomb lift was massive, to the Cold War period when the individual effect of atomic weapons meant that the numbers of aircraft were less significant but the strategic value was enormous. Only the types used in the Second World War had to test themselves in a major war and their reputations, as passed down to history have varied from the 'superlative' for the Avro Lancaster to the 'heroic failure' of the Fairey Battle. What, however, cannot be denied for any of the wartime types is the courage and tenacity of their aircrew and the hardwork and dedication of their ground crew. Mention must also, of course, be made of the designers and manufactures, some of whom battled against official indifference to produce aircraft that subsequently became key components of Bomber Command.

The Avro Lancaster is remembered as the most important and effective RAF bomber of the Second World War.

Summary of Operational Types

Aircraft	Period of service	Sqns	First Op	Last Op	Crew
Pre 1939					
Virginia	(May 1924)–Feb 1938	3			4
Heyford	(Nov 1933)–Aug 1939	11			4
Overstrand	(Jan 1935)–Aug 1938	2			5
Hind	(Dec 1935)–Sep 1939	40			2
Hendon	Nov 1936–Jan 1939	2			5
Harrow	Jan 1937–Dec 1939	5	(Op use outside Bomber Command)		5
Wellesley	Apr 1937–Apr 1939	6	(Op use Middle East/Africa)		2
Second World War					
Whitley	Mar 1937–Dec 1942	9	3/4 Sep 1939	27/28 Apr 1942	5
Battle	May 1937–Aug 1941	21	(*see notes)	(*see notes)	3
Blenheim	Mar 1937–Nov 1942	24	3 Sep 1939	18 Aug 1942	3
Hampden	Feb 1939–Sep 1942	14	3 Sep 1939	14/15 Sep 1942	4
Wellington	Oct 1939–Jan 1945	45	3 Sep 1939	8/9 Oct 1943	5 or 6
Stirling	Aug 1940–Mar 1945	14	10/11 Feb 1941	Mar 1945*	7
Manchester	Nov 1940–Jun 1942	7	24/25 Feb 1941	25/26 Jun 1942	7
Halifax	Nov 1940–Nov 1945	32	10/11 Mar 1941	2/3 Mar 1945	6 or 7
Fortress	May 1941–	3	8 Jul 1942	May 1945	10
Boston	Jul 1941–May 1943	4	22 Feb 1942	Post May 1943	4
Mosquito	Nov 1941–Jan 1953	13	31 May 1942	2/3 May 1945	2
Lancaster	Dec 1941–Mar 1950	60	10/11 Mar 1942*	25/26 Apr 1945	7
Ventura	May 1942–May 1943	4	3 Nov 1942	Post May 1943	5
Mitchell	Sep 1942–	4	22 Jan 1943	Post May 1943	5
1945-1968					
Lincoln	Aug 1945–Dec 1955	24	*Op* use in Malaya and Kenya		7
Washington	Aug 1950–Mar 1954	8			10
Canberra	May 1951–(current)	24	BC *Op* use Malaya and Suez		3
Valiant	Jan 1955–Dec 1964	10	*Op* use Suez		5
Victor	Apr 1958–(Oct 1993)	7	*Op* use in tanker role*		4 or 5
Vulcan	Jul 1957–(Mar 1984)	9	*Op* use 1982 (Falklands)*		5
Thor	Sep 1958–Aug 1963	20			0

Notes

1. Period of service refers to numbered squadrons; in some cases aircraft entered service with the Command prior to this date and continued beyond it, usually in a training or support role. The medium bombers of No. 2 Group (Boston, Mitchell, Ventura) transferred with that Group to Tactical Air Force at the end of May 1943.
2. Number of squadrons refers to operational squadrons and does not include training units or specialist units. The figure is the total number of squadrons in the Command that used the type.
3. Operational dates for the Battle are difficult as they were operating with the Advanced Air Striking Force in France from late 1939, including sorties near the border with Germany; it was not until May 1940 that the real operational period began. Battles also operated from the UK attacking invasion ports in summer 1940.
4. Last Stirling *Op* September 1944 bombing, March 1945 RCM.
5. First Lancaster *Op* was minelaying on 3/4 March; this is the first bombing *Op*.
6. The final *ops* do not take account of Operation *Exodus* (26 Apr–7 May 1945) and *Manna* (29 Apr–7 May 1945) as these were 'peaceful' sorties with no bombs.
7. Operational use refers to Bomber Command use, although notes are made in respect of other operational use of the type for pre-war and post-war types only.
8. Crew is the average crew for the type; some variants had different crew levels – for example RCM variants invariably carried an extra 'special operator'.
9. Both the Victor and the Vulcan saw operational use after the Bomber Command period; the former playing a key role as a tanker in various campaigns, most notably the Falklands (1982) and the first Gulf War (1991).

This chapter is divided into the same three periods we have used throughout this book: Pre-1939, the Second World War and the Cold War (1945–1968). The most significant aircraft types (and one missile) are included and reference is made in each section to other aircraft if this is appropriate. Aircraft tables concentrate on the period of use of the type by Bomber Command: this is reflected in service dates by placing start or end dates in brackets if it occurred outside of the period of Bomber Command use; for example the aircraft types that were part of No. 2 Group at the end of May 1943 when the Group transferred to the Tactical Air Force. The entries are not therefore a mini history of the type as in many instances the type was used outside of Bomber Command. Occasional notes are included if considered relevant; for example the operational use of the Vulcan and Victor in their later, post Bomber Command years. The tables do not show individual Marks of aircraft and the airfield list is main bases only and not detachments. Airfields are only listed for the period the type was in use with Bomber Command use.

Pre-1939

When Bomber Command was formed from Central Area, Western Area and No. 1 Air Defence Group in May 1936 it acquired three operational Groups equipped with a variety of biplane bomber, from the light-bomber Hawker Hinds, the most common type within the Command, to the large bomber types such as the Virginia and Heyford, which were concentrated in No. 3 Group. The fourth operational Group, No. 2 Group formed in May 1936, was also primarily equipped with Hinds, although some squadrons had Fairey Gordons. Considering that the Second World War was only three years away it was not an impressive Order of Battle. The Fairey Gordon is best known for its overseas service with the RAF and it was in the Middle East and Africa (Sudan) that the type spent most of its career in the 1930s; although, a number of Bomber Command squadrons were equipped with the aircraft for a short period of time in 1936–1937 it has been omitted from the list of types. A number of squadrons also acquired other types as expedients whilst waiting for their real equipment; some were aircraft, such as the Avro Anson, that were operational types, albeit not as true bombers, but they too have been omitted from this list.

Vickers Virginia

The Virginia had entered service with 7 Squadron in May 1924 and was to be the RAF's main home-based strategic bomber for almost 15 years, eventually equipping eight squadrons. Designed to Specification 1/21 the Virginia first flew in November 1922 and was intended as a night bomber, although bomber doctrine also claimed that it could operate by day. Over the next few years the Virginia was produced in a large number of Marks, the final operational variant being the Mk X. Production came to an end in December 1932 by which time the RAF had received 124 aircraft, fifty of which had been built as the Mk X with its fabric-covered metal structure (the early variants had been wooden structure); most of the surviving examples of the early Marks were upgraded to Mk X standard.

By the time that Bomber Command formed only three squadrons were still equipped with Virginias, the other five having re-equipped, although two of the long-serving Virginia units, 7 Squadron and 9 Squadron, both of which had used the type since 1924, had only given them up in spring 1936.

Virginia of 9 Squadron, March 1927; the airmen are in the 'fighting tops', each of which carried a single machine gun.

Vickers VIRGINIA
Prototype, first flight: J6856, 24 November 1922
Entry to service: 7 Sqn, May 1924

Squadron	Dates	Airfield
51 Sqn	Mar 1937–Feb 1938	Driffield, Boscombe Down
58 Sqn	(Dec 1924)–Jan 1938	Worthy Down, Upper Heyford, Driffield
214 Sqn	(Sep 1935)–Apr 1937	Boscombe Down, Andover, Scampton

Handley Page Heyford

The lumbering shape of the Heyford first took to the air in 1930 and at the time was a reasonable day bomber with its 'fighting tops' with gunners who could protect the aircraft against the manoeuvrable but under-armed fighters of the day. This was still true – just – in November 1933 when the Heyford 5 entered service with 99 Squadron. However, it is amazing to think that Bomber Command still had five squadrons equipped with this bomber well into 1939; if war had come with the Munich Crisis of September 1938 this would have been one of the front-line bombers!

The Handley Page Heyford was the culmination of a generation of large biplane bombers that had started in the First World War with the Handley Page 0/100 and 0/400. These types had helped pioneer the doctrine of strategic bombing and were followed by the likes of the Vimy and the Virginia. The Handley Page HP.38 (the Heyford) was designed to Specification 22/32 and first flew in June 1933; its most unusual feature was that the fuselage was attached to the underside of the top wing rather than the more usual arrangement of it sitting on the lower wing. It was a massive aircraft and with its large wheel spats was not the most attractive of aircraft. Its performance of 142 mph, 21,000 ft and a 1,600 lb bomb load over a range of 920 miles was not bad for the period. The maximum bomb load was 3,500 lb, part of which was carried in internal bomb cells – one of the first aircraft with a bomb bay. Self defence was provided by three gun stations each with a Lewis gun. By late 1936 Bomber Command had nine squadrons of Heyfords in service; the concept of operations involved stooging around in formation at 10,000 ft looking for their targets. In exercises the gunners 'fought off' the attacking Demons and Furies and the bombing theory appeared practical.

Heyford K6898 on its nose having overshot on landing when diverted due to bad weather.

Handley Page HEYFORD
Prototype, first flight: J9130, June 1930
Entry to service: 99 Sqn, November 1933

Squadron	Dates	Airfield
7 Sqn	(Mar 1935)–Apr 1938	Worthy Down, Finningley
9 Sqn	(Feb 1936)–May 1939	Aldergrove, Scampton, Stradishall
10 Sqn	(Aug 1934)–June 1937	Boscombe Down, Dishforth
38 Sqn	(Sep 1935)–Apr 1937	Mildenhall
78 Sqn	Nov 1936–Jun 1938	Boscombe Down, Dishforth
97 Sqn	(Sep 1935)–Aug 1937	Boscombe Down, Leconfield
99 Sqn	(Nov 1933)–Nov 1938	Upper Heyford, Mildenhall
102 Sqn	(Oct 1935)–May 1939	Worthy Down, Finningley, Honington, Driffield
148 Sqn	Nov 1938–May 1939	Stradishall
149 Sqn	Apr 1937–Aug 1939	Mildenhall
166 Sqn	Nov 1936–Jul 1939	Boscombe Down, Leconfield

The RAF had received 124 Heyfords by the time production ceased in July 1936, these being made up of three main variants, the Mk I/Ia, Mk II, and Mk III. The type appeared in the news a number of times, two such instances being the Royal Review of 1935 and the loss of three of 102 Squadron's aircraft when returning to Finningley from Aldergrove in mid December 1935. Seven Heyfords left for the flight back to their base but in poor weather only one made it; of the others, three crashed and three landed elsewhere, although one ended up its nose having overshot the runway. With its replacement in front-line units the Heyford remained in second-line service to summer 1941 when the type was finally declared obsolete.

Boulton Paul Overstrand

If there was a prize for the ugliest Bomber Command aircraft the Overstrand would almost certainly be the runaway winner, which in some ways is unfair as its ugliest feature – the 'greenhouse' on the nose was actually the RAF's first power-operated gun turret and as such pointed the way to the future armament of bombers. When first developed to Specification 29/33 it was known as the Sidestrand V but in March 1934 the name was changed to Overstrand (a small village on the Norfolk coast and thus not far from Boulton Paul in Norwich). Only twenty-four service aircraft were produced under Specification 23/34 and only one squadron was fully equipped with the Overstrand, 101 Squadron acquiring the type in January 1935 to supplement and then replace the Boulton Paul Sidestrand. However, when the Squadron's 'B Flight' became the nucleus of 144 Squadron at Bicester in January 1937 they took their four Overstrands with them, although they were given up the following month in favour of Ansons (the Ansons too were a temporary measure pending equipment with Blenheims).

Overstrands of 101 Squadron; despite its antiquated appearance the Overstrand included a number of advanced features.

Boulton Paul OVERSTRAND
Prototype, first flight: J9186, 1933
Entry to service: 101 Sqn, January 1935

Squadron	Dates	Airfield
101 Sqn	(Jan 1935)–Aug 1938	Bicester
144 Sqn	Jan 1937–Feb 1937	Bicester

The Overstrand had a crew of five, a top speed of 153 mph, a ceiling of 22,500 ft (on a good day) and a maximum bomb load of 1,600 lb. When 101 Squadron re-equipped with Blenheims a number of the remaining Overstrands continued to be used for support roles.

Hawker Hind

At the peak of its service with the light bomber squadrons (spring 1937) there were 452 Hinds in service, an incredible total – especially when they had all vanished from the front-line within two years. The Hawker Hind is very much one of the ignored aircraft types in the history of Bomber Command but its importance to the Command during this period of rapid expansion cannot be overstated. It was always intended as an interim aircraft but it enabled squadrons to form, train and gain experience prior to receiving more appropriate aircraft; for that reason alone it deserves a place in the Bomber Command record – and as a derivative of the delightful Hart it had an excellent pedigree. It is worth mentioning here that a number of Hart-equipped squadrons joined Bomber Command when it was formed, although they re-equipped with Hinds during 1936.

The Hind was designed to Specification G.7/34 for a General Purpose day bomber and the prototype first flew on 12 September 1934 and looked almost identical to the Hart, although it had a supercharged Kestrel engine and a different gunner's cockpit. First unit was 21 Squadron at Bircham Newton but equipment of squadrons proceeded at a rapid pace. The Hind had a top speed of 186 mph, a ceiling of 26,400 ft and a minute bomb load of 500 lb and two machine guns: this performance, and a range of only 430 miles meant that this was certainly not a truly operational type for Bomber Command but as with other members of the Hawker family of biplanes it was said to be a delight to fly and was well liked by its crews. Having been taken out of 'front-line' service, although the last squadron did not lose its aircraft until 1940, the Hind continued in use throughout the war in support roles, primarily training. This included 139 light-bombers that were converted to dual-control Hind Trainers.

The Hawker Hind had a brief spell with Bomber Command but for a few months it equipped a large number of squadrons; 98 Squadron had Hinds for nearly two years.

Hawker HIND
Prototype, first flight: K2915, 12 September 1934
Entry to service: 21 Sqn, December 1935

Squadron	Dates	Airfield
12 Sqn	Oct 1936–Feb 1938	Andover
15 Sqn	(Mar 1936)–Jul 1938	Abingdon
18 Sqn	(Apr 1936)–May 1939	Bircham Newton, Upper Heyford
21 Sqn	(Dec 1935)–Aug 1938	Bircham Newton, Abbotsinch, Lympne, Eastchurch
34 Sqn	(Jan 1936)–Jul 1938	Bircham Newton, Abbotsinch, Lympne, Upper Heyford
40 Sqn	(Mar 1936)–Aug 1938	Abingdon
44 Sqn	Mar 1937–Dec 1937	Wyton, Andover, Waddington
49 Sqn	(Feb 1936)–Dec 1938	Bircham Newton, Worthy Down, Scampton
50 Sqn	May 1937–Jan 1939	Waddington
52 Sqn	Jan 1937–Dec 1937	Abingdon, Upwood
57 Sqn	May 1936–May 1938	Upper Heyford
62 Sqn	May 1937–Mar 1938	Abingdon, Cranfield
63 Sqn	Feb 1937–Apr 1937	Andover, Upwood
83 Sqn	Aug 1936–Dec 1938	Turnhouse, Scampton
90 Sqn	Mar 1937–Jun 1937	Bicester
98 Sqn	(Feb 1936)–Jun 1938	Abingdon, Hucknall
103 Sqn	Aug 1936–Aug 1938	Andover, Usworth
104 Sqn	Jul 1936–May 1938	Abingdon, Hucknall, Bassingbourn
106 Sqn	Jun 1938–Jul 1938	Abingdon
107 Sqn	Sep 1936–Sep 1938	Andover, Old Sarum, Harwell
108 Sqn	Jan 1937–Jun 1938	Upper Heyford, Farnborough, Cranfield, Bassingbourn
110 Sqn	May 1937–Jan 1938	Waddington
113 Sqn	May 1937–(Jun 1939)	Upper Heyford, Grantham
114 Sqn	Dec 1936–Mar 1937	Wyton
139 Sqn	Sep 1936–Jul 1937	Wyton
142 Sqn	Jan 1937–Apr 1938	Andover
185 Sqn	Mar 1938–Jul 1938	Abingdon
211 Sqn	Aug 1937–(May 1939)	Mildenhall, Grantham
500 Sqn	Feb 1937–Mar 1939	Manston, Detling
501 Sqn	Mar 1938–Mar 1939	Filton
502 Sqn	Apr 1937–Apr 1939	Aldergrove
503 Sqn	Jun 1938–Nov 1938	Waddington
504 Sqn	May 1937–Nov 1938	Hucknall
602 Sqn	Jun 1936–Nov 1938	Abbotsinch
603 Sqn	Feb 1938–Mar 1939	Turnhouse
605 Sqn	Aug 1936–Jan 1939	Castle Bromwich
609 Sqn	Jan 1938–Aug 1939	Yeadon
610 Sqn	May 1938–Sep 1939	Hooton Park
611 Sqn	Apr 1938–May 1939	Speke
616 Sqn	Nov 1938–Jan 1939	Doncaster

A total of 528 aircraft were produced; the Hind was the RAF's last biplane bomber and from an aesthetic if not operational point of view it was not a bad way to go out. A small number of aircraft (Harts and Hinds) have been preserved, including an immaculate airworthy Hind operated by the Shuttleworth Collection.

Fairey Hendon

Only fourteen Fairey Hendon night bombers were produced but it has a place in Bomber Command, and indeed RAF history as the first all-metal low-wing monoplane to enter service. The Fairey Night Bomber (it was not called the Hendon until November 1934)

The Fairey Hendon night bomber was slow and had a small bomb-load but it did incorporate a number of advanced features.

Fairey HENDON
Prototype, first flight: K1695, November 1930
Entry to service: 38 Sqn, November 1936

Squadron	Dates	Airfield
38 Sqn	Nov 1936–Jan 1939	Mildenhall, Marham
115 Sqn	Jun 1937–Aug 1937	Marham

---

was designed to Specification B.19/27 for a 'heavy' night bomber and the prototype flew in November 1930. The fabric-covered metal structure gave a rugged aircraft and its performance of 155 mph, ceiling of 21,500 ft and bomb load of 1,600 lb met the Specification.

The Hendon entered service with 38 Squadron at Marham in November 1936. However, the development period having taken longer than expected meant that there were better options becoming available by this time and the main contract for another sixty aircraft was cancelled.

In June 1937, 'B Flt' of 38 Squadron became the nucleus of 115 Squadron and took four Hendons across the airfield with them, although the new unit was re-equipped with Harrows in June. The short career of the Hendon came to an end in January 1939 when 38 Squadron received Wellingtons.

Handley Page Harrow

The Handley Page origins of this high-wing monoplane were obvious; indeed at first glance it might be thought that the manufacturers had simply taken the lower wing off the Heyford. The Harrow was designed to Specification 29/35 for a heavy bomber and the prototype flew in October 1936, although orders had already been placed the previous year. There were no significant problems in the development and the aircraft entered service with 214 Squadron at Scampton the following January. By the end of the year five Bomber Command squadrons had equipped with the type; all of them kept the Harrow in service to mid 1939, with 215 Squadron being last to lose the type, in December, although its first Wellingtons had arrived in the summer.

Despite its somewhat ungainly appearance, not helped by the spatted undercarriage, the Harrow had a reasonable performance with top speed of around 200 mph, ceiling of 22,800 ft and bomb load of 3,000 lb. It also had three power-operated turrets, although the mid-upper turret was not fitted to all aircraft. These figures would have been fine for

Atmospheric shot of a 115 Squadron Harrow at Marham; note the squadron number painted on the fuselage of the aircraft. The powered turrets in the nose and tail were a pointer to the future but the rest of the aircraft was grounded in the past.

Handley Page HARROW
Prototype, first flight: K6933, 10 October 1936
Entry to service: 214 Sqn, January 1937

Squadron	Dates	Airfield
37 Sqn	Apr 1937–Jun 1939	Feltwell
75 Sqn	Sep 1937–Jul 1939	Driffield, Honington
15 Sqn	Jun 1937–Jun 1939	Marham
214 Sqn	Jan 1937–Jun 1939	Scampton, Feltwell
215 Sqn	Aug 1937–Dec 1939	Driffield, Honington

the early 1930s but by 1938, when the five squadrons were very much in the front line, they would have been little short of disastrous should war have broken out.

Bomber Command gave up its Harrows before the shooting war started but the aircraft served with other units and did see active service during the war as well as being used for various support roles. The most unusual utilisation was that of 93 Squadron, which used Harrows to sow aerial minefields as part of the night defence of England. The major user of the Harrow was 271 Squadron in the transport and later medical evacuation role, the type usually being referred to as the Sparrow.

Vickers Wellesley

The Wellesley was a private venture not intended for an Air Ministry Specification but with the hope that in the mid 1930s period of a desperate rush to expand the RAF there was a good chance of acquiring a contract. The prototype flew in June 1935 and was the first Vickers design to use the fabric-covered metal geodetic structure. In September the 'expected' contract was received, ninety-six aircraft being ordered to Specification 22/35. The Wellesley entered service with 76 Squadron at Finningley in April 1937 as a two-seat day General Purpose bomber.

It was a strange-looking aircraft with its twin cockpit arrangement and very long wing. Despite being single-engined the overall performance was reasonable with a top speed of 228 mph, ceiling of 33,000 ft and bomb load of 2,000 lb – not too bad for a GP type. Self-defence armament was not very impressive, comprising single machine guns fore and aft.

The Wellesley had a very short career with Bomber Command; by autumn 1937 there were six squadrons but by the end of the following year this had reduced to a single squadron. This was not the end of the Wellesley's service and a large number of aircraft were transferred to squadrons in the Middle East and Africa, where they saw active service against the Italians. The type finally left front-line service in August 1943 but a number of aircraft remained in use in support roles.

The one notable achievement of the Wellesley was the autumn 1938 flight by three Wellesleys of the Long Range Development Flight; two of the aircraft completed a record-breaking non-stop flight from Egypt to Australia – a distance of 7,162 miles in around forty-eight hours.

Formation of Wellesleys of 76 Squadron airborne out of Finningley. The Wellesley was a two-crew day bomber and when it entered service in 1937 was totally out of date from an operational point of view.

Vickers WELLESLEY
Prototype, first flight: K7556, 9 June 1935
Entry to service: 76 Sqn, April 1937

Squadron	Dates	Airfield
7 Sqn	Apr 1937–Apr 1938	Finningley
35 Sqn	Jul 1937–May 1938	Worthy Down
76 Sqn	Apr 1937–Apr 1939	Finningley
77 Sqn	Nov 1937–Nov 1938	Honington, Driffield
148 Sqn	Jun 1937–Nov 1938	Scampton, Stradishall
207 Sqn	Sep 1937–Apr 1938	Worthy Down

Second World War

As mentioned above, Bomber Command was in a poor position in respect to its Order of Battle in the late 1930s. The aircraft that had entered service in the earlier part of the decade were definitely obsolete and the new types under development in the mid 1930s were only just starting to arrive on squadrons in the late 1930s, and even then they were based on what was soon to prove a flawed doctrine of daylight operations. Despite the fact that the expansion plans of the early 1930s had placed the greatest emphasis on bombers over other types, and despite large orders being placed, often straight off the drawing board, the Command was poorly equipped in 1939. Whilst a number of new types were coming on line the advanced nature of those types caused its own problems; for example, the high incidence of wheels-up landings by Blenheim pilots who were not used to having a retractable undercarriage. Bomb loads had increased but the bombs, with their origins in the First World War, were to prove woefully inadequate in the new war. Bombers had started to sprout more self-defence guns but the concept of 'impenetrable massed firepower' from formations of bombers had yet to be tested. Furthermore, most of the new medium bombers required two pilots and the strain on the training system was enormous.

All the four-engined bombers were under development before war broke out and by 1940 the RAF was planning an all-heavy bomber force of 4,000 aircraft to be achieved by 1944–1945; if this had come to fruition the bomb lift, and thus the destructive potential of the Command would have been enormous.

The Halifax had a mixed record with Bomber Command but the overall assessment of it being inferior to the Lancaster is in large measure unjustified. The Command's desire from 1940 onwards was for a bomber force comprising thousands of four-engine bombers.

Armstrong-Whitworth Whitley

The Armstrong-Whitworth Whitley entered service with 10 Squadron at Dishforth in March 1937, one of the new heavy bombers for Bomber Command and the only one designed as a night bomber. The aircraft was designed to Specification B.3/34 and first flew on 17 March 1936 (prototype K4586), by which time its top speed of less than 200 mph and an operational ceiling of less than 20,000 ft, and limited defensive armament, were beginning to look inadequate. As with all the other bomber types entering service around this same period it was an improvement over the existing front-line types but was nevertheless verging on obsolete. The one saving grace when it entered service was that it had been designed for night operations and as night fighters were a rarity in the late 1930s the fighter threat was almost non-existent.

Nevertheless, a number of armament improvements were made to the variants entering service over the first few years of the Whitley's service, including the Mk IV with the impressive Nash and Thompson four-gun powered rear turret. More powerful engines were also introduced and the Whitley V had a maximum speed of 222 mph. The initial order for eighty aircraft was costed at an average of around £25,000 per aircraft. Orders were soon increased and the unit price reduced to £17,000 per aircraft.

At the outbreak of war No. 4 Group, with whom the type was concentrated, had a well established operational routine with its squadrons as most had re-equipped with the type by late 1938. The Whitleys were airborne on the first night of the war with Linton-on-Ouse despatching aircraft of 51 and 58 Squadrons to drop leaflets over the Ruhr. This first *nickelling* sortie set the scene for the Group for the first months of the war, including a trip to Berlin on the night of 1/2 October 1939 – the first British aircraft over the German capital being a Whitley of 10 Squadron. Between the start of the war and late December 1939 the Whitleys operated, in small numbers, on twenty-two nights with leaflet-dropping the main activity, although 'night reconnaissance' was also tasked. Losses were low and the crews, and Bomber Command in general, gained experience and information on night operations. This factor was to be highly significant when the Command abandoned daytime attacks in favour of the cover of night.

With the launching of the bombing campaign against land targets the Whitley units began dropping other cargo than leaflets, although the 3,000 lb bomb load was not impressive by later standards. The Whitleys also took part in the maritime war both with mine-laying and anti-submarine operations, the latter with units detached to Coastal Command. Sidney Munns was an experienced Observer: 'Compared with the Fairey

Whitley of 7 Squadron at Finningley; the Squadron re-equipped from Heyfords in March 1938. The Whitley became standard equipment for No. 4 Group and pioneered night leaflet-dropping operations.

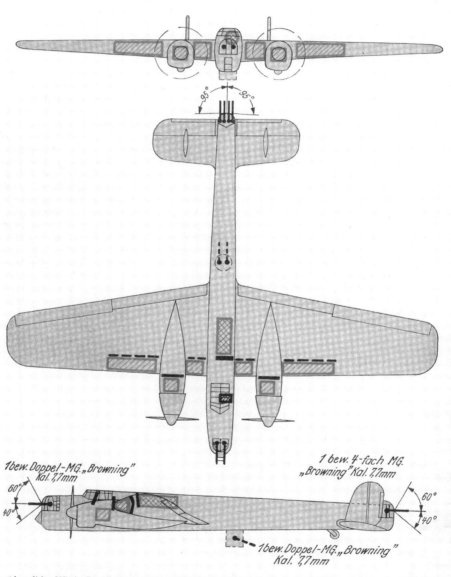

Die Kriegsflugzeuge der Feindmächte

Großbritannien

Anlage 31 a

Armstrong-Whitworth „Whitley V"
Kampfflugzeug

1bew. Doppel-MG.„Browning" Kal. 7,7mm

1 bew. 4-fach MG. „Browning"Kal. 7,7mm

1bew.Doppel-MG.„Browning" Kal. 7,7mm

1 bewegliches MG. im Rumpfbug. 1 bewegliches Vierfach-MG. im Rumpfheck in hydraulisch betätigtem Drehturm, manchmal auch 1 bewegliches Doppel-MG. in ausfahrbarem, handbetätigtem Drehturm an Rumpfunterseite. Antrieb des hydraulisch betätigten Drehturmes im Rumpfheck von einer Pumpe am **rechten** *Motor.*

Armstrong-Whitworth WHITLEY
Prototype, first flight: K4586, 17 March 1936
Entry to service: 10 Sqn, March 1937

Squadron	Dates	Airfield
7 Sqn	Mar 1938–May 1939	Finningley
10 Sqn	Mar 1937–Dec 1941	Dishforth
51 Sqn	Feb 1938–Oct 1942	Linton-on-Ouse, Dishforth, Chivenor
58 Sqn	Oct 1937–Dec 1942	Boscombe Down, Linton-on-Ouse, St Eval
77 Sqn	Nov 1938–Oct 1942	Driffield, Linton-on-Ouse, Topcliffe, Leeming
78 Sqn	Jul 1937–Mar 1942	Dishforth, Linton-on-Ouse, Croft
97 Sqn	Feb 1939–Apr 1940	Leconfield, Abingdon
102 Sqn	Oct 1938–Feb 1942	Driffield, Leeming, Linton-on-Ouse, Topcliffe, Dalton
138 Sqn	Aug 1941–Nov 1942	Newmarket, Stradishall
161 Sqn	Feb 1942–Dec 1942	Newmarket, Graveley, Tempsford
166 Sqn	Jun 1939–Apr 1940	Leconfield, Abingdon

Battle, the navigator's station in a Whitley was to me like a palace: a comfortable seat to sit on, and a proper plotting table to work on, with instruments conveniently to hand and even an angle-poise lamp to see by. The bomb-aiming position in the nose of the aircraft was equally well equipped and comfortable by comparison. With its longer range, navigating in a Whitley was a more satisfying experience and by the end of August 1940 I was navigating on night-time exercises of eight hours' duration, similar in length to typical operational sorties over Germany.'

The Whitley flew its last Bomber Command operational sortie over Germany (five aircraft of 58 Squadron) on the night of 27 April 1942 the target being Rostock, the fourth night that week that Main Force had attacked this Baltic port. The final sortie was made by two of the Squadron's aircraft the following day against Dunkirk. This was not the end of the Whitleys career with Bomber Command and the type continued to serve with the OTUs for some time; it also served with other Commands, especially Coastal Command – the other major user – to the end of the war. The Mk V was the only variant built in significant numbers (1,466) and of the over 1,600 Whitleys built there are no survivors, although a number of major airframe components have been salvaged in recent years. The Whitley even had a 'ditty' that was popular with the crews of No. 4 Group and was sung to the tune of Waltzing Matilda:

Ops in a Whitley

The first silly blighter got into his aeroplane,
Said he would fly over Germany,
And he sang as he swang and pranged it on the boundary,
'Who'll come on Ops in a Whitley with me?'
    Chorus:
    Ops in a Whitley, Ops in a Whitley,
    Who'll come on Ops in a Whitley with me?
    And he sang as he swang and pranged it on the boundary,
    'Who'll come on Ops in a Whitley with me?'

The second silly blighter got into the air all right,
Flew over Flamborough and crashed it in the sea,
And they sang as they swam right up and down the coast and back,
'Who'll come on Ops in a Whitley with me?'
    Chorus:

The third silly blighter got out over Germany,
Up came the flak like a Christmas tree,
And the Wireless Op, cried as the Captain quite forgot himself,
'Who'll come on Ops in a Whitley with me?'
  Chorus:

The fourth silly blighter flew out over Hanover,
Up came the fighters, one, two, three,
And the Rear Gunner cried as he buckled on his parachute,
'Who'll come on Ops in a Whitley with me?'
  Chorus:

The fifth silly blighter he got over Magdeburg,
They couldn't find the target and dropped 'em in the sea,
And the Navigator cried as the Captain tried to shoot himself,
'Who'll come on Ops in a Whitley with me?'
  Chorus:

The sixth silly blighter he got there and back all right,
They gave him a Green but he couldn't see the 'T',
And he sang midst the flames as he pranged it on the hangar-roof,
'Who'll come on Ops in a Whitley with me?'

Fairey Battle

The Fairey Battle is not an aircraft that is usually associated with Bomber Command and yet the role of the aircraft was important – as well as tragic. The Battle, like the Blenheim, was produced in response to Specification P.27/32 for a Light Bomber and like the Blenheim initially showed promise. Prototype K4303 first flew on 10 March 1936 and entered service in May 1937 with 63 Squadron at Upwood. Replacing biplane light bombers such as the Hart and Hind the Fairey Battle was a definite improvement with its 241 mph speed and 1,000 lb bomb load. The sleek lines and stressed-skin construction gave it an advanced appearance and pilots considered that it was a responsive aircraft; however, they were to add that, 'Despite its agreeable qualities it was not an operational machine. It could only carry four 250 lb bombs and was far too slow if enemy fighters were around.' Fairey was given an initial instruction to proceed with an average price of £7,250 per aircraft, the initial ten being costed at £22,009. The initial order for 155 aircraft was almost immediately increased to 339.

When the Battle came to fight its war there proved to be far too many enemy fighters around that were well-armed and fast. The Battles equipped No. 1 Group and as war approached all ten squadrons were allocated to the Advanced Air Striking Force (AASF) for deployment to France in support of British operations. They duly deployed in September 1939 and over the next few months were primarily used on reconnaissance missions, although the occasional contact was made with the enemy. During this phase of the Phoney War the bombers were not allowed to attack strategic targets as bombing of land targets was still prohibited. When the Germans launched their offensive in the West in May 1940 the Fairey Battles of the AASF entered the fray in a series of daring attacks on lines of communication, mainly bridges, and troop movements. In the face of heavy German defences, fighters and anti-aircraft fire, the Battles were shot out of the sky; over half of the available aircraft were lost in a single day. For one of these attacks

Battles of 218 Squadron; the Fairey light-bomber was a revolution when it entered service and its 'place in history' as a disaster (ops in connection with the German attack on May 1940) is not fully justified.

on 12 May 1940 two members of the crew of 12 Squadron Battle P2204 were each awarded the Victoria Cross.

The remnants of the Battle force were withdrawn to the UK for rest and re-equipment. This was not the end of the aircraft's participation in bomber operations and the Battles continued in the front-line with No. 1 Group, although some squadrons began to re-equip with Wellingtons. Attacks on the ports being used for the invasion build-up were prime targets and the Battles, along with all other Bomber Command types, made

---

Fairey BATTLE
Prototype, first flight: K4303, 10 March 1936
Entry to service: 63 Sqn, May 1937

Squadron	Dates	Airfield
12 Sqn	Feb 1938–Nov 1940	Andover, Bicester, Finningley, Binbrook
15 Sqn	Jun 1938–Dec 1939	Abingdon
35 Sqn	Apr 1938–Feb 1940	Worthy Down, Cottesmore, Cranfield, Bassingbourn
40 Sqn	Jul 1938–Dec 1939	Abingdon
52 Sqn	Nov 1937–Apr 1940	Upwood, Abingdon, Benson
63 Sqn	May 1937–Apr 1940	Upwood, Abingdon, Benson
88 Sqn	Dec 1937–Aug 1941	Boscombe Down, Driffield, Sydenham
98 Sqn	Jun 1938–Jul 1941	Hucknall, Scampton, Finningley
103 Sqn	Jul 1938–Oct 1940	Usworth, Abingdon, Benson, Honington, Newton
105 Sqn	Aug 1937–May 1940	Harwell, Honington
106 Sqn	Jul 1938–May 1939	Abingdon, Thornaby, Grantham
142 Sqn	Mar 1938–Nov 1940	Andover, Bicester, Binbrook
150 Sqn	Aug 1938–Sep 1940	Boscombe Down, Benson, Stradishall, Newton
185 Sqn	Jun 1938–Jun 1939	Abingdon, Thornaby, Grantham
207 Sqn	Apr 1938–Apr 1940	Cottesmore, Cranfield, Cottesmore
218 Sqn	Jan 1938–May 1940	Upper Heyford, Boscombe Down, Mildenhall
226 Sqn	Oct 1937–May 1941	Harwell, Sydenham, Wattisham
300 Sqn	Jul 1940–Nov 1940	Bramcote, Swinderby
301 Sqn	Jul 1940–Nov 1940	Bramcote, Swinderby
304 Sqn	Aug 1940–Nov 1940	Bramcote
305 Sqn	Aug 1940–Nov 1940	Bramcote

frequent attacks on this type of target. Whilst it was appreciated that the Battle would have to be removed from front-line Bomber Command service as soon as possible it was still used as initial equipment for new squadrons. The Battle flew its last Bomber Command operation on the night of 15/16 October 1940, nine aircraft being part of a force that attacked the Channel ports. After its final departure from the operational Groups the Battle was used in a variety of training roles and as such continued to play a part in the development of the Command. There are two surviving – or rather restored/rebuilt – examples of the Fairey Battle, one in the RAF Museum at Hendon and one in Belgium.

Handley Page Hampden

The Handley Page Hampden is one of the forgotten aircraft of Bomber Command and yet it played a major role in the first two years of the war, perhaps its most significant contribution being the development of the Command's air-dropped minelaying campaign. The Hampden was designed to the same twin-engine bomber specification, B.9/32, as the Wellington; and the Handley Page HP.52 was an impressive sleek-looking monoplane when it was first unveiled in the mid 1930s, a time when Bomber Command was equipped with lumbering biplanes. Prototype K4240 first flew on 21 June 1936 and its early performance was promising: it was faster than the Wellington and had a better bomb load and range than the Blenheim. An initial order was placed for 180 aircraft and the Hampden entered service with 49 Squadron at Scampton in August 1938. The initial order was soon increased to 320. Two more Bomber Command squadrons had re-equipped by the end of the year and by the outbreak of war there were ten squadrons in service.

The Hampden had a crew of four and from a purely flying point of view it was popular with pilots because of its manoeuvrability, which proved valuable during evasion of searchlights over Germany. It was considered to be an aircraft with no vices, although the cramped cockpit made a tight fit for the crew. From the defensive point of view the Hampden was not so well served; the early manually-operated 0.303 inch guns were typical of bomber armament of the late 1930s, but even though they were upgraded and their numbers increased, with twin guns in upper and ventral positions and one fixed and one movable gun forward, they were still inadequate. Losses on early daylight raids were heavy but this appears to have been primarily due to anti-aircraft and operational hazards such as weather rather than enemy fighters. From the offensive perspective the Hampden had a small load for a 'strategic bomber' of only 2,000 lb.

The Hampden was the main equipment of No.5 Group during the early years; its limited bomb-load was a major limitation but it remained in service with the Command to late 1942.

Handley Page HAMPDEN
Prototype, first flight: K4240, 21 June 1936
Entry to service: 44 Sqn, February 1939

Squadron	Dates	Airfield
7 Sqn	Apr 1939–Apr 1940	Finningley, Upper Heyford
44 Sqn	Feb 1939–Dec 1941	Waddington
49 Sqn	Aug 1938–Apr 1942	Scampton
50 Sqn	Dec 1938–Apr 1942	Waddington, Lindholme, Swinderby, Skellingthorpe
61 Sqn	Feb 1939–Oct 1941	Hemswell
76 Sqn	Mar 1939–Apr 1940	Finningley, Upper Heyford
83 Sqn	Nov 1938–Jan 1942	Scampton
106 Sqn	May 1939–Mar 1942	Thornaby, Cottesmore, Finningley, Coningsby
144 Sqn	Mar 1939–Apr 1942	Hemswell, North Luffenham
185 Sqn	Jun 1939–May 1940	Thornaby, Cottesmore
207 Sqn	Jul 1941–Aug 1941	Waddington, Bottesford
408 Sqn	Jun 1941–Sep 1942	Lindholme, Syerston, Balderton, Leeming
420 Sqn	Jan 1942–Aug 1942	Waddington, Skipton-on-Swale
455 Sqn	Jul 1941–Apr 1942	Swinderby, Wigsley

The Hampden suffered an additional problem in that its long pencil shape and bulbous front end, which led to its nickname of the 'flying panhandle', meant that it was frequently mistaken for the German Dornier Do.17. There were numerous instances of Hampdens being engaged by British fighters and anti-aircraft guns.

Hampdens flew the Command's first minelaying sortie on 13/14 April 1940; the operation was flown by fifteen aircraft, with fourteen reporting successful laying of mines in the sea lanes off Denmark between the Norwegian coast and the German ports. One Hampden was lost from this mission. No. 5 Group became the operational Group for the Hampden but it was obvious from 1940 that the type had severe limitations; however, with few options in terms of an immediate replacement the type remained in the front-line for three years, the last Bomber Command operation taking place on 14/15 September 1942.

No Hampdens have survived but at least two restoration projects are underway using wreckage recovered from various locations.

Bristol Blenheim

The Blenheim stunned the aviation world when it first appeared in 1936 as it was superior in performance to the current front-line fighters of the RAF. However, the highly-manoeuvrable but slow bi-planes were themselves in the process of giving way to modern types – and the *Luftwaffe* was already re-equipping with types such as the Bf 109. Without detracting from the importance of the Blenheim and the splendid achievement it represented as a private venture development it, like all of Bomber Command's new aircraft, was fine in 1937 for the planned doctrine but a mere two years later the situation had dramatically changed – and the Blenheim squadrons were to suffer very high losses as a result.

The Blenheim was under development in the early 1930s at a period when the RAF was desperate for new aircraft and it looked so impressive on paper that 150 were ordered 'off the drawing board' in August 1935, the prototype (K7033) not making its first flight until 25 June 1936. Destined to join Bomber Command as a light bomber the first Blenheims went to 114 Squadron at Wyton in March 1937 and the type became standard equipment for No. 2 Group. The concept of operations for the light bombers was daylight low-level attacks and although the Blenheim I had been replaced by the Mk IV in Bomber Command by the outbreak of war both its performance and armament were to prove inadequate. The first Mk IV unit, 90 Squadron, re-equipped in March 1939 and it was a Blenheim IV of Bomber Command that was the first British aircraft to intentionally cross the German border, a 139 Squadron aircraft flying a reconnaissance mission on 3 September 1939.

The Blenheims shouldered the burden of the daylight campaign for the first two years of the war, initially with anti-shipping operations but following the German invasion in May 1940 and clearance to attack land targets with an increasing variety of targets in Occupied Europe.

Some of the early anti-shipping sorties demonstrated the vulnerability of the Blenheim to both *flak* and fighters and although additional armour plating was added in the Mk IV the aircraft was, in common with all Bomber Command types at this period, ill-provided with passive defensive aids such as armour plate and self-sealing fuel tanks. The limitations of the Blenheim were known and attempts were made from 1941 to find a replacement, the Purchasing Commission in America eventually acquiring a number of American light and medium bombers – some of which were proved equally limited in operational terms. In the meantime the Blenheim units of No. 2 Group soldiered on and a number of notable attacks were made, including one led by Wing Commander Hughie Edwards of 105 Squadron against Bremen on 4 July 1941; an attack for which Edwards was awarded the Victoria Cross.

The last Bomber Command Blenheim *op* was flown on 18 August 1942, an intruder operation flown by 18 Squadron from Wattisham against German night fighter airfields in Holland. Bomber Command was only one of the users of the Blenheim and the aircraft served with Army Co-operation, Coastal and Fighter Commands in the UK, playing a key role with the latter in the development of radar for night fighting, as well as with overseas Commands and in training roles.

Over 4,000 Blenheims, mainly Mk IVs, were built and the type remained in service to the end of the war. A number of airframes have survived, although most of these are the Canadian-built Bolingbroke variant, including one airworthy aircraft that flies out of Duxford, Cambridgeshire.

Blenheim of 107 Squadron: when it first appeared in 1936 the Blenheim was a vast improvement in every respect over the aircraft then in service with Bomber Command; however, in daylight operations in the early years of the war it suffered heavy losses.

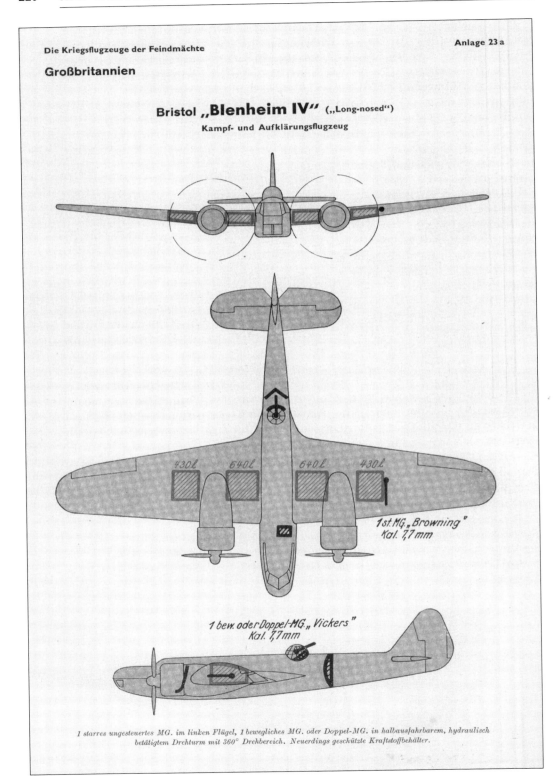

Die Kriegsflugzeuge der Feindmächte

Großbritannien

Anlage 23 a

Bristol „Blenheim IV" („Long-nosed")
Kampf- und Aufklärungsflugzeug

430 ℓ   640 ℓ   640 ℓ   430 ℓ

1st.MG.„Browning"
Kal. 7,7mm

1 bew. oder Doppel-MG.„Vickers"
Kal. 7,7mm

1 starres ungesteuertes MG. im linken Flügel, 1 bewegliches MG. oder Doppel-MG. in halbausfahrbarem, hydraulisch betätigtem Drehturm mit 360° Drehbereich. Neuerdings geschützte Kraftstoffbehälter.

Bristol BLENHEIM
Prototype, first flight: K7033, 25 June 1936
Entry to service: 114 Sqn March 1937

Squadron	Dates	Airfield
15 Sqn	Dec 1939–Oct 1940	Wyton, Alconbury
18 Sqn	May 1939–Apr 1943	Upper Heyford, Great Massingham, Oulton, Wattisham, West Raynham
21 Sqn	Aug 1938–Mar 1942	Eastchurch, Watton, Lossiemouth, Bodney
34 Sqn	Jul 1938–Aug 1939	Upper Heyford, Watton
35 Sqn	Nov 1939–Apr 1940	Cranfield, Bassingbourn, Upwood
40 Sqn	Dec 1939–Nov 1940	Wyton
44 Sqn	Dec 1937–Feb 1939	Waddington
57 Sqn	Mar 1938–Nov 1940	Upper Heyford, Wyton
61 Sqn	Jan 1938–Mar 1939	Hemswell
62 Sqn	Feb 1938–Aug 1939	Cranfield
82 Sqn	Mar 1938–Mar 1942	Cranfield, Watton
88 Sqn	Feb 1941–Feb 1942	Sydenham, Swanton Morley
90 Sqn	May 1937–Apr 1940 Oct 1941–Feb 1942	Polebrook, Bicester, West Raynham, Upwood
101 Sqn	Jun 1938–Jul 1941	Bicester, West Raynham
104 Sqn	May 1938–Apr 1940	Bassingbourn, Bicester
105 Sqn	Jun 1940–Dec 1941	Honington, Watton, Swanton Morley
107 Sqn	Aug 1938–Feb 1942	Harwell, Wattisham, Great Massingham
108 Sqn	Jun 1938–Apr 1940	Bassingbourn, Bicester
110 Sqn	Jan 1938–Mar 1942	Waddington, Wattisham
114 Sqn	Mar 1937–Nov 1942	Wyton, Wattisham, Horsham St Faith, Oulton
139 Sqn	Jul 1937–Dec 1941	Wyton, Horsham St Faith, Oulton
	Jun 1942–Nov 1942	Horsham St Faith
144 Sqn	Aug 1937–Apr 1939	Hemswell
218 Sqn	Jul 1940–Nov 1940	Mildenhall, Oakington
226 Sqn	May 1941–Dec 1941	Wattisham

Vickers-Armstrongs Wellington

The Wellington was one of the most important aircraft in Bomber Command but its role in the war is overshadowed by the four-engined 'heavies' of the second half of the war. For its four years of operational service and its role as the most important type in service with the Operational Training Units, the Wellington deserves far greater recognition. Designed to Specification B.9/32 for a twin-engined heavy bomber (although the designation was changed to Medium Bomber with the advent of the four-engined types) the prototype Wellington (K4049) first flew in 15 June 1936. With its performance and payload it was a massive improvement on the front-line types such as the Heyford and the Air Ministry placed an initial order for 180 aircraft. The concept of operations remained that of formation day bombing and the Wellington was provided with defensive armament of twin guns in nose and tail turrets plus single guns in the beam positions, all being 0.303 inch calibre. Various alternate gun positions were tested, including a retractable ventral turret but the general principle that was applied to all of the later 1930s bombers was that fighters were nothing more than a moderate threat and that anti-aircraft fire was unlikely to be accurate at the operational heights of the bombers. Both of these tactical tenets were soon proved to be false.

The most distinctive feature of the Wellington was its fabric-covered geodetic structure, designed by Barnes Wallis for strength and lightness but one that also proved resilient to enemy fire – as witnessed by many a badly damaged Wellington that made it back to base with fabric burnt away or part of the geodetic structure destroyed. When 99 Squadron at Mildenhall became the first squadron to re-equip, October 1938, Bomber Command entered a new era with the first true modern bomber in its inventory. By the outbreak of war the Command had six Wellington squadrons in service and over the next few months additional squadrons re-equipped or formed. The poor showing of the aircraft in the anti-shipping attacks of autumn 1939 was not the fault of the Wellington or its crews; rather, it was a simple case of inappropriate tactics and a lack of appreciation of enemy defensive potential.

The Mk 1C became the Command's standard equipment and of the 2,685 of this variant that were built most served with Bomber Command. When the Wellington Groups turned to night operations the major problem was that of weather and crew comfort, although it was no worse than the other bombers operating in the cold night skies of a European winter. Normal bombing heights were 10,000–12,000 ft, although the Pegasus-powered Mk 1C had a ceiling of 18,000 ft, and standard bomb load was 4,000 lb over a range of 1,200 miles. Throughout 1940 and 1941 the Wellington squadrons, increasing in number up to mid 1942, were responsible for the majority of night sorties over Germany and although the accuracy and effectiveness of those attacks, due to lack of navigation aids, has often been called into question, they did provide invaluable training for Bomber Command as well as their direct effect on the German war effort caused by diversion of resources into air defence. Other Marks of Wellington, primarily the Mk II and Mk III entered service with the Command but in each case there was little significant improvement in overall performance or capability.

By early 1942 it was obvious that future operational potential for the Wellington was limited, it simply didn't have the defensive firepower or operational ceiling to cope with the increased German night defences; also, its bomb lift was too small in comparison with that of the new bomber types. The Wellington would soldier on for another year, in part as initial equipment for new squadrons, and it was not until the night of 8/9 October 1943 that the last operational Wellington sortie was flown, the target being Hanover and twenty-six Wellingtons from 300 Squadron and 432 Squadron were part of the total force of 504 bombers; all the Wellingtons returned safely.

It would be safe to say that the majority of Bomber Command aircrew, with the exception of those destined for the light bomber force, had contact with the Wellington

Wellington of 149 Squadron.

Die Kriegsflugzeuge der Feindmächte

Anlage 30 a

Großbritannien

Vickers „Wellington III"[1]

Kampfflugzeug

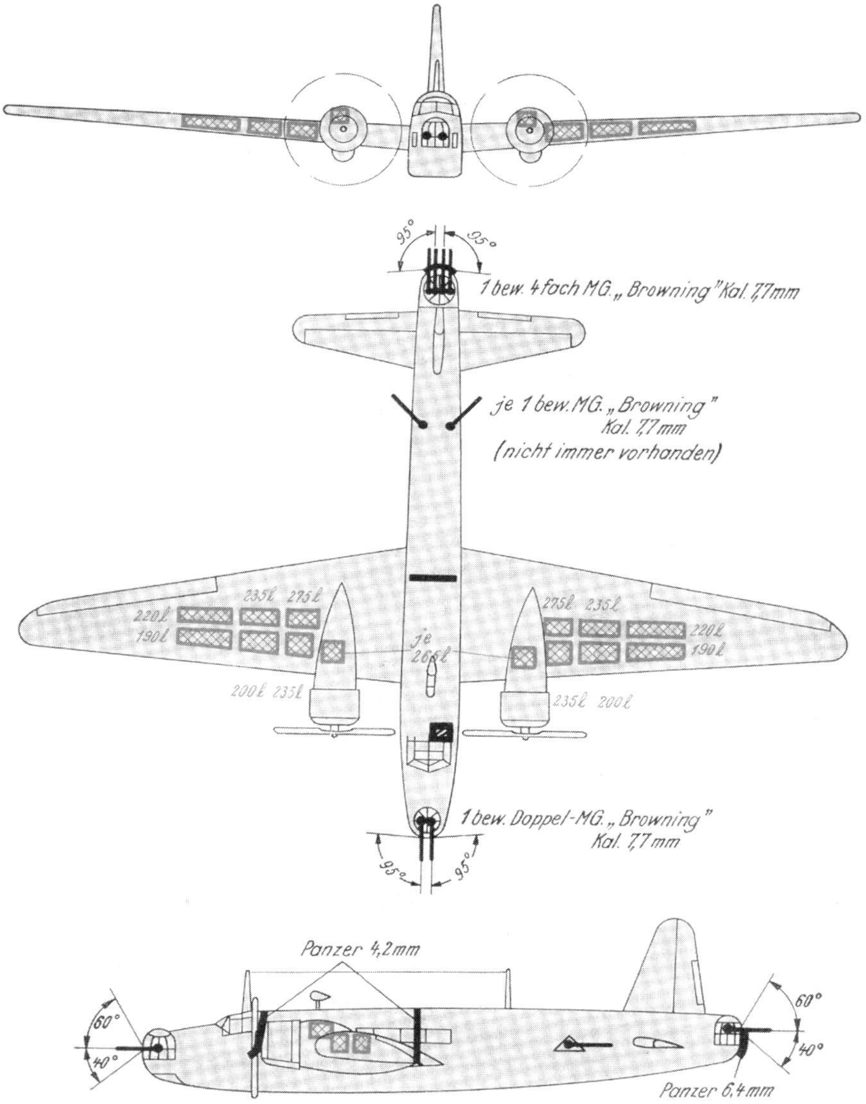

95°
95°
1 bew. 4fach MG. „Browning" Kal. 7,7mm
je 1 bew. MG. „Browning" Kal. 7,7 mm (nicht immer vorhanden)
235 l 275 l
220 l
190 l
275 l 235 l
220 l
190 l
je 266 l
200 l 235 l
235 l 200 l
1 bew. Doppel-MG. „Browning" Kal. 7,7 mm
95°
95°
Panzer 4,2mm
60°
40°
60°
40°
Panzer 6,4mm

[1]) „Wellington II" hat 3 flüssigkeitsgekühlte 12 Zyl.-V-Motoren Rolls Royce „Merlin X" (s. Anlage 30c).

Vickers-Armstrongs WELLINGTON
Prototype, first flight: K4049, 15 Jun 1936
Entry to service: 99 Sqn, October 1938

Squadron	Dates	Airfield
9 Sqn	Jan 1939–Aug 1942	Stradishall, Honington
12 Sqn	Nov 1940–Nov 1942	Binbrook, Wickenby
15 Sqn	Nov 1940–May 1941	Wyton
37 Sqn	May 1939–Nov 1940	Feltwell
38 Sqn	Nov 1938–Nov 1940	Marham
40 Sqn	Nov 1940–Oct 1941	Wyton, Alconbury
57 Sqn	Nov 1940–Sep 1942	Feltwell
75 Sqn*	Jul 1939–Nov 1942	Honington, Stradishall, Harwell, Feltwell, Mildenhall
99 Sqn	Oct 1938–Feb 1942	Mildenhall, Newmarket, Waterbeach
101 Sqn	Apr 1941–Oct 1942	West Raynham, Oakington, Bourn, Stradishall
103 Sqn	Oct 1940–Jul 1942	Newton, Elsham Wolds
104 Sqn	Apr 1941–Feb 1942	Driffield
109 Sqn	Dec 1940–Jul 1942	Boscombe Down, Tempsford, Stradishall
115 Sqn	Mar 1939–Mar 1943	Marham, Mildenhall, East Wretham
142 Sqn	Nov 1940–May 1943	Binbrook, Waltham, Kirmington
148 Sqn	Mar 1939–May 1940	Stradishall, Harwell
149 Sqn	Jan 1939–Dec 1941	Mildenhall
150 Sqn	Oct 1940–Jan 1943	Newton, Snaith, Kirmington
156 Sqn	Feb 1942–Jan 1943	Alconbury
158 Sqn	Feb 1942–Jun 1942	Driffield, East Moor
166 Sqn	Jan 1943–Sep 1943	Kirmington
192 Sqn	Jan 1943–Jan 1945	Gransden Lodge
196 Sqn	Dec 1942–Jul 1943	Leconfield, Witchford
199 Sqn	Nov 1942–Jun 1943	Blyton, Ingham
214 Sqn	May 1939–Apr 1942	Feltwell, Methwold, Stradishall, Honington
215 Sqn	Jul 1939–Feb 1942	Honington, Bramcote, Bassingbourn
218 Sqn	Nov 1940–Feb 1942	Oakington, Marham
300 Sqn	Dec 1940–Mar 1944	Swinderby, Hemswell, Ingham, Faldingworth
301 Sqn	Oct 1940–Apr 1943	Swinderby, Hemswell
304 Sqn	Nov 1940–Dec 1945	Bramcote, Syerston, Lindholme
305 Sqn	Nov 1940–Aug 1943	Bramcote, Syerston, Lindholme, Hemswell, Ingham
311 Sqn	Aug 1940–Jun 1943	Honington, East Wretham
405 Sqn RCAF	May 1941–Apr 1942	Driffield, Pocklington
419 Sqn RCAF	Jan 1942–Nov 1942	Mildenhall, Leeming, Topcliffe, Croft
420 Sqn RCAF	Aug 1942–Oct 1943	Skipton-on-Swale, Dalton
424 Sqn RCAF	Oct 1942–Oct 1943	Topcliffe, Leeming, Dalton, Skipton-on-Swale
425 Sqn RCAF	Aug 1942–Oct 1943	Dishforth, Tholthorpe
426 Sqn RCAF	Oct 1942–Jun 1943	Dishforth, Linton on Ouse
427 Sqn RCAF	Nov 1942–May 1943	Croft, Leeming
428 Sqn RCAF	Nov 1942–Jun 1944	Dalton, Middleton St George
429 Sqn RCAF	Nov 1942–Aug 1943	East Moor, Leeming
431 Sqn RCAF	Dec 1942–Jul 1943	Burn, Tholthorpe
432 Sqn RCAF	May 1943–Nov 1943	Skipton-on-Swale, East Moor
458 Sqn	Aug 1941–(Jun 1942)	Holme-on-Spalding Moor
460 Sqn RAAF	Nov 1941–Sep 1942	Molesworth, Breighton
466 Sqn RAAF	Oct 1942–Sep 1943	Driffield, Leconfield

Note: * 75 Squadron became 75 (RNZAF) Sqn in April 1940 when the New Zealand Flight at Feltwell was given the number plate.

Wellingtons of 9 Squadron, which was one of the first bomber squadrons to re-equip. After a disastrous introduction to daylight operations in late 1939 the Wellington was moved to night bombing and for three years was the mainstay of the Command's bombing offensive.

during their training. From 1940 to the end of the war the Wellington was the single most important aircraft in service with the Operational Training Units, and there were hundreds of aircraft in service at any one time as a full-size OTU would have a strength of fifty to sixty aircraft. Not that this contact was also looked on favourably as many of the OTU aircraft were cast-offs no longer considered fit for operational duties!

It would be unfair to this great aircraft not to mention its other roles, especially with Coastal Command – both with units loaned from Bomber Command and with Coastal's own squadrons, especially the Leigh Light Wellingtons that played an important part in the anti-submarine war. Whilst other bombers of its generation – such as the Hampden and Whitley – had vanished into obscurity by the end of the war, the Wellington remained in RAF service into the early 1950s. One final statistic that shows the aircraft's importance is that 11,461 Wellingtons were built, the largest total for a British multi-engined type: sad then that so very few survive in museums today. The best examples are in the RAF Museum at Hendon and the Brooklands Museum, the latter being a partially restored aircraft recovered from Loch Ness.

Like the Whitley, the Wellington had its own song; not perhaps as interesting as that of the Whitley but obviously sung with feeling. Judging by the words it was probably being sung in the later years of the aircraft's use, and perhaps by OTU crews for whom old and tired airframes were a matter of routine. The nickname *Wimpey* was taken from the cartoon character.

Old Fashioned *Wimpey*
Tune: 'That Old Fashioned Mother of Mine'

There's an old-fashioned Wimpey
With old-fashioned wings,
With a fuselage tattered and torn.
She's got old-fashioned engines

All tied up with strings,
It's a wonder she was ever airborne.
Still, she's quite safe and sound
'Cos she won't leave the ground,
And there's something that makes her divine;
For the Huns up above were all taught how to love
That old-fashioned Wimpey of mine.

Short Stirling

Of the four-engined British types to serve with Bomber Command the Short Stirling acquired the worst reputation and is often virtually ignored in histories as being an insignificant and ill-fated bomber. Whilst there is some truth in aspects of this statement it does, however, paint too bleak a picture of the aircraft. Designed to Specification B.12/36, the four-engined 'heavy' bomber specification that spawned all the Command's operational aircraft of this type, the prototype Stirling (L7600) first flew on 14 May 1939, the first of the new types to fly. Despite the crash of the prototype at the end of that first flight and despite early indications that the Stirling would suffer from certain operational limitations there was an urgent need to replace old twin-engined types and increase the bomb lift. The Stirling certainly fitted the latter category as its 14,000 lb load was a massive increase over the 4,000 lb of its predecessors.

No. 7 Squadron at Leeming became the first operational unit with the Stirling, August 1940, and it was some months before any other units re-equipped. The Squadron had given up Hampdens for the new bomber and were initially delighted as it seemed that they now had a powerful bomber with which to take the war to the enemy rather than the somewhat limited Hampden. It was on the night of 10/11 February 1941 that the Stirling made its first operational bombing mission, aircraft of No. 7 Squadron bombing the oil storage targets at Rotterdam. The Stirling was a difficult aircraft to produce and entry to service was slow, it was not until April 1941 that a second squadron was equipped. The decision was taken to concentrate all Stirling units in No. 3 Group and over the next few months the Group's units duly re-equipped, although not without problems and the AOC wrote a number of memos concerning the unsatisfactory rate of aircraft delivery and poor aircraft serviceability.

Despite the indications of performance problems the early showing of the Stirling was good and the aircraft appeared to be able to take a reasonable level of punishment

Although the Stirling was the first of the 'heavies' to enter service, build-up was slow because of production problems.

Stirling R9358 of 214 Squadron at Stradishall, September 1942; the Squadron operated Stirlings from April 1942 to August 1944.

from flak and fighters, although there was some concern over the Hercules engines. After early fin problems had been overcome the manoeuvrability of the aircraft, an important aspect in evasive manoeuvres, was considered reasonable by pilots and the airframe was definitely strong. This latter aspect owed much to the designers having used knowledge gained with other Shorts types such as the Sunderland, although in the longer run this was to prove detrimental to attempts at improving the aircraft's performance. Likewise, the unique cell arrangement in the bomb bay initially looked like a good idea but as the maximum bomb in any cell was 4,000 lb this later became a problem.

Stirlings of No. 3 Group formed part of Main Force on a large number of attacks over Occupied Europe and Germany and by 1942 questions were being asked as to why the type appeared to have a higher loss rate than the other 'heavies.' As more Lancasters and Halifaxes entered service the statistics certainly supported the view that the Stirling loss rate was higher, with a number of instances when the loss rate exceeded 10 per cent. The conclusion was that the lower all-round performance, especially in terms of operational ceiling, with the Stirling flying at around 15,000 ft, meant that they were more likely to be engaged by flak and more likely to be picked up by night fighters. The introduction of the Mk III did little to improve the overall situation and the loss rates, combined with continued production problems and the restrictions of the bomb bay led to a decision to replace the type in the front-line at the earliest opportunity. The final squadrons re-equipped in late 1943 – after the decision to replace Stirlings had been made but with no choice if the planned expansion of the Command and its bomb lift were to be maintained. However, by mid 1944 the aircraft's role in Main Force was coming to an end, the final bombing sortie taking place in September.

This was not the end of the Stirling with Main Force as two squadrons of the specialist No. 100 Group used the type for Radio Counter Measures operations. These specially equipped Stirlings continued to operate to the latter part of the war and with its large sturdy airframe and reasonably spacious interior the Stirling was well suited to this role. No. 199 Squadron took on the new role on 1 May 1944, the aircraft being equipped with *Mandrel* and *Shiver* equipment, the former being the main system. The Squadron was operational by June, the first *op* taking place on the night of 5/6 June, and its *Mandrel* screens became a routine part of the Group's protective work. A second RCM Stirling was created in September when 'C Flight' of 199 Squadron became 171 Squadron, also at North Creake.

Die Kriegsflugzeuge der Feindmächte   Anlage 29a

Großbritannien

Short „Stirling"

Kampfflugzeug

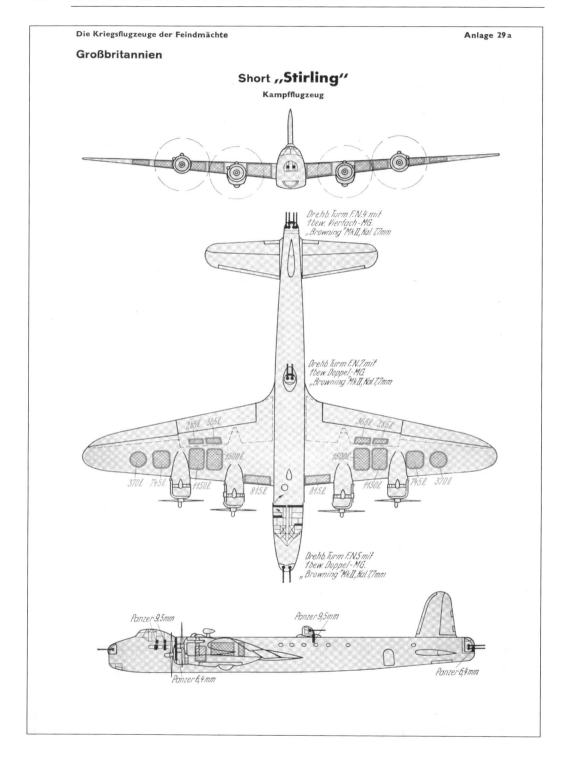

Drehb. Turm F.N.4 mit
1 bew. Vierfach-MG.
„Browning" Mk II, Kal. 7,7mm

Drehb. Turm F.N.7 mit
1 bew. Doppel-MG
„Browning" Mk II, Kal. 7,7mm

285ℓ 365ℓ   365ℓ 285ℓ

1500ℓ   1500ℓ

370ℓ 745ℓ   1150ℓ   815ℓ   815ℓ   1150ℓ   745ℓ 370ℓ

Drehb. Turm F.N.5 mit
1 bew. Doppel-MG.
„Browning" Mk II, Kal. 7,7mm

Panzer 9,5mm   Panzer 9,5mm

Panzer 6,4 mm   Panzer 6,4 mm

Short STIRLING
Prototype, first flight: L7600, 14 May 1939
Entry to service: 7 Sqn, August 1940

Squadron	Dates	Airfield
7 Sqn	Aug 1940–Aug 1943	Leeming, Oakington
15 Sqn	Apr 1941–Dec 1943	Wyton, Bourn, Mildenhall
75 Sqn	Nov 1942–Apr 1944	Newmarket, Mepal
90 Sqn	Nov 1942–Jun 1944	Bottesford, Ridgewell, Wratting Common, Tuddenham
138 Sqn	Jun 1944–Mar 1945	Tempsford, Tuddenham
149 Sqn	Nov 1941–Sep 1944	Mildenhall, Lakenheath, Methwold
161 Sqn	Sep 1944–Jun 1945	Tempsford
171 Sqn	Sep 1944–Jan 1945	North Creake
196 Sqn	Jul 1943–Mar 1946	Witchford, Leicester East, to transport
199 Sqn	Jul 1943–Mar 1945	Lakenheath, North Creake
214 Sqn	Apr 1942–Jan 1944	Stradishall, Chedburgh, Downham Market, Sculthorpe
218 Sqn	Jan 1942–Aug 1944	Marham, Downham Market, Woolfox Lodge, Methwold
513 Sqn	Oct 1943–Nov 1943	Witchford
620 Sqn	Jun 1943–Jul 1945	Chedburgh, to transport
622 Sqn	Aug 1943–Jan 1944	Mildenhall
623 Sqn	Aug 1943–Dec 1943	Downham Market

Almost 1,800 Mk I and Mk III bombers were built but in addition to use with Bomber Command the Stirling played a key role with the airborne forces, for paratroop dropping and as a glider tug, and two later variants, the Mk V and Mk VI, were developed for the transport role. In the latter role the Stirling continued to serve with the RAF into mid 1946.

There are no surviving Stirlings but a group of enthusiasts is determined to find enough parts – or build them from scratch – to ensure that this bomber is not completely forgotten.

Avro Manchester

The twin-engined Avro Manchester has gone down in aviation history as a disaster but one whose failure gave rise to the greatest RAF bomber of the war, the Lancaster: both statements are partly true and partly overstated. Designed to Specification P13/36 as a medium bomber the prototype first flew on 25 July 1939, a contract for 200 aircraft having been issued in July 1937. The basic airframe was sound, although a central fin had to be added after initial trials showed lateral stability problems. However, it was the Rolls-Royce Vulture engines that were to prove the key failing of the Manchester; the twenty-four-cylinder engines were of a new design and they proved both unreliable and under-powered, with a tendency to catch fire!

The Manchester entered service with 207 Squadron at Waddington in November 1940, the Squadron having re-formed to become the first Manchester unit. After a few months of familiarisation the Squadron flew its first *op* with the type on the night of 24/25 February 1941, six Manchesters took part in this attack on warships at Brest.

As more aircraft entered service the engine problems became frustratingly common, although questions were also asked about the aircraft's overall performance. The notional 10,000 lb bomb load was good for an aircraft of its class and self-defence armament was standard for the time, but within months of the type becoming operational it was obvious that the problems would be hard to overcome, although serviceability did increase in the

Skellingthorpe-based 50 Squadron only spent three months with the Manchester before re-equipping with Lancasters.

Avro MANCHESTER
Prototype, first flight: L7246, 25 July 1939
Entry to service: 207 Sqn, November 1940

Squadron	Dates	Airfield
49 Sqn	Apr 1942–Jun 1942	Scampton
50 Sqn	Apr 1942–Jun 1942	Skellingthorpe
61 Sqn	Jun 1941–Jun 1942	Hemswell, North Luffenham, Woolfox Lodge
83 Sqn	Dec 1941–Jun 1942	Scampton
97 Sqn	Feb 1941–Feb 1942	Waddington, Coningsby
106 Sqn	Feb 1942–Jun 1942	Coningsby
207 Sqn	Nov 1940–Mar 1942	Waddington, Bottesford

Avro Manchester of 83 Squadron; the Manchester operated with No. 5 Group and flew 1,185 operational sorties for a loss of sixty-nine aircraft (5.8 per cent).

latter months of the Manchester's operational service. Follow-on orders for 300 aircraft were cancelled and production ended in November 1941. The final operational sortie took place on the night of 25/26 June 1942 with twenty Manchesters as part of the Thousand Bomber (actually 960 aircraft) force that attacked Bremen.

A number of Manchesters remained with Bomber Command in the training role but the short period of operations was over and the type entered the history books as a failure. One Victoria Cross was awarded to a Manchester crewman, Flying Officer Leslie Manser, a pilot with 50 Squadron being awarded the VC for his actions on the Cologne raid of 30/31 May 1942.

Only 209 Manchesters were built and, not surprisingly, there are no survivors.

Handley Page Halifax

The Handley Page Halifax's wartime career has always been compared with that of the Lancaster and it is invariably written up as 'inferior'; whilst there is some truth in this, especially for the Mk I Halifax it is an over-generalisation. One Squadron Commander stated: 'We were very favourably impressed by the flying qualities of the Halifax B.III with its powerful Bristol Hercules engines, which gave it a lively climbing ability and good all-round performance.'

As one of the trio of four-engined bombers designed to Specification P13/36 the Halifax first flew on 25 October 1939 (L7244). The type entered service with 35 Squadron in November 1940, the second of the 'heavies'. The first operational sortie by the Handley Page Halifax (35 Squadron) took place on the night of 10/11 March 1941, the target being Le Havre. Six aircraft took part, four of which bombed the primary target. One aircraft aborted the mission because of hydraulic problems and one was shot down by a British night fighter.

Over the next few months the other squadrons of No. 4 Group re-equipped and the Halifax began to take an increasing role in bomber operations. Initial impressions of the Halifax were favourable but within weeks the first problems occurred and the aircraft were temporarily withdrawn from operations for modifications to hydraulic pumps and undercarriages. An attempt was also made to regulate the cabin heat as excessive heat had given rise to a good deal of sickness amongst crews. Modifications were also made to the front escape hatch as this tended to fly off in the air. Whilst the latter two points appear to have been cured, at least they do not crop up again in the official records, the undercarriage remained troublesome.

Halifax MZ910 of 433 Squadron at Skipton-on-Swale.

Two French squadrons, 346 and 347, operated Halifaxes from the summer of 1944 to the end of the war.

However, by early 1942 the Halifax was already under investigation as its loss rate was higher than that of the other four-engined bomber, the Stirling. An ORS report looked at loss rates for the period July 1941 to June 1942 with the Halifax having a 50 per cent higher loss rate on all except lightly-defended targets. The conclusion was that the aircraft was more vulnerable to fighter attack and that a major factor was the 'greater visibility of the Halifax exhausts and its rather doubtful stability in making evasive turns.' With a loss rate of over 6 per cent, rising to 10 per cent for August 1942, the decision was taken to reduce the scale of Halifax operations until the majority of aircraft had received additional modifications, including weight reduction. A new fin and rudder were tested on the prototype Mk III and when engine and propeller improvements were added the new variant was far better than its predecessors; indeed, it was close to the Lancaster in overall performance.

In October 1942 the Bomber Command Operational Research Section (ORS) was again investigating why the Halifax had a higher loss rate than other operational types. Once more it was the aircraft's poor manoeuvrability that was highlighted as the most significant defect. The conclusion recommended that in order to gain experience and confidence, 'The pilots posted to Halifax squadrons should be detailed to complete at least three, preferably five, sorties as 2nd Pilot or against lightly defended targets before being employed on main operations.' However, this laudable aim was not always possible, indeed it was seldom achieved, and the higher than average loss rates of the early Halifax variants continued. The bomb load of 13,000 lb was a great improvement on that of the medium bombers and unlike the Stirling the bomb bay was of standard design and gave good flexibility of bomb load. The self-defence armament of four-gun rear turret and twin-gun front turret, with beam guns in some aircraft, was inadequate but was soon improved with the addition of a mid-upper turret.

The first Mk IIIs entered service with 466 Squadron at Leconfield in October 1943 and this 'definitive' variant gradually replaced the older variants and was to remain in service until the end of the war. By early 1944 the new aircraft had demonstrated their superior performance and the plan to replace all squadrons with Lancasters was re-considered – or at least delayed. The Halifax was the standard equipment of No. 6 (RCAF) Group based in Yorkshire and the Canadian squadrons had few problems with serviceability or operational difficulties; loss rates stabilised and the Group was happy with its Halifaxes, although in recent years an ill-informed debate has been reopened as to why the Canadians were given 'inferior aircraft.'

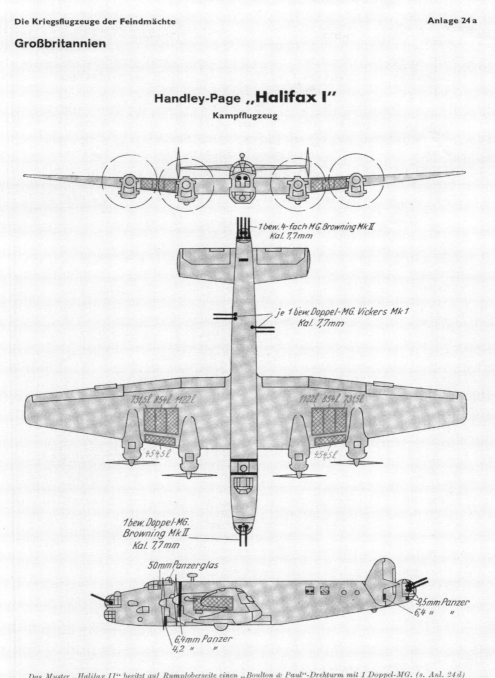

Die Kriegsflugzeuge der Feindmächte

Anlage 24 a

Großbritannien

Handley-Page „Halifax I"
Kampfflugzeug

1 bew. 4-fach M.G. Browning Mk II
Kal. 7,7 mm

je 1 bew. Doppel-M.G. Vickers Mk 1
Kal. 7,7 mm

731,5 l 854 l 1122 l   1122 l 854 l 731,5 l

454,5 l   454,5 l

1 bew. Doppel-MG.
Browning Mk II
Kal. 7,7 mm

50 mm Panzerglas

9,5 mm Panzer
6,4 "   "

6,4 mm Panzer
4,2 "   "

Das Muster „Halifax II" besitzt auf Rumpfoberseite einen „Boulton & Paul"-Drehturm mit 1 Doppel-MG. (s. Anl. 24 d) und beiderseits im Flügel noch je 1 Kraftstoffbehälter mit 550 l Fassung.

An ORS report in July 1943 related loss rates to training as the Halifax had acquired a bad reputation for instability during hard manoeuvres. As the corkscrew manoeuvre was the standard tactic by which bomber pilots avoided enemy defences it was vital that pilots had the confidence to undertake the hard manoeuvring demanded by this technique. Report B160 looked at the, 'Effect of operational experience on No. 4 Group Halifax losses' and concluded that: 'There is no reasonable doubt that pilots on their first two operations have a casualty rate well above the average and that those who have survived twenty sorties had a rate well below the average. This must be aircraft related as the Lancaster does not suffer the same problem.' The report stated that the major problem occurred when aircraft attacked heavily defended targets. 'New pilots are a bit nervous of the aircraft as it had gained a bad name for instability in manoeuvre. It thus may happen that a new pilot is reluctant, when he meets defences, to manoeuvre his machine sufficiently in combat or that in a sudden emergency he puts his machine into an attitude in which he has had no previous experience of controlling it.'

Handley Page HALIFAX
Prototype, first flight: L7244, 25 October 1939
Entry to service: 35 Sqn, November 1940

Squadron	Dates	Airfield
10 Sqn	Dec 1941–May 1945	Leeming
35 Sqn	Nov 1940–Mar 1944	Leeming, Linton-on-Ouse, Graveley
51 Sqn	Nov 1942–May 1945	Snaith, Leconfield
76 Sqn	May 1941–May 1945	Linton-on-Ouse, Middleton St George
77 Sqn	Oct 1942–Aug 1945	Elvington, Full Sutton
78 Sqn	Mar 1942–Jul 1945	Croft, Middleton St George, Linton-on-Ouse, Breighton
102 Sqn	Dec 1941–Sep 1945	Dalton, Topcliffe, Pocklington
103 Sqn	Jul 1942–Oct 1942	Elsham Wolds
138 Sqn	Aug 1941–Aug 1944	Stradishall, Tempsford, Tuddenham
158 Sqn	Jun 1942–May 1945	East Moor
161 Sqn	Sep 1942–Oct 1944	Tempsford
171 Sqn	Oct 1944–Jul 1945	North Creake
192 Sqn	Mar 1943–Aug 1945	Gransden Lodge, Feltwell, Foulsham
199 Sqn	Feb 1945–Jul 1945	North Creake
346 Sqn	May 1944–Nov 1945	Elvington
347 Sqn	Jun 1944–Nov 1945	Elvington
405 Sqn RCAF	Apr 1942–Sep 1943	Pocklington, Topcliffe, Beaulieu, Leeming, Gransden Lodge
408 Sqn RCAF	Sep 1942–Oct 1943	Leeming
	Sep 1944 – May 1945	Linton-on-Ouse
415 Sqn RCAF	Jul 1944–May 1945	East Moor
419 Sqn RCAF	Nov 1942–Apr 1944	Croft, Middleton St George
420 Sqn RCAF	Dec 1943–May 1945	Tholthorpe
424 Sqn RCAF	Dec 1943–Jan 1945	Skipton-on-Swale
425 Sqn RCAF	Dec 1943–May 1945	Tholthorpe
426 Sqn RCAF	Apr 1944–May 1945	Linton-on-Ouse, Driffield
427 Sqn RCAF	May 1943–Mar 1945	Leeming
428 Sqn RCAF	Jun 1943–Jun 1944	Middleton St George
429 Sqn RCAF	Aug 1943–Mar 1945	Leeming
431 Sqn RCAF	Jul 1943–Oct 1944	Tholthorpe, Croft
432 Sqn RCAF	Feb 1944–May 1945	East Moor
433 Sqn RCAF	Nov 1943–Jan 1945	Skipton-on-Swale
434 Sqn RCAF	Jun 1943–Dec 1944	Tholthorpe, Croft
460 Sqn RAAF	Aug 1942–Oct 1942	Breighton
466 Sqn RAAF	Sep 1943–Aug 1945	Leconfield, Driffield, Bassingbourn
578 Sqn	Jan 1944–Mar 1945	Snaith, Burn
640 Sqn	Jan 1944–May 1945	Leconfield

The Halifax Mk III was the most effective of the variants but by the time it entered service the earlier reputation of the Halifax as being inferior to the Lancaster had been established.

The Halifax also saw action with Bomber Command as part of No. 100 Group, the airframe proving well-suited to this RCM usage and at one stage became the main type used by the Group. The main role of the Halifax RCM squadrons was *Mandrel*, although 462 Squadron was fitted with ABC, and the first effective mission was flown by 171 Squadron from North Creake in late October 1944. Indeed, it was 171 and 199 Squadrons from this Group that flew the Command's last Halifax operation of the war, on 2 May 1945 against Kiel.

Total Halifax production was 6,176 aircraft and whilst some of these were specialist Coastal or Transport variants, the majority were bomber variants, including 2,238 of the Halifax MK III. There is no surviving complete Halifax today, although a number of well-preserved aircraft have been recovered from lakes in Norway and the museum at Elvington, Yorkshire has 'built' a Halifax, with parts coming from a variety of sources. This is an appropriate location as Elvington was home to two Free French Halifax squadrons. One of the recovered aircraft is being rebuilt in Canada as a tribute to No. 6 (RCAF) Group.

Boeing B-17 Fortress

On 8 July 1941 Wing Commander MacDougall, OC of 90 Squadron led the RAF's first B-17 Fortress I attack, the target being shipping at Wilhelmshaven. The RAF had decided to acquire the Boeing B-17 as part of its search for new bombers and in the spring of 1941 twenty B-17C variants were flown to Britain. The Boeing B-17 was designed for the US Army Air Corps and first flew on 28 July 1935, the concept of operations being for high-level daylight bombing. By the outbreak of war the Americans were claiming that their 'Flying Fortress' would be able to protect itself from enemy fighters and with its new bombsight could, 'Drop bombs into a pickle barrel from 30,000 ft'. These bold claims appealed to the RAF and the Fortress seemed an ideal strategic bomber – despite its very low bomb load of 2,500 lb.

The new aircraft went to 90 Squadron at West Raynham and after a short work-up the Squadron flew its first operation, sending three aircraft to Wilhelmshaven. Two aircraft bombed the target and all returned safely. The RAF only employed small numbers of Fortresses, a concept alien to the American doctrine of massed mutually-

Boeing B-17 FORTRESS
Prototype, first flight: 28 July1935
Entry to service: 90 Sqn, May 1941

Squadron	Dates	Airfield
90 Sqn	May 1941–Oct 1941	West Raynham, Polebrook
214 Sqn	Jan 1944–Jul 1945	Sculthorpe, Oulton
223 Sqn	Apr 1945–Jul 1945	Oulton

defensive formations of bombers. Over the next few months the Squadron continued to mount daylight operations but the aircraft were proving troublesome, with numerous serviceability problems that meant a very poor sortie rate and a high percentage of aborts; the Norden bombsight and the guns proving particularly troublesome. By September Bomber Command had decided to abandon this experiment with the Fortress and for the next few years Coastal Command was the RAF's main user of the type, gradually acquiring, as the Fortress II, the much improved B-17E and F.

With the growth of the Radio Counter Measures war the Fortress once more returned to Bomber Command with 214 Squadron of No. 100 Group acquiring Fortress IIIs (B-17G) in January 1944. It took some while for the aircraft to be given their special equipment and it was not until the 20/21 April that the Squadron mounted its first sortie. The Fortresses were equipped with various jamming devices including *ABC*, *Jostle* and *Mandrel* but they spent much of their time operating with the Special *Window* Force. In March 1945 a second Fortress unit was formed in No. 100 Group, 223 Squadron being based alongside 214 Squadron at Oulton. By the end of the war the RCM *Fortresses* had flown around 1,000 operational sorties. Although both units disbanded in July 1945 the RCM Fortress continued in service for a while longer with the Radio Warfare Establishment.

Dozens of B-17s have survived, including a fair number of airworthy examples but all are preserved in memory of USAAF usage and particular the 8th Air Force.

Douglas Boston

The Douglas Boston was one of the American types selected in 1940 as a replacement for the light and medium types in Bomber Command, particularly the Blenheim. In summer 1940 the RAF received 20 DB-7 Boston Is but although a number of these were issued to squadrons it was primarily used for conversion training. Having been chosen as the first Boston squadron in the Command 88 Squadron received a number of Boston Is, which it used for training whilst the Blenheim was used as the operational type. The first Boston IIIs, with an improved all-round performance, arrived in the summer of 1941 and the first were issued to 88 Squadron at Swanton Morley. The first operational sorties were flown on 12 February 1942 and from then on the Bostons flew anti-shipping missions as well as day low-level sorties against industrial and military targets in Europe, including a number of spectacular raids. By the time that No. 2 Group transferred to the Tactical Air Force in May 1943 it had four squadrons equipped with Bostons, and with some of these the type continued in service to spring 1945, albeit in later variants.

The Boston, and its Havoc derivative, also served in a number of other capacities with the RAF, most notably – albeit short-lived and with limited success – as a 'night fighter' using the Turbinlite searchlight system. Of more relevance to Bomber Command was the limited use as a night intruder to attack German night-fighter airfields, with

Unusual shot of a Boston of 226 Squadron, May 1942. This was one of four Bomber Command squadrons to use the type and in its career with No. 2 Group, as part of Bomber Command, the Boston flew 1,215 operational sorties.

Douglas BOSTON
Prototype, first flight:
Entry to service: 88 Sqn, Feb 1941

Squadron	Dates	Airfield
88 Sqn	Feb 1941–(Apr 1945)	Sydenham, Swanton Morley, Attlebridge, Oulton
107 Sqn	Jan 1942–(Mar 1944)	Great Massingham
226 Sqn	Nov 1941–(Jun 1943)	Wattisham, Swanton Morley
342 Sqn	Apr 1943–(Apr 1945)	West Raynham

23 Squadron specialising in this role. Over 1,000 Bostons were delivered to the RAF but overall it was not considered to be a very successful aircraft, although better than many of the other 'new' bombers acquired by No. 2 Group.

De Havilland Mosquito

The Mosquito was without doubt one of the great British aircraft of the war and it performed astoundingly well in a variety of roles, of which the pure bomber role was in many ways the least significant. It served with the Coastal Command Strike Wings and Fighter Command, especially as a night fighter, as well as performing a variety of other roles. The Mosquito was produced in an impressive number of Marks and served into the post-war period. With Bomber Command it performed three main roles – target marker, bomber and night fighter, but was also used in the reconnaissance role.

The de Havilland Mosquito started life in late 1938 as a private venture for a high-speed, unarmed all-wooden bomber and there was little initial interest from an Air Staff that was looking towards a heavy bomber force. Planned to have no self-defence armament, relying on its speed and height, and with no real thought of a bomb load, the initial RAF reaction was poor but under Specification B.1/40 an order was placed for fifty aircraft able to carry a 1,000 lb bomb load. The prototype flew on 25 November 1940 and its startling performance convinced any doubters that this aircraft had a future and fighter and photo-reconnaissance variants prototypes were soon underway.

First of the bombers was the Mosquito IV, the prototype of which flew on 8 September 1941 and with its top speed of 380 mph and ceiling of 40,000 ft was unlike any previous bomber. Entry to service was with 105 Squadron at Swanton Morley in November 1941 where it replaced the Blenheim. It was not until 31 May 1942 that the Squadron made the first operational sorties with the Mosquito, five aircraft being sent to Cologne the day after the Thousand Bomber attack to take photographs and drop a few nuisance bombs. One aircraft was damaged by flak and later crashed into the North Sea with the loss of its two crewmen. This single loss would equate to a 20 per cent loss rate but of course that figure means nothing as the average loss rate for the Mosquito with Bomber Command for the duration of the war was less than 1 per cent, by far the lowest of any type (although the short period of *ops* with No. 2 Group had a 5 per cent loss rate over 793 sorties).

No. 2 Group was desperate for new aircraft and the Mosquito seemed to be the answer to the problem of low-level daylight attacks on pinpoint targets; however, such was the demand for the new type that deliveries were slow. However, it was not long before the Mosquito was in the news, such as the dramatic attack on the Gestapo HQ in Oslo by four aircraft of 105 Squadron on 25 September 1942. One pilot at Marham remarked, although not in connection with this raid, that they didn't read the news, they made the news. The Mosquito had the range to reach Berlin and the first such attack was made on 31 January 1943 – by 105 Squadron again, although followed by 139 Squadron the same afternoon – and from then on Berlin was a regular target for the *Mossies* as they were reasonably immune from the German defences.

The more powerful Mk IX variant entered service in April 1943 and it was this variant that was initially equipped with the *Oboe* navigation system for use on target marking. April 1943 also brought the Mosquito into action with Bomber Command in two new tactics: firstly, the formation of No. 1409 Flight, a specialist unit tasked with

Prototype Mosquito W4050 first flew in November 1940; a 4,000 lb bomb load and the range to reach Berlin added a new dimension to Bomber Command for diversionary and nuisance raids.

Anlage 6   Nr. 43

De Havilland D. H. 98 „Mosquito"

Mehrzweckeflugzeug (Aufklärer, leichtes Kampfflugzeug und Zerstörer)

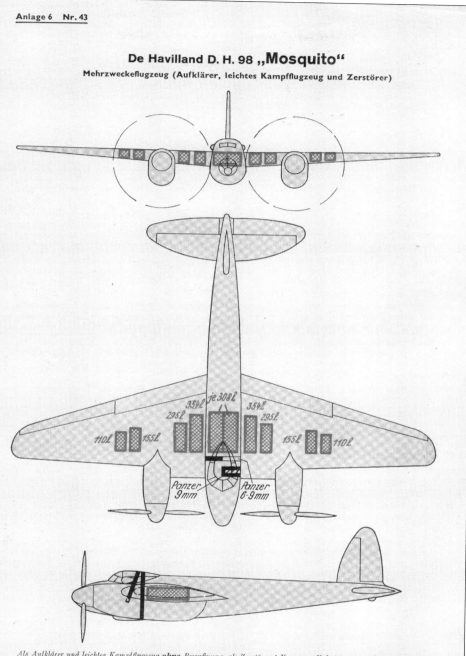

Als Aufklärer und leichtes Kampfflugzeug **ohne** *Bewaffnung, als Zerstörer 4 Kanonen, Kal. 20 mm, und 3—4 starre MG., Kal. 7,7 mm, im Rumpf. Keine bewegliche Bewaffnung. (Bilder des Flugzeugs noch nicht vorhanden.)*

The Mosquito IV was the first of the operational bomber variants, entering service with 105 Squadron at Swanton Morley in November 1941.

Met reconnaissance (*Pampas*) over Europe; and, secondly, the employment of the *Mossie* for night harassing raids. The idea behind the latter was twofold: help confuse the defences as to the Command's target for the night and to keep the air raid sirens going over as wide an area as possible. The first such operation took place on 13/14 April when six Mosquitoes of 105 Squadron flew raids to Bremen, Hamburg and Wilhelmshaven. This was the forerunner of what was to become the highly effective Light Night-Striking Force (LNSF). The *Mossie's* ability to carry a 4,000 lb bomb, find pinpoint targets with great accuracy, and its incredibly low loss rate (with the added benefit that if lost it was only two crew and not the six of a 'heavy' bomber) has led many post war commentators to remark that an all Mosquito bomber force would have been far more effective. Whilst there is some truth in this, as there invariably is with the benefit of hindsight, it would not

De Havilland MOSQUITO
Prototype, first flight: W4050, 25 November 1940
Entry to service: 105 Sqn, November 1941

Squadron	Dates	Airfield
23 Sqn	Jul 1944–Sep 1945	Little Snoring
85 Sqn	May 1944–(Oct 1951)	Swannington
105 Sqn	Nov 1941–Feb 1946	Swanton Morley, Horsham St Faith, Marham, Bourn, Upwood
109 Sqn	Dec 1942–Jul 1952	Wyton, Marham, Little Staughton, Woodhall Spa, Wickenby, Hemswell, Coningsby
128 Sqn	Sep 1944–Mar 1946	Wyton, Warboys
139 Sqn	Jun 1942–Jan 1953	Horsham St Faith, Oulton, Marham , Wyton, Upwood, Hemswell, Coningsby
141 Sqn	Nov 1943–Sep 1945	West Raynham, Little Snoring
142 Sqn	Oct 1944–Sep 1945	Gransden Lodge
157 Sqn	(Jan 1942)–Aug 1945	Swannington
162 Sqn	Dec 1944–Jul 1946	Bourn, Blackbushe
163 Sqn	Jan 1945–Aug 1945	Wyton
169 Sqn	Jan 1944–Aug 1945	Little Snoring, Great Massingham
192 Sqn	Jan 1943–Aug 1945	Gransden Lodge, Foulsham
239 Sqn	Jan 1944–Jul 1945	West Raynham
515 Sqn	Feb 1944–Jun 1945	Little Snoring
571 Sqn	Apr 1944–Sep 1945	Downham Market, Oakington, Warboys
608 Sqn	Aug 1944–Aug 1945	Downham Market
613 Sqn	Oct 1943–Aug 1945	Lasham, Swanton Morley, Hartford Bridge
627 Sqn	Nov 1943–Sep 1945	Oakington, Woodhall Spa
692 Sqn	Jan 1944–Sep 1945	Graveley, Gransden Lodge

have suited the doctrine of the time of overall bomb lift and tonnage on target – it would have required a fresh doctrine more along the lines of that used by the 8th Air Force.

The Mosquito appeared in so many variants, performed so many roles and served with so many squadrons that a short overview can never do justice to the part it played in RAF history and the campaigns of the Second World War. With Bomber Command the Mosquito operated in No. 2, No. 5 and No. 100 Groups, the latter primarily as a night intruder or night fighter in which it flew 8,814 missions for the loss of 75 aircraft.

The Mosquito continued in RAF service into the 1950s and with overseas air forces even longer than that. A reasonable number of airframes have survived, with the collection at the Mosquito Aircraft Museum being particularly impressive. Sadly there is no airworthy aircraft at present, or at least not one that actually flies, although a number of restorations are underway.

Avro Lancaster

In his post-war Despatch on War Operations Sir Arthur Harris expressed his preference for the Lancaster: 'The Lancaster, however, coming into operation for the first time in March 1942 soon proved immensely superior to all other types in the Command. The advantages which it enjoyed in speed, height and range enabled it to attack with success targets which other types could attempt only with serious risk or even the certainty of heavy casualties.' This was written in 1945 with the benefit of the C-in-C's comprehensive knowledge of the aircraft that served with his squadrons.

The Avro Lancaster made its maiden flight (BT308) on 9 January 1941, a few months after the Halifax entered service as the last of the 'heavies'. The type entered service with 44 Squadron in December and flew its first operational bombing sortie on 10/11 March 1942 to Essen, although minelaying *ops* had been flown earlier in the month. With its 14,000 lb bomb load (although special loads carried later in the war by the likes of 617 Squadron included the 22,000 lb *Grand Slam* bomb) and excellent all-round performance, speed of just under 300 mph and ceiling of 24,500 ft, the Lancaster was an immediate success. There were a number of teething troubles but with the Manchester as a predecessor these were of a minor nature and did not affect the overall introduction to service. Nevertheless, production remained slower than the bomber chiefs would have liked and even though by 1943 there was general agreement to switch bomber production to the Lancaster this process would take at least two years: 'Hence

Powered by four Rolls-Royce Merlins and with an excellent all-round performance the Avro Lancaster was the best strategic bomber of the Second World War.

Lancaster LM217 of IX Squadron at Bardney; the Squadron had been operating Lancasters since September 1942 and in the latter part of the war was a special squadron equipped with Tallboy bombs.

the constant pressure brought by Bomber Command HQ for concentration on Lancaster production at the expense of other types and hence the policy to employ every available Lancaster in the front line, even at the expense of an uneconomical training set-up.'

Whilst the Lancaster's first year of operations had appeared relatively trouble free, despite some initial production problems, in March 1943 the ORS was reporting that Lancaster loss rates had increased to near the 4 per cent average of the other bombers. This change was put down to improvements in the Halifax but also an increased effectiveness of the German defences. In other words the decreasing vulnerability of the Halifax had increased the vulnerability of the Lancaster.

Although the Lancaster has generally acquired a reputation in the historical record of low loss rates the type was not always immune from heavy losses on particular raids; for example, an attack on Berlin on 2/3 December 1943 made by 458 aircraft, primarily Lancasters, suffered forty aircraft lost (a rate of 8.7 per cent). However, averaged across all the Groups for the period of *ops* with Bomber Command the loss rate was around 2 per cent. It could be argued that this figure is somewhat false because of very low loss rates in the final months of the war when the bulk of sorties were being flown by Lancasters – but it was ever thus with statistics!

In addition to the one special raid that everyone had heard off – Operation *Chastise*, the Dams Raid of May 1943, Lancaster squadrons carried out a number of other daring raids, such as the daylight attack on the MAN works at Augsburg for which John Nettleton received the Victoria Cross. It was, however, its work with Main Force and with the Pathfinder Force that the Lancaster was most involved and in which it made its greatest contribution to Bomber Command's war. As the Order of Battle shows, by late 1944 the bulk of the Command's front-line strength comprised Lancasters. The main variants were the Mk I and Mk III, including the Canadian-built Mk X, and the RAF eventually received around 7,500 Lancasters.

Großbritannien

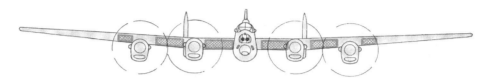

Avro „**Lancaster**"
Kampfflugzeug

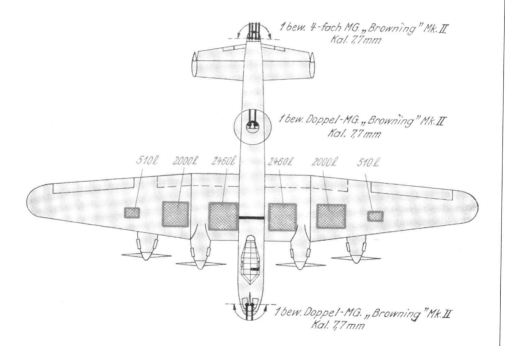

1 bew. 4-fach MG „Browning" Mk. II
Kal. 7,7mm

1 bew. Doppel-MG „Browning" Mk. II
Kal. 7,7mm

510ℓ   2000ℓ   2460ℓ   2460ℓ   2000ℓ   510ℓ

1 bew. Doppel-MG „Browning" Mk. II
Kal. 7,7mm

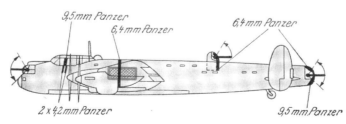

9,5mm Panzer

6,4mm Panzer

6,4mm Panzer

2 x 4,2mm Panzer

9,5mm Panzer

Avro LANCASTER
Prototype, first flight: BT308, 9 January 1941
Entry to service: 44 Sqn, December 1941

Squadron	Dates	Airfield
7 Sqn	May 1943–Jan 1950	Oakington, Mepal, Upwood
9 Sqn	Sep 1942–Jul 1946	Waddington, Bardney, Binbrook
12 Sqn	Nov 1942–Jul 1946	Wickenby, Binbrook
15 Sqn	Dec 1943–Mar 1947	Mildenhall, Wyton
35 Sqn	Mar 1944–Sep 1949	Graveley, Stradishall, Mildenhall
44 Sqn	Dec 1941–Sep 1947	Waddington, Dunholme Lodge, Spilsby, Mepal, Mildenhall
49 Sqn	Jun 1942–Mar 1950	Scampton, Fiskerton, Fulbeck, Syerston, Mepal, Upwood
50 Sqn	May 1942–Oct 1946	Skellingthorpe, Swinderby, Sturgate, Waddington
57 Sqn	Sep 1942–May1946	Feltwell, Scampton, East Kirkby, Elsham Wolds
61 Sqn	Apr 1942–Jun 1946	Woolfox Lodge, Syerston, Skellingthorpe, Coningsby, Sturgate, Waddington
75 Sqn RNZAF	Mar 1944–Sep 1945	Mepal, Spilsby
83 Sqn	May 1942–Jul 1946	Scampton, Wyton, Coningsby
90 Sqn	May 1944–Sep 1947	Tuddenham, Wyton
97 Sqn	Jan 1942–Jul 1946	Coningsby, Woodhall Spa, Bourn
100 Sqn	Dec 1942–May 1946	Waltham, Elsham Wolds, Scampton
101 Sqn	Oct 1942–Aug 1946	Holme, Ludford Magna, Binbrook
103 Sqn	Oct 1942–Nov 1945	Elsham Wolds
106 Sqn	May 1942–Feb 1946	Coningsby, Syerston, Metheringham
115 Sqn	Mar 1943–Nov 1949	East Wretham, Little Snoring, Witchford, Graveley, Stradishall, Mildenhall
138 Sqn	Mar 1945–Sep 1947	Tuddenham, Wyton
149 Sqn	Aug 1944–Nov 1949	Methwold, Tuddenham, Stradishall, Mildenhall
150 Sqn	Nov 1944–Nov 1945	Fiskerton, Hemswell
153 Sqn	Oct 1944–Sep 1945	Kirmington, Scampton
156 Sqn	Jan 1943–Sep 1945	Warboys, Upwood, Wyton
166 Sqn	Sep 1943–Nov 1945	Kirmington
170 Sqn	Oct 1944–Nov 1945	Kelstern, Dunholme Lodge, Hemswell
186 Sqn	Oct 1944–Jul 1945	Tuddenham, Stradishall
189 Sqn	Oct 1944–Nov 1945	Bardney, Fulbeck, Metheringham
195 Sqn	Oct 1944–Aug 1945	Witchford, Wratting Common
207 Sqn	Mar 1942–Aug 1949	Bottesford, Langar, Methwold, Tuddenham, Stradishall, Mildenhall
214 Sqn	Nov 1946–Mar 1950	Upwood
218 Sqn	Aug 1944–Aug 1945	Methwold, Chedburgh
227 Sqn	Oct 1944–Sep 1945	Bardney, Balderton, Strubby, Graveley
300 Sqn	Apr 1944–Oct 1946	Faldingworth, Skipton-on-Swale
405 Sqn RCAF	Aug 1943–Sep 1945	Gransden Lodge, Linton-on-Ouse
408 Sqn	Oct 1943–Sep 1944	Linton-on-Ouse
419 Sqn RCAF	Mar 1944–Sep 1945	Middleton St George
420 Sqn RCAF	Apr 1945–Sep 1945	Tholthorpe
424 Sqn RCAF	Jan 1945–Oct 1945	Skipton-on-Swale
425 Sqn RCAF	May 1945–Sep 1945	Tholthorpe
426 Sqn RCAF	Jul 1943–May 1944	Linton-on-Ouse
427 Sqn RCAF	Mar 1945–May 1946	Leeming
428 Sqn RCAF	Jun 1944–Sep 1945	Middleton St George
429 Sqn RCAF	Mar 1945–May 1946	Leeming
431 Sqn RCAF	Oct 1944–Sep 1945	Croft
432 Sqn RCAF	Oct 1943–Feb 1944	East Moor
433 Sqn RCAF	Jan 1945–Oct 1945	Skipton-on-Swale
434 Sqn RCAF	Dec 1944–Mar 1945	Croft
460 Sqn RAAF	Oct 1942–Oct 1945	Breighton, Binbrook, East Kirkby
463 Sqn RAAF	Nov 1943–Sep 1945	Waddington, Skellingthorpe
467 Sqn RAAF	Nov 1942–Sep 1945	Scampton, Bottesford, Waddington, Metheringham
514 Sqn	Sep 1943–Aug 1945	Foulsham, Waterbeach
550 Sqn	Nov 1943–Oct 1945	Waltham, North Killingholme
576 Sqn	Nov 1943–Sep 1945	Elsham Wolds, Fiskerton
582 Sqn	Apr 1944–Sep 1945	Little Staughton
617 Sqn	Mar 1943–Sep 1946	Scampton, Coningsby, Woodhall Spa, Waddington, Binbrook
619 Sqn	Apr 1943–Jul 1945	Woodhall Spa, Coningsby, Dunholme Lodge, Strubby
622 Sqn	Dec 1943–Aug 1945	Mildenhall
625 Sqn	Oct 1943–Oct 1945	Kelstern, Scampton
626 Sqn	Nov 1943–Oct 1945	Wickenby
630 Sqn	Nov 1943–Jul 1945	East Kirkby
635 Sqn	Mar 1944–Aug 1945	Downham Market

The Lancaster II was powered by four Bristol Hercules engines rather than the usual Merlins and entered service with 61 Squadron in October 1942.

The Lancaster made its final wartime attack on the night of 25/26 April, the target being an oil facility at Vallo in Norway, whilst other Lancasters dropped mines in the Oslo fjord. More fitting perhaps was the attack on 25 April that targeted Hitler's Bavarian retreat at Berchtesgaden in which 359 Lancasters (and 16 Mosquitoes) took part; two of the Lancasters were lost. The final operational Lancaster loss occurred on the Vallo raid, an aircraft of 463 Squadron having to force-land in Sweden (with all crew safe).

With the war in Europe over a number of Bomber Command Lancaster squadrons were earmarked for *Tiger Force* and the Far East's final campaign against the Japanese. The war ended before any significant movement took place and for the Lancaster the next few years presented the sad picture of squadron disbandments and scrapping of aircraft. The Lancaster remained in Bomber Command service for a number of years, some having been converted to PR.1 standard for photo reconnaissance.

A number of airframes have survived, most notably in Canada, but also including one of the Century aircraft (more than 100 ops) now in the RAF Museum, Hendon. There are two airworthy Lancasters, one in Canada flown in memory of Andrew Mynarski VC and the other operated by the RAF's Battle of Britain Memorial Flight.

Lockheed Ventura

In the summer of 1940 the British Purchasing Commission placed an order for 675 Lockheed Ventura bombers as part of the search for additional sources of aircraft, and with a view to replacing older types such as the Battle and Blenheim. Based on the successful Hudson design, although actually a militarised version of the Lodestar transport, the Ventura looked promising; however, in the crucible or war in daylight operations over Europe it was to prove almost as vulnerable as the types it was meant to replace.

Designed as a light bomber with a crew of five the Ventura had a bomb load of 2,500 lb, a speed of 260 mph and a range of 950 miles but for an aircraft of its size was well armed with 0.303 inch and 0.5 inch guns. Development of the aircraft was slower than planned and first deliveries were not made until May 1942, with 21 Squadron at Bodney being the first Bomber Command unit to re-equip. It was not until 3 November that the Squadron flew is first *op* with the Ventura, with three aircraft tasked to attack a

The Lockheed Ventura was not a popular aircraft during its short career with No. 2 Group, although, despite one or two disastrous raids, its overall loss rate was only 3.6 per cent.

factory at Hengelo; all had to bomb a secondary target having failed to locate the primary but all returned safely. From then on the Venturas of 21 Squadron, soon joined by two other squadrons in Bomber Command, undertook daylight raids on a variety of targets, including some of the most famous of daylight attacks such as the Philips factory at Eindhoven on 6 December.

The most notable Ventura raid was the one that all but wiped out 487 Squadron on 3 May 1943. The Squadron despatched twelve aircraft to attack a power station near Amsterdam and of the eleven that crossed the enemy coast – with a Spitfire escort – nine were shot down by German fighters, one managed to limp back to England and one proceeded to the target. This lone Ventura, flown by Sqadron Leader L. H. Trent managed to release its bombs in the target area but was then shot down, only two of the crew, including Trent, surviving. It was not until after the war that the full story became clear, following which Leonard Trent was awarded the Victoria Cross.

By the time that No. 2 Group transferred to the Tactical Air Force there were four squadrons of Venturas in service, although most of these would re-equip in autumn that year having had a less than successful career with the aircraft. The initial order for 675 aircraft was stopped after 349 had been produced. The Ventura continued to serve with Coastal Command, Transport Command and in a number of overseas theatres but the career of the *Pig*, its RAF nickname, was not a memorable one.

Lockheed VENTURA
Prototype, first flight: AE658, 31 July 1941
Entry to service: 21 Sqn, May 1942

Squadron	Dates	Airfield
21 Sqn	May 1942–(Sep 1943)	Bodney, Methwold, Oulton
140 Sqn	Apr 1943–(Jan 1944)	Hartford Bridge
464 Sqn	Sep 1942–(Nov 1943)	Feltwell, Methwold
487 Sqn	Sep 1942–(Sep 1943)	Feltwell, Methwold

North American B-25 Mitchell

The North American B-25 Mitchell was another of the American types acquired by the RAF during its search for a new medium bomber to equip No. 2 Group. The Mitchell was developed from the NA-40 and in its B-25 guise first flew on 19 August 1940, entering service with the USAAF the following year as the B-25B. The RAF had already expressed an interest and the first aircraft arrived in late summer 1942, going to 98 Squadron and 180 Squadron at West Raynham in September. After a short work-up period the Mitchells were declared operational and made their first sortie on 22 January 1943 when twelve aircraft from the two squadrons attacked the oil facilities at Terneuzen, near Ghent. It was not an auspicious start as three aircraft were lost, including that of the CO of 180 Squadron, Wing Commander C. Hodder.

The Mitchell had a crew of five and with its top speed of 292 mph and bomb load of 6,000 lb it was a good medium bomber, although the ceiling of only 20,000 ft made it vulnerable to flak. Self-defence was provided by 0.5 inch guns in nose, tail, dorsal (turret) and ventral positions and the aircraft was also reasonably manoeuvrable.

Two further squadrons formed whilst the Group was with Bomber Command but in May 1943 all the Mitchell units transferred with No. 2 Group to the Tactical Air Force. The aircraft went on to have a fine career with the TAF and established a reputation for highly accurate attacks. The final wartime mission was flown on 2 May 1945 and soon

North American B-25 MITCHELL
Prototype, first flight: 19 August 1940
Entry to service: 98 Sqn, September 1942

Squadron	Dates	Airfield
98 Sqn	Sep 1942–(Sep 1945)	West Raynham, Foulsham
180 Sqn	Sep 1942–(Sep 1945)	West Raynham, Foulsham
226 Sqn	May 1943–(Sep 1945)	Swanton Morley
320 Sqn	Mar 1943–(Aug 1945)	Methwold, Attlebridge

Of the American bomber types acquired for No.2 Group as Blenheim replacements, the Mitchell was the most effective and four squadrons were re-equipped.

after the end of the war the Mitchells were replaced in RAF units by Mosquitoes. The RAF eventually acquired over 800 Mitchells, the majority being Mk II and Mk III variants, the latter did not enter service until May 1944 and so were never part of Bomber Command.

The B-25 had a comprehensive career with the American military serving with distinction in most theatres of war as well as performing valuable training roles. Post-war use of the B-25 in a variety of military and civil roles meant that examples of the type survived long enough for the interest in aircraft preservation to ensure that their long-term preservation. Various museums around the world, but mainly the USA, have B-25s on display and airworthy aircraft make regular appearances at airshows in the USA and Europe.

The Cold War

With the war over the immediate interest of the politicians was in saving money and returning the country to a semblance of peace and prosperity. Disbandment of squadrons had started in early 1945 and although a number of new aircraft types had been under development in the latter years of the war there was suddenly no great urgency to bring them into service. For the next few years rationalisation was the name of the game; the Avro Lincoln entered service having narrowly missed the war and development of the first jet bombers continued, work on the English Electric Canberra having started in 1944.

However, by the late 1950s Europe had started to look less secure once more as relations with the Russians cooled to such an extent that the Cold War was 'declared'. This, and the outbreak of the Korean War in 1950, led to renewed interest in giving the RAF up to date equipment, which was one of the reasons for the acquisition of Boeing B-29 Washingtons on loan from the Americans. The piston types soon gave way to the jets – and the new bombers were unarmed, relying on speed and height to avoid the enemy. Offensive power took a leap forward with the introduction of nuclear bombs and Bomber Command became the focus of the British nuclear deterrent. With some pundits predicting that ballistic missiles were the future, the RAF acquired American *Thor* missiles. By the time Bomber Command was disbanded to become part of Strike Command it had virtually lost its strategic nuclear role but with its array of long-range bombers, supporting by air-refuelling, it remained a potent weapon.

Avro Lincoln

As the Lancaster was starting to prove its worth with Bomber Command in the middle years of the war, Avro's designers were looking at the requirement of Specification B.14/43, which was essentially a replacement for the current range of four-engined heavies. The design they came up with showed its Lancaster origins, indeed it was originally known as the Lancaster IV and V and the prototype first flew at Ringway on 9 June 1944. Development was reasonably straightforward and the aircraft entered service as the Avro Lincoln I in August 1945, the first unit to re-equip being 57 Squadron at East Kirkby. Too late for active service in Europe, the first Lincoln units were designated as part of Tiger Force for the final operations against Japan, However, the end of the war overtook this plan and the Lincolns saw no active service in the Second World War. Bomber Command's replacement programme was fairly rapid and twenty-four squadrons were re-equipped with the Lincoln in its Mk I and Mk II versions, the

Avro Lincoln of 100 Squadron: the Lincoln was the RAF's main bomber in the immediate post-war period and remained in service to the mid 1950s.

Avro LINCOLN
Prototype, first flight: PW925, 9 June 1944
Entry to service: 57 Sqn, August 1945

Squadron	Dates	Airfield
7 Sqn	Aug 1949–Dec 1955	Upwood
9 Sqn	Jul 1946–May 1952	Binbrook
12 Sqn	Aug 1946–Apr 1952	Waddington, Binbrook, Hemswell
15 Sqn	Feb 1947–Nov 1950	Wyton, Marham, Coningsby
35 Sqn	Aug 1949–Feb 1950	Mildenhall
44 Sqn	Oct 1945–Jan 1951	Mildenhall, Wyton
49 Sqn	Oct 1949–Jul 1955	Upwood, Waddington, Wittering
50 Sqn	Jul 1946–Jan 1951	Waddington
57 Sqn	Aug 1945–May 1951	Elsham Wolds, Scampton, Lindholme, Waddington
58 Sqn	Nov 1950–Oct 1951	Benson
61 Sqn	May 1946–Aug 1954	Waddington, Wittering
75 Sqn	Sep 1945–Oct 1945	Spilsby
83 Sqn	Jul 1946–Dec 1955	Coningsby, Hemswell
90 Sqn	Apr 1947–Aug 1950	Wyton
97 Sqn	Jul 1946–Dec 1955	Coningsby, Hemswell
100 Sqn	May 1946–Apr 1954	Lindholme, Hemswell, Waddington, Wittering
101 Sqn	May 1946–Jun 1951	Binbrook
115 Sqn	Jul 1949–Feb 1950	Mildenhall
138 Sqn	Jul 1947–Aug 1950	Wyton
148 Sqn	Sep 1949–Jun 1955	Upwood
149 Sqn	Oct 1949–Mar 1950	Mildenhall
207 Sqn	Jul 1949–Feb 1950	Mildenhall
214 Sqn	Feb 1950–Dec 1954	Upwood
617 Sqn	Sep 1946–Jan 1953	Binbrook

former being powered by the Merlin 85 and the latter by the Merlin 86. It was a typical heavy bomber of the period with a large bomb bay for a maximum load of 14,000 lb and with front, mid-upper and rear gun turrets, some with 20 mm and some with 0.5 inch guns. Maximum speed was 295 mph, ceiling 22,000 ft and range 1,470 miles with the maximum bomb load. The figures were average for the period but as air forces starting looking towards jet options with speed and operational ceiling as the main considerations the Lincoln was to be the last of its breed.

Although it missed operational service in the Second World War, the Lincoln did go into 'action' during the Mau Mau operations in Kenya and in Malaya, with the RAF and RAAF. The Lincoln's active period was short-lived for a peacetime aircraft and Bomber Command had given them up in favour of B-29 Washingtons and Canberras by the mid 1950s, although the type remained in service with Signals Command to 1963.

Boeing B-29 Washington

The Boeing B-29 Superfortress had seen operational service in the Far East theatre with the bombing campaign against Japan and had made its name at the end of the war as the aircraft that dropped the Atom bombs on Hiroshima and Nagasaki. It was in the conventional heavy bomber role that Bomber Command acquired its fleet of B-29s, duly named the Washington B.1 in a political gesture, in the early 1950s. The reason for the acquisition was the Command's shortage of effective bombers at a time when the Cold War was starting to acquire sinister overtones; the formation of NATO and then the Soviet-led Warsaw Pact had created two monolithic power blocks facing each other in Europe.

The Americans offered refurbished B-29s and the RAF accepted, the first unit, 115 Squadron at Marham, re-equipping from Lincolns in August 1950 (the first aircraft had arrived at Marham in March for the Washington Conversion Unit). With its higher performance and better armament the Washington was superior to the Lincoln and was liked by its crews, the pressurised and comfortable cockpit environment being a massive improvement over the cold and noisy Lincoln. The aircraft could carry up to 6,000 lb of bombs (a typically low American bomber load), although for long-range operations (3,000 nm) this reduced to a mere 1,000 lb, which was acceptable if the bomb was a

The B-29 Washington was stop-gap loan bomber from the Americans to give Bomber Command an enhanced capability in the early 1950s; trio of B-29s of 115 Squadron.

Boeing B-29 WASHINGTON
Prototype, first flight: 21 September 1942
Entry to service: 115 Sqn, August 1950

Squadron	Dates	Airfield
15 Sqn	Feb 1951–Apr 1953	Coningsby
36 Sqn	Sep 1951–Feb 1954	Marham
44 Sqn	Feb 1951–Jan 1953	Marham, Coningsby
57 Sqn	Apr 1951–Mar 1953	Marham, Waddington, Coningsby
90 Sqn	Jan 1951–Mar 1954	Marham
115 Sqn	Aug 1950–Mar 1954	Marham
149 Sqn	Nov 1950–Feb 1953	Coningsby
207 Sqn	Jun 1951–Mar 1954	Marham

nuclear one but of no value otherwise. The crew of ten was larger than anything the RAF had employed to that time and caused some problems with training and constitution, but the heavy radar-controlled armament was seen as a bonus. Further squadrons formed at Marham and a second Wing formed at Coningsby.

The RAF eventually acquired some eighty-eight B-29s but it was only a short-term arrangement pending the introduction of the RAF's first jet bombers, Canberras, in the early 1950s.

English Electric Canberra

Design work commenced in 1944 for the RAF's first jet bomber, the intention being to produce a high-speed, high-flying bomber equipped with a radar bombing system. Over the next four years 'Teddy' Petter and his team refined the design, settling on a circular fuselage and straight, tapering wing, power being provided by two Rolls-Royce Avon engines set in the mid-wing position. In its bright blue finish, prototype English Electric A.1 VN799 took to the air, flown by Roland Beamont, on 13 May 1949, for a very successful first flight. However, problems with the radar bombing system led to a redesign of the front end with the incorporation of a glazed nose with optical panel – the Bomb Aimer would have to lie down in the nose to use a traditional visual bombsight. The official naming ceremony took place on 19 January 1951 when Mr R. Menzies, the Prime Minister of Australia, gave the aircraft the name 'Canberra'. The average cost of a Canberra was £80,000 to £100,000 depending on the number ordered. That same year the first production variant, the B.2 entered RAF service, 101 Squadron at Binbrook receiving its first aircraft on 25 May. The overall plan for Canberra re-equipment within Bomber Command was for twenty-four squadrons, each with ten aircraft, organised in Wings of four squadrons at six bases.

With its 6,000 lb bomb load, 45,000 ft operational ceiling, crew of three, and high-speed, the Canberra was a great improvement on Bomber Command's existing types (Lincoln, B-29 Washington and Mosquito), albeit its range was somewhat less. This latter aspect was not important as the Command was due to take delivery of its long-range strategic jet bombers (the V-bombers) in the mid 1950s. A trainer version, the T.4, was given side-by-side seating, in a somewhat crowded cockpit, and proved invaluable over the years for pilot conversion.

Such was the success of the basic airframe that a photo reconnaissance variant was built; the Canberra PR.3 was in essence a lengthened B.2 equipped with a variety of

Intended as a interim bomber prior to introduction of the V-bomber force, Canberras equipped a number of bomber Wings for much of the 1950s. This Warton line-up illustrates both bomber and reconnaissance variants.

cameras: the first PR.3s were delivered to 540 Squadron in December 1952. Although to many senior officers in the Air Staff the Canberra was seen as an 'interim' aircraft, it proved so effective and so adaptable that over the next forty years it was to serve with over sixty RAF squadrons, become an export success, and be one of very few British types licence-built by the Americans (as the Martin B-57).

The original plan for Bomber Command Wings underwent a number of changes but by 1954 the main Wings had formed at Binbrook, Coningsby, Honington, Scampton and Marham, and with two target-marker squadrons at Hemswell. Canberras were soon in the news for record-breaking flights and overseas tours of a 'show the flag' nature; the RAF was justly proud of its new aircraft, although from an operational perspective of putting bombs on target its capability was no better than that of previous types as the promised bombing aids failed to materialise. The B.2 version was followed in June 1954, with 101 Squadron being first to re-equip with the more powerful (bigger engines) variant. This still had a crew of three as, once again, the blind-bombing system was not available. The basic bombing technique was for medium to high level bombing (20,000 ft to 40,000 ft) using either visual aiming or *Gee-H* and crew spent most of their time practising these arts. If bombing accuracy was little improved, survivability was better and many an RAF fighter squadron was frustrated at being unable to intercept the bombers. The PR squadrons also received a new variant, the PR.7 entering service with 82 Squadron in June 1953. By this time the Canberra was also trying out its hand at low-level tactics, for which 101 Squadron formed an 'Intruder Flight' to evaluate the tactics. In part this was in response to changing requirements, one of which was the introduction of the Low Altitude Bombing System (LABS), although this did not enter service, with 9 Squadron, until 1957.

From 1956 the Bomber Command Canberra force entered a decline as the first of the V-bombers entered service, the first full Wing disbanding in early 1957. However, this mid 1950s period was also when the Canberra went to war, at first in Malaya and then during the Suez crisis.

It was the early 1960s before the bomber force had finally gone, although the PR Canberras remained in service. This was far from being the end of the Canberra as the

Formation of Canberra B.6s of 9 Squadron (or IX Squadron – the preferred designation). The Canberra provided an interim jet bomber for Bomber Command but did see operational service in the mid 1950s.

English Electric CANBERRA
Prototype, first flight: VN799, 13 May 1949
Entry to service: 101 Sqn, May 1951

Squadron	Dates	Airfield
9 Sqn	May 1952–Jul 1961	Binbrook, Coningsby
10 Sqn	Jan 1953-Dec 1956	Scampton, Honington
12 Sqn	Mar 1952–Jul 1961	Binbrook, Coningsby
15 Sqn	May 1953–Apr 1957	Coningsby, Cottesmore, Honington
18 Sqn	Aug 1953-Jan 1957	Scampton, Upwood
21 Sqn	Sep 1953-Jan 1959	Scampton, Waddington, Upwood
27 Sqn	Jun 1953-Dec 1957	Scampton, Waddington
35 Sqn	Apr 1954–Sep 1961	Marham, Upwood
40 Sqn	Oct 1953-Feb 1957	Coningsby, Wittering, Upwood
44 Sqn	Apr 1953–Jul 1957	Coningsby, Cottesmore, Honington
50 Sqn	Aug 1952–Oct 1959	Binbrook, Upwood
57 Sqn	May 1953–Dec 1957	Coningsby, Cottesmore, Honington
61 Sqn	Aug 1954–Mar 1958	Wittering, Upwood
76 Sqn	Dec 1953–Dec 1960	Wittering, Hemswell, Upwood
90 Sqn	Nov 1953–May 1956	Marham
100 Sqn	Apr 1954-Sep 1959	Wittering
101 Sqn	May 1951–Jan 1957	Binbrook
109 Sqn	Aug 1952–Jan 1957	Hemswell, Binbrook
115 Sqn	Feb 1954–May 1957	Marham
139 Sqn	Nov 1952–Dec 1959	Hemswell, Binbrook
149 Sqn	Mar 1953–Aug 1956	Coningsby, Cottesmore
207 Sqn	Mar 1954–Feb 1956	Marham
542 Sqn	May 1954-Oct 1958	Wyton, Weston Zoyland, Hemswell, Upwood
617 Sqn	Jan 1952–Dec 1955	Binbrook

type served in all the main RAF theatres, RAF Germany, the Middle/Near East and the Far East, as well as adopting a variety of support roles, most notably target facilities. No less than sixty-three RAF squadrons used Canberras and in what is a record for the RAF the type is still in front-line service – the PR.9s of 39 (1 PRU) Squadron remaining operational at Marham, and with an out-of-service date predicted as 2006/7.

Vickers Valiant

The Vickers Valiant will only be remembered for one thing – the dramatic and sudden end to its flying career at the end of 1964 following the discovery of critical structural fatigue. In many ways this is as sad epitaph as the aircraft was one of the most attractive of its era and up until the fatigue problem it had played a major role in the development of Bomber Command's Cold War capability.

As the first of the V-bombers to enter service, the Valiant joined 138 Squadron at Gaydon in January 1955, for which purpose the Squadron had re-formed. Designed to Specification B.9/48 the prototype Valiant flew in May 1951 but development was slowed down when this aircraft (WB210) was destroyed early the following year. The aircraft was designed to carry up to 21,000 lb of conventional bombs or an unspecified nuclear load and with its speed of 414 mph and ceiling of 54,000 ft it was intended to operate above enemy defences and as such was unarmed. A reconnaissance variant of the B.1, as the B(PR).1, joined 543 Squadron in July 1955 for strategic reconnaissance and aerial survey. The sole operational use of the Valiant occurred in 1956 when four squadrons detached aircraft to Malta to take part in the Suez campaign, although it was not an inspiring debut as bombing was reported as poor.

Another claim to a place in the history books came with the Valiant's participation in nuclear bomb trials; aircraft from 49 Squadron dropping the first British atomic bomb

Valiant WP223 of 90 Squadron dropping a 10,000 lb bomb on the range at Jurby.

Valiants of 214 Squadron on air-to-air refuelling training; the aircraft's involvement in the development of the AAR capability was vital to Bomber Command and its successor, Strike Command.

(11 October 1956) and the first British hydrogen bomb (15 May 1957). The final bomber squadron formed in May 1957, shortly before the last of 104 Valiants left the production line. A final squadron formed the following year when 18 Squadron acquired a number of Valiants for its ECM role.

The tanker role had arrived in 1956 when a number of aircraft became B(PR)K.1s, the 'K' being the designation for a tanker. The squadron in effect became the RAF's trials and evaluation unit for air refuelling and over the next few years worked hard to develop the techniques and tactics of what was to become a key role for strategic air power. It also meant that the Squadron, and the Valiant, could notch up a number of record-breaking flights; for example, four distance/time records were claimed in 1959. On 7 March 1960 a Valiant remained airborne for 18 hours and 5 minutes having flown around the UK a number of times on its 8,500 mile 'journey'.

The major rationale for the Command's Valiants remained that of nuclear QRA and stations such as Marham kept aircraft at the required readiness states during this

Vickers VALIANT
Prototype, first flight: WB210, 18 May 1951
Entry to service: 138 Sqn, January 1955

Squadron	Dates	Airfield
7 Sqn	Nov 1956–May 1963	Honington, Wittering
18 Sqn	Dec 1958–Mar 1963	Finningley
49 Sqn	May 1956–Dec 1964	Wittering, Marham
90 Sqn	Mar 1957–Dec 1964	Honington
138 Sqn	Jan 1955–Apr 1962	Gaydon, Wittering
148 Sqn	Jul 1956–Dec 1964	Marham
199 Sqn	May 1957–Dec 1958	Hemswell, Honington
207 Sqn	Jun 1956–Dec 1964	Marham
214 Sqn	Jan 1956–Dec 1964	Marham
543 Sqn	Jun 1955–Dec 1964	Gaydon, Wyton

Cold War period. However, for the Valiant it was all about to end, as recorded in one of the squadron diaries: 'Inspection of WP217 after landing at Gaydon showed only too plainly that the aircraft had suffered major damage. The fuselage below the starboard inner plane had buckled, popping the rivets; the engine door had cracked on the top surface of the mainplane between the engines, the rivets had been pulled and the skin buckled. The primary cause of the damage was a broken rear spar on the starboard side. All Valiants of a similar age and life pattern were grounded forthwith.' By the time the manufacturer's working party had assessed all the aircraft twelve had been give Cat. A (fit to fly), nineteen Cat. B (flyable only in an emergency) and five Cat. C (grounded). Further examination of two Cat. B aircraft that were broken up showed that the problem was worse than expected and all aircraft were grounded, although non-flying QRA was maintained until January. The squadrons disbanded and Marham became a scrapyard for Valiants, although one was preserved on the base and many years later (1982) was moved to the RAF Museum where it was put into 49 Squadron markings in commemoration of the atom bomb trials.

Handley Page Victor

Although the Victor was an impressive bomber it was its second career as an air-to-air refuelling aircraft that assured its place in RAF history. The first part of this tanker story fell within the Bomber Command period but the operational employments in this role took place long after Bomber Command had become Strike Command.

Developed to the same Specification as the other V-bombers, the Victor was superior to its two counterparts in that its conventional bomb load was 35,000 lb, the greatest of any RAF bomber and an impressive sight when it carried out a full drop of thirty-five 1,000 lb bombs. The prototype flew in December 1952 and the Victor B.1 entered Bomber Command squadron service at Cottesmore in April 1958 with 10 Squadron, although the training unit, 232 OCU at Gaydon had been operating Victors since the previous November. The initial plan was for two Wings, each with two squadrons, to be based at Cottesmore and Honington and both were operational by summer 1960.

The B.1 had a top speed of Mach 0.9 and a ceiling of 55,000 ft, although like a number of aircraft at this period its ceiling was limited by the performance of crew equipment such as oxygen systems. This performance was slightly improved on by the

The Victors of 543 Squadron at Wyton were used in the Strategic Reconnaissance role with Bomber Command.

Handley Page VICTOR
Prototype, first flight: WB771, 24 December 1952
Entry to service: 10 Sqn, April 1958

Squadron	Dates	Airfield
10 Sqn	Apr 1958–Mar 1964	Cottesmore
15 Sqn	Sep 1958–Oct 1964	Cottesmore
55 Sqn	Sep 1960–(Oct 1993)	Honington, Marham
57 Sqn	Mar 1959–(Jun 1986)	Honington, Marham
100 Sqn	May 1962–Sep 1968	Wittering
139 Sqn	Feb 1962–(Dec 1968)	Wittering
543 Sqn	May 1965–(May 1974)	Wyton

B.2 variant that entered service in February 1962 with 139 Squadron, the OCU once again having been flying them since the previous year. The conventional bomb load was unchanged but the B.2 was also able to carry the *Blue Steel* nuclear missile. The final Victor, of 83 built, was delivered in May 1963 and as the bomber role started come to an end the Victor found new roles as a strategic reconnaissance aircraft, 543 Squadron with the B/SR.2 and its incredible endurance and range capability courtesy of no bombs and with extra fuel tanks, and as an air refueller.

Two ex bomber units, 55 and 57 Squadrons, came to specialise in the tanker role, the first tanker conversions having entered service in June 1965. This role was to keep the Victor in front-line service for another twenty-eight years during which time it continued the development work started by the Valiant and flew countless 'trails' with fighter-type 'chicks' in tow on a world-wide commitment. After a fine career, including a number of operational deployments, the Victor's long and distinguished career as a tanker came to an end in October 1993 with the disbandment at Marham of 55 Squadron.

It was sad to see the aircraft being scrapped at Marham but a number were preserved; Marham keeps one as 'gate guard' but the most impressive is at Bruntingthorpe where it is kept 'live', taking part in fast taxi runs.

Avro Vulcan

Of all the aircraft associated with Bomber Command and the Cold War the Vulcan is probably the best known, even though from a historical perspective it was by no means the most significant – but it did look 'the business!' As one of the trio of V-bombers the Avro Vulcan had its origins in the same late 1940s requirement and as such had to meet the 45,000 ft and 21,000 lb bomb load criteria, which it did easily. Avro's design was unique in that it used a massive delta wing, this distinctive feature giving rise to the aircraft's nickname of 'tin triangle'. The prototype flew in August 1952 but it was not until January 1957 that the Vulcan finally entered service, when No. 230 OCU at Waddington received its first two aircraft (XA895 and XA898), with training of students commencing in late February. No. 1 Course graduated on 21 May and became 'A Flight' of 83 Squadron, the designation for the first operational unit; the Lincoln-equipped 83 Squadron had disbanded in January. The Squadron received its first Vulcan (XA905) on 11 July, having previously borrowed OCU aircraft, and also received the graduates of No. 2 Course. Finningley was chosen as the base for the second unit and 101 Squadron started to form in October, with four aircraft being on strength with the unit by the end of the year. The crews on both squadrons got down to the business of settling the new aircraft down and evaluating performance and tactics; however, as with any new type

The delta-wing of the Vulcan – the 'tin triangle'; by no means the most effective of the V-bombers but the one that survived in operational bomber service into the 1980s.

there was also a fair amount of politics – although the overseas 'flag waving' tours were both valuable and popular. Bomber Command had a global commitment so the capability of deploying to and operating from various RAF and Allied bases was vital.

The introduction to service of the Vulcan B.1 was relatively trouble-free, except for the loss of XA908 and most of its crew on 24 October 1958 when the aircraft went out of control following loss of electrical power – a critical failure for an aircraft with powered flying controls. Prototype VX770 had crashed four weeks before but the structural failure in this case was put down to the aircraft being operated outside its performance clearance during an air display.

The primary role for the all-white Vulcans was part of the strategic deterrent and as such the main weapon was a free-fall nuclear bomb, although in a conventional role the Vulcan could drop twenty-one 1,000 lb bombs. Cruising at high subsonic speed and, in theory, above the defences (45,000 ft), and with long range, the bombers would be able to attack their targets with impunity. With the early Olympus engines the B.1s were underpowered and even the 13,500 lb thrust of the Olympus 104, which became standard for the B.1, was not ideal. Avro was working on a new Vulcan variant to take advantage of the promised higher thrust Olympus under development, but this also required a redesign of the wing for the high-speed/high-altitude environment. There were numerous other changes throughout the aircraft but the most obvious was the engine and wing. Vulcan VX777 first flew as a B.2 on 31 August 1957, although this was an airframe test as it was not flying with the 16,000 lb Olympus 200 series engines. A number of aircraft took part in the development work, which included a new rear fuselage to accommodate Electronic Counter Measures (ECM) equipment. The first production B.2, XV533, flew on 19 August 1958, although the first aircraft with operational engines (Olympus 201s of 17,000 lb thrust) and an ECM fit did not fly until January. The aircraft showed great promise with an all-round improvement in performance, including up to 30 per cent increase in range – bringing more targets within the coverage of Bomber Command's nuclear weapons.

The first B.2 was delivered to No. 230 OCU in July 1960 and once more 83 Squadron became the lead squadron, converting to B.2s later in the year and handing its B.1s to one of the newly-forming squadrons. In October 1960 the Squadron had moved to Scampton and by September 1962 two more Vulcan units (27 and 617) had equipped with B.2s at the Lincolnshire base, completing the planned Wing of three squadrons. The

The Vulcan in two of its guises: the original all white anti-flash scheme of the nuclear era and the later camouflaged scheme for low-level operations.

Waddington Wing, equipped with B.1As, comprised 44, 50 and 101 Squadrons and a second B.2 Wing was established at Coningsby in 1962, comprising 9, 12, 35 Squadrons. With a strength of nine Vulcan squadrons Bomber Command had a very potent strike force by the early 1960s and it remained the cutting edge of the Command throughout the decade. The free-fall nuclear weapons were joined in late 1962 by the stand-off missile *Blue Steel* and with this weapon the Vulcan's capability was given a major boost. A planned follow-on version was abandoned in favour of ballistic missiles but when this decision was reversed the acquisition of a new American stand-off missile, *Skybolt* was initiated. Vulcan trials showed that a standard B.2 could carry one missile under each wing but Avro put forward a proposal for the Vulcan Phase Six, which would have become the B.3, capable of carrying up to six missiles. However, with the cancellation of *Skybolt* the 'next generation' Vulcan also vanished, even though it was also being promoted as a conventional bomber with thirty-eight 1,000 lb bombs.

Avro VULCAN
Prototype, first flight: VX770, 30 August 1952
Entry to service: 83 Sqn, May 1957

Squadron	Dates	Airfield
9 Sqn	Mar 1962–Jan 1969	Coningsby, Cottesmore
12 Sqn	Jul 1962–Dec 1967	Coningsby, Cottesmore
27 Sqn	Apr 1961–Mar 1972	Scampton
35 Sqn	Dec 1962–Jan 1969	Coningsby, Cottesmore
44 Sqn	Aug 1960–Dec 1982	Waddington
50 Sqn	Aug 1961–Mar 1984	Waddington
83 Sqn	May 1957–Aug 1969	Waddington, Scampton
101 Sqn	Oct 1957–Aug 1982	Finningley, Waddington
617 Sqn	May 1958–Dec 1981	Scampton

These events tied in with a tactical change for the Vulcan with the decision to move from high-level, which was now too vulnerable in the face of the increased air defence capability of SAMs and fighters, to low-level. So for the remaining years of its front-line service with Bomber Command the Vulcan, changing from its white anti-flash paint scheme, to a green-grey camouflage became a low-level bomber. This tactic was used for both nuclear and conventional roles, although in the former it usually involved a pop-up technique to deliver the weapon and then a dart back down to low-level to run away from the target area. The main addition in terms of equipment was a terrain-following radar and additional ECM, as evidenced by the fairing on top of the fin.

The run-down of the force commenced in 1967 when 12 Squadron disbanded, although the following year all squadrons had equipped with B.2s. The subsequent development of the Vulcan force is outside the scope of this book as the disbandment of Bomber Command in 1968 took place whilst the Vulcan was still a major part of the Order of Battle. The table shows the UK deployment of the aircraft and ignores the move of some squadrons to Cyprus.

Douglas Thor IRBM

The 1950s were the decade in which nuclear weapons came to dominate strategic thinking and by the mid 1950s that thinking including ground-launched ballistic missiles. The British Air Estimates for 1958 stated that: 'Ballistic missiles will gradually come to play an increasingly important part in the offensive deterrent. Agreement in principle has been reached with the United States Government to make a number of American IRBMs available to this country.' This statement took the RAF into the ballistic missile era and in September that year the first Douglas *Thor* missiles arrived, the first unit to equip being 77 (Strategic Missile) Squadron at Feltwell. The deployment concept was for four Wings, each with five launch Stations and with three missiles at each Station. By the time deployment was complete in late 1950 Bomber Command's missile Order of Battle was:

1. Driffield (HQ and 98 Sqn): Stations at Carnaby (150 Sqn), Catfoss (226 Sqn), Breighton (240 Sqn), Full Sutton (102 Sqn).
2. Hemswell (HQ and 97 Sqn): Stations at Caistor (269 Sqn), Ludford Magna (104 Sqn), Bardney (106 Sqn), Coleby Grange (142 Sqn).
3. North Luffenham (HQ and 144 Sqn): Stations at Folkingham (223 Sqn), Melton Mowbray (254 Sqn), Polebrook (130 Sqn), Harrington (218 Sqn).
4. Feltwell (HQ and 77 Sqn): Stations at North Pickenham (220 Sqn), Mepal (113 Sqn), Tuddenham (107 Sqn), Shepherds Grove (82 Sqn).

Thor sites were very distinctive as massive concrete walls were needed at each of the launch platforms for blast protection, along with the triple barbed wire fence and constant Military Police patrols. The warheads were controlled by the Americans and so every site had a number of American personnel. *Thor* had been developed in a very short space of time, thirty months from drawing board to first deliveries; the first trial launch had taken place in January 1957. Deployment in the UK was part of a NATO chain of missiles, although this was the only *Thor* location in Europe and the missiles were capable of reaching targets in Russia. This was very much Cold War stuff and Britain was planning its own follow-on system, *Blue Streak*. Personnel posted to the missile force were told that this was the future and that they were at the cutting edge of Bomber Command.

The missile was protected by a sliding hangar - this was a weather protection and not designed to withstand attack.

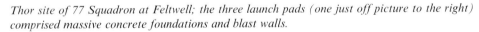

Thor site of 77 Squadron at Feltwell; the three launch pads (one just off picture to the right) comprised massive concrete foundations and blast walls.

Douglas THOR
Entry to Service: 77 Sqn, September 1958

Squadron	Dates	Airfields
77 Sqn	Sep 1958–Jul 1963	Feltwell
82 Sqn	Jul 1959–Jul 1963	Shepherds Grove
97 Sqn	Dec 1959–May 1963	Hemswell
98 Sqn	Aug 1959–Apr 1963	Driffield
102 Sqn	Aug 1959–Apr 1963	Full Sutton
104 Sqn	Jul 1959–May 1963	Ludford Magna
106 Sqn	Jul 1959–May 1963	Bardney
107 Sqn	Jul 1959–Jul 1963	Tuddenham
113 Sqn	Jul 1959–Jul 1963	Mepal
130 Sqn	Dec 1959–Aug 1963	Polebrook
142 Sqn	Jul 1959–May 1963	Coleby Grange
144 Sqn	Dec 1959–Aug 1963	North Luffenham
150 Sqn	Aug 1959–Apr 1963	Carnaby
218 Sqn	Dec 1959–Aug 1963	Harrington
220 Sqn	Jul 1959–Jul 1963	North Pickenham
223 Sqn	Nov 1959–Aug 1963	Folkingham
226 Sqn	Aug 1959–Mar 1963	Catfoss
240 Sqn	Aug 1959–Jan 1963	Breighton
254 Sqn	Dec 1959–Aug 1963	Melton Mowbray
269 Sqn	Jul 1959–May 1963	Caistor

The daily routine was one of maintaining alert status and practising procedures. From time to time a missile was withdrawn and sent to Vandenburg for live firing. The first RAF crew to fire a missile was from 98 Squadron under Operation *Lion's Roar* in April 1959. The Squadron diarist recorded the launch process: 'Attention all stations. This is the Launch Control Officer. On my mark the terminal launch countdown will begin … 5-4-3-3-1-Mark. On the executive word the sequence key is turned and the auto sequence starts. The guidance system is aligned and checked, the missile shelter is moved back and the missile rises to the vertical launch position. The propellants are fed into the missile. The amber light comes on indicating engines about to start and 5 seconds later off it goes.' A successful launch was made on 16 April to the delight of the 98 Squadron crew. The twenty-first, and last, RAF firing was made on 19 June 1962 and of those twenty-one launches only two were unsuccessful.

That last launch took place a month after the US Secretary of Defense announced that the Americans would cease to provide technical support for *Thor* after 31 October 1964, the missile having been replaced in the USAF inventory. With the cancellation of *Blue Streak* this spelled the end of Bomber Command's missile era and in August 1962 it was announced that the RAF would disband its *Thor* organisation the following year. The run-down commenced in December 1962 with a trial dismantling of facilities at Breighton; the last *Thor* missile left the UK on 27 September 1963.

Annexes

Annex A

AOC-in-C Bomber Command

Command from:

14 July 1936	ACM Sir John Steel
12 Sep 1937	ACM Sir Edgar Ludlow-Hewitt
2 Apr 1940	AVM C. F. Portal
5 Oct 1940	AM Sir Richard E. Peirse
8 Jan 1942	(acting AOC) AVM J. E. Baldwin
22 Feb 1942	AVM A. T. Harris
15 Sep 1945	AM Sir Norman Bottomley
16 Jan 1947	AM Sir Hugh W. L. Saunders
8 Oct 1947	AM A. B. (later Sir Aubrey) Ellwood
2 Feb 1950	AM (later ACM) Sir Hugh P. Lloyd
9 Apr 1953	AM G. H. (later Sir George) Mills
22 Jan 1956	AM (later ACM) Sir Harry Broadhurst
20 May 1959	AM Sir Kenneth Cross
1 Sep 1963	AM Sir John Grandy
19 Feb 1965	ACM Sir Wallace Kyle

A number of Bomber Command airfields have memorials to the squadrons that operated from them in the Second World War; this memorial to 462 and 466 Squadrons RAAF is situated in North End Park at Driffield.

Annex B

Operational Squadrons

During the period of the Second World War 128 operational squadrons (plus No. 1409 Met Flight as an operational unit) served with Bomber Command, some throughout the war and others for only a matter of weeks, with two forming but not becoming operational before being transferred.

Squadrons of Bomber Command: Second World War

Sqn	Aircraft	Period	Ops	Loss	Remarks
7 Sqn	Whitley	Mar 1938–May 1939	0	0	
	Hampden	Apr 1939–Apr 1940	0	0	
	Stirling	Aug 1940–Aug 1943	1,744	78	
	Lancaster	May 1943–Jan 1950	3,316	87	
9 Sqn	Wellington	Jan 1939–Aug 1942	2,333	66	
	Lancaster	Sep 1942–Jul 1946	3,495	111	VC (Thompson)
10 Sqn	Whitley	Mar 1937–Dec 1941	1,430	47	
	Halifax	Dec 1941–May 1945	4,803	109	
12 Sqn	Battle	Feb 1938–Nov 1940	36	1	VC (Garland), AASF VC (Gray) AASF Not inc. AASF ops
	Wellington	Nov 1940–Nov 1942	1,242	59	
	Lancaster	Nov 1942–Jul 1946	3,882	111	
15 Sqn	Blenheim	Dec 1939–Oct 1940	543	27	
	Wellington	Nov 1940–May 1941	173	3	
	Stirling	Apr 1941–Dec 1943	2,231	91	
	Lancaster	Dec 1943–Mar 1947	2,840	45	
18 Sqn	Blenheim	May 1939–Apr 1943	1,242	40	
21 Sqn	Blenheim	Aug 1938–Mar 1942	1,050	29	
	Ventura	May 1942–(Sep 1943)	369	10	
23 Sqn	Mosquito	Jul 1944–Sep 1945	1,067	8	
35 Sqn	Halifax	Nov 1940–Mar 1944	2,493	100	
	Lancaster	Mar 1944–Sep 1949	2,216	27	
37 Sqn	Wellington	May 1939–Nov 1940	688	15	
38 Sqn	Wellington	Nov 1938–Nov 1940	659	7	
40 Sqn	Blenheim	Dec 1939–Nov 1940	526	22	
	Wellington	Nov 1940–Oct 1941	730	31	
44 Sqn	Hampden	Feb 1939–Dec 1941	2,043	43	
	Lancaster	Dec 1941–Sep 1947	4,362	149	VC (Nettleton)
49 Sqn	Hampden	Aug 1938–Apr 1942	2,636	55	VC (Learoyd)
	Manchester	Apr 1942–Jun 1942	47	6	
	Lancaster	Jun 1942–Mar 1950	3,818	102	
50 Sqn	Hampden	Dec 1938–Apr 1942	2,299	57	
	Manchester	Apr 1942–Jun 1942	126	7	VC (Manser)
	Lancaster	May 1942–Oct 1946	4,710	112	
51 Sqn	Whitley	Feb 1938–Oct 1942	1,806	50	
	Halifax	Nov 1942–May 1945	4,153	108	
57 Sqn	Blenheim	Mar 1938–Nov 1940	58	10	
	Wellington	Nov 1940–Sep 1942	1,056	54	
	Lancaster	Sep 1942–May 1946	4,037	108	
58 Sqn	Whitley	Oct 1937–Dec 1942	1,757	49	
61 Sqn	Hampden	Feb 1939–Oct 1941	1,339	28	
	Manchester	Jun 1941–Jun 1942	197	12	
	Lancaster	Apr 1942–Jun 1946	4,546	116	VC (Reid)
75 Sqn	Wellington	Jul 1939–Nov 1942	2,540	74	VC (Ward)

(continued)

Squadrons of Bomber Command: Second World War (*continued*)

Sqn	Aircraft	Period	Ops	Loss	Remarks
	Stirling	Nov 1942–Apr 1944	1,736	72	
	Lancaster	Mar 1944–Oct 1945	3,741	47	
76 Sqn	Halifax	May 1941–May 1945	5,123	139	1st 4,000lb bomb Most Halifax Ops
77 Sqn	Whitley	Nov 1938–Oct 1942	1,687	56	Most Whitley losses
	Halifax	Oct 1942–Aug 1945	3,692	75	
78 Sqn	Whitley	Jul 1937–Mar 1942	1,117	34	
	Halifax	Mar 1942–Jul 1945	5,120	158	Most Halifax losses
82 Sqn	Blenheim	Mar 1938–Mar 1942	1,436	62	Most Blenheim losses
83 Sqn	Hampden	Nov 1938–Jan 1942	1,987	43	VC (Hannah)
	Manchester	Dec 1941–Jun 1942	152	9	
	Lancaster	May 1942–Jul 1946	3,382	91	
85 Sqn	Mosquito	May 1944–(Oct 1951)	1,190	7	
88 Sqn	Blenheim	Feb 1941–Feb 1942	96	5	
	Boston	Feb 1941–(Apr 1945)	559	6	1st Boston Ops
90 Sqn	Fortress	May 1941–Oct 1941	52	3	1st Fortress Ops
	Stirling	Nov 1942–Jun 1944	1,937	58	
	Lancaster	May 1944–Sep 1947	2,624	25	
97 Sqn	Manchester	Feb 1941–Feb 1942	151	8	
	Lancaster	Jan 1942–Jul 1946	3,783	101	
98 Sqn	Mitchell	Sep 1942–(Sep 1945)	70	2	1st Mitchell Ops
99 Sqn	Wellington	Oct 1938–Feb 1942	1,786	43	
100 Sqn	Lancaster	Dec 1942–May 1946	3,984	92	
101 Sqn	Blenheim	Jun 1938–Jul 1941	618	15	
	Wellington	Apr 1941–Oct 1942	1,253	43	
	Lancaster	Oct 1942–May 1946	4,895	113	ABC
102 Sqn	Whitley	Oct 1938–Feb 1942	1,372	52	
	Halifax	Dec 1941–Sep 1945	4,734	140	
103 Sqn	Battle	Jul 1938–Oct 1940	51	1	Not inc. AASF ops
	Wellington	Oct 1940–Jul 1942	1,116	31	
	Halifax	Jul 1942–Oct 1942	137	12	
	Lancaster	Oct 1942–Nov 1945	4,536	135	
104 Sqn	Wellington	Apr 1941–Feb 1942	373	13	
105 Sqn	Blenheim	Jun 1940–Dec 1941	692	22	
	Mosquito	Nov 1941–Feb 1946	5,495	36	1st Mosquito Ops Most Mosquito Ops VC (Edwards)
106 Sqn	Hampden	May 1939–Mar 1942	1,230	55	1st minelaying
	Manchester	Feb 1942–Jun 1942	151	9	
	Lancaster	May 1942–Feb 1946	4,364	105	VC (Jackson)
107 Sqn	Blenheim	Aug 1938–Feb 1942	1,442	61	Most Blenheim Ops
	Boston	Jan 1942–(Mar 1944)	157	23	
109 Sqn	Mosquito	Dec 1942–Jul 1952	5,421	18	1st Oboe Ops VC (Palmer)
110 Sqn	Blenheim	Jan 1938–Mar 1942	1,402	38	
114 Sqn	Blenheim	Mar 1937–Nov 1942	731	39	
115 Sqn	Wellington	Mar 1939–Mar 1943	3,075	98	Most Wellington losses
	Lancaster	Mar 1943–Nov 1949	4,678	110	
128 Sqn	Mosquito	Sep 1944–Mar 1946	1,531	2	
138 Sqn	Halifax	Aug 1941–Aug 1944	1,788	47	
	Stirling	Jun 1944–Mar 1945	503	10	
	Whitley	Aug 1941–Nov 1942	219	1	
	Lancaster	Mar 1945–Sep 1947	105	1	
139 Sqn	Blenheim	Jul 1937–Dec 1941 Jun 1942–Nov 1942	1,112	33	

(*continued*)

Squadrons of Bomber Command: Second World War (*continued*)

Sqn	Aircraft	Period	Ops	Loss	Remarks
	Mosquito	Jun 1942–Jan 1953	4,432	37	
141 Sqn	Beaufighter	(Jun 1941)–Jan 1944	12		1st Serrate Ops BC from Dec 1943
	Mosquito	Nov 1943–Sep 1945	1,202	11	
142 Sqn	Battle	Mar 1938–Nov 1940	63	4	Not inc. AASF ops
	Wellington	Nov 1940–May 1943	1,073	47	
	Mosquito	Oct 1944–Sep 1945	1,095	2	
144 Sqn	Hampden	Mar 1939–Mar 1943	2,045	62	Most Hampden Ops Most Hampden losses
149 Sqn	Wellington	Jan 1939–Dec 1941	1,647	40	
	Stirling	Nov 1941–Sep 1944	2,628	87	Most Stirling Ops VC (Middleton)
	Lancaster	Aug 1944–Nov 1949	1,630	4	
150 Sqn	Battle	Aug 1938–Sep 1940	50	nil	Not inc. AASF ops
	Wellington	Oct 1940–Jan 1943	1,667	50	
	Lancaster	Nov 1944–Nov 1945	840	6	
153 Sqn	Lancaster	Oct 1944–Sep 1945	1,041	22	
156 Sqn	Wellington	Feb 1942–Jan 1943	651	39	
	Lancaster	Jan 1943–Sep 1945	3,933	104	
157 Sqn	Mosquito	(Jan 1942)–Aug 1945	1,122	5	BC from May 1944
158 Sqn	Wellington	Feb 1942–Jun 1942	207	14	
	Halifax	Jun 1942–May 1945	5,161	145	Most Halifax Ops
161 Sqn	Halifax	Sep 1942–Oct 1944	786	17	Also used Havoc and Albemarle
	Stirling	Sep 1944–Jun 1945	379	6	
	Lysander	Feb 1942–Jun 1945	266	10	
	Hudson	Sep 1943–Jun 1945	179	10	
	Whitley	Feb 1942–Dec 1942	139	6	
162 Sqn	Mosquito	Dec 1944–Jul 1946	913	1	
163 Sqn	Mosquito	Jan 1945–Aug 1945	636	3	
166 Sqn	Whitley	Jun 1939–Apr 1940	nil	nil	
	Wellington	Jan 1943–Sep 1943	789	39	
	Lancaster	Sep 1943–Nov 1945	4,279	114	
169 Sqn	Mosquito	Jan 1944–Aug 1945	1,247	13	BC from Dec 1943
170 Sqn	Lancaster	Oct 1944–Nov 1945	980	13	
171 Sqn	Stirling	Sep 1944–Jan 1945	87	nil	
	Halifax	Oct 1944-Jul 1945	1,496	4	
180 Sqn	Mitchell	Sep 1942–(Sep 1945)	151	4	1st Mitchell Ops
186 Sqn	Lancaster	Oct 1944–Jul 1945	1,254	8	
189 Sqn	Lancaster	Oct 1944–Nov 1945	652	16	
192 Sqn	Wellington	Jan 1943–Jan 1945	880	5	1st 100 Gp Ops
	Halifax	Mar 1943–Aug 1945	992	11	
	Mosquito	Jan 1943–Aug 1945	592	2	
	Lightning		101	2	
195 Sqn	Lancaster	Oct 1944–Aug 1945	1,384	14	
196 Sqn	Wellington	Dec 1942–Jul 1943	517	13	
	Stirling	Jul 1943–Mar 1946	166	11	
199 Sqn	Wellington	Nov 1942–Jun 1943	475	12	
	Stirling	Jul 1943–Mar 1945	2,059	18	
	Halifax	Feb 1945–Jul 1945	329	2	
207 Sqn	Manchester	Nov 1940–Mar 1942	360	17	1st Manchester Ops Most Manchester losses
	Lancaster	Mar 1942–Aug 1949	4,203	131	
214 Sqn	Wellington	May 1939–Apr 1942	1,532	45	
	Stirling	Apr 1942–Jan 1944	1,432	54	

(*continued*)

Squadrons of Bomber Command: Second World War (*continued*)

Sqn	Aircraft	Period	Ops	Loss	Remarks
218 Sqn	Fortress	Jan 1944–Jul 1945	1,225	13	
	Blenheim	Jul 1940–Nov 1940	122	2	
	Wellington	Nov 1940–Feb 1942	854	21	
	Stirling	Jan 1942–Aug 1944	2,600	91	Most Stirling losses VC (Aaron)
223 Sqn	Lancaster	Aug 1944–Aug 1945	1,726	16	
	Liberator	Aug 1944–Jun 1945	615	3	
226 Sqn	Fortress	Apr 1945–Jul 1945	0	0	
	Blenheim	May 1941–Dec 1941	241	16	
227 Sqn	Boston	Nov 1941–(Jun 1943)	499	12	
239 Sqn	Lancaster	Oct 1944–Sep 1945	815	15	
300 Sqn	Mosquito	Jan 1944–Jul 1945	1,394	9	BC from Dec 1943
	Battle	Jul 1940–Nov 1940	7	nil	
	Wellington	Dec 1940–Mar 1944	2.421	47	
301 Sqn	Lancaster	Apr 1944–Oct 1946	1,216	30	
	Battle	Jul 1940–Nov 1940	40	nil	
304 Sqn	Wellington	Oct 1940–Apr 1943	1,220	29	
305 Sqn	Wellington	Nov 1940–Dec 1945	464	18	
311 Sqn	Wellington	Nov 1940–Aug 1943	1,063	30	
320 Sqn	Wellington	Aug 1940–Jun 1943	1,029	19	
342 Sqn	Mitchell	Mar 1943–(Aug 1945)	nil	nil	No Ops flown
346 Sqn	Boston	Apr 1943–(Apr 1945)	nil	nil	No Ops flown
347 Sqn	Halifax	May 1944–Nov 1945	1,371	15	
	Halifax	Jun 1944–Nov 1945	1,355	15	
405-434 Sqn – see RCAF					
455-467 Sqn – see RAAF					
487 Sqn	Ventura	Sep 1942–(Sep 1943)	273	15	VC (Trent)
513 Sqn	Stirling	Oct 1943–Nov 1943			Not operational
514 Sqn	Lancaster	Sep 1943–Aug 1945	3,675	66	
515 Sqn	Mosquito	Feb 1944–Jun 1945	1,366	21	BC from Dec 1943
550 Sqn	Lancaster	Nov 1943–Oct 1945	3,582	59	
571 Sqn	Mosquito	Apr 1944–Sep 1945	2,681	8	
576 Sqn	Lancaster	Nov 1943–Sep 1945	2,788	66	
578 Sqn	Halifax	Jan 1944–Mar 1945	2,721	40	VC (Barton)
582 Sqn	Lancaster	Apr 1944–Sep 1945	2,157	28	VC (Swales)
608 Sqn	Mosquito	Aug 1944–Aug 1945	1,726	9	
617 Sqn	Lancaster	Mar 1943–Sep 1946	1,478	32	VC (Gibson) VC (Cheshire)
619 Sqn	Mosquito	Apr 1944–Mar 1945	75	nil	
620 Sqn	Lancaster	Apr 1943–Jul 1945	3,011	77	
622 Sqn	Stirling	Jun 1943–Jul 1945	339	17	
	Stirling	Aug 1943–Jan 1944	195	7	
623 Sqn	Lancaster	Dec 1943–Aug 1945	2,805	44	
625 Sqn	Stirling	Aug 1943–Dec 1943	150	10	
626 Sqn	Lancaster	Oct 1943–Oct 1945	3,385	66	
627 Sqn	Lancaster	Nov 1943–Oct 1945	2,728	49	
630 Sqn	Mosquito	Nov 1943–Sep 1945	1,535	19	
635 Sqn	Lancaster	Nov 1943–Jul 1945	2,453	59	
640 Sqn	Lancaster	Mar 1944–Aug 1945	2,225	34	VC (Bazalgette)
692 Sqn	Halifax	Jan 1944–May 1945	2,423	40	
1409 Flt	Mosquito	Jan 1944–Sep 1945	3,237	17	
	Mosquito		1,364	3	

RCAF Squadrons of Bomber Command

Sqn	Aircraft	Period	Ops	Loss	Remarks
405 Sqn	Wellington	May 1941–Apr 1942	522	20	
	Halifax	Apr 1942–Sep 1943	781	42	
	Lancaster	Aug 1943–Sep 1945	2,549	50	
408 Sqn	Hampden	Jun 1941–Sep 1942	1,233	35	
	Halifax	Sep 1942–Oct 1943	2,009	53	
		Sep 1944–May 1945			
	Lancaster	Oct 1943–Sep 1944	1,210	41	
415 Sqn	Halifax	Jul 1944–May 1945	1,526	13	
419 Sqn	Wellington	Jan 1942–Nov 1942	648	24	
	Halifax	Nov 1942–Apr 1944	1,616	66	
	Lancaster	Mar 1944–Sep 1945	2,029	39	VC (Mynarski)
420 Sqn	Hampden	Jan 1942–Aug 1942	535	19	
	Wellington	Aug 1942–Oct 1943	467	16	
	Halifax	Dec 1943–May 1945	2,477	25	
424 Sqn	Wellington	Oct 1942–Oct 1943	332	5	
	Halifax	Dec 1943–Jan 1945	1,811	23	
	Lancaster	Jan 1945–Oct 1945	388	5	
425 Sqn	Wellington	Aug 1942–Oct 1943	482	11	
	Halifax	Dec 1943–May 1945	2,445	28	
426 sqn	Wellington	Oct 1942–Jun 1943	467	18	
	Lancaster	Jul 1943–May 1944	579	28	
	Halifax	Apr 1944–May 1945	2,161	22	
427 Sqn	Wellington	Nov 1942–May 1943	270	10	
	Halifax	May 1943–Mar 1945	2,800	58	
	Lancaster	Mar 1945–May 1946	239	1	
428 Sqn	Wellington	Nov 1942–Jun 1944	350	17	
	Halifax	Jun 1943–Jun 1944	1,406	32	
	Lancaster	Jun 1944–Sep 1945	1,677	18	
429 Sqn	Wellington	Nov 1942–Aug 1943	542	28	
	Halifax	Aug 1943–Mar 1945	2,519	49	
	Lancaster	Mar 1945–May 1946	114	1	
431 Sqn	Wellington	Dec 1942–Jul 1943	321	18	
	Halifax	Jul 1943–Oct 1944	1,461	46	
	Lancaster	Oct 1944–Sep 1945	796	11	
432 Sqn	Wellington	May 1943–Nov 1943	494	16	
	Lancaster	Oct 1943–Feb 1944	190	8	
	Halifax	Feb 1944–May 1945	2,416	41	
433 Sqn	Halifax	Nov 1943–Jan 1945	1,926	28	
	Lancaster	Jan 1945–Oct 1945	390	3	
434 Sqn	Halifax	Jun 1943–Dec 1944	2,038	53	
	Lancaster	Dec 1944–Mar 1945	559	5	

RAAF Squadrons of Bomber Command

Sqn	Aircraft	Period	Ops	Loss	Remarks
455 Sqn	Hampden	Jul 1941–Dec 1943	424	14	
458 Sqn	Wellington	Aug 1941–(Jun 1942)	65	3	Left BC Mar 1942
460 Sqn	Wellington	Nov 1941–Sep 1942	538	29	
	Lancaster	Oct 1942–Oct 1945	5,700	140	Most ops by RAAF sqn
462 Sqn	Halifax	Aug 1942–Oct 1942	1,165	13	
463 Sqn	Lancaster	Nov 1943–Sep 1945	2,525	69	
464 Sqn	Ventura	Sep 1942–(Nov 1943)	226	6	
466 Sqn	Wellington	Oct 1942–Sep 1943	844	25	
	Halifax	Sep 1943–Aug 1945	2,484	40	
467 Sqn	Lancaster	Nov 1942–Sep 1945	3,833	104	

Annex C

Accuracy of Bomber Command night attacks on German cities (excluding Berlin)

The table below is a post-war Bomber Command assessment using the plotting of target photographs to assess the accuracy of attacks; it starts with mid-1941 as it was not until then that sufficient numbers of cameras had been fitted to make this kind of analysis possible.

| Period | Total number of photographs plotted | | | Photographs plotted within 3 miles of A.P. | | | Percentage plotted within 3 miles of A.P. | | |
| | Weather | | | Weather | | | Weather | | |
	Good	Mod.	Total	Good	Mod.	Total	Good	Mod.	Total
1941									
August–September	121	90	211	47	20	67	39	22	32
October–November	61	31	92	13	2	15	21	6	16
December–January	52	74	126	39	17	56	75	23	44
1942									
February–March	69	185	254	54	24	78	78	13	31
April–May	370	152	522	247	16	263	67	11	50
June–July	475	487	962	175	97	272	37	20	28
August–September	386	902	1,288	152	295	447	39	33	35
October–November	88	192	280	22	48	70	25	25	25
December–January	18	88	106	11	20	31	61	23	29
1943									
February–March	581	416	997	148	208	356	25	50	36
April–May	2,070	403	2,473	1,475	147	1,622	71	36	66
June–July	3,399	33	3,432	2,277	17	2,294	67	52	67
August–September	2,027	534	2,561	829	260	1,089	41	49	43
October–November	1,290	674	1,964	1,106	397	1,503	86	59	77
December–January	261	496	757	180	108	288	69	22	38
1944									
February–March	973	624	1,597	667	466	1,133	68	75	71
April–May	607	477	1,084	562	261	823	93	55	76
June–July	–	287	287	–	271	271	–	94	94
August–September	1,625	675	2,300	1,547	502	2,049	95	74	89
October–November	1,715	684	2,399	1,624	671	2,295	95	98	96
December–January	1,381	354	1,735	1,258	344	1,602	91	97	92
1945									
February–March	1,633	269	1,902	1,613	252	1,865	99	94	98

Annex D

Order of Battle, 1 August 1939

Squadron	Airfield	Establishment	Strength	Notes
No. 1 Group (Abingdon)				
15	Abingdon	Battle		
40	Abingdon	Battle		
105	Harwell	Battle		
225	Harwell	Battle		
88	Boscombe Down	Battle		
218	Boscombe Down	Battle		
12	Bicester	Battle		
142	Bicester	Battle		
103	Benson	Battle		
150	Benson	Battle		
No. 2 Group (Wyton)				
90	West Raynham	Blenheim IV		
101	West Raynham	Blenheim IV		
62	Cranfield	Blenheim IV		To Far East
82	Cranfield	Blenheim IV		
107	Wattisham	Blenheim IV		
110	Wattisham	Blenheim IV		
21	Watton	Blenheim I		
34	Watton	Blenheim I		To Far East
114	Wyton	Blenheim IV		
139	Wyton	Blenheim IV		
18	Upper Heyford	Blenheim		
57	Upper Heyford	Blenheim		
No. 3 Group (Mildenhall)				
37	Feltwell	Wellington		
99	Mildenhall	Wellington		
149	Mildenhall	Wellington		
9	Stradishall	Wellington		
38	Marham	Wellington		
115	Marham	Wellington		
No. 4 Group (Linton-on-Ouse)				
10	Dishforth	Whitley		
78	Dishforth	Whitley		
77	Driffield	Whitley		
102	Driffield	Whitley		
51	Linton-on-Ouse	Whitley		
58	Linton-on-Ouse	Whitley		
No. 5 Group (Grantham)				
61	Hemswell	Hampden		
144	Hemswell	Hampden		
49	Scampton	Hampden		
83	Scampton	Hampden		
50	Waddington	Hampden		
44	Waddington	Hampden		

TOTAL 40 squadrons

Annex E

Order of Battle, 16 June 1940

Squadron	Airfield	Establishment	Strength	Notes
No. 2 Group (Huntingdon)				
18	West Raynham	Blenheim IV		Non-op
101	West Raynham	Blenheim IV		Non-op
107	Wattisham	Blenheim IV		
110	Wattisham	Blenheim IV		
21	Bodney	Blenheim IV		
82	Watton	Blenheim IV		
40	Wyton	Blenheim IV		
57	Wyton	Blenheim IV		Non-op
15	Alconbury	Blenheim IV		
114	Horsham St Faith	Blenheim IV		Non-op
139	Horsham St Faith	Blenheim IV		Non-op
No. 3 Group (Exning)				
37	Feltwell	Wellington IA, IC		
75 NZ	Feltwell	Wellington IA, IC		
99	Newmarket	Wellington IA, IC		
149	Mildenhall	Wellington IA, IC		
214	Stradishall	Wellington IA, IC		Non-op
38	Marham	Wellington IA, IC		
115	Marham	Wellington IA, IC		
9	Honington	Wellington IA, IC		
No. 4 Group (York)				
51	Dishforth	Whitley IV, V		
58	Linton-on-Ouse	Whitley V		
10	Topcliffe	Whitley IV, V		
77	Driffield	Whitley V		
102	Cottam	Whitley V		At Driffield
78	York	Whitley IVA, V		Non-op
No. 5 Group				
61	Hemswell	Hampden		
144	Hemswell	Hampden		
49	Scampton	Hampden		
83	Scampton	Hampden		
44	Waddington	Hampden		
50	Waddington	Hampden		
106	Finningley	Hampden		Non-op

TOTAL 32 squadrons

Note: No. 1 Group is excluded as they were in France with the Advanced Air Striking Force

Annex F

Order of Battle, 23 February 1941

Squadron	Airfield	Establishment	Strength	Notes
No. 1 Group (Hucknall)				
103	Newton	Wellington 16+2		
150	Newton	Wellington 16+2		
300	Swinderby	Wellington 16+2		
301	Swinderby	Wellington 16+2		
12	Binbrook	Wellington 16+2		Non-op
142	Binbrook	Wellington 16+2		Non-op
304	Syerston	Wellington 16+2		Non-op
305	Syerston	Wellington 16+2		Non-op
No. 2 Group (Huntingdon)				
107	Wattisham	Blenheim IV 16+4		
110	Wattisham	Blenheim IV 16+4		
21	Watton	Blenheim IV 16+4		
82	Bodney	Blenheim IV 16+4		
114	Oulton	Blenheim IV 16+4		
139	Horsham St Faith	Blenheim IV 16+4		
18	Great Massingham	Blenheim IV 16+4		
101	West Raynham	Blenheim IV 16+4		
105	Swanton Morley	Blenheim IV 16+4		
No. 3 Group (Exning)				
99	Mildenhall	Wellington I 16+2		
149	Mildenhall	Wellington I 16+2		
115	Marham	Wellington I 16+2		
9	Honington	Wellington I 16+2		
75 NZ	Feltwell	Wellington I 16+2		
214	Stradishall	Wellington I 16+2		
57	Feltwell	Wellington I 16+2		
311	Honington	Wellington I 16+2		
15	Wyton	Wellington I 16+2		
40	Wyton	Wellington I 16+2		
218	Marham	Wellington I 16+2		
7	Oakington	Wellington I 16+2		
No. 4 Group (Linton-on-Ouse)				
51	Dishforth	Whitley V 16+2		
58	Linton-on-Ouse	Whitley V 16+2		
10	Leeming	Whitley V 16+2		
77	Topcliffe	Whitley V 16+2		
102	Topcliffe	Whitley V 16+2		
78	Dishforth	Whitley V 16+2		
35	Linton-on-Ouse	Halifax		Non-op
No. 5 Group (Grantham)				
61	Hemswell	Hampden 16+2		
144	Hemswell	Hampden 16+2		
49	Scampton	Hampden 16+2		
83	Scampton	Hampden 16+2		
44	Waddington	Hampden 16+2		
50	Lindholme	Hampden 16+2		
106	Coningsby	Hampden 16+2		
207	Waddington	Manchester		Non-op
97	Waddington	Manchester 8+2		Non-op

TOTAL 45 squadrons

Annex G

Order of Battle, 13 February 1942

Squadron	Airfield	Establishment	Strength	Notes
No. 1 Group (Bawtry)				
103	Elsham Wolds	Wellington 16+2	17 Wellington IC	
150	Snaith	Wellington 16+2	19 Wellington IC	
300	Hemswell	Wellington 16+2	19 Wellington IV	
301	Hemswell	Wellington 16+2	19 Wellington IV	
12	Binbrook	Wellington 24+3	25 Wellington II	
142	Grimsby	Wellington 16+2	17 Wellington IV	
304	Lindholme	Wellington 16+2	19 Wellington IC	
305	Lindholme	Wellington 16+2	16 Wellington II	
460	Breighton	Wellington 16+2	16 Wellington IV	Non-op
No. 2 Group (Huntingdon)				
110	Wattisham	Blenheim IV 16+4	21 Blenheim IV	
21	Watton	Blenheim IV 16+4	1 Blenheim IV	Det overseas
82	Bodney	Blenheim IV 16+4	21 Blenheim IV	
18	Wattisham	Blenheim IV 16+4	6 Blenheim IV	
105	Horsham St Faith	Blenheim IV 16+4	3 Blenheim IV	Non-op on
			5 Mosquito	Mosquito
107	West Raynham	Boston 16+4	3 Blenheim IV	Non-op on
			18 Boston III	Boston
114	West Raynham	Blenheim IV 16+4	19 Blenheim	
226	Swanton Morley	Boston 16+4	21 Boston III	
88	Swanton Morley	Boston 16+4	20 Boston III	
No. 3 Group (Exning)				
57	Feltwell	Wellington I 16+2	21 Wellington III	Non-op
101	Oakington	Wellington I 16+2	16 Wellington III	Non-op
419 RCAF	Mildenhall	Wellington I 16+2	14 Wellington IC	
115	Marham	Wellington I 16+2	20 Wellington III	Non-op
9	Honington	Wellington I 16+2	22 Wellington III	Non-op
75 NZ	Feltwell	Wellington I 16+2	22 Wellington III	Non-op
214	Stradishall	Wellington I 16+2	19 Wellington IC	
311	Honington	Wellington I 16+2	19 Wellington IC	
156	Wyton	Wellington I 16+2	19 Wellington IC	
218	Marham	Stirling 16+2	18 Stirling	Non-op
7	Oakington	Stirling 16+2	10 Stirling	Non-op
15	Wyton	Stirling 16+2	12 Stirling	
149	Mildenhall	Stirling 16+2	7 Stirling	
No. 4 Group (York)				
51	Dishforth	Whitley 24+3	23 Whitley V	
102	Topcliffe	Whitley 24+3	6 Whitley V	Non-op on
		Halifax 16+2	14 Halifax	Halifax
58	Linton-on-Ouse	Whitley 24+3	16 Whitley V	
77	Leeming	Whitley 24+3	17 Whitley V	
78	Middleton St George	Whitley 24+3	15 Whitley V	Non-op on
			2 Halifax	Halifax
158	Driffield	Halifax 16+2	21 Wellington II	
405 RCAF	Pocklington	Halifax 16+2	15 Wellington II	
35	Linton-on-Ouse	Halifax 16+2	22 Halifax	Non-op
76	Middleton St George	Halifax 16+2	16 Halifax	
10	Leeming	Halifax 16+2	19 Halifax	

(continued)

Squadron	Airfield	Establishment	Strength	Notes
138	Stradishall		12 Whitley V	
			1 Lysander	
			1 Wellington	
			3 Halifax	
No. 5 Group (Grantham)				
420 RCAF	Waddington	Hampden 16+2	17 Hampden	
144	North Luffenham	Hampden 24+3	27 Hampden	
49	Scampton	Hampden 24+3	22 Hampden	
83	Scampton	Manchester 16+2	16 Manchester	Non-op
50	Swinderby	Hampden 24+3	23 Hampden	
106	Coningsby	Hampden 24+3	12 Hampden	Non-op on
		Manchester 16+2	4 Manchester	Manchester
408 RCAF	Syerston	Hampden 24+3	20 Hampden	
455 RCAF	Swinderby	Hampden 24+3	23 Hampden	
207	Bottesford	Manchester 16+2	19 Manchester	
97	Coningsby	Lancaster 16+2	5 Lancaster	Non-op
61	North Luffenham	Manchester 16+2	15 Manchester	
44	Waddington	Lancaster 16+2	19 Lancaster	Non-op

TOTAL 54 squadrons

Note: Airfield is Parent Station, actual location may vary.

Annex H

Order of Battle, 18 February 1943

Squadron	Airfield	Establishment	Strength	Notes
No. 1 Group (Bawtry)				
12	Wickenby	Lancaster 16+2	20 Lancaster	
101	Holme-on-S-M	Lancaster 16+2	17 Lancaster	
103	Elsham Wolds	Lancaster 16+2	17 Lancaster	
460 RAAF	Breighton	Lancaster 16+2	21 Lancaster	
166	Kirmington	Wellington 16+2	19 Wellington III	
199	Ingham	Wellington 16+2	17 Wellington III	
			3 Wellington X	
300	Hemswell	Wellington 10+2	8 Wellington III	
			2 Wellington X	
301	Hemswell	Wellington 10+2	14 Wellington IV	
305	Hemswell	Wellington 10+2	10 Wellington IV	
100	Grimsby	Wellington 16+2	20 Lancaster	Non-op
No. 2 Group (Huntingdon)				
88	Oulton	Boston 16+2	17 Boston III	Note 5
107	Great Massingham	Boston 16+2	16 Boston III	Note 5
226	Swanton Morley	Boston 16+2	18 Boston III	Note 5
105	Marham	Mosquito 16+2	20 Mosquito	
139	Marham	Mosquito 16+2	20 Mosqutio	
			13 Blenheim V	
21	Methwold	Ventura 16+2	20 Ventura	
464	Feltwell	Ventura 16+2	22 Ventura	
487	Feltwell	Ventura 16+2	20 Ventura	
98	Foulsham	Mitchell 16+2	19 Mitchell	
180	Foulsham	Mitchell 16+2	20 Mitchell	
No. 3 Group (Exning)				
15	Bourn	Stirling 24+3	22 Stirling	Note 6
75 NZ	Newmarket	Stirling 16+2	17 Stirling	
90	Ridgewell	Stirling 16+2	15 Stirling	
149	Lakenheath	Stirling 16+2	19 Stirling	Note 6
214	Chedburgh	Stirling 16+2	15 Stirling	Note 6
218	Downham Market	Stirling 24+3	20 Stirling	
115	Ridgwell	Lancaster 16+2	2 Lancaster	1 Flt op on
			15 Wellington	Wellington
138	Tempsford	Halifax 15+2	18 Halifax	Note 1
161	Tempsford	Lysander 7+0	9 Lysander	Note 1
		Halifax 5+0	5 Halifax	
		Hudson 1+0	1 Hudson	
		Havoc 2+0	2 Havoc	
		Albemarle 2+0	2 Albemarle	
192	Grasnden Lodge	Wellington 8+2	12 Wellington	Note 1
		Mosquito 3+0	2 Wellington Ic	
		Halifax 1+0	3 Mosquito	
			2 Halifax	
No. 4 Group (York)				
10	Melbourne	Halifax 16+2	23 Halifax	
51	Snaith	Halifax 24+3	25 Halifax	
			2 Whitley	
76	Linton-on-Ouse	Halifax 16+2	21 Halifax	
77	Elvington	Halifax 16+2	20 Halifax	
			1 Whitley	

(continued)

Squadron	Airfield	Establishment	Strength	Notes
78	Linton-on-Ouse	Halifax 16+2	19 Halifax	
102	Pocklington	Halifax 16+2	17 Halifax	
158	Rufforth	Halifax 24+3	25 Halifax	
			1 Wellington II	
196	Leconfield	Wellington 16+2	17 Wellington X	
429 RCAF	East Moor	Wellington 16+2	12 Wellington III	
			4 Wellington X	
466 RCAF	Leconfield	Wellington 16+2	15 Wellington X	
431 RCAF	Burn	Wellington 16+2	20 Wellington X	Non-op
No. 5 Group (Grantham)				
9	Waddington	Lancaster 16+2	17 Lancaster	
44	Waddington	Lancaster 16+2	19 Lancaster	
49	Fiskerton	Lancaster 16+2	18 Lancaster	
50	Skellingthorpe	Lancaster 16+2	17 Lancaster	
57	Scampton	Lancaster 16+2	19 Lancaster	
61	Syerston	Lancaster 16+2	19 Lancaster	
97	Woodhall Spa	Lancaster 16+2	20 Lancaster	
106	Syerston	Lancaster 16+2	21 Lancaster	
207	Langar	Lancaster 16+2	23 Lancaster	
467 RAAF	Bottesford	Lancaster 16+2	19 Lancaster	
No. 6 (RCAF) Group (Allerton)				
405 RCAF	Beaulieu	Halifax 16+2	20 Halifax	Note 2
408 RCAF	Leeming	Halifax 16+2	18 Halifax	
419 RCAF	Middleton St George	Halifax 16+2	20 Halifax	
420 RCAF	Middleton St George	Wellington 16+2	14 Wellington III	
			1 Wellington X	
424 RCAF	Topcliffe	Wellington 16+2	16 Wellington III	
			1 Wellington X	
425 RCAF	Dishforth	Wellington 16+2	21 Wellington III	
426 RCAF	Dishforth	Wellington 16+2	19 Wellington III	
			1 Wellington X	
427 RCAF	Croft	Wellington 16+2	15 Wellington III	
			2 Wellington X	
428 RCAF	Dalton	Wellington 16+2	14 Wellington III	
			6 Wellington X	
No. 8 (PFF) Group (Wyton)				
7	Oakington	Stirling 24+3	24 Stirling	Note 3
35	Graveley	Halifax 24+3	27 Halifax	
83	Wyton	Lancaster 16+2	21 Lancaster	
156	Warboys	Lancaster 16+2	21 Lancaster	
			3 Wellington III	
109	Wyton	Mosquito 18+3	22 Mosquito	Note 4
			1 Wellington 1C	

TOTAL 65 squadrons

Notes:
1. These three squadrons under the control of ACAS (Assistant Chief of Air Staff).
2. Attached to Coastal Command.
3. Lodger on a No. 3 Group airfield.
4. Includes training flight of 2+1 Mosquito.
5. Squadron trained in gas spraying.
6. Squadron trained in gas bombing.

Annex I

Order of Battle, 24 February 1944

Squadron	Airfield	Establishment	Strength	Notes
No. 1 Group (Bawtry)				
12	Wickenby	Lancaster 16+4	19 Lancaster	
100	Grimsby	Lancaster 16+4	19 Lancaster	
101	Ludford Magna	Lancaster 24+6	29 Lancaster	
103	Elsham Wolds	Lancaster 16+4	19 Lancaster	
166	Kirmington	Lancaster 24+6	30 Lancaster	
460 RAAF	Binbrook	Lancaster 24+6	30 Lancaster	
550	Nth Killingholme	Lancaster 16+4	21 Lancaster	
576	Elsham Wolds	Lancaster 16+4	19 Lancaster	
625	Kelstern	Lancaster 16+4	21 Lancaster	
626	Wickenby	Lancaster 16+4	19 Lancaster	
300	Ingham	Lancaster 8+1	8 Wellington X	Op on Wellington
		Wellington 8+2	4 Lancaster	
No. 3 Group (Exning)				
75	Mepal	Stirling 24+6	32 Stirling	
90	Tuddenham	Stirling 24+6	30 Stirling	
149	Lakenheath	Stirling 16+4	18 Stirling	
218	Lakenheath	Stirling 16+4	19 Stirling	
15	Downham Market	Stirling 16+4	20 Stirling	
115	Mildenhall	Lancaster 16+4	21 Lancaster	
622	Witchford	Lancaster 24+6	24 Lancaster	
	Waterbeach	Lancaster 24+6	26 Lancaster	
	Mildenhall	Lancaster 16+4	19 Lancaster	
138	Tempsford	Halifax 14+2	19 Halifax II/V	
161	Tempsford	Lysander 7+3	7 Lysander	
		Halifax V 6+0	6 Halifax	
		Hudson 5+0	7 Hudson	
No. 4 Group (York)				
10	Melbourne	Halifax 24+6	25 Halifax II	
102	Pocklington	Halifax 24+6	23 Halifax II	
76	Holme-on-S-M	Halifax 24+6	28 Halifax III	Non-op
77	Elvington	Halifax 24+6	23 Halifax V	
			6 Halifax II	
51	Snaith	Halifax 24+6	29 Halifax III	1 Flt No-op
			1 Halifax II	
158	Lissett	Halifax 16+4	17 Halifax III	
			1 Halifax II	
466 RAAF	Leconfield	Halifax 16+4	18 Halifax III	
			3 Halifax II	
578	Burn	Halifax 16+4	19 Halifax III	
640	Leconfield	Halifax 16+4	17 Halifax III	
78	Breighton	Halifax 24+6	26 Halifax III	
			2 Halifax II	
No. 5 Group (Swinderby)				
9	Bardney	Lancaster 16+4	19 Lancaster	
44	Dunholme Lodge	Lancaster 16+4	21 Lancaster	
49	Fiskerton	Lancaster 16+4	16 Lancaster	
50	Skellingthorpe	Lancaster 16+4	17 Lancaster	
57	East Kirkby	Lancaster 16+4	19 Lancaster	
61	Coningsby	Lancaster 16+4	19 Lancaster	
106	Metheringham	Lancaster 16+4	19 Lancaster	

(*continued*)

Squadron	Airfield	Establishment	Strength	Notes
207	Spilsby	Lancaster 16+4	18 Lancaster	
463 RAAF	Waddington	Lancaster 16+4	19 Lancaster	
467 RAAF	Waddington	Lancaster 16+4	17 Lancaster	
619	Coningsby	Lancaster 16+4	20 Lancaster	
630	East Kirkby	Lancaster 16+4	18 Lancaster	
617	Woodhall Spa	Lancaster 16+4	28 Lancaster	
No. 6 (RCAF) Group (Allerton)				
420 RCAF	Tholthorpe	Halifax 16+4	19 Halifax III	
424 RCAF	Skipton-on-Swale	Halifax 16+4	19 Halifax III	
425 RCAF	Tholthorpe	Halifax 16+4	19 Halifax III	
427 RCAF	Leeming	Halifax 16+4	17 Halifax III	
			1 Halifax V	
432 RCAF	East Moor	Halifax 16+4	20 Halifax III	
			1 Lancaster II	
433 RCAF	Skipton-on-Swale	Halifax 16+4	22 Halifax III	
419 RCAF	Middleton St George	Halifax 16+4	13 Halifax II	
			1 Lancaster X	
428 RCAF	Middleton St George	Halifax 16+4	17 Halifax II	
429 RCAF	Leeming	Halifax 16+4	18 Halifax V	
431 RCAF	Croft	Halifax 16+4	16 Halifax III	
434 RCAF	Croft	Halifax 16+4	16 Halifax III	
408 RCAF	Linton-on-Ouse	Lancaster 16+4	20 Lancaster II	
426 RCAF	Linton-on-Ouse	Lancaster 16+4	22 Lancaster II	
No. 8 (PFF) Group (Huntingdon)				
35	Graveley	Halifax 24+6	28 Halifax III	
			9 Halifax II	
7	Oakington	Lancaster 24+6	30 Lancaster	
83	Wyton	Lancaster 16+4	23 Lancaster	
97	Bourn	Lancaster 24+6	30 Lancaster	
156	Warboys	Lancaster 24+6	30 Lancaster	
405	Gransden Lodge	Lancaster 16+4	23 Lancaster	
105	Marham	Mosquito 16+2	17 Mosquito	
109	Marham	Mosquito 24+6	30 Mosquito	
139	Upwood	Mosquito 16+2	15 Mosquito	
627	Oakington	Mosquito 16+2	8 Mosquito	
692	Graveley	Mosquito 16+2	5 Mosquito	1 Flt Non-op
No. 100 (SD) Group (West Raynham)				
141	West Raynham	Mosquito 16+2	18 Mosquito II	
169	Little Snoring	Mosquito 16+2	14 Mosquito II	Non-op
			3 Beaufighter	
239	West Raynham	Mosquito 16+2	17 Mosquito II/V	Non-op
192	Foulsham	Wellington 6+1	8 Wellington	
		Mosquito 3+0	3 Mosquito	
		Halifax 8+2	12 Halifax	
515	Little Snoring	Mosquito 16+2	10 Beaufighter	
214	Sculthorpe	Fortress 12+2	21 Fortress	Non-op

TOTAL 73 squadrons

Annex J

Order of Battle, January 1945

Squadron	Airfield	Establishment	Strength	Notes
No. 1 Group (Bawtry)				
12	Wickenby	Lancaster 20		
100	Elsham Wolds	Lancaster 20		
101	Ludford Magna	Lancaster 30		
103	Elsham Wolds	Lancaster 20		
150	Hemswell	Lancaster 20		
153	Scampton	Lancaster 20		
166	Kirmington	Lancaster 30		
170	Hemswell	Lancaster 20		
300	Faldingworth	Lancaster 20		
460 RAAF	Binbrook	Lancaster 30		
550	North Killingholme	Lancaster 30		
576	Fiskerton	Lancaster 30		
625	Scampton	Lancaster 20		
626	Wickenby	Lancaster 20		
No. 3 Group (Exning)				
15	Mildenhall	Lancaster		
75 NZ	Mepal	Lancaster		
90	Tuddneham	Lancaster		
115	Witchford	Lancaster		
138	Tempsford	StirlingHudson		
149	Methwold	Lancaster		
161	Tempsford	StirlingHudson		
186	Stradishall	Lancaster		
195	Wratting Common	Lancaster		
218	Chedburgh	Lancaster		
514	Waterbeach	Lancaster		
622	Mildenhall	Lancaster		
No. 4 Group				
10	Melbourne	Halifax		
51	Snaith	Halifax		
76	Holme-on-S-M	Halifax		
77	Full Sutton	Halifax		
78	Breighton	Halifax		
102	Pocklington	Halifax		
158	Lissett	Halifax		
346 French	Elvington	Halifax		
347 French	Elvington	Halifax		
462 RAAF	Foulsham	Halifax		
466 RAAF	Driffield	Halifax		
578	Burn	Halifax		
640	Leconfield	Halifax		
No. 5 Group				
9	Bardney	Lancaster		
44	Spilsby	Lancaster		
49	Fulbeck	Lancaster		
50	Skellingthorpe	Lancaster		
57	East Kirkby	Lancaster		
61	Skellingthorpe	Lancaster		
83	Coningsby	Lancaster		
97	Coningsby	Lancaster		

(continued)

Squadron	Airfield	Establishment	Strength	Notes
106	Metheringham	Lancaster		
189	Fulbeck	Lancaster		
207	Spilsby	Lancaster		
227	Bardney	Lancaster		
463 RAAF	Waddington	Lancaster		
467 RAAF	Waddington	Lancaster		
619	Woodhall Spa	Lancaster		
630	Strubby	Lancaster		
617	Woodhall Spa	Lancaster		
627	East Kirkby	Lancaster		
No. 6 (RCAF) Group				
408 RCAF	Linton-on-Ouse	Halifax		
415 RCAF	East Moor	Halifax		
419 RCAF	Middleton St George	Halifax		
420 RCAF	Tholthorpe	Halifax		
424 RCAF	Skipton-on-Swale	Halifax		
425 RCAF	Tholthorpe	Halifax		
426 RCAF	Linton-on-Ouse	Halifax		
427 RCAF	Leeming	Halifax		
429 RCAF	Middleton St George	Halifax		
429 RCAF	Leeming	Halifax		
431 RCAF	Croft	Halifax		
432 RCAF	East Moor	Halifax		
433 RCAF	Skipton-on-Swale	Halifax		
434 RCAF	Croft	Halifax		
No. 8 (PFF) Group				
7	Oakington	Lancaster		
35	Graveley	Lancaster		
105	Bourn	Lancaster		
109	Woodhall Spa	Mosquito		
128	Wyton	Mosquito		
139	Upwood	Mosquito		
142	Gransden Lodge	Mosquito		
156	Upwood	Mosquito		
405 RCAF	Gransden Lodge	Lancaster		
571	Oakington	Mosquito		
582	Little Staughton	Lancaster		
608	Downham Market	Mosquito		
692	Graveley	Mosquito		
1409 Flt		Mosquito		
No. 100 (BS) Group				
23	Little Snoring	Mosquito		
85	Swannington	Mosquito		
141	West Raynham	Mosquito		
157	Swannington	Mosquito		
169	Great Massingham	Mosquito		
171	North Creake	Halifax		
192	Foulsham	HalifaxMosquito		
199	North Creake	Halifax		
214	Oulton	Fortress		
239	West Raynham	Mosquito		
515	Little Snoring	Mosquito		

Total 95 squadrons and 1 Flight

Annex K

Bomber Command organisation, October 1944–April 1945

Main Force

No. 1 Gp (Bawtry) – 4 bases, 14 stations, 14 squadrons
No. 3 Gp (Exning) – 3 bases, 17 stations, 11 squadrons
No. 4 Gp (York) – 3 bases, 12 stations, 12 squadrons
No. 5 Gp (Newark) – 4 bases, 12 stations, 18 squadrons
No. 6 (RCAF) Gp (Knaresborough) – 3 bases, 7 stations, 14 squadrons

Pathfinder Group

No. 8 (PFF) Gp (Huntingdon) – 9 stations, 16 squadrons

Countermeasures Group

No. 100 Gp (Norfolk) – 9 stations, 12 squadrons

Training Groups

No. 7 (HC) Gp (Grantham) – 6 bases, 22 stations, 16 HCU, 2 LFS
No. 91 (OTU) Gp (Abingdon) – 11 stations, 7 OTU
No. 92 (OTU) Gp (Winslow) – 14 stations, 9 OTU
No. 93 (OTU) Gp (Eggington) – 4 stations, 3 OTU

Annex L

Bomber Command airfield maps 1939 and 1945

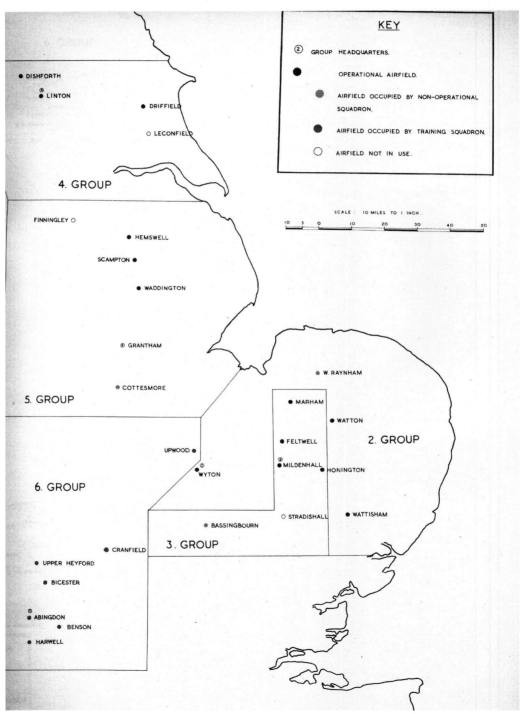

Bomber Command airfield map 1945

Annex M

Aircraft in Squadrons, daily availability with crews: Monthly Average, February 1942–April 1945

	Light	Medium	Heavy	All types		Light	Medium	Heavy	All types
1942									
February	55	275	44	374	August	62	152	174	388
March	52	301	68	421	September	44	109	178	331
April	56	247	86	389	October	47	136	225	408
May	70	210	136	416	November	45	118	234	397
June	80	181	141	402	December	46	111	262	419
July	76	198	153	427					
1943									
January	53	148	313	514	July	26	88	662	776
February	57	173	363	593	August	35	67	685	787
March	37	213	413	663	September	35	37	654	726
April	44	199	466	709	October	41	24	742	807
May	48	182	560	790	November	47	16	816	879
June	24	117	632	773	December	46	11	776	833
1944									
January	44	7	818	869	July	107	–	1,178	1,285
February	43	6	897	946	August	110	–	1,135	1,245
March	58	–	942	1,000	September	113	–	1,210	1,323
April	72	–	980	1,052	October	119	–	1,336	1,455
May	84	–	1,048	1,132	November	137	–	1,339	1,476
June	102	–	1,162	1,264	December	148	–	1,381	1,529
1945									
January	147	–	1,287	1,434	March	192	–	1,262	1,454
February	166	–	1,283	1,449	April	201	–	1,424	1,625

Annex N

Available Bomb lift in tons, by aircraft type: February 1942–April 1945

	Light	Medium	Heavy	All types		Light	Medium	Heavy	All types
1942									
February	33	340	137	510	August	44	215	538	797
March	39	391	199	629	September	39	152	486	677
April	43	311	229	583	October	42	187	552	781
May	51	273	381	705	November	52	118	469	639
June	58	241	424	723	December	63	94	667	824
July	51	287	471	809					
1943									
January	72	159	915	1,146	July	17	113	2,225	2,355
February	91	203	1,074	1,368	August	24	88	2,032	2,194
March	66	254	1,180	1,500	September	24	59	2,229	2,312
April	61	182	1,325	1,568	October	28	36	2,542	2,606
May	77	201	1,864	2,142	November	42		2,864	2,906
June	14	153	2,179	2,346	December	36		2,930	2,966
1944									
January	34		3,013	3,047	July	108		5,116	5,224
February	37		2,682	2,719	August	101		5,086	5,187
March	60		3,837	3,897	September	107		5,832	5,939
April	78		4,393	4,471	October	139		6,315	6,454
May	92		4,768	4,860	November	167		6,354	6,521
June	95		4,986	5,081	December	169		6,132	6,301
1945									
January	167		5,097	5,264	March	198		5,356	5,554
February	185		5,031	5,216	April	232		6,004	6,236

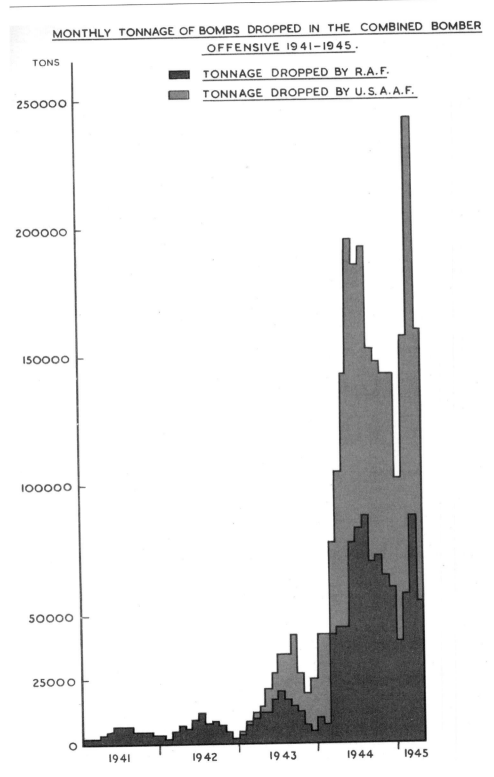

MONTHLY TONNAGE OF BOMBS DROPPED IN THE COMBINED BOMBER OFFENSIVE 1941–1945.

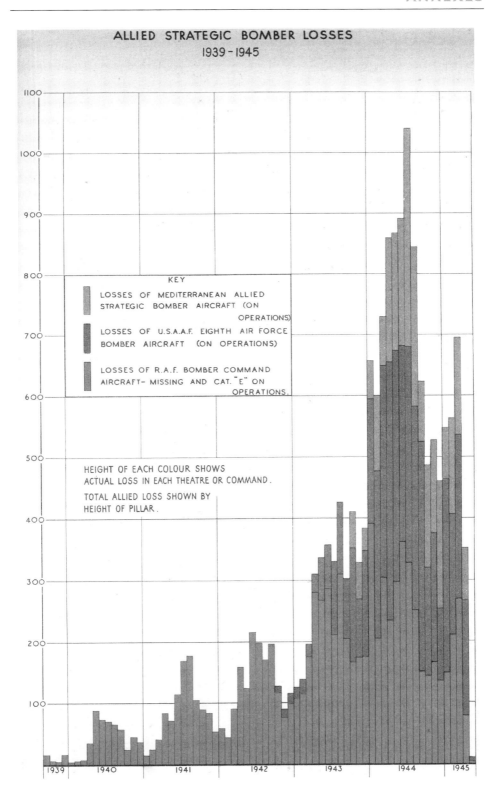

ALLIED STRATEGIC BOMBER LOSSES
1939 - 1945

KEY

LOSSES OF MEDITERRANEAN ALLIED
STRATEGIC BOMBER AIRCRAFT (ON
                    OPERATIONS)

LOSSES OF U.S.A.A.F. EIGHTH AIR FORCE
BOMBER AIRCRAFT (ON OPERATIONS)

LOSSES OF R.A.F. BOMBER COMMAND
AIRCRAFT– MISSING AND CAT. "E" ON
                    OPERATIONS.

HEIGHT OF EACH COLOUR SHOWS
ACTUAL LOSS IN EACH THEATRE OR COMMAND.

TOTAL ALLIED LOSS SHOWN BY
HEIGHT OF PILLAR.

Annex O

Cumulative monthly totals of tonnage of bombs, sorties despatched, and aircraft missing, February 1942–May 1945

	Bomb raids			Bombs (tons)	
	Tonnage	Sorties	Missing	H.E.	Incend
1942					
February	48,071	53,872	1,439	42,885	5,089
March	50,746	55,921	1,512	44,993	5,624
April	55,179	59,509	1,649	47,997	7,051
May	58,413	61,806	1,750	49,630	8,634
June	65,258	66,230	1,946	52,174	12,928
July	71,626	69,993	2,129	56,357	15,109
August	75,788	72,225	2,271	58,755	16,864
September	81,383	75,387	2,431	61,698	19,511
October	85,192	77,540	2,525	63,450	21,564
November	87,615	79,133	2,577	64,737	22,694
December	90,329	80,619	2,662	65,967	24,177
1943					
January	94,674	82,930	2,746	68,066	26,423
February	105,633	87,869	2,845	73,204	32,242
March	116,224	92,739	2,995	78,647	37,385
April	127,691	97,860	3,234	85,187	42,310
May	140,611	102,904	3,482	92,392	48,103
June	155,882	108,155	3,750	100,651	55,021
July	172,712	113,869	3,940	109,590	62,912
August	192,861	121,044	4,229	120,496	72,155
September	207,716	126,057	4,420	128,507	78,999
October	221,489	130,177	4,578	135,556	85,724
November	235,984	134,830	4,734	143,489	92,286
December	247,786	138,499	4,902	149,718	97,859
1944					
January	266,214	144,148	5,219	160,391	105,614
February	278,268	148,277	5,406	166,774	111,286
March	305,966	156,474	5,686	183,348	122,410
April	339,462	165,034	5,876	209,860	129,304
May	376,714	174,940	6,131	244,197	132,210
June	443,981	190,926	6,459	301,096	132,581
July	491,596	206,549	6,759	357,081	134,211
August	557,451	224,342	6,972	416,290	140,856
September	610,038	238,885	7,089	461,898	147,835
October	671,242	254,314	7,205	512,572	158,364
November	724,264	267,569	7,337	560,628	163,330
December	773,304	281,153	7,449	604,504	168,494
1945					
January	806,227	290,782	7,568	632,736	173,185
February	852,116	305,847	7,721	666,555	185,255
March	919,753	324,699	7,923	723,866	195,581
April	954,707	335,895	7,985	758,218	196,173
May	955,044	336,037	7,985	758,408	196,256

Annex P

Distribution of effort and casualties – cumulative totals: (a) Sorties despatched and (b) Aircraft missing on various types of operations

	Sorties					Aircraft missing		
	Bomb raids	Sea mining	Counter measures	Misc.	Total	Bomb raids	Sea mining	Total
1942								
February	53,872	2,761		2,175	58,808	1,439	57	1,496
March	55,921	3,027		2,254	61,202	1,512	68	1,580
April	59,509	3,371		2,338	65,218	1,649	78	1,727
May	61,806	3,821		2,399	68,026	1,750	94	1,844
June	66,230	4,337		2,455	73,022	1,946	103	2,049
July	69,993	4,771		2,493	77,257	2,129	114	2,243
August	72,225	5,153		2,530	79,908	2,271	130	2,401
September	75,387	5,621		2,540	83,548	2,431	147	2,578
October	77,540	6,082		2,566	86,188	2,525	161	2,686
November	79,133	6,664		2,657	88,454	2,577	176	2,753
December	80,619	7,085		2,710	90,414	2,662	183	2,845
1943								
January	82,930	7,681		2,765	93,376	2,746	199	2,945
February	87,869	8,221		2,842	98,932	2,845	208	3,053
March	92,739	8,732		2,921	104,392	2,995	226	3,221
April	97,860	9,423		3,027	110,310	3,234	259	3,493
May	102,904	9,791		3,190	115,885	3,482	267	3,749
June	108,155	10,217		3,255	121,627	3,750	274	4,024
July	113,869	10,530		3,555	127,954	3,940	280	4,220
August	121,044	11,032		3,743	135,819	4,229	290	4,519
September	126,057	11,429		3,896	141,382	4,420	293	4,713
October	130,177	11,796		4,089	146,062	4,578	298	4,876
November	134,830	12,148		4,340	151,318	4,734	306	5,040
December	138,499	12,404	11	4,569	155,483	4,902	311	5,213
1944								
January	144,148	12,777	51	4,817	161,793	5,219	314	5,533
February	148,277	13,547	140	5,295	167,259	5,406	323	5,729
March	156,474	14,065	423	6,175	177,137	5,686	326	6,012
April	165,034	14,919	827	6,907	187,687	5,876	345	6,221
May	174,940	15,745	1,175	7,700	199,560	6,131	354	6,485
June	190,926	16,205	2,194	8,088	217,413	6,459	355	6,814
July	206,549	16,389	4,707	8,748	236,393	6,759	357	7,116
August	224,342	16,803	6,728	9,179	257,052	6,972	369	7,341
September	238,885	16,988	8,503	10,048	274,424	7,089	373	7,462
October	254,314	17,245	10,030	10,397	291,986	7,205	381	7,786
November	267,569	17,415	11,414	10,596	306,994	7,337	382	7,719
December	281,153	17,675	12,754	10,745	322,327	7,449	385	7,834
1945								
January	290,782	17,834	13,873	10,808	333,297	7,568	391	7,959
February	305,847	18,126	15,910	11,023	350,906	7,721	400	8,121
March	324,699	18,402	17,968	11,178	372,247	7,923	405	8,328
April	335,895	18,682	19,525	12,248	386,350	7,985	408	8,393
May	336,037	18,725	19,686	15,362	389,810	7,985	408	8,393

Annex Q

Progress of the Bomber Offensive against German industrial towns schedule, by towns, of attacks and devastation resulting

Town	Date of first Main Force attack	Date of last Main Force attack	Total no. of Main Force attacks	Acreage 40% or more built-up (target) area	Acreage destroyed in built-up (target) area	Destroyed % of built-up (target) area
Aachen	5/6.10.42	13/14.7.43	2	1,030	605	59
Augsburg	25/26.2.44		1	1,535	445	29
Berlin	16/17.1.43	24/25.3.44	24	19,423	6,427*	33
Bochum	29/30.3.43	4/5.11.44	6	640	532	83
Bonn	18.10.44	4/5.2.45	5	708	240	34
Bremen	3/4.6.42	22.4.45	12	1,744	1,042	60
Bremerhaven	18/19.9.44		1	375	297	79
Brunswick	14/15.1.44	14/15.10.44	5	1,400	655	47
Chemnitz	14/15.2.45	5/6.3.45	2	1,452	590	41
Coblenz	6/7.11.44		1	523	303	58
Cologne	13/14.3.42	2.3.45	22	3,250	1,994	61
Darmstadt	25/26.8.44	11/12.9.44	2	745	516	69
Dessau	7/8.3.45	8/9.4.45	2	542	331	61
Dortmund	14/15.4.42	12.3.45	9	1,720	923	54
Dresden	13/14.2.45		1	2,844	1,681	59
Duisburg	13/14.7.42	21/22.2.45	18	2,955	1,424	48
Dusseldorf	31/1.8.42	2/3.11.44	10	3,115	2,003	64
Emden	6/7.6.42	6.9.44	5	485	270	56
Essen	8/9.3.42	11.3.45	28	2,630	1,319	50
Frankfurt a/Main	24/25.8.42	28/29.12.44	11	2,200	1,145	52
Freiburg	27/28.11.44		1	694	257	37
Friedrichshafen	27/28.4.44		1	148	99	67
Gelsenkirchen	25/26.6.43	22/23.1.45	4	757	360	48
Giessen	2/3.12.44	6/7.12.44	2	398	130	33
Hagen	1/2.10.43	15/16.3.45	4	486	325	67
Hamburg	15/16.1.42	13/14.4.45	17	8,315	6,200	75
Hamm	5.12.44		1	355	140	39
Hanau	6/7.1.45	18/19.3.45	2	275	190	69
Hannover	22/23.9.43	25.3.45	16	2,519	1,517	60
Harburg	11/12.11.44		1	286	153	53
Heilbronn	4/5.12.44		1	430	351	82
Hildesheim	22.3.45		1	378	263	70
Kaiserslautern	27/28.9.44		1	369	134	36
Karlsruhe	2/3.9.42	2/3.2.45	6	1,237	398	32
Kassel	27/28.8.42	8/9.3.45	6	905	620	69
Kiel	27/28.2.42	23/24.4.45	10	1,466	725	50
Konigsberg	26/27.8.44	29/30.8.44	2	824	435	53
Krefeld	2/3.10.42	21/22.6.43	2	1,529	714	47
Leipzig	20/21.10.43	19/20.2.44	3	3,183	625	20
Lubeck	28/29.3.42		1	633	190	30
Magdeburg	21/22.1.44	13/14.2.45	4	1,884	774	44
Mainz	11/12.8.42	27.2.45	4	971	593	61
Mannheim–Ludwigshaven	14/15.2.42	1.3.45	13	1,911	1,213	64
Mulheim	22/23.6.43		1	303	193	64
Munchen-Gladbach and Rheydt	30/31.8.43	1.2.45	4	1,176	633	54
Munich	19/20.9.42	7/8.1.45	9	3,634	1,547	42
Munster	28/29.1.42	25.3.45	6	997	650	65
Neuss	23/24.9.44	28/29.11.44	4	225	17	8
Nuremberg	28/29.8.42	16/17.3.45	11	2,255	1,146	51
Oberhausen	14/15.6.43	4.12.45	3	502	100	20

(continued)

Town	Date of first Main Force attack	Date of last Main Force attack	Total no. of Main Force attacks	Acreage 40% or more built-up (target) area	Acreage destroyed in built-up (target) area	Destroyed % of built-up (target) area
Osnabruck	9/10.8.42	25.3.45	5	658	441	67
Pforzheim	23/24.2.45		1	369	304	83
Plauen	10/11.4.45		1	712	365	51
Potsdam	14/15.4.45		1	559	75	13
Remscheid	30/31.7.43		1	339	281	83
Rostock	23/24.4.42	26/27.4.42	4	634	200	32
Saarbrucken	29/30.7.42	5/6.10.44	4	866	418	48
Schweinfurt	24/25.2.44	26/27.4.44	2	293	126	43
Solingen	4.11.44	5.11.44	2	343	169	49
Stettin	20/21.4.43	29/30.8.44	4	1,386	736	53
Stuttgart	4/5.5.42	12/13.2.45	18	2,514	1,152	46
Trier	21.12.44	23.12.44	2	492	48	10
Ulm	17/18.12.44		1	562	155	28
Wiesbaden	2/3.2.45		1	605	90	15
Witten	18/19.3.45		1	207	129	62
Wilhelmshaven	10/11.1.42	15/16.10.44	9	972	130	13
Worms	21/22.2.45		1	328	127	39
Wuppertal-Barmen	29/30.5.43	13.3.45	2	1,139	655	58
Wuppertal/Elberfeld	24/25.6.43		1	929	870	94
Wurzburg	16/17.3.45		1	477	422	89

Annex R

Bomber Command nuclear weapons

Weapon	Dates	Aircraft
Project E*	1958–?	Valiant, Canberra
Red Beard	1960–?	Valiant
Blue Danube	1960–?	Valiant, Vulcan, Victor
Violet Club	1958–1959	Vulcan
Yellow Sun 1	1960–1963	Vulcan
	1960–1963	Victor
Yellow Sun 2	1961–1970	Vulcan
	1961–1966	Victor
Blue Steel	1963–1970	Vulcan
	1964–1968	Victor
WE.177	Late 1960s	Vulcan
US Mk 28	1960s	Valiant
US Mk 43	1963–?	Valiant

Notes

* Project E involved a number of US weapons from the Mk 5 to the Mk 43 for carriage by the Valiants and Canberras.

This list does not include main Canberra nuclear capability held by the Germany-based Canberra B(I)8s and the Cyprus-based B.15s/B.16s, the former using US Mk 7 and Mk 43 weapons and the latter, Red Beard.

Index

To some extent this book is self-indexing in terms of general subject by the arrangement of chapters and the following index references are only a guide; for example, the Lancaster references point the reader to pages where the aircraft is specifically named – but to obtain an overall picture of the Lancaster's role requires the whole book to be read. The same is true of general subjects such as loss rates and the index only points at a specific mention of the subject. For references to people, targets, airfields and the like it is of course more relevant.